HENRY JAMES

LETTERS

Volume I
1843–1875

Henry James at seventeen

HENRY JAMES
LETTERS

Edited by

Leon Edel

Volume I

1843-1875

SBN 333 17324 5
SBN 333 17234 5

This edition first published in the United Kingdom by
MACMILLAN LONDON LIMITED

London and Basingstoke
Associated companies in New York, Dublin,
Melbourne, Johannesburg, & Delhi

Printed in the United States of America

The best letters seem to me the most
delightful of all written things—
and those that are not the best the
most negligible. If a correspondence
has not the real charm I wouldn't have
it published even privately; if it has, on
the other hand, I would give it the
glory of the greatest literature.

Henry James

Acknowledgments

My debt to the many institutions in different parts of the world, to librarians, collectors, booksellers, and private individuals who guided me to letters of Henry James over many years, has been acknowledged in the five volumes of my *Life of Henry James* (New York and London, 1953–1972) as well as in the *Bibliography of Henry James* (1957) which I compiled in collaboration with Professor Dan H. Laurence.

In the present volumes of the "general correspondence" of Henry James I hope readers will recognize that, when I list the institutions which have generously granted me permission to use their letters, I am at the same time expressing the gratitude of many years—to universities, libraries, librarians, and to all other institutions and individuals to whom I am deeply indebted. When letters are in institutions I label these at the head of each letter; when they are in private hands I designate them simply as "Ms Private." Letters change hands, when they are not in institutions—where one thinks of them as placed in a relative perpetuity. To avoid too much "obsolescence" of description, I prefer not to attach such letters to the individuals who own them. However, in my acknowledgments, I will name these individuals and with a large sense of indebtedness.

In these volumes my abbreviations are:

Ts—typescript
Mf—microfilm
Ms—holograph

In the present volume the designations are as follows:

Brown—John Hay Library, Brown University
Colby—Colby Library, Colby College
Congress—Library of Congress, Manuscript Division

Duke—Duke University Library
Harvard—Houghton Library, Harvard College
N. Y. Historical—New York Historical Society
NYPL—New York Public Library, Astor, Lenox, and Tilden
        Foundations, Manuscript Division
Yale—Beinecke Library, Yale University
Vaux—Robertson James Archive

I wish to thank in particular Alexander R. James, the present holder of the copyrights, for maintaining the priorities given me by his predecessors in the James family. I would like to recall the help given me for many years by the late William A. Jackson, Director of the Houghton Library, his successor, Dr. W. L. Bond, and the Houghton's librarian, Carolyn E. Jakeman. Professor Richard Cary of Colby College gave me particular assistance in my work on the rare manuscripts gathered in by himself and his predecessor Dr. Carl J. Weber.

I wish to thank also Professor Donald Gallup, and Herman W. Liebert, former librarian of the Beinecke Library, at Yale; also Professors Earl Daniels of Colgate, Virginia Harlow of DePauw, and Henry James Vaux of Berkeley. My debt to others will be acknowledged in their relevant place in the succeeding volumes.

L. E.

New York and Honolulu
1974

Contents

Illustrations

Introduction

The Relics of the Master

Letters are burned in "The Aspern Papers" and in "Sir Dominick Ferrand," one by one, as a kind of act of sadism on posterity: nothing must escape destruction; secrecy and mystery must be maintained. The relics of John Delavoy are held from the trumpeting press as long as possible. And in "The Abasement of the Northmores" the fables of the posthumous life take a particular turn: publication deflates—it shows up the Great Personality for the windbag he has been. But the letters of his private friend and schoolmate, such as survived, are masterpieces. They are not for the sensation-seeking public. James describes them—he might have been describing his own. The correspondent "played with the lightest idlest hand up and down the whole scale. His easy power—his easy power; everything that brought him back brought that." In fact, "if many pages were too intimate to publish, most others were too rare to suppress."

After the funeral in Chelsea Old Church early in March of 1916, Henry James's friends—in the midst of war, in the midst of death—wondered what could bring him back and how to bring him back. They had felt the "easy power" in his letters; and they knew also his elaborate discretions. The Master had died in the belief that his friends were as reticent as he was. If he burned the letters he received, surely they burned his letters as well, those spontaneous indiscretions scrawled across the notepapers of his decades, in Bolton Street, in De Vere Gardens, at his clubs, or on the various small sheets of continental hotels. He had hardly anticipated unanimous agreement with his words. A James letter was "too rare to suppress." That seems to have been the general verdict. And even his demand "burn, burn, burn"—made in certain of his letters early and late—was only an inducement to preservation, in the era when there were fireplaces in every room. The Master's friends clung to his letters as they clung to his memory. It was a little like possessing some small part of James himself. They saved even his thank-you notes and his apologies for not coming to dinner; they found the touch of his style everywhere, his "easy power" extended to epistolary courtesies. There was also his endless playful irony.

Mrs. William James, the novelist's sister-in-law, and her daughter Peggy were with the novelist at the end. They had crossed the war-time Atlantic to keep a promise made to William that his bachelor brother would not die alone. During the days after the funeral, as condolences poured in and obituaries were written, they were questioned about the relics—the manuscripts, notebooks, letters. They responded with a touch of awe and bewilderment. Little in their previous experience had prepared them for their discovery that Henry James was anything more than a dear, temperamental, fussy member of the James family, charmingly literary, whose books did not sell and who would leave a certain inheritance for his niece and nephews. They were accustomed to the aura of Harvard and national eminence which surrounded William, the philosopher. They had not envisaged a legendary brother. Moreover, Henry had been ambivalent about his private papers. He had reviewed Balzac's letters long before feeling that he was eavesdropping—but hugely enjoying the experience. He had read Flaubert's general correspond-ence with the close attention of a craftsman seeking to discover how a fellow-artist lived and worked. He had read critically all of Stevenson's letters; and he reveled in the sex and anguish of George Sand's life and loves. Still, an author had to clear the approaches to his privacy, and Mrs. William James knew that during his final visit to Rye, ill and suffering, the novelist had ruthlessly burned anything he found in old drawers and desks. What remained, usually by accident, could be "fair game." James would have liked to organize this game, the whole game of biography and letter pub-lishing. In a notable passage, in one of his half-dozen essays on George Sand, he argued for a duel between the dead author and the living biographer. Only such a duel could restore a sense of fair play; otherwise the dead author was too easy a quarry, a sitting duck for the curious huntsman of letters. "There are secrets for privacy and silence," wrote Henry James, "let them be cultivated on the part of the hunted creature with even half the method with which the love of sport—or call it the historic sense—is cultivated on the part of the investigator." Only then would the game be equal. The sleuth would have to be genuinely cunning, "envenomed with resistance," and his inquiry could exceed in "subtlety and ferocity" the biographical hunt as hitherto practiced: "with every track covered, every paper burnt and every letter unanswered," the victim of the hunt could "in the tower of art, the invulnerable granite, stand, without a sally, the siege of all the years."

Every letter unanswered! The biographer disarmed would indeed have to reach far for his substance. James's mixture of sport and strategy, of hunt and siege, suggested his will to give himself to posterity on his own terms. He offered in effect a challenge to biography; and no less to the editors of his posthumous papers. Yet if certain letters were unanswered, others had to be written—to publishers, editors, friends, hostesses, relatives. He did not have the safety of the telephonic age. He had, as a civilized person, duties of civility and consanguinity. He had always obeyed these duties, in his highly individual way and always in the grand style. His correspondence ends up like his tale of "The Turn of the Screw." The reader gets to know the governess in that tale only by the account she has left of the strange happenings in her life. She is the sole witness, and the reader has to decide on her reliability. So, with all the letters to James burned, and those he wrote preserved, *his* reader must deduce the integral James from his personal documents and the anecdotes or memories of others. Nevertheless James's letters, kept in such abundance, provide vivid pictures of character and personality, and glimpses into art, into life, into the meaning of literary genius and literary power. They belong, as James demanded, to literature; and also to literary psychology. Within the well-organized game of reporter and reported, hunter and hunted, James's letters constitute one of the greatest self-portraits in all literature.

Henry James had given thought to the question of his literary relics beyond the fictional statements in his tales. But with human resistance to the idea of personal extinction, he had done less than he might to protect his privacy. Mrs. William James's unpublished diary records a troubled last visit to Rye; and the novelist himself described in a letter the huge bonfire in his garden which reduced to ashes his literary archive of forty years. He had planned to make specific allusion in his will about his letters; he delayed too long, however. In the end the decisions were left to his executor, his nephew and namesake, William James's oldest son. However, in one letter to Harry James (so called to distinguish him from his famous uncle), he explicitly enjoined him to act as "a check and frustrator" against the "post-mortem exploiter." Pronouncing Shakespeare's curse on such individuals, he declared his "utter and absolute abhorrence of any attempted biography or the giving to the world by 'the family' or by any person for whom my approval has any sanctity, of any part or parts of my private correspondence." Mrs. William James did not know of this when questions began to be asked in London in March of 1916 about Henry James's letters; and while she announced that her son would have to make all the decisions, she gathered what information she could. The celebrated hostess of Hill Hall, Mrs. Charles Hunter (her name was apposite for the image of the chase invoked by James), arranged a special luncheon at which Mrs. James met Max Beerbohm, with whom Mrs. Hunter had been freely discussing the question of a suitable editor of the James papers. Beerbohm began by proposing the most obvious figure, old Edmund Gosse. Gosse had known James for four decades; he was not only librarian of the House of Lords but a formidable literary-establishment figure. He had written biographies which James had criticized but read with lively interest. The two had gossiped in London clubs year after year about their fellow-writers. They had worked together on one of the committees of the Royal Society of Literature. Gosse had elegant and fastidious—and decidedly dogmatic—tastes; yet he was dedicated as few men of his time to the "literary history" that begins from the moment a stylist's pen touches paper. Mrs. James listened in silence. She knew Gosse. She knew also what James's literary agent, J. B. Pinker had told her —"how he had tried to find out what Uncle Henry did want, but that all he knew was that he did *not* want Gosse." This settled Gosse for the James family. Beerbohm wrote after the lunch to Mrs. Hunter, "I hope Mrs. William James hasn't got her eye on some earnest and illiterate Christian Scientist. Gosse, on the whole, seems to me the very best man for the task and Mrs. Wharton the very best woman. Failing either of them, I wish it could be Desmond MacCarthy, who has fine taste and insight and enthusiasm."

Gosse, however, was ruled out; and Mrs. Wharton was ruled impossible. The "incomparable Max" could not have known how thoroughly—and morbidly—Mrs. William James hated Edith Wharton. She hated her with all her Puritan soul because Mrs. Wharton not only wrote novels about adultery, but was reputed to have lovers; or, as Peggy James put it in a letter to her mother some years earlier, she had heard "things about Mrs. Wharton of which I had not dreamed. Her morals are scarcely such as to fit her to be the companion of the young and the innocent." Mrs. James's heart had told her so. And then the devoted and imperious Edith had tried to raise a large purse for Uncle Henry's seventieth birthday! James himself had squelched this act of misguided generosity. When Mrs. James discovered that Theodora Bosanquet, James's amanuensis, was writing daily health bulletins to Mrs. Wharton during her employer's last illness, she dismissed the secretary from Carlyle Mansions where she had served James long and faithfully. Peggy reported to her brother that the amanuensis had "enjoyed the running of things" and had been "getting a bit above herself." An objective observer would say Miss Bosanquet had simply done her duty after James had his stroke until the arrival of next of kin; she had answered the inquiries of friends; but the answers to Mrs. Wharton brought about her exile from her regular tasks. Peggy undertook to answer inquiries and Miss Bosanquet was to come only when summoned.

Miss Bosanquet, who was herself distinctly literary, and would in later life attain a very particular reputation in London's literary world, knew at once from her talks with James's close friends—persons like Mrs. Clifford, Gosse himself, Howard Sturgis, Mrs. Wharton— who the ideal editor of the James letters should be. Desmond

MacCarthy had been mentioned and Peggy James adored him. He was a critic of probity and charm, and a genius of conversation. But would he see the job through with the promptness required? Miss Bosanquet seems to have felt that such a conversational "charmer" would not be capable of editorial self-effacement. There was however the young Percy Lubbock, of Eton and Cambridge, who had reviewed the New York Edition of James's novels and tales in the *Times Literary Supplement* with a genuine feeling for the Master's work. He was a man of energy and also a thorough Jamesian disciple. The matter was none of her affair; but she had taken dictation too long from Henry James not to feel involved, and not to feel a certain bitterness at Mrs. James's proceedings. Percy Lubbock himself was interested. He called on Miss Bosanquet to find out the lay of the land before going to see Mrs. James. He told the amanuensis that he had casually broached the matter to the Jameses and found Mrs. William moving "in a cloud of fine discretions and hesitations and precautions." His remark was worthy of the Master.

Miss Bosanquet went to see James's literary agent, J. B. Pinker, about the choice of an editor. The agent told her he had discovered that Mrs. Wharton had transferred some of her royalties—had subsidized—James's last novel, the incomplete *Ivory Tower*, by having Charles Scribner in New York offer a large advance for which she provided the funds. Miss Bosanquet noted wryly that Mrs. James would be "unwittingly benefitting to a pretty good tune from the gift of her hated enemy." Pinker's theory was that Mrs. James "will always be accessible to the argument of pecuniary profit and that by means of it he can deal with Mr. James's things in the way most in accordance with his wishes." Miss Bosanquet added with a touch of bitterness that Mrs. James showed an "utter lack of understanding"; she had told Pinker that James's autobiographical fragment, *The Middle Years,* describing the novelist's early days in London, wasn't worth publishing. It had been dictated to Miss Bosanquet, who knew what vivid pictures it contained of Tennyson and Browing, George Eliot, a glimpse of Swinburne, a sense of late pre-Raphaelite London.

Percy Lubbock became the candidate of James's intimate friends.

He moved in part within Mrs. Wharton's orbit, but Mrs. William James was not aware of this. He had given proof of his distinction not only in his writings about James but in a study of Pepys, fruit of his librarianship during 1906–1908 of the Bibliotheca Pepysiana at Magdalene College, Cambridge. Lubbock approached literature with the finely attuned English amateurism which is the despair of Americans. He had the aristocratic touch, an assurance of life and manners and an ingrained discretion and delicacy. Miss Bosanquet, recording her interview with Lubbock in her diary, wrote that he "joined with me in a regret that Mrs. Wharton hadn't been left in charge. He feels that it's awfully difficult to offer advice to people like the Jameses and yet that they do need some very badly! He's full of sensitive feeling himself that he can't go boldly trampling on their reserves as Mr. Pearsall Smith more easily can." Logan Pearsall Smith had come to tea a few days earlier in Carlyle Mansions, and "I heard him offering advice by the gallon." The anecdotal Logan could speak freely; he was uninvolved; he was genial; he was a fellow-American and he had known James in his later years (although less well than he would, in the future, make out). His candidate was Desmond MacCarthy.

By midsummer of 1916—by the time Mrs. James returned to Cambridge, smuggling the ashes of Henry James to keep an espionage-conscious America from examining them—the editorial question had been settled. The nephew, Harry, who would always try to do "the real right thing," read Lubbock's writings and was impressed, among other things, by the obituary notice Lubbock contributed that summer to the *Quarterly Review*. To make doubly sure that Mrs. Wharton's imperious hand might not descend from some Olympus on the James papers, Lubbock was instructed to use Edmund Gosse as consultant. He was glad to do this; Gosse knew all literary London and was a fund of ancient gossip. He himself had received half a thousand letters from James; and he had a lifetime's experience in biography. His knowledge of the technical side of book production would be useful to the younger man. Mrs. William James agreed to read the family letters in America, and Peggy agreed to copy the relevant portions—those deemed relevant by the family—for the editor. Lubbock thus never saw the originals. In England he engaged Miss Bosanquet to copy such letters as he could gather in from James's friends. Her familiarity with the sweeping, rushing handwriting assured accuracy. It was agreed that he should work as rapidly as possible, in spite of the delays occasioned by the war. The agent Pinker was aware of the way in which reputations can slip once a writer is dead; it was necessary to put the posthumous writings into print—the two unfinished novels, the autobiographical fragment, and finally the representative collection of the correspondence. Lubbock edited these works while the letters were being assembled; later he would see through the press the thirty-five-volume set of James's fiction, enlarging the New York Edition by eleven volumes, those James had omitted. The Master was available to posterity—at a time when his reputation sank to its lowest point.

Hesitations and Discretions

Percy Lubbock worked rapidly in the midst of difficulties created by the war—the inability to communicate with holders of Henry James letters and indeed his not knowing the full history of James's friendships. The Master had survived so many; Mrs. James and her children knew James's Edwardian world, but the Victorian world was already beginning to be dim and distant. Edith Wharton would later say that James had been extremely secretive about his friends; there were "the friends of the friends" but there were also little cubbyholes, she said, in which certain intimates were kept from other intimates. An appeal for letters was made: but Lubbock could proceed only on the basis of generous cooperation. This he had from all of the late friends. The largest part of his assembling and editing was completed in three years. Both he and his sponsor, Henry James of New York (by this time an important foundation executive and involved with various war tasks), could only work with what they had. They decided the important thing was to recreate the distinctive image which London and New York had known in the twentieth century. The James of mid-century Victorian London—of Bolton Street and De Vere Gardens—was more shadowy, blurred in a middle and far distance. Harry James argued, however, that *A Small Boy and Others* and *Notes of a Son and Brother* and the fragment *The Middle Years* opened up the earlier vistas; and the letters could begin just before *The Middle Years*, 1869, from the time of the "grand tour," James's first adult journey to Europe at twenty-six.

Peace came, and Lubbock put the manuscript into the hands of the executor. Two volumes were scheduled for publication in London and New York in 1920. The text was carefully gone over by Harry, by Mrs. James, by Peggy, and by Harry's younger brother, Billy. The family scrutiny was thorough. Their natural desire was to see their Uncle Henry portrayed in key with the figure *they* remembered from their earlier years. The nephews had first met him in 1892, during one of Willaim James's sabbaticals in Europe; and later Peggy, on emerging from infancy, had come to know her uncle at Lamb House. They were aware of Lubbock's problems, and they were justifiably concerned lest references to the living might cause hurt—or give rise to charges of libel.

Some of the correspondents in England brought their bundles of letters to Lubbock eagerly; genius has a way of exalting the humble, and to have received a letter from the Master singled one out. Others, like the actress Elizabeth Robins, told Lubbock her letters were too "private." A dozen years later she produced her own volume. Still other letters remained locked away. Old friends, like Howells, sent characteristic documentary letters, and Edith Wharton, whose marital problems were spread across many of the 177 letters she had received, chose 50 of the more impersonal ones and had them typed up for Lubbock. Lubbock thus had little opportunity for neutral selection. He used a goodly number of the Wharton letters, not entirely with the approval of Mrs. William James. "Mother thought there was too much Edith Wharton in Lubbock's second volume," one of her sons said years later. How scrupulously Lubbock worked may be seen in the typescripts of the letters copied for him. These he ultimately gave to Harvard. They are far from complete, even less complete than they were in 1919, for during the second world war the Germans occupied his Italian villa and some of the file boxes were used to start fires. Among those that survived are copies of letters the originals of which have disappeared. Deciphering the letters was a problem; James's handwriting seems legible enough; it is large and often a fast scrawl, but his bunchings of words and his rapid pen strokes can make for easy misreadings. The word "your" in one letter to Gosse was read by one biographer as "queer," with astonishing results. There were of course many repetitions; and many letters duplicated passages in other letters on nights when James was too tired to mint new phrases. The Lubbock volumes enshrined for posterity the Johnsonian image of the Master of Rye and Chelsea rather than a younger Henry James who rode horseback on the Campagna and climbed mountains in Switzerland. Lubbock made no attempt to search out James's letters to editors and publishers. He dealt exclusively with the literary and social, the friendly Henry James, the figure of "Master" rather than the tough professional.

To this day Lubbock's volumes remain the most important collection of Henry James letters in print. The present edition is the first to draw upon the full *epistolarium*, now available, after half a century. There are still some James letters hidden from sight; but there are now representative letters for all the decades of his maturity and certain illuminating letters out of his adolescence. The few peripheral collections, published since Lubbock, not all authorized, have added minor glimpses of the protean artist. Lubbock's image of James was set for fifty years, the figure of the fictional lawgiver, as well as the gregarious expatriate. But James was never seen in these volumes as relaxed and unbuttoned: he is always in a top hat. The editing was sparse and objective: James was allowed— and this was a merit—to talk, unencumbered by irrelevant footnotes. An occasional headnote gave some guidance where necessary.

The correspondence of Lubbock and James's nephew Harry furnishes an interesting gloss to the whole question of the original editing of the letters. The nephew seems to have been concerned first and foremost with his uncle's spontaneity in his intimate correspondence, and there is a long and charming passage on this subject. Harry described how his uncle "reacted vigorously against the Anglo-Saxon incapacity for emotional expression." He remembered his "telling twice with great enjoyment of going to see James Russell Lowell off on a New York steamer—some French or Spanish friends of Lowell appeared and embraced, and Henry James heard an Englishman say to his wife 'look at those two dirty Frenchmen kissing each other.' Considering," said Harry, "what orthodox British manners and prejudices are, there was something almost splendid in his disregard of bystanders and listeners when he wished to express his goodwill to anyone for whom he cared at all." This was confirmed by Bernard Shaw, who told once how Henry James had kissed him on both cheeks when he arrived to pay a call at Lamb House—and there was a kind of childish surprise in Shaw's eyes and voice even in telling his anecdote many years after—he who was always accustomed to distance and to a barricade of words between himself and his listeners.

But Harry's question to Lubbock was, would readers understand? How would they interpret a letter to Hugh Walpole beginning "most retrocessive but incurably beloved Hugh," or another that began "dearest, dearest, darlingest Hugh"? Harry characterized this as his uncle's impulse "to begin and end the letter to anyone for whom he cared, by enveloping the person addressed in some kind of affectionate hug." And the nephew continued, "I wonder whether sometimes the evidence may not be heaped up in ways which will be misunderstood . . . Is there any danger of giving occasion for silly joking at their expense?" In blunter terms, Harry was worried about his uncle's relaxed homoerotism. Hendrik Andersen, the sculptor James loved in so troubled a way, would later ask permission to publish the novelist's letters to him: they were filled with intensities of affection; and permission was refused on the ground that the letters were not sufficiently literary or historical. The letters written by James to Walpole were selected for Lubbock by Walpole himself and received thorough editing. "Ah, Hugh Walpole needn't be alarmed!" Lubbock wrote to Edmund Gosse. "I most carefully cut out very nearly all the extravagances he has in mind, and only left in one or two that struck me as pleasant and easy. (But they shall go too if he doesn't like them.) You may be quite sure I shall watch this point attentively and indeed I had it in mind throughout. But don't you find that such things don't *now* strike outsiders as they would have a generation or so ago?—that kind of effusive expression is so much commoner among people of all sorts than it used to be."

Victorian reticence and New England puritanism nevertheless joined hands in Lubbock's editing, with his reluctant consent. We must take care in judging the volumes, however, for we look back from an unbuttoned age to an era more inhibited, but also more delicate in its approach to privacy. Lubbock spoke of "the perpetual discretion question." Many letters wholly gossipy were set aside by the family. Harry explained that his uncle had made people his study and "during one of the earlier years in Cambridge he made it a rule to see somebody or other outside of the family every day." The rule may have been—during those long, dull seasons in Cambridge—one way of escaping from the oppressive atmosphere of Quincy Street; but it had become a way of life. The overflow of intimate talk in the letters about persons and personalities is indeed constant.

Another element in the correspondence troubled the novelist's nephew. His uncle too frequently pleaded poverty, without justification. James's earliest letters, not made available to Lubbock but printed here, show how scrupulously he kept his accounts with his parents who lent him money initially for his life abroad—sums he repaid by constant publication. James always spent freely, but cautiously. He never denied himself creature comforts; he did refuse deluxe accommodations. First-class hotels were more than sufficient for novelistic comfort, and he complained later in life when he had to accept luxury while motoring with the Whartons. In his earlier years he had stinted at times and revealed a certain thriftiness. He was generous to a fault when appeals were made to him, as we know from sums sent not only to relatives but to authors in need. His own needs as a writing bachelor were modest. For years he lived in simple lodgings in Piccadilly at a time when other writers of his reputation and earnings would have chosen more commodious quarters. In late middle life he finally furnished his own flat and engaged servants; and he waited until he was sixty before buying a house in the country. Yet to his literary friends he spoke always of his small earnings, and this gave his nephew pause. "He was always better off than he trusted himself to believe," he told Lubbock, and he urged the editor to tone down some of the pleas of poverty. In fact he found the allusions so frequent that "I can't much wonder now, as I once did, at Mrs. Wharton's attempt to raise a fund on his 70th birthday." The nephew went on: "His father had inherited what was a fortune for that day, was always utterly careless or indifferent, wasted most of it thro' sheer inattention to what was happening and launched my father and Uncle Henry into the world with the conviction that such things were perversely fatal and beyond their comprehension and control."

Harry further explained that James's complaints of small royalties overlooked a significant fact. The novelist invariably demanded and received very large advances from publishers. Sales of his books seldom caught up with the sums advanced, or did so very slowly. The nephew remembered on one occasion receiving an urgent cable from Henry James for funds and sent $1,000 at once. Later he discovered that the appeal was the fruit of a sudden anxiety and that his uncle had a comfortable balance in his London bank and a sizable fund for petty cash needs at Rye. What the nephew failed to understand, however, was that James's royalties were indeed small compared with the best-selling Kipling or his constantly successful friend Howells. The revenues of a popular writer like F. Marion Crawford or the successes of certain playwrights made James feel like an impoverished country cousin or one of the poor relations in Balzac. His own books rarely went into second editions, and when he heard how often Mrs. Wharton's books were reprinted, he ironically pointed to the little cart on which her luggage was placed (when she came to visit) and said that this was what *his* last novel had earned. As a craftsman James waxed ironic at public success; what could one say about success?—it was like a good dinner—one simply had had it. Yet he felt, as tales such as "The Death of the Lion" or "The Next Time" show, that his genius was not sufficiently rewarded. The author of "The Next Time" dreams of the moment when he will write a smashing work, but the next time never comes; and the lady novelist whose works sell in millions calls to discover how she might for once at least, in *her* "next time," have a "distinguished failure." She desires the great author's distinction; he wants her flat-footed success. Deep in his heart James believed in his ultimate triumph, in the ultimate judgment of literary history. But in that artist's "love affair" with the world of which Freud wrote, James felt himself distinctly to be the rejected lover. What sustained him was his philosophy of "doing." Failure never discouraged him from trying again; and trying always to surpass himself.

Harry James read Lubbock's manuscript during a voyage from Europe to America in 1919. Surveying the letters as assembled, with the admirable connective tissue written by Lubbock uniting the different periods of the Master's life, it dawned on the practical yet sensitive Harry at last what manner of man his uncle had been. There had always existed in the William James family a touch of condescension toward the fiction-writing relative of Lamb House; the children had picked up from William his easy tolerance of an idiosyncratic younger brother who troubled so little with the facts in which William was interested, those of science and the laboratory —those of expository writing and of philosophical speculation. William had defined Henry as "powerless-feeling," and later had spoken in a humorous vein that scarcely disguised his feeling that Henry was "vain" and "frivolous." William's children could not see that Uncle Henry was powerless only in the presence of his dynamic elder brother. Left to himself he possessed unlimited power in the management of his art and his career. William's sense of reality did not allow him to have empathy for his brother's realities of imaginative being. They were foreign to his pragmatic, scientific, investigative mind. He used explicit, forceful similes and striking analogies. He had criticized Henry's early writings for their slightness and he criticized the late for their density. He was impatient with the textured and symbolic metaphors of his brother, his nuances of feeling, his impressionistic prose. The William James children had grown up to an image of an overly fastidious uncle. And this sets in relief the letter written by Harry to his sister when he had completed his reading of Lubbock's manuscript:

> During the voyage I've had leisure to read Lubbock's collection of Henry James letters carefully. I shall turn the type-copy over to mama on landing and she will doubtless soon send the bundle to you ... The book makes a deeper and bigger impression on careful reading [as a whole]. It will, I rather think, make Uncle Henry count very much more than he did already. For it's full of literature as well as character. In fact I suspect that these letters will become, in the history of English literature, not only one of the half dozen greatest epistolary classics, but a sort of milestone —the last stone of the age whose close the Great War has marked. They are a magnificent commentary on the literary life of his generation, and they're done in a style which will never be used naturally again. Indeed in the matter of style they're not exactly characteristic of Henry James's time. It's fairer to say that they sustain the massive and abundant suavity of earlier days down to the latest date to which the modern world *could* have allowed it a genuine survival. Nobody could have, would have had a right, to express himself that way who hadn't been born nearly eighty years ago. That particular thing died with Uncle Henry. If the letters of any of his contemporaries are still to be published, their correspondence will prove them to have been more modern, or to have been inferior in this art. These letters will be the final, classic and magnificent manifestation of their kind.

In recognizing the distinction of the letters, the nephew confused the individual voice of Henry James with the voice of his age. Perhaps he did not grasp, being more a man of practical affairs, that his uncle was not using the style of his era, but a style created by himself. Still, the nephew's letter showed a capacity to look for the truth of things. He had often been depreciatory, but now he could see—it was spread before him—that his uncle had been from the first a constituted and integrated artist, even in his letters. This made them, in certain ways, no less significant than other works that issued from his pen. Written spontaneously, but with the ingrained habit of "writing," the correspondence showed the novelist's sense of reality—the reality of emotion—a salient and fanciful mind, a manner of saying things that was memorable. For James survives, above the materials of his fiction, above the "invulnerable granite" of his art, and above the critical controversies, as one of America's supreme stylists. His letters represent an overflow of this style into his daily life. People who would otherwise be unknown found their little niche by the touch of the Master's pen; it gave him almost a kind of literary "papal" power. Had James not traveled, had he not isolated himself in his later years from London, had he lived in our age of the telephone (he did install a primitive phone during his last years), we might have fewer letters and a less lively and less abundant account of his active life. His early travels were chronicled to amuse his family and his friends. There was a moment when Emerson carried copies of the young Henry's letters in his pocket, to read to his friends, and Norton sent them to Ruskin who was enchanted with them. In America the epistolary pen ceased to write; and we have sparse records of his seasons in Cambridge or his sojourns in New York. But we have enough to show that these were not fallow periods; we can discover traces of his reading, and his tales of these periods supply all the evidence we need of his incessant fertility and his untamed ambition. If he chronicled in letters the small happenings of his literary life to amuse, these today become the picture of an age; they contain the penetrating glimpses by a pair of American eyes into the manners and society of England and Europe, so that gossip often becomes history. In later years, during his continental wanderings, his friends received the full bounty of his writing portfolio. The masses of letters in Gosse's archive, the Norton family papers, the correspondence with Stevenson especially after the latter's "secession" to the South Pacific, the late letters to Mrs. Wharton, the sporadic yet substantial epistolary tête-à-têtes with Howells, the Curtises, or Jessie Allen, provide a vast hoard and in the high literary and social style. James had challenged his future biographers to find him in his art; but his art was in his letters as well as in his tales and he may be seen in many moods. Among his foreign friends, Paul Bourget and Alphonse Daudet saved his letters, and one was found recently in the archive of Gustave Flaubert. Lubbock's two fat volumes, as the nephew realized, provided a splendid "sampling." Thousands more would turn up in the ensuing years.

The Real Right Thing

To do "the real right thing" of James's ghost story of that name was to leave dead writers alone, to read them only in their works. Henry James's executor believed that he had done the real right thing in commissioning the Lubbock volumes. He hoped that this would take care of his uncle's reputation for the rest of the century. However in the 1920s and 1930s he began to receive requests from Henry James's friends who came upon bundles of old letters in their desks or attics. Could these not be published? They seemed so warm, so filled with the voice of the Master. He also received copies of letters found by professors and students in research libraries, individuals who sought to wrap themselves (so Harry believed) in the glory of his uncle's prose. "Lately," wrote James's nephew to Percy Lubbock, "almost everybody who ever received a letter or two from my Uncle Henry seems to have conceived plans for publishing them. The effect is not happy." His first experience involved his tenant in Lamb House, E. F. Benson, writer of light fiction and popular historian of the Edwardian and Georgian periods. Benson came upon a packet of letters written by the novelist to his brother Arthur Christopher Benson and asked whether he might not print these in a limited edition. Harry James knew of his uncle's casual friendship with A. C. Benson, a don at Eton and then at Cambridge. The request seemed reasonable and Harry gave permission spontaneously without asking for copies of the correspondence. He received a shock when the volume arrived. The letters were trivial; the volume was trivial; and Harry felt his uncle was trivialized in the process. They showed the novelist trying to say gracious things about Benson's turgid verses, or making dates for lunch at his club. There was no discussion of literature to speak of; the correspondence was insubstantial—it was, as we might say, telephone talk. Harry wrote an irritated comment, on the flyleaf, recording the history of the book, and deposited it at Harvard. From then on he was alert to the dangers of easily given permissions. Shortly after, Elizabeth Robins, the American actress, asked to print James's letters to her about Ibsen and the theater. Harry James knew her; she was beautiful and imperative and he found it difficult to refuse. But he enjoined her to supply a gloss, a context, a background. This she did in a sparse and elusive way, making the volume seem mysterious and greatly exaggerating her intimacy with James. The best letters in the volume were written not to her but to her friend Mrs. Hugh Bell (later Lady Bell) for whom James had a high regard as a writer of witty closet comedies. But from this time the nephew drew a firm line. He told Lubbock, "One reason for trusting you with the delicate task of editing a couple of volumes and for rejoicing when they have been done the way you did them, is that one can say 'let those volumes stand.'" And this was what Harry James did thereafter. He permitted only letters of substance to be put into print and then only after careful consultation with Lubbock. "Most of these people who want to print now are merely reaching out for a few shillings or ministering to their own vanity." I find in Harry's correspondence with Lubbock that he took the same careful and "correct" attitude when I inquired whether I might collect James's plays. But once his decision was made, he gave me all possible assistance and access to the family papers. In 1937, seven years before the family archive was given to Harvard, I first examined the thousands of letters and other papers then deposited in the basement of Widener Library and also found in a large old-fashioned wooden chest—which doubtless had served James on his early sea voyages—the composition books that constitute his notebooks (later edited by Matthiessen and Murdock).

The second world war inevitably interrupted many literary and scholarly enterprises. The centenaries of William and Henry James in 1942 and 1943 brought a new wave of interest in the brothers and many new readers. Thus began what came to be called "the James revival." It was in reality the first discovery of Henry James as an artist: his role had previously been as a culture figure who "turned his back" on America. A later generation could take a wider view. In 1943, the year of the novelist's centenary, Harry James presented to Harvard, for deposit in the Houghton Library, the materials I had seen six years before in the basement of the Widener. This was after Ralph Barton Perry had used them for his substantial study of the "thought and character" of William James. In his letter of gift to Harvard, a copy of which he sent to me, the executor stipulated that the manuscript material and the letters be reserved exclusively for post-doctoral research. He did not want (as he put it to me) "my father and Uncle Henry writing dissertations for inexperienced students." It was at this time that certain priorities in the materials were established for Professors Perry, Matthiessen, and myself. Even before Matthiessen's tragic death, I had proposed to the executor the publication of volumes of letters designed to be "complementary to the notebooks and supplementary to Lubbock." My decision in 1950 to write the life of James caused me to postpone the editorial project. However, I issued, with the consent of the James heirs, a small volume of *Selected Letters* (1955), in Louis Kronenberger's series of "Great Letter Writers" designed to serve as a guide to Henry James's epistolary styles and strategies. It contained 120 letters. During my work on the biography many thousands of letters became available to me which had been locked away during Lubbock's editing, and it became clear with the lapse of the decades and the deaths of all those who had known James that my original idea for a volume or two of supplementary letters should be expanded to the publication of the novelist's "general" correspondence, as had been done for Flaubert long ago. I discussed this project with the representatives of the family, first with Billy James, who succeeded his brother as head of the family, later with his son John, and still later with John's cousin, Alexander R. James, in whom the rights are now vested. The Jameses felt that the general policies set down by Harry should be maintained. Billy James in particular, who had known his uncle, was firm in refusing to allow publication of letters James had termed "the mere twaddle of graciousness." Permission to publish was also limited for another reason—one which James's agent originally gave to Miss Bosanquet —to protect the future statutory copyrights of valuable literary material. The general theory subscribed to by the James heirs was to publish a comprehensive selection of James's literary letters; this would put the entire correspondence into perspective; the original material excised by Mrs. William James could be restored, and readers would better understand the range of James's friendships as well as his calculated art in the epistolary medium—his cultivated irony, his spontaneities, his loyalties, as well as his social duplicities which made some of his correspondence seem more friendly than it really was. Indiscriminate publication tends to fragment and create erroneous impressions; and the social letters read in great accumulation tended to nullify the serious artistic side of his personal expression. As Billy James put it, "I feel I have to protect the dear Uncle from his own generosities and volubilities." By this he meant that some balance was required between James the artist and James the mandarin.

The present collection is taken from the large stores of letters I found in many countries, but mainly from the family papers at Harvard. It constitutes only a part of the entire corpus. My guiding thought has been that in an age of photo-duplication we no longer need total publication, and in any event, in the case of James, such publication would be difficult, costly, and redundant, certainly out of proportion to the needs of the general reader. Scholars can read for themselves the holographs which today are so easily copied. When I print an archetypal letter giving directions and trains to Rye—the speedy express from Charing Cross, the "dilatory" local at Ashford—there is no need to print another hundred resembling it. The letters I have selected have been chosen either because they are documentary, throw light on character or personality, or furnish a picture of family background. I have used literary content as my primary criterion; and I give importance to James's "working" letters—the correspondence of the artist and the "professional."

Even the earliest letters, those of the schoolboy, show an ear for the rhythms of prose and James's close power of observation and description. The adolescent James is unusually alert, extremely precocious in his verbalizations, and shrewdly watches human behavior. When James, in later letters, describes J. T. Fields as deeply melancholy in spite of his Dickensian cheerfulness he demonstrates an ability to cut through social masks. And when in repeated letters he counsels friends like Grace Norton to "live through" the disasters of experience, to consult the "algebra" of themselves, he seems almost to be talking, in a literary sense, the modern modes of therapy, his full understanding of catharsis. James's sense of "reality" is nowhere better illustrated than in his constant study of the English. The "observant stranger" who took Victorian England in his stride, seeing its philistines with good-natured irony, adhered to his humane aestheticism and with clairvoyance predicted certain forms of English decay. And this at times in language that was Gibbonesque or, after the fact, we might say "Churchillian." We can trace in the letters the gradual evolution of the personal style, the search for delicacies of feeling, and the ultimate complexity which spoke for the intricacies of his own mind. "I hate American simplicity," James one day told his niece Peggy. "I glory in the piling up of complications of every sort. If I could pronounce the name of James in any different and more elaborate way I should be in favor of doing it."

James's feelings about publication of letters were consistent with his professionalism. He opposed truncation. "One has the vague sense of omissions . . . one *smells* the thing unprinted," he remarked after reading Colvin's edition of Stevenson's letters. He wasn't sure that Colvin had not erred on the side of "over-suppression." By the same token he protested to Charles Eliot Norton because he had edited the letters of Lowell without discrimination. The second volume, he wrote Norton, "might have contained more letters illustrative of his London life . . . It was the richest period of his existence, surely, in the particular way in which letters are an expression of 'richness' and would have given a picture, very delightful to possess, of the play of his mind in a far greater multitude

xxxiii

of contacts than he had ever had before." James added, "I may be invidious—but I care comparatively so little for the play of his mind in contact, say, with R. W. Gilder or T. B. Aldrich."

If "play of mind" seems to be the primary concern of James in published letters, there is no problem in garnering the correspondence in this and the succeeding volumes. The play of mind is constant—even when James writes to Gilder or Aldrich—and it is never more active and imaginative than when he is showing his plumage to his fellow stylists. "I live with my pen in my hand," he once wrote, "which is perhaps why I am always answering the letters I haven't wanted particularly to get." On another occasion, James told Henry Adams, "in writing to my relatives I ransack my memory for every adventure that has befallen me and turn my pockets inside out, so that they receive, and possibly propagate, an exaggerated impression of my social career." He may have turned out the small change in his pockets; but it was this change that became literary capital; and now it is socio-historical capital as well. All the vulnerable parties are gone from the scene, and in this respect I enjoy a freedom no editor of James's letters has had hitherto. Lubbock was forced to eliminate remarks in James's letters to Howells which the Jameses felt might touch sensitive feelings, and Harry asked that a certain letter criticizing his brother-in-law for believing in the Shakespearian ciphers be suppressed. Lubbock fought back and sent the letter to Gosse. Gosse ruled that any letter in which James spoke of Shakespeare belonged to posterity. Moreover the recipient, Bruce Porter, had made the letter available to Lubbock. I remember removing a letter dealing with *Guy Domville* from the *Selected Letters* because Billy James found it "too sad"—it showed Uncle Henry in a fit of deep depression. I had gone to great pains to run down this document, but I felt that Billy's feelings should be respected. The letter now will appear in its chronological place.

Among scholars the discussion is interminable: how should letters be edited? Some seem to believe that modern letters should be reproduced almost as if they were photographs of the original.

Is this valid in an age of photography? It seems to me when letters are translated from handwriting to print, they should be edited to be read as one reads books: with an avoidance of brackets and an economy of footnotes. The & should certainly read "and," and all abbreviations and shortcuts of hasty writing deserve to be spelled out. Simon Nowell Smith, in a charming lecture on "Authors, Editors and Publishers," raised his voice rightly I think against the bracketed *sic* when used immoderately, or the reproduction of obvious spelling mistakes anyone might make when writing in a hurry. Modern scholarship has perhaps been rigid in believing that what applies to ancient manuscripts may be applied to the modern. I have made silent corrections where they were obviously called for; but where there has been a significant slip of the pen I have indicated it in footnotes or kept it in the text. In the letters of the young Henry James I have retained relevant misspellings; they are a part of the flavor of the letters. As for the footnotes, I have preferred to be simply informative, with a strong feeling that if one carried footnotes to the extreme one could end up writing a history of all civilization. I see no need to give full names and dates for every name mentioned in the letters. Most intelligent readers know who Shakespeare is; and the names of Cambridge worthies to whom Henry James sends regards have as little need of dating as certain of the better known painters James mentions. Such footnotes as I have included are bibliographical or historical; identifications are made when they involve persons whom we meet repeatedly. I have tried to offer an answer wherever the reader might ask a question.

At the risk of some redundancy I have printed in each instance, where it was available, the total letter. Each letter has its particular integrity; it is written to a separate individual and it must be allowed its repetitions of matter in other letters. But I have been selective among letters containing redundancies.

Where possible each letter has been taken from the holograph, and even when I have used photocopies I have sought to verify my transcript against the original. I have told myself that books of letters are often dipped into rather than read consecutively, and I have therefore proceeded on the assumption that each letter stands by itself, even while it belongs in a continuum. No system has yet been devised by which the gloss can be movable; and the index remains the best resort for those who like to read letters methodically and attentively.

I have tried to select the "best" letters; and in such an embarrassment of riches the choice, the taste, the discrimination is personal; but in this instance it can claim a particular circumstance: it is informed by my long-sustained biographical enterprise. Certain omissions, as well as calculated inclusions, became inevitable for me; however, the large James archives in many libraries will provide opportunities for amplification and further collections in the years to come. The present and ensuing volumes are designed to be "representative" and "useful," serving also as a guide to the "epistolary James," both the novice and the Master; showing his evolution in a literary form which is at once "interpersonal" and also in a certain sense self-exhibiting. The electronic age is making our communications more audible and thus more ephemeral; this fact alone renders even more precious these records of one age in which letters were a supreme and highly particular form—especially when they were written with the pen of art.

Brief Chronology

1843: Born April 15, No. 21 Washington Place, New York City, second son of Henry James, writer and lecturer.

1845–1855: Lives in New York and Albany, goes to school in both cities, plays in lower Fifth Avenue area, much theater-going and reading.

1855–1858: James family goes abroad. Travel and study, Switzerland, England, France. Attends French school at Boulogne-sur-mer.

1858: Returns to America, residence at Newport, R. I.

1859: Studies at Geneva and Bonn.

1860: Returns to Newport. Dabbles in art. Friendship with John LaFarge. Reads Balzac and Merimée.

1861: Receives back injury while helping to extinguish a fire.

1862: Enters Harvard Law School (Dane Hall), September 2.

1863: Abandons law for letters.

1864: Family moves from Newport to Boston. James submits first writings to Charles Eliot Norton and becomes friend of William Dean Howells. First known book review appears unsigned in *North American Review*, October; anonymous tale, "A Tragedy of Error," in *Continental Monthly*, February.

1865: First signed tale, "The Story of a Year," appears in *Atlantic Monthly*, March.

1866: Family settles in Cambridge.

1869: First adult trip to Europe: England, Switzerland, Italy.

1870: Returns to Cambridge. Writes first novel *Watch and Ward*.

1872–1874: Travels in England, Switzerland, Germany, writing articles for the *Nation*. Stays in Paris, Rome, Florence.

1874–1875: Spends winter in New York writing art and theater notes for the *Nation*. Decides to settle in Europe.

1875: Completes *Roderick Hudson*. Publishes first two books, *Transatlantic Sketches* and *A Passionate Pilgrim*. Sails for England en route to a residence in Paris.

I
Boyhood and Youth

1843-1861

1
Boyhood and Youth

Henry James was born 15 April 1843 at No. 21 Washington Place, a little street between the Square and Broadway and in a house located where the Brown Building of New York University now stands. He was the second son of five children, William, the elder (born in 1843), Garth Wilkinson, his junior (1845), Robertson (1846), and Alice (1848). His father, Henry James Sr. (1811–1882) for whom he was named, had purchased the house expecting to live continuously in New York: but the word "continuous" was not in his vocabulary. During the birth-year of his second son he took his family abroad and immediately sold this house. Henry James Jr. learned to walk and talk in England, in a commodious cottage in Windsor Park. Small wonder that English parks and houses loom so large in his work; they were the earliest landscape to which his eyes were exposed. He himself has recorded his precocious memory of the Place Vendôme in Paris and its Napoleonic obelisk. Europe was Henry's initial experience; but there followed a return to New York in 1845 and a shuttling back and forth between Manhattan and his grandmother's house in Albany, celebrated in the opening pages of *The Portrait of a Lady*. In New York, little Henry James's walks in the Square were attended by maids and governesses; these are described in the opening pages of *Washington Square*, where James in particular remembers—in an autobiographical passage—the peculiar odor of the ailanthus trees. We glimpse the small boy kicking autumn leaves along the lower reaches of Fifth Avenue and (like Proust after him in Paris) spelling out the theatrical billboards. He remembered vividly the small parochial world of Manhattan with its muddy streets, its chickens on the sidewalks and pigs rooting in the gutters. He and his brother William went to various schools on Broadway and lived in a large house in 14th Street off Fifth Avenue. The streets of Manhattan were the playground of the James boys; the daughter Alice, like many little girls of the time, was reared decorously at home. In the household were the father, his wife (the former Mary Walsh; 1810–1882) and her sister Catherine (1808?–1889). James thus had two mothers—both formidable—the quiet but firm Mary and the assertive and ever-present Aunt Kate.

The elder Henry James was a mystic and a Swedenborgian, though remaining a worldly, secular figure in all that he did. He was, however, impractical, voluble, gregarious, possessed of much originality of expression and a great deal of Irish verbal aggressiveness. He had lost a leg in a fire when he was thirteen, and Henry always had memories of his stomping about on his wooden and later his cork leg. The longish stay in Manhattan between little Henry's third and twelfth years came to an end when the elder James decided to take his children abroad again in 1855, first to Geneva, then to London, and later to Paris. They needed a "better sensuous education" than New York's streets could give them—so the father said in a famous letter to his friend Ralph Waldo Emerson. The single extant letter from James's boyhood shows him reaching from Paris to New York, to accept membership in a youthful theatrical enterprise.

The Jameses returned from abroad in 1858 during a period of financial slump and settled in Newport, R.I. Here James formed his friendship with Thomas Sergeant Perry, John La Farge the painter, and other young and promising Americans. Then, after a year of Newport, the restless father for a third time took his family abroad. The letters here given record the 1859–1860 school experience of the future novelist and his period of study in Bonn. He was homesick for America—for Newport. The wandering father, in carrying his children back and forth, ultimately found them rebellious, and their joy at their return to America is clearly told in the letters. These vividly document for us the itinerant nature of the family of those years and Henry's sense of being a "hotel-child." Yet these were the journeys which launched James as a cosmopolite. The rest of his education would be the private school of the artist, the mysterious school of the imagination.

The letters of Henry James's boyhood are sparse; one survives out of the time in New York which the novelist celebrated in *A Small Boy and Others*. But we possess a correspondence which lights up his adolescence—the letters he wrote to his Newport friend, Thomas Sergeant Perry. Curiously enough, Perry did not make these letters available to Percy Lubbock. When Lubbock asked him for assistance he received a 2,000 word memorandum which is reproduced in the first volume of the Lubbock edition, describing Perry's early acquaintance with the Jameses at Newport, their vast reading at the Redwood Library, and the future novelist's shyness and reticence. The letters, which would have vividly documented this, were allowed to remain in attic and barn; they are stained and smudged and not easily deciphered. Fortunately Virginia Harlow, while working on a dissertation on Perry, was able to obtain the correspondence from Perry's daughter and she printed them in an appendix to the biography she published in 1950. I have established their definitive text from those deposited by Perry's daughter, Margaret, in Colby College Library, in Waterville, Maine, but was unable to locate the originals of the earliest of these letters, those written from Geneva. Fortunately Duke University Library microfilmed the Perry letters when Miss Harlow was working on them. The texts of these particular letters are based on the microfilm copy.

To Edgar Van Winkle

Ms Harvard   ฿
[Paris 1856]

Dear Eddy[1]

As I heard you were going to try to turn the club into a Theatre And as I was asked w'ether I wanted to belong here is my answer. I would like very much to belong.

Yours Truly
H. James

1. This is the earliest Henry James letter extant, written to a former playmate when the Jameses lived in 14th Street in New York. Edgar Beach Van Winkle

5

(1842–1920) was later chief engineer of the Department of Public Parks in New York. See *A Small Boy and Others* (1913), Chap. XVII.

To Thomas Sergeant Perry

Mf Duke

New York. [by]
Oct. 8. [1859]
9 o'clock

Dear Perry[1]

I have been postponing answering your welcome letter in the hope that something would turn up that would be worth relating; but as yet nothing has occured to make my heart beat faster than usual, to make my hair stand on end, or to plunge my family into tears of solicitude about my fate, as indeed would be difficult, for I have spent most of my time between the omnibi and the buildings in and about Wall St.

You see by the date that this is our day for sailing. I write now in case I am not able to do so on board. I can scarcely sit still to write this and feel myself thinking much more of what I leave behind than what I expect to find. Newport and the Newporters are surrounded with a halo, in my mind which grows brighter and brighter as two o'clock draws near.

Mother and the children arrived safely and soundly on Thursday morning, and they join with me in begging to be remembered to your mother and sisters and all our other friends. I will write from the Vanderbilt[2] if possible; and if not as soon after we arrive as I can.

Good bye to you and every body and every thing!

Yours very truly
H. James Jr.

Our address is Care of Baring Bros. London England.

Excuse these blots and hurried writing and torn paper.

1. Thomas Sergeant Perry (1845–1928) was HJ's fellow student in Newport at a private school before the Civil War. His ancestors included the two famous Commodores—the Perrys of Lake Erie and of Japan. He was for a number of years an active critic, editor, and translator.

2. The James family sailed on the S.S. *Vanderbilt*, New York to Le Havre. The voyage lasted from 8 to 20 October 1859.

To Thomas Sergeant Perry

Mf Duke

Geneva November 18*th* [1859].

Dear Perry

/ I had commenced a letter to you a day or two ago when yours arrived, and as it renders a great many things that I said useless I have torn it and now commence another. I had begun with a great many excuses for not having written sooner and I feel inclined to redouble them when I see how much more exemplary you have been. You received, wonderful to relate, my letter written from New York, and would have been gladdened with another written off Southampton had not the very necessary point of sending it off to the Arago which passed us there been neglected. When we arrived in Geneva five days after landing there was a prospect of becoming so soon settled at school that I thought I had better postpone till I could enrich my letter with an account of the thrilling event.

It came to pass three weeks ago, and since then I haven't had the time to write—yes, for the first time in my life almost I can really say I haven't had the time. I will give you an account of my manifold occupations in a few minutes; and first tell you what sort of a journey we have had. Our passage was of eleven days in length and of scarcely more than eleven hours in fine weather. The Demon of the Sea was not behindhand in paying me a visit, and a very long and tedious one he made, indeed I don't think there was a passenger who didn't have a little taste of his delightful society. We had our share of the storms which have been working such mischief within the last month, but as they did no worse than proove to us what an excellent sailer the Vanderbilt is I do not regret them now I'm on land. We spent a day in Havre, plenty of time to find out what a nice little place it is, two days in Paris, which I devoted to the revisiting of certain familiar spots, and one on the journey from Paris here, which I devoted principally to looking out of the

Henry James and his father, 1854

window and going to sleep, the latter let me add, being a necessary consequence of the former. We arrived here in good season for the opening of the schools and we boys are disposed of as follows: Wilky and Robbie are installed at boarding school out in the country.[1] They've a very nice place, capital play ground and provisions for fun out of doors; their teacher M. Maquelin is a very good man, and Americans and English are in the minority which is very rare here in Geneva. Willie goes to the Courses of the Academy which he finds to suit him exactly. I have become a member of the school of M. Rochette, which thus far I have no cause to regret; I have to work harder than I have ever done before, the school-hours being from eight A.M. to 5 P.M. with but an hour's intermission. Hitherto I have had to study all the evening, and on my holidays which are Thursday afternoon and Sunday and have therefore no time of my own at all. But I shall be soon able to have most of the evenings free, as I have caught up with my class, which was a couple of weeks ahead of me and have given up one study for which I had no time. There are twenty scholars who attend as I do from eight to five, and several who only come for certain classes, and leave as soon as they are over. The school is intended for preparing such boys as wish to be engineers, architects, machinists, "and the like" for other higher schools, and I am the only one who is not destined for either of the useful arts or sciences, although I am I hope for the art of being useful in some way. I get on there nevertheless very well.

When we first came here we could find no apartments to suit us and have taken rooms at the Hotel de l'Écu for the Winter—and this I believe is all, about ourselves.

The first question that occurs to me to ask about you is whether you have gone South yet or not. If you have you are enjoying the same pleasure that I am, that of dreaming about Newport. If you are not gone tell me all that is passing there, and how every body and every thing is getting along. You don't know what pleasure the slightest scrap of news would give. How is the Redwood[2] getting along; I miss it very much for there is no place of the kind here, except a venerable old institution, with none but the oldest of books (not that I object to that, for the older the better I think) and an old librarian who looks as if he derived his being from all that was most sanctimonious and respectable in them. Give my respects to Messrs. Clark and Rhoades and tell them that I think they would make a rapid fortune by transporting their interesting and valuable collection to this benighted town. Father found out just now that I am writing to you, which causes him to exclaim again as he often does, "what a pity that good (?) boy Sargy Perry shouldn't be out here enjoying the advantages of these schools!" He told me to give his love to your mother and to say how gladly he would take charge of you if she would only send you out and would deal with you as faithfully as he would with his own boys. I know this would interfere with some of your plans, but I can't help enumerating the benefits which arise from it. You could go to the *Gymnase* here, an excellent school, which I would have gone to but for being so backward in Latin, you could learn French very well here and go to Germany with us and learn German, and when your mother comes out as she spoke of doing before we left I am sure she will have no cause to be sorry for having let you come. I say all this without knowing any of your own reasons for not wishing to come, but I only hope they are few and easily overbalanced.

Here I must end. Please remember us all to your mother and sisters; and to all our Newport friends, particularly to Mr. Leverett; to the boys, MacKaye, Robeson, Wetmore, Porter, Pell and De Jongh,[3] and to the Porters if you are with them. Good bye, *please* write soon and believe me

ever affectionately yours.

H. James Jr.

P. S. Your letter written on the 9 Oct. arrived here about the 10*th* of November, having come by a Packet owing to your not having written per Steamer on the cover. This is the way
Per Steamer
of such and such   in the corner.
date from New York

H. J.

P. P. S. I saw your brother at the sailing of the Vanderbilt, but he disappeared before I had time to speak to him.

1. Wilky and Robbie were Garth Wilkinson James and Robertson James the younger brothers who were placed in a boarding school, the Pensionnat Maquelin, near Geneva. William James attended the Academy, which later became the University of Geneva, and HJ was enrolled in the Institution Rochette, a preparatory school for engineers and architects. For details of this schooling see Edel, *The Untried Years* and also Robert LeClair, *Young Henry James* (1955).

2. The Redwood Library and Athenaeum in Newport much used by HJ and T.S. Perry.

3. Newport playmates, neighbors, friends. George Peabody Wetmore (1846–1921) would later be U.S. senator from Rhode Island. Steele MacKaye (1842–1894), was to become the actor, playwright, stage designer, and producer.

To Thomas Sergeant Perry

Mf Duke

Geneva, 26 Jan. 1860.

Dear Perry,

I received your letter about ten minutes ago, and behold me already answering it. Was such a pitch of virtue ever before attained? I had been expecting to hear from you for a long time and had intended to consecrate this afternoon which is Thursday and a holiday to writing to find out what had become of you, but I now have the pleasure of doing so with a mind relieved of all anxiety. I supposed you were established at the South by this time, and from your acct. of it you must be having a very jolly time. Nothing of moment has transpired in our family since I last wrote. Wilky and Robby are still at boarding-school, Willie still at the Academy and I stillest at M. Rochette's. I am getting on very well there, and am studying very hard. I have never had a life of such routine as during the past three months. Every day is the same, and an account of one would be an account of all. I rise every day except Sunday at half-past six o'clock, break fast alone, go to school at eight, return at twelve, lunch, go back again at one, come home at five, dine and study till bed time. On Thursday I go to school at eight, home at twelve and stay for the rest of the day. After twelve I walk as I did today, read, look out of the window, or make the purchases for which I have no time on other days. This morning I wint[1] with Willie to "the Junction" a place where the rivers Rhone and Arve meet, one of the deepest blue, and the other sluggish and muddy, and flow on side by side without their waters mingling. Sometimes I go along the borders of the Lake, sometimes out to see the boys at school and these are my perambulations. Perhaps you would like to know about my school. The building is wholly unlike that of the Berkeley Institute.[2] It is a dilapidated old stone house in the most triste[3] quarter of the town. Scarcely a soul passes by it all day, and I do not remember to have seen a wheeled vehicle of any kind near it since I've been there. Beside it is the prison and opposite the Cathedral of St. Peter, in which Calvin used to preach. It seems to me that none but the most harmless and meekest men are incarcerated in the former building. While at my lesson in a class room which looks out on the door, I have once in a while seen an offender brought up to his doom. He marches along with handcuffs on his wrists followed by a gendarme in "spick and span" uniform. The gendarme knocks on the door, which is opened by some internal spring, shoves in his charge, the door closes, the gendarme retraces his steps. What happens after the prisoner is inside I don't know, but as the only officer I have ever seen about the prison is a diminutive little porter with a most benign countenance, I am inclined to think that the most inoffensive subjects are sent to him to deal with. The Scholars are divided into what are here called Internes and externes. The former are the regular scholars who stay at the school all day take all their lessons there etc. I am one of these. The others are those who only come for certain lessons, which they recite and leave as soon as they've done so. There are about twenty of the Internes, and a dozen externes. The principal study of the school is mathematics, as it is intended to prepare young men to be Engineers, Architects &c. One can study other things though, if he wants. The School course is divided into three years, and I take the studies of the first year with Latin in addition, there being but two or three of the regular scholars who study Latin. They have most of them a pretty good knowledge of the classics though as in the schools here, where boys go till they are about fifteen and sixteen, those are the principal studies. I fully intended to study Greek when I came here, but I have not now the time. I shall commence it as soon as I possibly can. I needn't be discouraged; I read the other day of a man with a good knowledge of Greek who didn't begin to study it till he was forty-six years of age. In the first year with me there are four other fellows, three sixteen or seventeen, the other I think a little older. Two of them are Genevese, one is a Russian and the other an Englishman. He is the only one with whom I have been able to become the least bit friendly. He seems to be a nice sort of a fellow, but as he is only an externe I do not see much of him. Of one of the Genevese I think I may say I never saw a more uninteresting individual, and of the other Genevese and the Russian that I have often seen more interesting. None of the other fellows have shown the least desire to make friends. When I first went there no one spoke to me, I had to commence every conversation myself. I think that if a Frenchman had come to Mr. Leverett's he would have been more hospitably received. The reason why I chose the School rather than any other was not because I was destined "à une carrière scientifique ou industrielle," but because it was the best *school* beside the Academy and the Gymnase neither of which I was prepared to enter. I might have had lessons at home, but I would have had no one to talk French with, and there were other causes for making that unsuitable. As for boarding in a Swiss family—which I told you of at Newport, that is a very good way to learn French, but I would have had to have learnt everything else elsewhere.

Here are five pages all about myself, but the reason I have written so much is because I like nothing better than for you to write about your own manners and customs, and suppose that you have the same taste in regard to me.

How did you leave all the Newporters? Have you any correspondent there, to furnish you with news? You've no idea what pleasure I have in thinking about the old place. I remember every little detail about it as well as if I'd only seen it yesterday. What ever news you get about it I wish you would transmit it to us if you think it would interest us. You say you saw McKaye, the painter-philosopher before you left. When you see him again, though as he is in New-York your chances for doing so are not very great, I wish you would remember us kindly to him, and tell him that we shall never forget him. As for LaFarge[4] we've heard nothing from him yet although Willie wrote to him a long time ago.

Sunday 29th

This has lain by from Thursday from today, I having had no time to take it up; in reading it over I think I have told you all there is to tell and in a very lugubrious manner. Please answer me soon, and our correspondence will perhaps be truly *voluminous*. Please also keep my letters, and I will yours, for I think it will be fun reading them over when we meet again. I had very little hope that my "insane" idea of your coming abroad would ever be realised, but I thought there was no harm in trying; you can do the next best thing, though, that is you can write as often as possible.

Yours very truly

Henry James

P.S. I was completely overcome by the hope of a letter from your sister. If she does not keep her promise and speedily I will not answer for the consequences. Please remember us all to the Porters and to your mother and sisters. Willie sends his love to you, and so I am sure would Wilky and Robby if they were to hum.[5]

1. In his early letters HJ on occasion imitates the spoken word.
2. The school attended by HJ and Perry was directed by the Rev. W. C. Leverett, curate of Trinity Church, Newport.
3. The bilingual HJ often used French words as if they were English.
4. John La Farge (1835–1910) American painter, an early friend and mentor of HJ.
5. Another example of HJ's imitation of speech—"to home."

To Thomas Sergeant Perry

Mf Duke

Geneva, March 27, [1860]
Hotel de l'Écu.

Dear Peri

Your letter of the 29 of Feb. came yesterday. What a jolly time you must be having. How I wish I were with you or you were here, although if you were I could promise you no midnight hunts, or play-acting or young ladies with beautiful eyes although I might indeed introduce you some with noses à la Becky Sharpe. I go twice a week to a dancing school (for reasons which I will hereafter explain) and seldom have I seen a more hideous collection of females than I do on those occasions. They all sit on benches ranged along one side of the room and the cavaliers stand up against the wall on the opposite side—for a fellow to sit down on one of their benches would be a most heinous crime. In the intervals of the dancing therefore we have occasion to contemplate them as they sit with their eyes modestly cast down upon the floor. I learned to dance because at the parties here that is the sole amusement—they do not even have supper but hand round little glasses of syrop and "helpings" of ice-cream about twice as large as a peach pit! Be thankful that you are born in our free and enlightened country.

I have become an "external" at my school, that is I am there but in class hours, and when the present Easter Vacation of two weeks is over I shall follow a couple of courses at the academy. I shall then tell you about it. This arrangement gives more time to myself, so that if you write me a letter every day I promise to answer it and not to find it too frequent.[1]

How you do make me wish to get back to America and Newport especially when you talk of the walks we used to take together! Geneva has endless lovely walks but I think Lily Pond, Cherry Grove, Purgatory, Paradise and Spouting Rock (how I delight to write the names) "take them all down." I think, I have as yet told you nothing of the town of Geneva itself. I like it best of all that I have been in—it has no Galleries or Museums or Churches but it is nevertheless very interesting. Such dingy old streets and courts and alleys, black with age some of them are, steep and dirty, such quaint old houses, high and sombre are very picturesque. If I was in sight of any of them I would try to draw one of them for you. But in this part of the town there are few. There is an odd-looking sort of an alley opposite the window where I am sitting, and I have made two or three attempts just now to give you a semblance of it but they are of no avail, and the alley is hardly worth the time too I think. You asked me in one of your letters whether there were many

English books in Geneva. I suppose there are in the Book-Stores but I have read very few. The reading time that I have had has consisted in little odd disconnected moments, so I have read mostly little bits from Magazines, Newspapers and "the like." I suppose that "down in Louisiana" you have not seen any numbers of the new "Cornhill Magazine" edited by Thackeray. I have seen the three numbers that are out and find it very good, and what is best of all and indicative of Thackeray setting up to be no more than it is and intends to be.

Wilky received a letter from Robeson not long ago, and Willie one from Lafarge so that with what you have told us we are quite well "posted up" in Newport news. *"B.,"* Robeson tell us, B. of the flashing eyes and rosy cheeks, B. of untarnished reputation, B. of Bull St. is still worshipped in her own temple and by her own admirers, notably by Wetmore (bless his little heart!) who promised, between ourselves, to *kiss her the next time he called at Bull-St!!* The letter from Lafarge was worth waiting so long for, just as in conversation his sentences when they do come forth are often worth the throes of concentration which attend their birth.

I suppose you have heard even in your uncivilized parts about the annexation of Savoy to France.[2] It has just taken place and the Swiss are in an "awful wax" about it, as there is danger of their being compromised by it. I don't suppose there will be any fighting on the subject although Switzerland *has* begun to marshall her troops. During yesterday and to day these streets have filled with Soldiers.

I have no idea when we shall go home. I think however it will be sooner than we expected when we came. I shouldn't wonder if we were to leave Geneva this summer and spend a shorter time than we thought to do in Germany, but in what place I can't say. Indeed the state of suspense in which I am living is very disagreeable. Sometimes I think nothing would be pleasanter than to wing freely over the world, tied down nowhere. I have lately become enamoured of the East and hope to go there "in the hereafter," but then I am afraid it will have become sacregligiously [sic] westernized.

Have you ever read "Eothen" a book of Eastern travels.[3] I have just been reading it. If you have not done so try to get a hold of it.

You asked me why I did not write to Mr. Leverett. I have often thought of him but it never exactly occurred to me to write to him. Wilky did so a little while ago, but as I did not know of it at the time I could not even send him a message.

28th I have just been to the Hotel de la Metropole, according to your request, to see Katrine's brother. He tells me to say that he and his sister are in excellent health, *he* evidently is as hearty as plenty of beef and beer can make him; he says, moreover, that he has written Katrine three letters lately—one at New-Years one in January, and one about a fortnight ago, and that she is coming for him in the month of June to take him to America. I have not yet seen either Vevey or Montreux but hope I soon shall. Farewell—please remember my parents and Aunt[4] to your mother and Mrs. Porter, and your sister, us also to them and mesdemoiselles Annie and Mary Porter and Miss Fannie Perry, Alice[5] particularly to the two latter and write before you return to Newport, and immediately afterwards.

Yours affectionately
H. James Jr.

P.S. I enclose a note to Miss. Margy[6] as she will not to me—You ask for My Address—it is *Hotel de l'Écu de Geneve, Geneve, Suisse,* but do not address me there, as I think we shall soon leave it. Address Barings as before for the present.

H. J.

1. HJ had been, as he would say in *Notes of a Son and Brother* (1914), "an obscure, a deeply hushed failure" in his scientific studies at the Institution Rochette. He was allowed by his parents to pursue only such subjects as he found congenial and also attended some of his brother's courses at the Academy.

2. Savoy and Nice had just been ceded to Napoleon III by Italy.

3. *Eōthen* (1844) a narrative of Near Eastern travels by A. W. Kinglake.

4. Catherine Walsh, maternal aunt of the Jameses, lived and traveled with the family.

5 Alice James (1848–1892), only sister to HJ.

6. Margaret Perry (1840–1925), T. S. Perry's sister. She later married John La Farge.

Henry James at Geneva, 1860

To Thomas Sergeant Perry

Mf Duke

Geneva, Sunday May 13 1860.

No 5 Quai du Mont Blanc

Faithless Tom!

I am afraid you are carrying into execution the threat conveyed in your last letter of not writing again before you returned to Newport. I write in the hope that I shall thereby bring in a letter from you in the course of the day—for it has come to pass on two different occasions that I had no sooner commenced to write to you and deplore your waning affection as I am doing now than a letter has arrived from you, giving peace to my troubled soul and banishing my doubts.

I have a little more news to relate than I have ever had before. The yoke, if the expression is not too tragic, has been considerably lightened. I had, a few weeks ago the pleasure of bidding adieu as an entire scholar to the Père Rochette. I go to his place now for German French and Latin lessons. I also take my place among the ranks of the learned at the Academia, and listen enraptured to the professors of Natural Philosophy (stupendous term!) of French Litterature, and of Human Anatomy. With the latter I went the other day in company with half a dozen other students to see a dissection at the Hospital. It was a most unlovely sight. The subject was a strapping big gendarme who had died of inflammation of the lungs. The smell was pretty bad, but I am glad to say that I was not in any way affected by the thing. Willie went the next day to see a drowned man dissected, and although the smell was not bad, one student fainted away, another turned a livid green and was obliged to leave and the rest only stood it by reinforcements of fresh air every little while.

Not long since Willie joined a society of Students the "Société des Zoffingues" which exists all over Switzerland. A few weeks ago they held one of their annual fêtes, and as any member can invite a friend I went to it along with Willie. It took place at the Village of *Moudon,*

19

about three quarters of a day's journey from Geneva, and 12 miles back of Lausanne. Drinking, smoking big German pipes and singing were the chief elements of the fun. It lasted three days. On the first night there was a grand concert given to the townsfolk by the students at the town hall, the like of which they had probably never seen. The second day there was a splendid banquet to which the mayor and aldermen were invited, and a lot of clergyman also. The latter had nothing of their calling about them but their white neckties for they drank as hard, sung as loud and gave as many toasts and jolly speeches as the most uproarious student—*medical* student, even there. On the same night took place the ceremony of the Landsvater which originated, I think, in the German Universities, but which this society has adopted. I cannot well make you understand what sort of an affair it is. It is a kind of oath of allegiance to their country and of brotherhood among themselves accompanied by a great swilling down of beer, of grasping of hands, of clashing of rapiers, and of glorious deep-mouthed German singing. Half the students were roaming in drunken ardour through the town and through the halls of the inns that night seeking whom they might devour. Willie, a German fellow, and I myself did not get scarcely a wink of sleep till near morning because of the constant attacks upon the door of the bed room which we shared together. The weather was fearful a driving storm of alternate hail and rain all the time. Summer dawning now upon Geneva makes quite another place of it, and I am becoming daily more and more convinced of its being one of the loveliest spots upon earth. The lake is capital for boating and swimming or I should say rather learning to swim, and the country about is full of splendid places for tramps on foot. There are however no such fields and meadows and groves as there are near Lily Pond, places where you can halt and lie out on the flat of your back and loll and loaf and reverise (Don't you remember?) There are beautiful roads on every side, lined with beautiful hedge rows and views of the snowy Alps and deep-blue waters of the lake, and of fine old country places. But you must pursue the even tenor of your way along these charming roads and stop but to contemplate and duly admire the lake and the mountains or peer through the iron gateways up the long avenue of trees that hides from you the treasures of the château. Everywhere there are *gardes champêtres* and bull-dogs. I suppose you will soon see the commencement of the annual migration to Newport. How I wish I was going to migrate there! It seems hardly a year since last May, and last September why it seems as yesterday.

According to my usual habit, having fully satisfied my egotism, I turn to humbler themes. Pray how may *you* be? What are your summer prospects. How are your mother and sisters? Mrs. Porter, Mesdemoiselles Annie and Mary, Mr. and Mrs. Pell and Archie, Deacon, Robeson and Wetmore? From the two last Wilky occasionally hears. Please remember us to them all. How is Mr. Leverett, and the little Leverett? Please remember us all particularly to him and to Mrs. L. Have you had any news lately of Lafarge or of Mackaye. We have only heard from *"Jno"* once and from the Mackaye we have not heard at all.

I believe I heard, I don't know how, that they were not to be at Newport this summer. We are expecting the Tweedies[1] every day; they arrived in England a fortnight ago and are at present in Scotland. I have no more time. Good-bye. Write as soon as you can, Willie and Wilky send you their love. Father and Mother and my Aunt desire to be remembered to your mother and sister, and Miss Alice to Miss Fanny. I direct to Newport. Direct you to Barings as always,—I don't know how long we shall remain at the present address—

Good-bye
Yours ever affectionately
H. James Jr.

WRITE SOON
and please remind your sister of her promise to do the same.

1. Edmund Tweedy was married to Mary Temple, step daughter of Catherine Margaret (James) Temple (1820–1854) a sister of the elder Henry James (1811–1882). Mrs. Tweedy reared the orphaned Temple cousins of the novelist.

To Thomas Sergeant Perry

Mf Duke

Bonn, on the Rhine, Prussia.
Wednesday, July 18*th*, 1860.

Mein lieber, schönster Peri—

If, on writing your letter of June 29th received by me this afternoon you had such an abundant stock of news to retail, that you did not know with which choice bit to commence, if *you* who have nothing but the gossip of a *little country village* to relate find yourself in such case, how much more perplexed must I be, *I* who can speak of the most hallowed spots of time-honoured historic Europe!!!!!! I think I must fire off my biggest gun first. One-two-three! Bung gerdee bang bang. . . . . !!! What a noise! Our passages are taken in the Adriatic, for the 11th of September!!!!!! We are going immediately to Newport, which is the place in America we all most care to live in. I'll tell you the reason of this as briefly as I can. Willie has decided to try and study painting seriously, and wished [to] return home and do so, if possible with Mr. Hunt.[1] That is the reason, at least in a great measure the reason (for his going home need not necessitate our all going) of this determination. Besides that, I think that if we are to live in America it is about time we boys should take up our abode there; the more I see of this estrangement of American youngsters from the land of their birth, the less I believe in it. It should also be the land of their breeding. I cannot devote my whole letter to this because I have so much more to say.

You ask me if I have made any of those courses[2] on foot which seem so pleasant to you, and if so to tell you about them. I am glad to say I have. Before leaving Switzerland Willie and [I] had about a week's walking among the mountains. Although we did but little compared with what many people do and have done, we enjoyed more in a week than I thought possible to cram into so short a time. We went first from Geneva to Chamouni. Have you heard of it? It is the rendezvous of travellers of all nations who wish to "do" a few Swiss Mountains. It is down at the foot of Mont-Blanc (in Savoy or what now *miserabile dictu,* is France.) We had but a day there, for the weather gave bad promise. We went over a mountain called the Moutonvert (two-hours) to the Mer de Glace. The M. de G. is a broad river of peaked, uneven ice that winds from the mountains down a deep ravine, and opens here and there into dark watery crevasses. We crossed—which with stout nails in your boots and a good spiked-pole is not a difficult business. We also crossed another glacier, the Gl. des Bassons which although smaller, is more beautiful than the M. de G. for the ice is much clearer and more sparkling. It is at the same time however, much more slippery and therefore I think more difficult of passage. We then crossed a mountain called the Tête-Noire to a place in the Canton du Valais called Martigny. It takes ten hours. We had a mule between us and I grieve to say that having hurt my foot the day before at Chamouni, I was obliged for a good part of the way to bestride the ugly beast. From Martigny we went up the great St. Bernard about whose good Father's and dogs we have both read, I am sure, in our primmers and geographys. The ascent takes about nine hours. I went almost all the way on foot for although we had a mule the guide profited most by him. At about three hours distance from the hospice the scenery becomes most wild dreary and barren. Everything indicates a great elevation. The growth of everything but the enormous rocks is stunted—not a blade of grass or straggling mountain pine. The tinkling of the last cattle bell dies away, you see the last hardy Alpine sheep climbing over desolate heights which would seem to afford no nourishment and then you enter upon the snow which lies all the year round. We had about an hour and a half's walk in it. It was very deep—far above our heads—but so hard on the surface that we didn't sink deeply in. It tires the legs to walk long in it, and it was bitter cold, so I was heartily glad when the high bleak hospice came in sight. We were received by one of the fathers who took us into a warm sitting-room, and gave us warm slippers and hot broth and roast mutton. He sat with us all the evening—a most kindly and courteous man. I asked him for pen and paper and sat me down to indite, by the light of a solitary tallow-candle a letter to you, dear friend. But sleep and chilliness with which I wrestled in vain soon overcame me and I retired to pass the night on a mattrass and pillow which were apparently stuffed with damp sand. In the morning we saw the dogs eight in number. They are noble majestic, tawny creatures and have (the old ones at least) the same stately courtesy in their bearing as the Fathers themselves. At a little distance from the Hospice is the house in which the corpses of those found in the snow are placed. As they cannot be buried they are stood around the walls in their shrouds and a grim and ghastly sight it is. They fall into all sorts of hideous positions, with such fiendish grins on their faces! faugh! I wish I could picture to you the appearance of that mournful region— I mean the colour. The sky is of a liquid twinkling sort of blue, and the gigantic gray and white rocks rise up against it so sharply-cut and so barren, and the stillness that reigns around and the apparent nearness of every object from the greater tenuity of the atmosphere! For all the courtesy and kindness which the priests expend nothing is asked. There is an alms-box in the chapel where one can drop what he pleases (nobody knows anything about it)—and that is all. The descent takes another day. On the following one we went by a carriage from Martigny to a place called Loèche-les-Bains, where there are warm medicinal baths which patients take in public tanks, sitting up to their chins in the nauseous places for hours together and reading and eating in them. Loèche stands at the foot of the ridge of the Gemmi over which one of the most wonderful passes in the Alps has been made; we crossed it the following day. From Loèche you see nothing but a vast towering surface of vertical rock naked and rugged. You cannot believe it possible that you can pass over it for no trace of a path can be discerned. And indeed the path is most curious. It is very narrow (5 feet at the widest and generally about 3) very steep and winds in such zigzags, that it turns so from right to left, that you never see whence you've come or whither you are going. In one place (so says the guide book, the spot escaped my notice) a plumb-line may be dropped over the precepice down a distance of 1600 ft. without any abutment to interfere. On the plateau on the summit we had for a little over an hour of snow, and were down on the other side in seven hours from the time we started. That same evening we reached Interlaken where we found all the "folks" except Robby whom at that young gent's own earnest solicitation father left at school in Geneva, but who now is gone with his teacher and mates to travel on foot among the mountains, and to go into Italy as far as Venice. I wish I were in his place. The rest had been already some time at Interlaken which is a strangers' summer place full of hotels and English people and had thoroughly "done" the place and its neighborhood. We remained there for three days longer, saw what there was to be seen and then set out for Germany. We came almost directly here, stopping for a couple of days only at Wiesbaden and Frankfort. At the former place of which I suppose you have heard, we drank of course of the hot waters, and witnessed the gambling for which it is famous. Then we sailed up (or down) the Rhine. I am not the first person who has been disappointed in the Rhine and have a better reason than many for such sacreligiousness inasmuch as I had just come from among the mountains of Switzerland whose high privilege it is to make everything else look mean and small.

We are all three of us installed in German families for the learning of the German tongue. Wilky and I together, Willie alone. The gentleman I am with is one Doctor Humpert[3] Latin and Greek professor at the Gymnasium here. His family is composed of his wife and sister who are to aid him in the task of conversing ceaselessly with us (a task for which they might seem to be but ill-qualified as I don't believe that between them they can muster, Germanlike, more than half a dozen teeth.) Also of his son Theodore aged seventeen, of whom I see little, as he is away at his lessons all day, and of five young Deutschers from six to fourteen years of age. With their company I am favoured only at meals. They are not his sons but are with him for intellectual cultivation, "all the comforts of a home" etc. This is an opportunity for me to see something of German life, in what would be called, I suppose the middle classes. I naturally compare it with the corresponding life at home, and think it truly inferior. The women stop at home all day, doing the housework, drudging, and leading the most homely and I should say joyless lives. I fancy they never look at a book, and all their conversation is about their pots and pans. The sister asked me the other day if we hadn't a king in the United States! The Doctor is a pleasant

25

genial man with very little force of character and more book-learning, that is knowledge of Greek and Sanscrit than anything else. The other day, Sunday last, I think we went all of us, wife, sister and little Dutchers (a nice little party of eleven) to a place called Godesberg within ten minutes of this, by rail, to see a little mound, or mountain they call it, with a ruin on the top. Notwithstanding the stifling heat of the weather, and the dust, we went under a shed on the dusty road and partook of some steaming coffee and boggy loaf-cake, then strolled about and came back to drink some sweetened wine and water.

When I see you, which will be you see, much sooner than we either of us hoped I can tell you more in an hour than I can do in fifty letters. Your plan for the first of August savours of "Rollo,"[4] did you get the idea from him? Of course I will write you what I do, but I'm sure I shall feel all day as if I had the sword of Damocles suspended above my head. A fearful vengeance awaits Wilky's foolhardy imprudence in disclosing, as he did, my secret employment. You ask upon what style of work I am employed. I may reply that to no style am I a stranger, there is none which has not been adorned by the magic of my touch. I shall be most happy to send you fifty copies of each work, the payment of which can await my return.

I must now close as I have written all this at one breath, that is at one sitting, and am rather tired. I shall of course write before we sail. Good bye. Remembrances to all.

Yours sincerely

Henry James Jr.

P.S. I forgot to say that I received your letter of June 1st while at Interlaken.

The date of our sailing is the *eleventh* of Sept. not 15th, as I had first put it. Tant mieux!

1. William Morris Hunt (1824–1879) French-influenced American painter had a studio in Newport.
2. Another example of HJ lapsing into French as if it were English.
3. Later recollections of this summer are recorded in the second chapter of *Notes of a Son and Brother* (1914).
4. An allusion to the "instructive" juvenile "Rollo" series by Jacob Abbott.

To Thomas Sergeant Perry

Mf Duke

Bonn AM Rhein, Preussen
Sunday the fifth day of August 1860.
Number one hundred an ninety Bongasse The Fust of August:
a Romance in 3 volumes. By 'Arry Jeames, alias G. P. R.[1] author
of the "beacon beacon, beacon light" etc. Vol. I. Part I. Book I.
Chap. I. The morning broke! High into the vast unclouded vault
of Heving rose the Awb of Day, chasing before it the fleeting
clouds that enshroud the slumbers of men. Nowhere shone it
brighter than on thy banks O! lovely Rhine! The rippling wavelets
of the noble river sparkled in its genial light, and the jew on the
vine-leaves which clothe with a garment of sweetest verdure its
fair encastled banks glittered with a rarer lustre than e'er did priceless diamond on a proud bewty's neck. It's golden golden rays
slanted through the casement of an apartment whose furniture
denoted a princeley wealth as did the appearance of its two occu-
pants bespeak noble blood. Full on the upturned countenance of
one of the latter glanced its rays as he lay enwrapped in slumber, on
a luxurious couch in an attitude, wherein with the listless grace of
the child was mingled somewhat of the sterner dignity of the man.
Through the long lashes of his drooped eyes pierced the radiant
glare, which though tempered by the rose-couloured hangings
through which it was shed, still caused those lashes slowly to turn
upwards and disclose a pair of eyes full at once of the liquid tenderness of the gazelle and the fierceness of the angered tiger. In sooth,
ne'er was seen a nobler form than that of 'Enry James de Jeames or
one which the most cunning sculptor might endeavour to imitate
with less hope of success. Born of a race who counted their ancestors
far back into the dim ages of chivalry he seemed to have been
endowed by the Wizard Nature, both with the fiery indomptable
spirit of those times and with their softer attributes of poesy and
romance. Turning as he woke upon his couch, covered with the
skin of a leopard, which he had killed with his own hands in the
burning wastes of Arabia, where he had already served, young as

he was under the crusading banner of Richard the Lion-heart, he stretched forth to a jewelled casket which lay at his bedside an arm in which the cerulean veins swelled like ivy creepers round a giant oak, and grasping a time piece more glittering with brilliants than an eastern monarch's diadem he,......nay—but a truce to this idiotic strain. This meaneth in plain English that your good friend Henry James Jr. Esquire was awakened by the sun at six o'clock on the morning of the first of August, that being so awakened he lept out of bed and made speed to don his accustomed *simple,* but SCRUPULOUSLY NEAT attire.

Now, ye, who demand a record of my humble doings prepare for no actions worthy to figure on history's storied page. If your appetite be for hairbreadth escapes and "exciting adventures by flood and field," you must apply elsewhere for wherewith to gratify it. *Some folks* may go trapesing about the country from *Rhode Island* to *Louisiana,* (indeed I might be more particular and say from *Newport* to *Oaklawn*), with a self-exploding gun on their shoulders, insinuating themselves into the society of their betters and frightening their lives out with *fibs* about their alligators, forsooth and their turtles, but I for my part, and Heaven be thanked for it! have no such tastes and if I had would scorn to thrust them under the notice of other people in *forward letters* and make a *parade* and *show* of them! *Some folks,* I say, but far be it from me to make any insinuations or *mention any names* as Heaven knows I well might. Let him as the shoe fits wear it. It is to those who admire a life of *strict morality* such as *some one* I know cannot boast of that I now address myself.

As I said, bien cher ami, I rose at six o'clock on Wednesday morning from a bed which is shapen more like a bird's nest than a human one, being deeply hollow in the middle and rising to a tremendous height round the sides, thereby causing me to feel when I enter it as if I were stepping into a well. I then dressed. My washstand deserves a line but I know not unto what to liken it unless it be a refrigerator which indeed, it strongly resembles both in form colour and above all in odour, it having once on an emergency been perhaps applied to that use. Having dressed I awoke the dormant Wilky who occupies a sort of baby's crib in the same room with me, and having received asseverate assurance of his immediate rising descended to breakfast. Breakfast is here a meal of no ceremony. It consists merely of bread and butter and coffee, which is placed upon the table at seven o'clock and lies there open to attack for about two hours, although toward nine, as you may imagine the coffee has begun to cool off. When I went down the doctor was eating and as people eat who are bereft of teeth, with his gums. Of course there were the usual salutations, the "Wie geht's?" and the everlasting "Haben Sie gut geschlafen?" which the members of this family never fail to ask you even if your first greeting does not happen to be untill dinner time. While we were engaged, the other young gents made their appearance, one by one, in a desperate hurry to gulp down their breakfast and escape being late for the Gymnasium which with the exception of two they all attend. I am afraid I did them injustice in my former letter. They are all bigger and older than I first thought them. They are almost a different race from boys of their own age at home. They have, if I may judge from these five specimens, more book learning, but less general knowledge which comes from unrestrained reading and less of the quality which we call *smartness*. They have no sports, which I have yet found out, except swimming (in which however they excel); and they have very few books to read. They study naught else than Latin and Greek. Their only recreations are going to bathe in the Rhine and going for a walk. They seldom make any jokes them-selves, though if you tell them one they do not seem incapable of enjoying it. Neither do they ever quarrel. Sometimes they have lively little discussions, but only raise their voices never their hands. All their ideas of America are taken from some German expurgated adaptations of Cooper's novels, the life therein depicted being as they imagine, the life that we lead when at home. But if, on an average, these little fellows are not so acute or clever as their brothers at home, I think that they are infinitely more comely mannered. There are no *Cozzenses*[2] among them. When I had finished break-fast, it being about half past seven, I went into the study. The study is the doctors library and the room where all the boys except Wilky and I get their lessons.. It is not a large room and their being book-shelves but on one side of it, the library is not extensive, and even such as it is it is not attractive. It has scarcely any but the Ancient Authors. In German there is nothing of any consequence but Goethe, Schiller, Lessing and Humboldt's Cosmos.[3] In English there are several of Fielding's and Smollet's novels and a few old fashioned books picked up I suppose at some sale or second hand book-stall, though for what purpose, I am at loss to determine, as the Doctor does not read English with any degree of facility. I sat down to read till our room should be made ready for me to go in and set to work. I looked over an odd volume of the "British Chronicle," a lot of bound weekly newspapers of the time of Byron, Shelley, Tom Moore and Walter Scott and which I had discovered in a corner the night before. Then I finished the Letters of Lady M. W. Montague which I had commenced a few days before from curi-osity and had continued from interest. By this time Wilky had come down breakfasted, and the hand-maiden flaxen haired blue-eyed Anna had set our room to rights. This was about nine o'clock. We both went up and commenced study, which simply consists in translating German into English. I am now working at Schiller's play of *Maria Stuart,* which I like exceedingly, although I do get along so slowly with it. I am convinced that German may take its stand among the difficult languages of the earth. I shall consider myself fortunate if I am able, when I leave Bonn, to translate even the simplest things. I worked on ploddingly till dinner-time which is at one o'clock. Shall I tell you what we had for dinner? I took particular note on purpose. Primo, some tepid cabbage-soup, its tepidity being the result of Fraulein Stamm's having poured it out almost a half an hour before we were called to dinner. (Fraulein Stamm is the sister of the Frau Doctorin—she sets the table and waits thereat) secundo—some boiled beef in rags and some excellent and greasy potatoes; tertio some Westphalia smoked ham and some black beans. Lastly some stewed cherries and tarts. Voilà. After dinner I went up stairs and set to work again, but had not been long occupied when Willie came in and told us that Mother proposed going to the Drachenfels, a mountain on the other side of the Rhine and commanded our attendance. This was cheerfully given. I went with Willie up to mothers lodgings. These are in a huge brick mansion built to imitate a feudal castle, situated immediately on the flat shore of the Rhine, so as that the water, I am told, sweeps in winter round its base. From M.'s sitting room which has a fine big stone balcony overlooking the river there is a lovely view. The Rhine is just here very broad. On its opposite bank are some fertile meadows and green hills called the Seven Mountains. The Drachenfels is one of these. Mother, my Aunt, Willie, Wilky, and Theodor the Doctor's son whom we asked to come with us formed our party. We took the steamboat for a place called Königswinter at the foot of the mountain. On the boat were a lot of students from the University here, who were going down the river to hold what they call a *Commerz* i.e. to go into a room and swill beer and wine with certain formalities and with emulative vigour till an advanced hour in the morning. I saw one of these entertainments in Switzerland and will tell you more about it when I see you. They had already commenced their work with huge ox-horns filled with Rhenish wine, and forced all the ladies on board (the German ones at least) to assist them therein at intervals of about ten minutes. We walked up the Drachenfels (it is not more than an hours ascent, with an excellent road), that is we all walked except mother who had the aid, if aid it truly be, of a donkey. On the top of the mountain, there stands a high crag with a ruined castle on the top of *it,* in truly Rhenish fashion. (Do you remember the picture in Brown Jones and Robinson of one of those gentlemen's preconception of the Rhine?[4]

[Drawing of river bordered on each side by many mountains of equal size, each topped with a castle.]

We went for the prospect, but the weather being cloudy, we had no prospect. We came home about eight o'clock, by the boat. I went back to Mother's with her. I went up in the tower with Alice, for the mansion can boast of a tower and a constellation of turrets. Then I came back here with Wilky. They had kept our tea for us. It was composed of boiled potatoes, rolls, cold-meat and stewed cherries, the "specialité" of this bill of fare. It being past nine when we had done and almost ten before I had finished the account of our excursion delivered to the other members of the family in the study I did not get till late at the letter which I intended to write you. The consequence was that after commencing I decided to leave the continuation of it till the morrow, the morrow however Willie, Wilky, Father and I went to Cologne which is about an hour's journey from Bonn by rail, and there in the contemplation of its manifold wonders we spent the whole day. On the following day Friday I left the letter purposely till to day when I could finish it without appropriating thereunto time which rightfully belonged to other things i.e. to *Maria Stuart* and the like.

At Cologne I saw several sights, foremost among which was the Cathedral, which is hardly a sight though, as while in it *you seem rather to feel than to see it.* I will reserve telling you about it till we get home as I am now in a hurry to close. Father, Mother and my Aunt and sister go to morrow to Paris there to remain until we sail, and I wish to give this to them to post there. I must therefore as they leave at seven A.M. be speedy for it is now near 7 P.M.

We were rather stunned at first by the thought of going home so soon, but now we have got accustomed to it. Father has written to Mr. Alf. Smith about a house in Newport. I have not the remotest idea of how I shall spend my time next winter. I don't wish to go back to Mr. Leverett, at least under the same conditions as before. I wish, although I've no doubt it is a very silly wish, that I were going to college. Although I have some prudential uneasiness about going back to Newport I have a delight of heart that stifles all such. The first thing on arriving I vote we go for a long walk to Lily Pond or Purgatory, or the Boat House. I can't find words to tell how glad I shall be to see you. Remember me to all of those of whom you think I can say that with equal truth—that is say it to everyone I knew there—Good bye. All send their love. I've no doubt, though they're not by to give it.

Believe me ever yr affectionate
Henry James Jr.

Wilky begs to send this scrap of paper. You see he is also guilty of beacon-becon light-ism.

   1. HJ had apparently been reading Thackeray's parodies. The "Jeames" is an allusion to the latter's "Jeames's Diary" (1845) and the G.P.R. to George Payne Rainsford James whose romances were parodied by Thackeray in "Novels by Eminent Hands." For the rest HJ is drawing upon his reading of the time, including Kinglake.
   2. An allusion to Frederick Swartwout Cozzens who wrote burlesques in the *Knickerbocker Magazine* under the name of Richard Haywarde. The popular New York magazine had been familiar to HJ from his childhood.
   3. Friedrich Heinrich Alexander von Humboldt whose *Cosmos* (1845–1862) was a physical description of the Universe.
   4. *The Foreign Tour of Brown, Jones and Robinson* (1854) by Richard Doyle, a book HJ kept all his life.

To Mrs. Henry James Sr.

Ms Harvard

[190] Bonngasse [Bonn]
Tuesday Evening [28(?) August 1860]

My very dear Mother

   We are going to see each other so soon that it seems hardly worth while to write,[1] but I must do so in order not to appear less meritorious than Willie and Wilky who are so free in their communications that I begin to suspect they simply despatch you blank sheets of paper, for what they can find to say about Bonn to fill so many pages is to me inconceivable—unless indeed they cover their epistles with protestations of love and admiration, which from occasional glimpses I have had of them seem to be in a tone much better suiting a young man who is writing a letter to his lady love than to his venerable mother.

   The three last days, however, have been a little more eventful than for some time past. On Sunday Wilky and I went to Roland-seck with the Humbards[2] "Kaffee trinken." It was a repetition of the performances, with a few alternations (for the better) which took place at Godesberg, the first Sunday we were here. There were about 800 people there all bent upon the same pleasure as ourselves and among them was an American lady who shone with the beauty of an angel among the 700 hideous German women.

We spent all yesterday in Cologne.[3] We were most of the time in the Cathedral. We also went to see the Collection of pictures which we visited on the previous occasion. I suppose you have been informed that we are not going to Strasbourg, (we think "le jeu ne vaut pas la chandelle").

This afternoon Wilky and I went up to Howenzberg and were shewn the corpses and staircase.

The weather for the past three or four days has been very fine. I hope it will continue so until our journey's over. The doctor entertained thoughts of accompanying us to America but his lady gave symptoms of such dread and horror at the idea that he has relinquished it. She and Miss Stamm seem to think that it is the exception in going to America not to be drowned and assurances to the contrary are received with uplifted eyes and hands and raised eyes and incredulous "Ohs!" and "achs," and pious ejaculations. I wish we could take Madame Humbart to America with us as cook. She is by far the best one I ever saw. I wish you could come on and take a few lessons from her; I shall bring you a lot of receipts by which I shall expect you to profit next winter. I shall look for a *marked improvement* in the cookery department.

We have not heard from Robby for a long time; his last communication was merely an official announcement of his intention to enter a dry-goods store on his return to New York, where he would receive a comfortable salary of from $500 to $1000.

We are all in the enjoyment of excellent health. I don't know what is the matter with me, but I have not been able to study for a few days past so well as I had hitherto done.

Please remember me most kindly to Father, Aunt Kate, and my sister and believe me ever, Madam, your

most obedient humble servt.
Henry James Jr.

1. HJ's letters to his parents are in the Houghton Library at Harvard. Mrs. James (1810–1882) had preceded her children to Paris before the family's sailing for the United States.

2. A misspelling of the Humperts, in whose home at 190 Bonn-Gasse HJ stayed in Bonn.

3. They had made an earlier excursion to Cologne on 2 August; see preceding letter.

To Thomas Sergeant Perry

Mf Duke

Paris, Hotel des Trois Empereurs
Rue de Rivoli
Monday 3d September 3 P.M. [1860]

My best of Péris:

You see I am thus far on my homeward journey, news of which you have already received as your last letter of August 11, which came to me at Bonn, informed me. Willie, Wilky and I arrived from Bonn on Saturday after a twelve hours ride on the rail in a carriage shared with us by a French lady's maid, valet and coachman and two Wallachian grandees. We passed through a part of Belgium which although it is more undulating than the Rhineland has none of that country's teeming richness and fertility. I am more than ever "penetrated" with Paris—a place not to be lightly spoken of or disposed of with two or three lines. The window at which I write is in the fifth storey and looks down on part of the Palais Royal and up at the New Louvre. Underneath is a wide open place upon which there is a ceaseless swarming movement. On one side there is a cab station. The drivers are snoozing with their bloated heads reclining on the tops of their square boxy fiacres, and the little low rats of horses are wearily stamping and whisking their feet and tails. Now, there is a group of warriors of the line receding across the place, little squat, brown men in blue and red who move with a gait formed of a mixture of a waddle and a swagger. Two Zouaves are coming this way. They too, are brown but not squat and neither waddle nor swagger.

Thursday 6th September

I was interrupted in this the other day and have been tramping the streets since to such a degree that I have hardly found time for the necessities, much less for the amenities of living such as writing to thee. Now I've only time to close if I wish my letter to reach Liverpool in time for Saturday's steamer; if I leave it I must myself be its bearer. When it reaches you I shall be on the

[drawing of ocean]

Good bye. À trois semaines!
Remember us to all.

Henry James Jr.

I met the other day the Tayloresses and Huntresses newly landed in the street.

To Thomas Sergeant Perry

Mf Duke

New York, Tuesday Sept 25 1860
9 1/2 A.M. 14th Street

Dear Sargey

I suppose you, on your way to school this morning (if to school you go) stopped at the P. O. in the full expectation of withdrawing therefrom a letter from me and were, I venture to believe, grievously disappointed in finding none such. We arrived at the wharf at 1 o'clock on Monday morning, and came ashore about nine. Willie and I came up here, the others are at the LaFarge Hotel. As soon as all the kissings and cetechisings were over, and Lafarge who called soon after our arrival, had delivered to me your blessed letter I scratched off a few lines to you and gave them to father who was going down town, to post. Imagine then the extremity of my horror at being informed by him at the eleventh hour last evening that he had forgotten to do so. I can't say when we shall be in Newport—I wish I *could* say to morrow morning. I wanted to go on last evening—mais il y a les convenances. Father has taken Mr. McKaye's house; we cannot go into it until Monday. Perhaps—I don't say *surely*, we shall leave here to morrow afternoon. At all events I will write to morrow if we decide not to do so—which is probable. The likelyhood is greatest of our leaving Friday. You ask about our voyage. My face elongates (if possible) as I make answer. It was one of dire tribulation, but I will tell you all when we meet. Goodbye. You cannot have harder work to keep your impatience under than I do. I am very sorry you got no letter this morning. I pictured to myself in writing yesterday, your joy in hearing we were at last so near—but you frighten me by telling me that you think of me so much, sleeping and waking—I am not so white as your imagination paints me. Indeed I am quite embrowned by eleven days of sun. Good bye, again. Excuse my using this paper. I can get no other unless I go into a room where there is company, and where for the twentieth time I must undergo the ordeal.

Remembrances to all
Ever truly yrs.
H. James Jr.

To Thomas Sergeant Perry

Mf Duke

Wednesday morning. 10 o'clock [Sept. 26 1860]
78 W. 14th Street.

My dear Child

If I write again it is not because I am able to inform you when I shall be in Newport, but because my departure hence appearing to be indefinitely postponed, I wish to soothe, to the best of the means allowed me, the grief with which this hope deferred must fill your heart. It is likely that Willie and I will remain at this comfortable abiding-place until the first of Next Week. My parents will perhaps go to Newpt. tomorrow. Wilky and Robertson are talking of going to see a paternal uncle who resides upon the river Hudson. Therefore you will have to curb your impatience until Tuesday morning, at least, when

[drawing of two men eagerly rushing to greet each other]
some such scene will occur. I saw La Farge yesterday, and gave him a long catechising relative to the state of things at the village. O!

how this heart of mine yearneth toward that same! Well do I remember its rustic lanes and by-ways, its simple unsophisticated inhabitants, who if they *are* ignorant of the delicate amenities of civilisation are also untainted by its sordid corruptions. They may have rough, inelegant exteriors but they have kindly hearts. The name of their little out of the way place may not be down on the map, mais ce sont de bonnes gens tout de même. I have little time to write and nothing more to tell, at least, nothing that won't keep till it can be told by word of mouth. My services as an able-bodied and willing young man are also greatly in demand in a family almost riven in twain by the austerities of an arrival just effected and a departure just about to be so. I think nothing of heaving a 60 pound trunk over my head.

Adoo, keep in good heart.

Your's heartily and hopefully
Henry James.

2
Beginnings

1861-1868

2

Beginnings

Henry James became a writer when the nation's strongest passions were engaged in the Civil War. The spectacle of the young, going forth to fratricidal strife, created a deep anguish in both Henry James and his older brother William. Their younger brothers enlisted. William withdrew into morbidities and illnesses but finally went to Harvard to study science. Henry, writing his *Notes of a Son and Brother* in his old age, felt a need to explain their non-participation in the conflict. He felt that he should have been "up and doing"— perhaps all the more keenly in a Boston in which so many friends actively committed their lives to the cause of the Union. The pressures on the brothers were considerable; but early in the war, the novice writer, helping to fight a stable fire, suffered a strained back: and this resolved the issue for him. To what extent the back pains were psychosomatic it is impossible to say. (This period is fully documented in Leon Edel, *The Untried Years* 1953). Henry's letters throw no light upon it; a fragment of a letter written by his father speaks of hanging on to the coat tails of his sons to keep them from going to the war; but one has a feeling that in the case of the two elder sons he did not have to hang on hard. The hypersensitive William and Henry both sank into themselves and at the same time envied their active younger brothers. Henry's visit to the military camps remained with him as a deep emotion, and ever after he read military memoirs and accounts of the Napoleonic campaigns (then so near to him in point of time) with an avidity one would not have attributed to so sedentary and pacifistic a person. A singular tale written in the 1890's, "Owen Wingrave," throws perhaps the best backward light. Owen, a second son, like Henry, whose older brother is a mental misfit, is asked to assume the burden of "family" and attend a military school. His ancestors have all been soldiers.

He prefers the poetry of Goethe to the hard prose of Clausewitz, but if he is a pacifist he is also brave. He fights for what he believes. And he dies defying a ghostly ancestor. Perhaps this was Henry James's way in middle life of laying old ghosts and family conflicts created by the Civil War. Toward the end of the war we discover him writing his first professional letters, reviewing for the *North American Review*, where Charles Eliot Norton proves to be his first mentor, and writing precocious tales. One story, unsigned, appeared in the *Continental Monthly* and was later identified thanks to the preservation of a Newport neighbor's letter which enjoined her son to read it and said it was by Harry James. His first signed tale appeared in the *Atlantic Monthly* in 1865, and after that the letters tell of his quiet periods of rumination in Cambridge, notably in a letter to T.S. Perry in which he sees American writers as children of history capable of using the freshness of the New World while assimilating the wisdom of the Old.

This sedentary life continued for four years after the end of the War Between the States. The James family, briefly installed in Ashburton Place in Boston, moved to 20 Quincy Street, opposite the Harvard Yard. In this large rambling house the young writer continued his apprenticeship, dreaming of the time when he could return to Europe.

To Thomas Sergeant Perry

Mf Duke

Newport, Friday
[6 June, 1862]

My dear T.S.P.

Your letter came. Much obliged for the note enclosed to you, that is not to the darned McClellan Club which sent it. Sorry that you should be so infested with caterpillars, and that you should sit upon them, as I suppose that is what you mean by saying that they attack your *person*. Never mind. There is an end to all things. Meanwhile I shall go hence unto Cambridge on Monday next.

I shall, belike, stop at Readville to see Robby on the way[1]—so I shall not see you till about 6, I suppose. Suppose you come to my room about that hour—or at least after your tea. No news. You speak of heat in Cambridge. 'Tis a thing unknown here.—I walked upon the cliffs this morning. I met Miss S. Newman. It was lovely—(not Miss N.) Met also two lunatics—(not counting Miss N.) One made a semblance of being a sentry with an old stick of wood, beside that stile between the beach and 40 steps which has the big druidical stone sticking out, and pretended to shoot me, forsooth, as I came up. But I was not to be intimidated *as you know*. The other was disporting himself wildly upon that beach at the bottom of the 40 steps. He is probably by this time a lifeless corpse among the waves—But as I am to see you so soon I will say no more—I enclose a letter Willie and I found yesterday morning floating about the harbour, when we were out sailing—thrown overboard by one of the midshipmen.

Yrs

H. James Jr.

1. Robertson James (1846–1910) had enlisted in the northern army and was in camp at Readville, Mass. See *Notes of a Son and Brother*, Chap. IX.

To Thomas Sergeant Perry

Mf Duke

New-York, Sunday [1 November 1863]

Dear Sargy,

I am well aware that I might have answered your last letter sooner; you are well aware that I have not done so. What more need be said? Fancies will not alter facts and facts can do without them. A delay of this kind is always fatally prolonged by the dread existing in the mind of the delinquent of the excuses he will have to make when he *does* write. I make no excuses—I have none to make. I wrap myself in my immaculate Virtue. My foolish delay is, like the emancipation act[1], a *fait accompli*. You know *that* cannot be receded from, need not be palliated etc etc; there it stands, stern, immutable, unchangeable.—Doubtless, if this strain is the result of my writing, you will prefer infinite silence.—Well, well, you know even Homer will sometimes nod.—Your letter is dated Oct. 24th—or rather 25th (Sunday). This also is Sunday—i.e. is a wet, nasty, black, horrid, damp-disgusting day. I have just finished breakfast and came up to my little roost to digest my rolls and coffee and pick my teeth, and gaze around at my four blank walls and at the white watery sky, and resolve the problem of extracting merriment—or at least, contentment, from these dismal surroundings. If my letter proves bald and blank and flat, revile it not—it will merely be from an excess of local colour. Here is a nice sentimental conundrum, such as free thinking young ladies would like: no, it is too nauseating; I will not give it.—I wish I had a novel to read. It cannot be denied that this desire is one of the elementary cravings of mankind. We take to it as to our mother's milk.—But I am destitute and can procure nothing approaching a Romance unless I go out in the rain and buy the Sunday Herald. I shall certainly not go to church. I went twice last Sunday. In the morning to hear an old Scotch presbyterian divine under whom my mother sat in her youth. Darkly must her prospect of Heaven have been obscured! The old man is now eighty, but he still finds strength with great reinforcements of tobacco-juice, to fulminate against back-sliders and evil doers. I may emphatically say that he gave us hell. It is curious. People may allege the existence of such sermons and doctrines as those as a proof of the immobility of human developement; but the real measure of progress is in the way they are received. Seventy years ago, people were really moved and frightened, and convulsed, convinced and converted I suppose, by all such grim anathemas; but now, even when they are willing to pay a man for grinding them out, they are willing to let them pass for what they are worth. The brimstone fizzles up in the pulpit but fades away into musk and cologne-water in the pews. (Don't it strike you that I'm very epigrammatic?)—Well, in the evening, at the instance of Bob Temple,[2] I went to listen to the preaching of Mrs. Cora V. L. Hatch. She holds forth in a kind of underground lecture room in Astor Place. The assemblage, its subterraneous nature, the dim lights, the hard-working, thoughtful physiognomies of everyone present quite realised my idea of the meetings of the early Christians in the Catacombs, although the only proscription under which the Hatch disciples labour is the necessity of paying 10 cents at the door. Three individuals from the audience formed themselves into a committee to select a subject for Cora to discuss—and they were marshalled out of the room by a kind of fat showman, who, as I wittily suggested, was probably Mr. Chorus V. L. Hatch.[3] They chose: "the Evidence of the continued existence of the Spirit after death." For some moments Cora remained motionless; probably, as Bob Temple said, "silently invoking her maker." Then she began to speak. Well, the long and short of it is, that the whole thing was a string of such arrant platitudes, that after about an hour of it, when there seemed to be no signs of a let-up we turned and fled. So much for Cora.

Your letter contains a little dissertation on prejudice, suggested by a book you had been reading (Locke on the Human Understanding), in which you do me the honour to ask me my opinion two or three times. It is a subject I have thought on not at all (like every other subject), and upon which I shrink from giving a judgement to you who have been reading Locke, even as a little child paddling among the chance waves that roll up about his feet on Newport beach, shrinks from following the strong man who ventures forth into the great ocean.—I agree with you perfectly that "prejudice is one of the worst evils which afflict humanity"; but I hardly think that it is one which each man can take in hand for himself and drive away. Every one knows the injustice of it, but few people are conscious that they possess it. Wilfully, intentionally prejudiced persons are very rare. Every one certainly is more or less prejudiced, but "unbeknown" to themselves. Is not a prejudice a judgement formed on a subject upon *data* furnished, not by the subject itself, but by the mind which regards it? (This is a very crude definition, but it will show you what I mean). These *data* are the fruits of the subtlest influences,—birth, education, association. Unless carefully watched they insinuate themselves into every opinion we form. They grow to be the substance of our very being. So far are they from being subjects of consciousness that they almost become vehicles thereof. They exercise, then, a great weight in our judgements. They are so intimately connected with every mental process, that they insidiously pervert our opinions, discolour and distort the objects of our vision. The opinion is consciously formed, perhaps; but not appreciatively, critically. That is we are conscious of it when formed, but not during formation. Now, all opinions which we consciously hold for any time, receive in a measure the sanction of conscience. And then—who shall gainsay them? They have been stamped at the royal mint: let them pass current. However false they may be, however base the metal of which they are composed, they have undergone an ordeal which renders them supremely valid in our eyes. You will say we cannot impose them on others. Certainly not. But when others reject them they become doubly dear to ourselves. We treasure them up. We gloat over them in private. We become millionaires of self-complacency.—This of course is the very height of prejudice.—But there is no-one whose judgements are *all* pre-conceived. And even the most prejudiced people when convinced that they *are* so are willing to correct themselves. But the question is to find out where the prejudice lies, to distinguish the true from the false. This is immensely difficult— so much so, that I should fear a man setting to work on his own hook would find it impossible. We know when we lie, when we kill, when we steal; when we deceive or violate others, but it is hard to know when we deceive or violate ourselves. You will say that a prejudice violates others—their rights, their claims, etc. Certainly it does when it is practically carried out; and *then* we can straightway take cognizance of it, measure it, reform it or cast it off. But as long as it is held as a mere opinion, I suppose it only violates some abstract standard of truth and justice. It cannot be denied, however, that we have mighty few opinions that we are not desirous to act upon.—Cannot you imagine the state of irresolution and scepticism and utter nothingness a man would be reduced to, who set to work to re-cast his old opinions, pick them clean of prejudice and build them up into a fairer structure? I'm afraid that he would find he had pulled out the chief corner stones, and that the edifice was prostrate, and he almost crushed in its ruins. In his desire to believe nothing but what his reason showed him to be true, I think he would end by believing nothing at all. It is a question whether he would not have attained the chief felicity of man; whether it is *not* better to believe nothing than to believe falsely; whether scepticism is not preferable to superstition. But it is a question which *I* can't answer. It seems to be like a choice between lunacy and idiocy,—death by fire—or by water. We were certainly born to believe. The truth was certainly made to be believed. Life is a prolonged reconciliation of these two facts. As long as we squint at the truth instead of looking straight at it—*i.e.* as long as we are prejudiced instead of fair, so long we are miserable sinners. But it seems to me that this fatal obliquity of vision inheres not wholly in any individual but is some indefinable property in the social atmosphere.—When by some concerted movement of humanity the air is purified then the film will fall from our eyes and (to conclude gracefully) we shall gaze undazzled at the sun!!!! How I *do* run on! You will certainly fear to broach any further question of morals THIS being the penalty. In reading the above over I am struck with its great dogmatism and crudity. It is probably all wrong or even all nothing. At all events, supply a query after every assertion and enclose the whole in a great parenthesis and interrogation point, or even scratch it all out.

9:30 P.M. I have just come in from another attempt at evening worship. *Monday morn.* My letter is delayed a day longer. I could not finish it last evening. I commenced to tell you about some religious performances I had just witnessed. As it had stopped raining and I was tired of having been in-doors so long I went with the ever faithful Bob Temple to a service held by the so-called "congregation of the new dispensation" just up Broadway. It was really wonderfully entertaining and worth telling about. I haven't time to describe it at length, tho' it was all extraordinary.—In fact my letter is so long already that I won't bother you with describing it at all. I enclose a little scribble of the platform. We had a grand oration (tremendous) from the female on the right and singing from her on the left. Love to Willie. *Is A. Porter in town?*

Yours very truly,
H.J.

47

1. Lincoln's Emancipation Proclamation of 1 January 1863.

2. Robert Emmet Temple Jr. (b. 1840), HJ's cousin. See *Notes of a Son and Brother*, Chap. V.

3. A foreshadowing of the secular preaching James would satirize a quarter of a century later in *The Bostonians*.

To Thomas Sergeant Perry

Mf Duke

13 Ashburton Place [Boston]
Monday Feb: [1864]

Dear Sarge:

I drop you a line out of the fulness of my heart and the emptiness of my head. It is a black drizzling day and I have been spending the morning with the dentist. Returning to my cheerless apartment with aching and throbbing jaws, I seek a ray of consolation in converse with you. Do drop me a line before you return. What's up in Philadelphia? Here, all is unchanged. Willy returned from Newport, after a ten-days' joyous sojourn. (My fire begins to crackle and blaze and my spirits to flicker responsive.) Haste thee back again and bring with you from your southern latitudes a little mite of spring. Black winter reigns, still. There was one day, recently, when a door seemed to have opened somewhere, several millions of miles away, and a whiff from the laboratory where they get up the flowers and vegetables, passed over this frozen town. The air was redolent with a smell as of rich damp earth: but it was but for a moment. Miss E. Van Buren[1] is here—pale, thin, and drooping. We taunt her facetiously with being in love—whereat she smiles languidly.— She has not yet come to us—being with a lady, down on the New Land. She comes shortly, when I hope that this rude climate will invigorate her.—I went t'other night to see the "Hunchback" privately performed, for charity, by Mrs. Agassiz, Miss Emily Russell, A. G. Sedgwick[2] and others. Truth compels me to state that it was d—d poor. What do you do at 1809 Spruce St.?—Have you made choice of a—etc.? Do you read, write, pay visits, "attend" parties! We hear from Wilky of his arrival and progress—buying cattle, tools, and "hiring" nigs.[3]—Do, I beseech thee, write me one of your inimitable effusions. I won't say in answer to this; for I

48

would fain have you forget it, ere the moment is out.—I close—lest I should grow more stupid. Fare well—A man can't smile gracefully when each particular tooth doth stand on end.—Regards to your mother and Miss Fanny.

Ever yours, dear S.

H. J. Jr.

1. Ellen James Van Buren (b. 1844), a cousin of HJ, daughter of Ellen King James (1823–1849) and Smith Thompson Van Buren, son of President Martin Van Buren.
2. Arthur George Sedgwick (1844–1915), brother-in-law of Charles Eliot Norton, later a member of the staff of the *Nation* in New York.
3. Garth Wilkinson James, invalided out of the war, was planning to run a farm or plantation in Florida with paid Negro labor.

To Thomas Sergeant Perry

Ms Colby

Newport Friday, March 25*th* [1864.]

Dear Sarge:—

Your second letter quite put me to the blush. (If you examine my paper with Willie's microscope you will see that it reflects a faint ruby tinge.) I had been meaning to give some sort of civil answer to your first, from day to day; but my pen, ink and paper—yea, even my small stock of wits—were engaged in advance. The printer's devil was knocking at the door. You know a literary man can't call his time his own: I wonder that you have enough for letter writing. What I mean is that I had made up my mind to finish a certain task or die in the attempt. The task is unfinished: and I have embraced the alternative. This is a spiritual, supernatural message. I write with a pen snatched from my angel-wing. It is very pleasant up here but rather lonely, the only other inhabitants being Shakespeare, Goethe and Charles Lamb. There are no women. Thackeray was up for a few days but was turned out for calling me a snob because I walked arm-in-arm with Shakespeare. I am rather sorry, for I am dying to hear the end of *Denis Duval:*[1] that is an earthly expression. Now I am immortal. Heigh-ho. I am lucky in having Goethe all to myself, for I am the only one who speaks German. I translate a good many of Elia's puns. I don't think G. quite relishes them. Elia is delicious.

He always flies about with a pen in his ear—a relic of his clerkship days. He looks a good deal like the picture of the harpies in Doré's Dante. He and W. S. have great times together. Elia is forever spouting out quotations from the Plays, which Shake. never recognises.——Nay, to speak seriously, or at least, soberly, the task I mentioned was to rewrite that modern novel I spoke of to you and get it off my hands within a certain number of days. To do this I had to husband my (physical) writing powers. I failed; still, it is almost finished and will go in a day or two. I have given it my best pains: bothered over it too much. On the whole, it is a failure, I think, tho' nobody will know this, perhaps, but myself. Do not expect anything: it is a simple story, simply told. As yet it hath no name: and I am hopeless of one. Why use that vile word novelette. It reminds me of chemisette. Why not say *historiette* outright? Or why not call it a bob-tale? I shall take the liberty of asking the *Atlantic* people to send their letter of reject. or accept. to you. I cannot again stand the pressure of avowed authorship (for the present.) and their answer could not come here unobserved.[2] Do not speak to Willie of this. I will not begin again the old song about being lonely; although just now I am quite so; Wilky is gone to New York. As for John La Farge, he comes to Newport so seldom that his company goes for little. I think I shall run up to Boston some day to see him. Do come down some Saturday, as you say. Now that the Spring is waking up to some sense of her duty it is good to be out of doors. I walk a little every day, and by sitting and standing and staring and lingering and sniffing the air, contrive to get a certain amount of exercise. The great event since you went off has been a grand sanitary concert: here the Rhodian Sappho loved—or at least, flirted,—and sung. Here your humble servant performed the duties of one: attired like an English footman, he showed folks to their seats.—I am impatient for your Wasson-killer.[3] My friend, read the 4th act of the Mercht. of Venice and be merciful. What a fearful state for a man! I wonder if he is aware of your presence in the world; if he sniffs you from afar. I suppose he is attacked with epileptic fits and unaccountable tremblings. He may die before your article comes out: in which case it could serve for an epitaph. *A propos* of Wasson, Father has been having quite a correspondence with your old love Miss Gail Hamilton, or Mary Abby Dodge.[4] I believe I told you while you were here that he had written her an anonymous letter, suggested by one of her articles. A short time ago he received a letter from her saying that she had just been reading the "Substance and Shadow",[5] and that she was convinced that the letter and the book were by the same hand; and thanking him warmly for both. Then he answered her; and yesterday heard from her again: a very good, healthy letter, with a promise of her next book.

Monday. So much I wrote yesterday. Today I saw John and got your 3rd letter!!! Oh beloved Friend! Oh joyous tidings! Oh magnanimous youth! Halleluia! Oh laggard time! Come! Come! Come to your H. J. jr.

1. Thackeray's unfinished novel. See HJ's essay, "Winchelsea, Rye and *Denis Duval*," *Scribner's Magazine*, XXIX (Jan. 1901).

2. His anonymous tale "A Tragedy of Error" was published in the *Continental Monthly*, V (Feb. 1864), 204–216 and "The Story of a Year," his first signed story, in the *Atlantic Monthly*, XV (March 1865), 257–281.

3. See the following letter.

4. Gail Hamilton was the pseudonym of Mary Abigail Dodge, essayist and critic of woman's suffrage. She edited *Our Young Folks*, 1865–1867.

5. HJ Sr's book *Substance and Shadow*, or, *Morality and Religion in Their Relation to Life: An Essay on the Physics of Creation* (Boston 1863).

To Thomas Sergeant Perry

Mf Duke

Newport R. I. Monday Apr. 18*th* [1864.]

My dear Sarge.—

What do you say to a pictorial letter? I have been sitting over my blank sheet for the last 20 minutes in this disconsolate posture [Drawing of frowning man sitting at table with ink and paper before him, quill in hand.] Language comes not at my bidding. How long did it take you to write that last letter of yours, hereby thankfully acknowledged? Heaven forbid that you should take this question as an insinuation!

I could not have written anything so brilliant had I laboured for an hour—for 24 hours! It had an easy elegant flow which my sputtering scratching pen refuses to master. But 'tis not given to any one to do every thing well. Some folks excel in letter writing—others in other departments of literature. I doubt not but Shakespeare and de Musset[1] were very poor fists at a letter; and there exists in the Archives of the family a stupid little note from Thackeray[2] of half dozen lines, in wh. there are as many erasures. To follow your own example you begin by stating that a N. E. wind of two weeks old was raging—then and there. Altho' (be it said in parenthesis) I don't see how you can speak so confidently of what had happened in your absence. Well, a violent hurricane is now roaring about my ears. Whence it cometh or whither it goeth I know not: but 'tis a bitter black wind and I hope it may blow somebody good. The sky is of a deep purple-black, as Gononome[3] would say, save at the horizon, which is lined with a broad zone of amber. My dear old Boy I have a confession to make—an apology to tender—a forgiveness to crave. I trust my sin is venial. Has it slipped your memory that you bade me take the Harv. Mag.,[4] THE H. M., to your sister ere she left town, so that she in turn might present it to your proud mother —proud at once of such a son and such a daughter? Now, be calm. It's nothing very frightful. On Thursday I presented myself at the door of the Lafarge house with my precious charge. It was opened by Miss Reilly—the ruby-haired A. R.[5] I immediately perceived that something had gone wrong. I was not slow to ascertain *what*. Mr. and Mrs. Lafarge had decamped that morning, (at day break, I suppose) none knew whither, leaving prodigious debts behind them, and one silver spoon in the side-board drawer; the servant's wages unpaid, the house dismantled of its richest ornaments. The "sar-cophagus" in the drawing-room, the carved chimney piece, the books, the paintings—all the furniture in short had been removed. Naught remained but the large photog. of T. S. P., the medicine-spoon above mentioned, and the remnant of a soda-cracker—a mere mouthful. Whither have the guilty pair fled? Shall I rescue the Harv. Mag. and send it to you? Or have you already provided your mother with another copy? The M. C.[6] was read with great pleasure and many outward signs of mirth by Miss Minny Temple,[7] who said that it was "exactly like you"—that is, the manner rather than the matter of the narration.—I got Brownings plays from J.'s [La Farge] and have been reading them with deep interest. I will possibly write you what I think, in as far as I can express it about them when I have read more. Think what a treat!—The dinner bell tolls—and I must close. I think I can do no more about this present letter after dinner, except posting it.

Ever your old young friend
H. James

In a fortnight from now I shall throw myself on yr. neck!

1. Perry later remembered HJ as having translated Musset's *Lorenzaccio* at this time, interpolating scenes of his own.
2. Thackeray had visited at the home of the Jameses in New York during his American tour of 1852. See *A Small Boy*, Chap. VII.
3. An allusion to a poem by Perry published in a Philadelphia paper, *Our Daily Fare*, 11 June 1864. The poem parodied contemporary verse.
4. The *Harvard Magazine* had published two pieces by Perry in the March and April issues of 1864, a short story, "Morning Call," and an essay on David A. Wasson (1823–1887) the transcendentalist.
5. Apparently the La Farge's Irish maid. The La Farge's had given up their Newport house.
6. The "M.C." was "Morning Call."
7. Mary (Minny) Temple, HJ's cousin, lived with the Tweedys at Newport. HJ and Minny were often together during these years.

To *North American Review*

Ms Harvard

Boston
13 Ashburton Place
July 30*th* [1864]

To the Editors of the
"North American Review"
Gentlemen—

I take the liberty of enclosing a very brief review of Senior's *Essays on Fiction*,[1] published in London a few months ago. Hoping that you may deem it worthy of a place among your Literary Notices, I remain yours respectfully

Henry James Jr.

1. The essay-review of Nassau W. Senior's *Essays on Fiction* appeared in the review, XCIX (October 1864), 580–587. Most of Henry James's early reviews were published anonymously.

To Charles Eliot Norton

Ms Harvard

Northampton,
Aug. 9th [1864]

Dear Sir,[1]

Your note of acceptance of my article has just been forwarded to me from home. I am very grateful for your kind opinion of my notice and your invitation to further attempts. May I request to see the proofs, at your convenience?

I have just been reading with great interest the Journals and Letters of Maurice and Eugénie de Guérin[1]—(Paris, 1864, 2d Edition.) I should like to write a notice of the two books combined; or at least of Maurice alone, as his seems to me the most interesting portion of the work. Would such a notice be acceptable to you?[2]— But perhaps this is an importunate question, and that you had better not trouble yourself to answer it. If I write the notice I will send it and then you can answer at your leisure. And I beg leave to add that if at any time you wish a particular work briefly reviewed, on learning your wish I shall be glad to undertake the task—if it comes within my narrow compass.—I am frequently in the way of reading French books.—

Respectfully yours
Henry James Jr.

1. Charles Eliot Norton (1827–1908) coeditor of the *North American Review* and the *Nation* would become professor of the history of fine arts at Harvard in 1873. From the time of this letter to his death, he remained a close friend of HJ and an early guide in forming his taste in the arts.

2. HJ's review of *The Journal of Eugénie de Guérin* (ed. Trebutiens) appeared in the *Nation*, I (14 Dec. 1865).

To Charles Eliot Norton

Ms Harvard

Northampton—October 15*th*
1864.

Dear Sir:

I take the liberty of writing to ask you whether you would like a notice of the novel "Emily Chester," just published, for the *North American Review?*[1] The book seems to me to have gained sufficient cont[inental] notoriety to justify a brief review. I make my application thus because it may be that you have committed the task to other hands, in which case my labour would be lost.—Some weeks ago in kindly answering a note of mine, you proposed that I should prepare some remarks on Miss Prescott's "Azarian."[2] I thought it unnecessary at the time to reply to your note otherwise than by a speedy practical assent to your proposal. I have written a little account of Miss P. and should have despatched it sometime since had I not been too unwell to give it the finishing touch. A patient in a "Water Cure" (which is my present dignity) cannot work very steadily.[3] I shall send my paper in a few days, hoping that in despair you have not closed the gates against it. Meanwhile awaiting your decision regarding "Emily Chester" I remain

most respectfully yours
Henry James Jr.

1. HJ's unsigned review of Mrs. A. M. C. Seemuller's *Emily Chester* (Boston 1864) appeared in the *North American Review*, C (Jan. 1865), 279–284.

2. Harriet E. Prescott Spofford, *Azarian: An Episode* (Boston 1864); unsigned review in *North American Review*, C (Jan. 1865), 268–277.

3. HJ was drinking the waters at Northampton to relieve the chronic constipation from which he suffered for some years during early manhood.

To Thomas Sergeant Perry

Mf Duke

Northampton, October 28*th 1864*

Dear T. S.—

I rec'd. your two letters with great pleasure. The news contained in the first was very welcome altho' as you say, "not unmingled

with misfortune." But I suppose I ought to be thankful for so much and not grumble that it is so little. One of these days we shall have certain persons *on their knees,* imploring for contributions.[1] Thus:
[Drawing of a man representing the *Atlantic Monthly* kneeling before a disdainful, bearded man.]

It was very kind, altho' not more so than I had a right to expect, of you, to write me a 2d time. The weather is dreadful—a true suicidal day. The black sky is voiding its blackness in grey diluted torrents. One ought to be in the city on such a day as this where the horizon is too narrow to be hidden by mist. But even as I write a white light declares itself over the distant fringe of leafless trees; and perhaps after all it will clear off. Life flows on as evenly as ever up here. Letters and scraps of news are very welcome. Sometimes it waxes so stupid that I swear a mighty oath that I will pack off the next day. The days *se ressemblent comme deux gouttes d'eau.* I got a letter from Willie recently wherein he spoke to me of John's *Enoch Arden:* I'm of course very anxious to see it. So John is to be "located" in Roxbury. I hope he will find the location agreeable. I suppose a great weight is off your mind. I, *too,* wrote to Miss Van Buren yesterday; and *also* requested a photog. I haven't read *Emily Chester;* but I intend to. My Uncle Howard James[2] who is here for the winter has just read it and having been strongly affected by it advises me to do the same. By all means. I want some strong sensation. It will be grand to get one from a non-sensation novel such as E. C.—How are matters and things in Cambridge? I hear they are going to give Colonel Lowell a grand funeral there. I hope it may be some comfort to his poor wife. By Jove, what an awful thing this war is! I mean for wives, &c. I went up Mount Holyoke t'other day for the 2d time. Of all the concentrated vulgarites it is the greatest. You ascend half way in carriages. Then you get into a little car, like that of a balloon and are hauled up the remainder on perpendicular grooves. On reaching the top, you find your self on a level with the floor of the elegant Prospect House where a lot of women are playing on the piano and curling their hair in the looking glass. It must be owned that the view is fine as such things go.—It must be charming up there today.—But the 1st dinner bell hath rung some time since and the second will ere long make itself heard. As I must mail this letter immediately after dinner, I will close it now. Write toujours. What are you reading? I have just read Vaughan's Eng. Revolutions in Religion. Interesting subject but middling book.

Ever your's, dear Sarge
Henry James Jr.

1. "The Story of a Year."
2. Howard James (1828–1887) youngest brother of HJ Sr.

To Charles Eliot Norton

Ms Harvard

Boston.
13 Ashburton Place
December 1st
Thursday [1864]

My dear Mr. Norton—

I had left Northampton the day before your letter arrived; as I received it only half an hour ago. Let me hasten to answer your question.—I shall be most happy to rewrite you a notice of *Lindisfarn Chase,* of the prescribed length, and with all despatch.[1] You shall have it by the beginning of next week.—I do *not* desire to notice novels exclusively, although I confess that that kind of criticism *comes most natural.* Other books which are not books of erudition, I shall always be glad to do my best for. Nothing would please me better, however, than to notice the novels of the next quarter in a lump, as you propose; so you may send me whatever it offers in that line. I am very grateful for your good opinion of the two notices last sent. You are right in saying that the Gypsy book does not deserve so elaborate a handling as I have given it.[2] You will of course cut out what you deem superfluous. But experience will cure me of the tendency to waste my substance upon worthless subjects, and teach me to write cheaply about cheap writing. I *did* receive your kind acknowledgement of the receipt of the *Azarian critique*. I meant to tell you so in sending the other criticisms, but on finishing them my time was so taken up with other engagements that I was unable to enclose a line to that effect.— My address for the present is in town, as above—

I remain in great haste,
most truly yours
Henry James Jr.

1. T. Adolphus Trollope, *Lindisfarn Chase* (New York 1864), unsigned review in the *North American Review*, C (January 1865), 277–278.

2. George S. Phillips, *The Gypsies of the Danes Dike* (Boston 1864). HJ's notice does not seem to have been published.

To Charles Eliot Norton

Ms Harvard

13 Ashburton Place
Monday, May 29. [1865]

My dear Mr. Norton.

I herewith forward you the notice of *Wilhelm Meister*, for which you asked a few weeks ago.[1] It is a little longer than you proposed; but not longer, I think than the subject demands. When we entertain a giant, it is a pity to cramp him: and I too have been so hospitable to little men, or rather—little women! I have received a copy of M. Arnold and have set to work to notice him.[2] Will it suit you to receive the results in four or five days?—I was very sorry not to have been able to spend last Monday evening with you. A charitable friend has told me of all that I lost—

Most truly yours
Henry James Jr.

1. Goethe, *Wilhelm Meister's Apprenticeship and Travels*, translated by Thomas Carlyle (Boston 1865), unsigned review in the *North American Review*, CI (July 1865), 281–285.

2. *Essays in Criticism* (Boston 1865), unsigned review in the *North American Review*, CI (July 1865), 206–213. Arnold read this review and praised it to his friends unaware that it was the work of a twenty-two-year-old novice.

Henry James in Boston, age sixteen or seventeen

To Oliver Wendell Holmes Jr.

Ms Harvard

Newport, R.I.
July 14*th* [1865]

Dear Holmes:[1]

Your kind letter just recd., together with one from our young friend[2] of the White Mts. I had been waiting for it to write you. It is I regret to say only half satisfactory. After superhuman efforts she had ferreted out a single room, the only one in the place, high or low—far or near. This the wretch who owned it refused to furnish with two beds; but she took it and when we get up there we can pull his own out from under him. At any rate we are sure of a shelter, and I will tell Minny T. to keep her "eye peeled" for another room or another bed. Room cheap—$2.50 per week; but we must dine etc. at a neighboring house to the tune of $5 or 6: which is not dear. It was the very best M. could do and I think we can bestow ourselves. At any rate, back out at your peril!

So much for "buz."[3] I shall be in town towards the end of the mo. and shall let you know when, and await your orders for marching. Meanwhile I am living a delicious life, far away from men women and newspapers, with a sky and sea of cobalt (to talk what is for the moment, shop) before the window at which I write; eating of the lotus, to repletion; rising at $9\frac{1}{2}$; loafing and talking aesthetics all day, &c. Glad your term is up, and that you liked my article. I shall certainly ask for "more"; don't be afraid. An invitation to meet Wilson was sent me from home, which I am sorry I missed. A friend is awaiting me to go a-walking and John LaFarge is waiting to go in town with my letter. Nevertheless I can't take up my pen. And yet what more have I to say? We can if need be, sit in silence; but it will hardly do to send a blank page of letter paper. Oh why art thou not here to come forth to the romantic sea girt glen to which I propose to direct my steps? You don't know what weather is my dear H., until you have been to this place. You who are susceptible thereunto should come here—You would soon ripen into absolute perfection.

My friend is wriggling in his seat; so I must close. As I say, I will write again. I pant for the 1st of August. I hope you will have a jolly interval. I will keep Minny Temple on the look out. We shall shift well enough. Farewell. Excuse unseemly haste.

Ever dear H. most truly yrs.

Henry James Jr.

1. Oliver Wendell Holmes Jr. the future Supreme Court Justice (1841–1935) had just returned from service in the Civil War and was studying law at Harvard.
2. Minny Temple.
3. HJ's abbreviation for "business."

To Charles Eliot Norton

Ms Harvard

Boston.

13 Ashburton Pl.

July 31*th* [1865]

My dear Mr. Norton.

Would the *N.A.R.* like a notice of *Thoreau's Letters*[1] fr. an outside, *i.e.* an extra-Concord point of view? Unless some such view is taken, I fear the lesson of the book will be lost. I will be glad to take it, if you so desire, according to my likes. I should also be well pleased to have you suggest any other book for criticism. As I start tomorrow for the White Mountains will you be so good as to address me at your leisure, *North-Conway, N.H.?*—

With kind regards to Mrs. Norton, believe me

Very faithfully yours

H. James Jr.

I importune you thus early, lest some Thoreau-ite should be before me.—Only remember my offer and answer at your perfect convenience.

1. Henry D. Thoreau, *Letters to Various Persons* (Boston 1865).

To Charles Eliot Norton

Ms Harvard

13 Ashburton Place, Boston
September 11*th* [1865]

My dear Mr. Norton—

Here at last are the *The Gayworthys,* whom I have entertained as hospitably as I could entertain so very uninteresting a set of people.[1] It is what the authoress would call "the old old story:" the book is very poor and she herself has as a matter of course plenty of talent. I hope the notice is still in season.—I shall send *Thoreau* to the *Nation* as you suggested.[2] He is not yet begun upon. It was easier to talk about a review of him before going to the White Mts. than to write one after getting there.—His nature is very good in town: but it will not stand juxtaposition with nature's own. If I should begin to talk about him now I am afraid I should be too savage.—With kind regards to Mrs. Norton, believe me

Very truly yours
H. James Jr.

1. Adeline Dutton (Train) Whitney, *The Gayworthys* (Boston 1865). Unsigned review in the *North American Review,* CI (October 1865), 619–622.
2. There is no evidence that HJ ever completed or published his notice of Thoreau's letters.

To Charles Eliot Norton

Ms Harvard

13 Ashburton Pl.
October 13 [1865]

My dear Mr. Norton

Begging you in the 1st place to excuse the hieroglyphics for the sake of a lame hand—I would like to ask you whether an article on "Recent French Criticism" (such as I remember speaking of with you some months ago) would find a place in the next N.A.R.? I would like to write a review say of Sainte-Beuve, Taine, Renan (as an Essayist) and Schérer.[1]—A remark in your last note leads me to suppose that you would like to have me give you a literary article of some kind; and I therefore suggest these gentlemen, with whom I am familiar: but if you in writing, had a particular subject in view, we may defer the Critics. Hoping to see you back in Cambridge before very long, I remain

most truly yours
Henry James Jr.

1. The article was not written. See HJ's unsigned review of Edmond Schérer's *Nouvelles Études sur la Littérature Contemporaine* (Paris 1865), in the *Nation*, I (12 October 1865), 468–470.

To Charles Eliot Norton

Ms Harvard

13 Ashburton Place
Nov. 28th [1865]

My dear Mr. Norton—

I have been subjected to so many interruptions of late, thro' occasionally not feeling well and thro' demands on my time from without when I *did* feel well, that I shall hardly be able to give you the promised notice of *Epictetus*[1] on the 1st inst. as you requested. I shall bring it to you in as few days thereafter as I possibly can.

Most truly yours
H. James Jr.

1. *The Works of Epictetus* edited by Thomas Wentworth Higginson from a translation by Elizabeth Carter (Boston 1865). Unsigned review in the *North American Review*, CII (April 1866), 599–606.

To Charles Eliot Norton

Ms Harvard

Boston, February 28th [1866]

My dear Mr. Norton:

I undertake a begging-letter. I beg in the first place that you will out of the abundance of your kindness, allow me to retract my proposal to deal critically with Mrs. Stowe, in the N.A.R. I have been re-reading two or three of her books and altho' I see them to be full of pleasant qualities, they lack those solid merits wh. an indistinct recollection of them had caused me to attribute to them; and it is only such merits as these that in my present state of intellectual exhaustion, consequent upon having popped up faint praise for a succession of vapid novels in the *Nation*, will restore vigour and enthusiasm to my pen. The fact of the proposal having been (as I believe) mine, makes me regret my indisposition both the more and the less: the less because it reminds me that you had probably not set your heart upon the article. If its omission will cause an aching void in the Review (or anywhere else) I will of course apply myself to the task. Otherwise I beseech you to avert your gaze and allow me to back out gracefully. I will promise for the future, not to undertake reviews without a better knowledge of the facts of the case.—And this remark applies somewhat to the second clause of my petition.—To come at it, at once: I am lothe, *moi chétif,* to engage with the French critics next June or at all, for the present. I honestly feel incompetant to the enterprise.[1] That is, I could of course put together a certain number of inoffensive commonplaces and uncontested facts about them, and the article would stand written. But I had rather not touch them till I feel that I can do it easily and without stretching: for except under these circumstances, what I should write would be stiff and laboured. I have written the Taine part of the review and it fails signally to satisfy me and would fail equally to satisfy you. I therefore would feel very grateful to you for sinking the scheme just now.—Do not think me either very lazy or very fastidious, but believe me simply tolerably shrewd where the interests of the Review are concerned. Do not trouble yourself, if my representations satisfy you, to answer. I will take your silence for a merciful assent, and not for that of contempt for the instability of my character, or as a token of your having cut my acquaintance—

Ever most truly yours
H. James Jr.

1. See HJ's letter to Norton of 13 October 1865.

To Thomas Sergeant Perry

Ms Colby

Swampscott. Sept 15 [1866].

Dear Sarge:

I recd. yesterday your letter from Vevey and devoured it with avidity. I can't tell you how odd it seems to hear from you in Europe. All our old Newport talk and visions relative to going thither swam into my head and made the reality seem like a dream. What a simple and rapid matter it is after all, I reflected: how much simpler is the future than the present will admit it to be! But I'll not pester you with my reflections. Still I have little that is more substantial to offer you.—This is a perfect September day, of the latter half and I picture you as treading the Alpine solitudes—if such they may be called—impelled by a love of the beautiful and the good—to eat. I don't understand.—Did you go to Baden-Baden and cut Switz. altogether, or did you break the bank at B.B. and then return to the bosom of Nature. Mind your steps on the A.s, or I shall be reading a paragraph about a young American in the *Advertiser*. My soul aches to think of the pictures which you have seen and I haven't.—Wendell Holmes has returned, but I haven't seen him. He was put thro' the Alps by the president of the Alpine club.—I heard this morn. from E. Van Buren, from Moscow—on her way to *Tartary—s'il vous plait*. She was (so to speak) having it all her own way in Russia, and carrying everything before her. Americans seem to be at a vast premium there. She spoke most earnestly of the sublime beauty of Norway. You may meet her. I have nothing whatever to tell you. I haven't heard of or from John since I parted from you. I rejoice that you found Ware so agreeable. Since you sailed, I have done nothing, but go to Campton N. H. for 3 days. But the idea of talking of Campton N. H.! *You* spoke of going to Spain. Perhaps you are there even now.—I could utterly hate you for your privilege, and yet I entreat that you will write as often, as fully, as *exasperatingly*, as you can. I thank the Lord that *someone* is seeing it all, if I'm not. Be keen of eye, retentive of memory, interrogative of tongue, copious of pen.—Don't you find that it's already pretty natural, mechanical and matter of fact?—I trust you are coming into France again and are going to see Oxford, too. You may imagine that I have nothing to recount. I could fill a quire with interjections of joy, sympathy, regret, envy, jealousy and baffled rage. But the dinner bell arrests my eloquence.——Sept. 17th. With dinner came Wendell Holmes and spent yesterday here. He spent his time, 8 weeks in London, Devonsh. and Scotland, 3 in Paris and 3 in Switz.——Adieu.——Write as often as you can.——Send in your letters any *striking* photo. of literary gent. Willie sends love.——

Your's
H. J. Jr

To Thomas Sergeant Perry

Ms Colby

Cambridge, Dec. 1st '66.

Dear Sarge:—

I rec'd your letter from Spain almost a month ago, and have deferred thus long answering it, from a deep conviction of the inherent impossibility of such a process. Can Cambridge answer Seville? Can Massachusetts respond unto Granada? Since then however, I have heard indirectly, from John, that you had "gone back" upon that romantic land and would advise no one to visit it. I shall probably follow your advice for the present. But what is the matter? Bed-bugs? Methinks that I would endure even them for a glimpse of those galleries and cathedrals of which you write.—I have been selfishly in hopes that undeterred by my silence you would have written me again relating your further adventures. All these I pant to hear. What became of you afterwards? Where are you now? Where will you be next week? Ah that I might follow your steps from afar, and catch at least some faint perfume of your pleasures.—But I heard also thro' Willie (who has recently seen John) that you had recrossed the Pyrenees and were established in Paris in the Latin Quarter and were elaborating a programme of study. I would have given much to see the letter in which this was shadowed forth. My dearest boy, for Heaven's sake don't mind my not writing you—what have I to write?—but keep me informed, if never so briefly of what you see, do and intend. In Paris now—I should have liked so much to know your impressions, circumstances, feelings, opinions, projects etc. Never mind; one of these days I expect a mighty report.—You have I suppose, by this time, waited upon your mother and sister, to whom, if they are within speaking distance, I should like to send my best regards. *Enfin*—but WHERE ARE YOU? How can I write without knowing that? I should be glad to know that you were fixing yourself in Paris. I should think you might easily feel as if you had seen sights enough for the present. And your mother and sister where are they, and how do they like it?—For myself, you will see that I date from Cambridge and that you have not even now escaped from its bondage. But I will not describe the spot. We have taken a house here, Mr. Thiess' in Quincy St,[1] and like it very well—better than town. I have not evolved any news within these five months past. I am leading a quiet life, not writing any, but reading as much as I can. Willie saw John 'tother day in Newport, who struck him as looking better than he had done for years. I believe he is to migrate in the Spring—but he has doubtless written you. Of your old friends I naturally see very few. Grinnell is back from Germany—I think he would have been glad to stay longer. I am told he saw you in Göttingen and will question him when next I see him. I see Arthur Sedgwick occasionally, who strikes me as a very pleasing fellow. I have not been to Newport since those melancholy days last July, too melancholy—and yet I know not altogether why—to recur to. Wilk and Bob are tilling the soil in Florida and Willie is still watching the auguries of opened bellies etc. I have read nothing new, and you I suppose, have read nothing but catalogues and guide books.—I return to the fact—to which I have not done justice—that my heart was mightily shaken by your letter from Spain. I went back to the time when we used to lie on the cliffs at Newport in the fulness of our innocent boyhood, and gaze upon that eternal—immortal—ocean line and feast upon its blue intense and prate about going where you in very sooth

67

have been. Has it really been a disappointment? is it a sell—like so much else? Or isn't it, taken for all in all, an experience worth the having? I understand very well that, once really started in Europe, and used to your new platform, the longed for sense of delight, the expected thrill and heart beat, should be easily superseded by a host of material cares and that the pleasure should only crop up at moments. But dont you reckon by these moments? Are they not frequent enough to characterize your course? Are they not, while they last, ineffable and sublime. Ah, thou who hast trod the pavement of Moorish shrines and gazed upon the olive cheek of dark-eyed Castilians, thou hast a mighty message for him who as he writes at his window, escapes not the distant towers of Bunker, and the eloquent dome of Boston State house. I hope you have picked up photos. Do you keep a diary, and is it copious? I should think all my talk would sound dismally irrelevant and rustic and am impelled to close. If you are really to be any time in Paris *do* make the most of it. And don't come and tell me you don't like it. And *do* wring in with some of the Mossers. And do familiarize yourself with the lingo. In short, live up to your privileges—especially to that of writing to me.—Farewell, friend of my innocent childhood—of my belle jeunesse. I shall write again as soon as I hear from you. I am pursuing a dreary hygienic course of no work and have plenty of vacuous hours to think of you in. Tout à toi:

H. James Jr.

1. From this time on and until the death of the James parents the family lived at 20 Quincy Street in a house situated where the Faculty Club of Harvard stands today.

To Alice James
Ms Harvard

Cambridge—Sunday
Feb. 3d [1867]

My dearest sister:[1]—

Long, long have I been meaning to write to you; but never, never have I been able. You see I have so much to do—so many duties, so many visitors, etc, that you will not be surprised at my not having found time. I seize a fleeting moment of accidental leisure.—Father and mother reached home safely on Wednesday evening; and the first thing father did on entering the library was to exclaim with religious fervour, "Good heavens! What a wonderful place this is!" But altho' glad to get home, I think they enjoyed themselves much in New York—We are delighted to hear such fine accounts of your improvement, the beauty of your character and so forth. Willie and I had a very pleasant time keeping house here together; altho' a much quieter one than last winter in Ashburton Place—having had neither Annie Watson nor Miss Eustis, staying with us.—This is Sunday morning as you see and marked by its usual exciting character. Outside, a raw drizzle: inside mother writing letters and fishballs lying heavy on my stomach.—I see nothing, hear nor do nothing worthy to be written to thee. I have not been out all winter—to speak of; I have not been into town once in the evening —since we went to see Ristori.[2] I should say there was very little party-giving or party-going in Cambridge; at least I hear of none. But this, you will say, is no proof. I am told that the wildest excitement prevails in New York about my literary *efforts*. Have patience yet awhile. A slight romance from my facile pen is to appear in the next *Atlantic* and another either in April or May[3]—I know not.— Did you read in the last *Atlantic* a thing called *Lago Maggiore*. "Tis by a Mr. Howells who lives here, and is a very nice gentleman.[4] If you haven't read it, do so; for it is very good.—Do you read Dr. Holmes's novel.[5]—I suppose the Temples have reached New York; and that you see them. If you do, give much love to them and tell Minny that I am on the verge of writing to her.—Mother brought me a great deal of "love"; I don't know who it was all from; but I wish you would distribute some of the same commodity impartially to whomsoever you suppose to be my creditors. She also gave me an urgent invitation from Cousin Helen to visit her; but I find that keeping quiet works so well that I think I will keep doing it for the rest of the winter at least, much rapture as it would give me to look upon your face and that of dear Aunt Kate. Would that you might return into our midst before very long! We sit in darkness without you.—But you will come with the spring, like a couple of lovely flowers, or birds. Embrace Aunt Kate and tell her I mean to write to her. Je t'embrasse, de fond en comble. Adieu soeur adorée.

Ton frère Henri

1. Alice James, was at this time in her nineteenth year and had apparently remained in New York with Aunt Kate while the parents returned to Quincy Street.
2. Adelaide Ristori (1822–1906), the Italian actress noted for her performance in Schiller's *Maria Stuart*.
3. "My Friend Bingham," *Atlantic*, XIX (March 1867), 346–358, and "Poor Richard," *Atlantic*, XIX (June 1867), 694–706; XX (July-August), 32–42, 166–178.
4. William Dean Howells (1837–1920) had settled in Cambridge to become sub-editor of the *Atlantic* under J. T. Fields.
5. Dr. Oliver Wendell Holmes (1809–1894). The novel was *The Guardian Angel*, then being serialized before its book publication in 1868.

To Thomas Sergeant Perry

Ms Colby

Cambridge Aug. 15 [1867].

Dear Sarge.—

Until the receipt of your letter from Loèche a silence had indeed reigned between us in which one might have heard a pin drop. I shall do my best to prevent its ever again becoming so appalling.— I remember spending a day and night at Loèche and seeing the people paddling together in their oleaginous tanks. I likewise remember the scenery as something grand, gloomy and peculiar. Am I mistaken? (Don't trouble yourself to answer this question). Your letter, dearest boy, was most welcome and acceptable. I had almost forgotten the look of your handwriting and the turn of your phraseology. I sympathise profoundly (out of the depths of my ignorance) with your Italian enthusiasm and don't despair of sometime feeling it in my own bosom. It must indeed be a delectable land and he must be a wiser and a better man who has felt its charms and glories.—I am very glad you saw things as thoroughly as you seem to have done and with so good a companion as Ware.—Whenever I think of you and your travels I think of long fireside talks and recollections in the vague sublime future. *Nous en aurons, de belles* I take it. I find myself curious to hear how you feel towards this America—how in your absence you have become affected towards it—alienated or the reverse. 'Tis after all no mean place. Willy writes as if he had already become in a certain degree Teutonized—or at least Europeanized—so that American papers, faces, talk etc seem strange and outlandish. I should think some of them easily might.—Your talk about the Italian—especially the Venetian—pictures, went to my soul. Of all and of all things, those are what I want most to see. Do you ever write to John and stir him up?—Your journey down through France—country of my love—I was also glad to hear of.—It will take you a lifetime to "read up" to all you have seen—if that is not a philistine speech.—Your friend Storey[1] had already lent me 3 of your letters and I have tried to get more but had not succeeded in finding him, and now of course he is away for the summer. I had mention of you of course from Willy, whom I was very glad to have you able to catch a glimpse of—sorry as I was to have it be in such accursed circumstances.—But these last are I firmly trust daily becoming better. We got a letter fm. him this ming.[2] in apparently very great spirits. It will be a great satisfaction to each of you, I take it, to be together next winter.—Of home news dear lad, and more especially of matters and things at Cambridge, what shall I tell you?—This place is at the present moment as empty as this blank page and as silent withal. Every human creature is away. Here have I been however, all summer and here I expect to stay. You may imagine that existence has not been thrilling or exciting. I have seen no one and done nothing—unless it be read; which I have done to some extent.—Take the whole year I have passed it as quietly as it was easily possible to have done. I like Cambridge very well, but at the end of another year I'm sure I shall have had enough of it. I doubt of the existence of any really satisfactory society here. The undergraduates are of course too young; the law students (in general) too stupid and common, the tutors and several of the professors too busy, and

Longfellow, Lowell, Norton and co. (in spite of great amiability), not at all to my taste, for the "bulk" of my society.—It is a question indeed whether a man gets the *bulk* of his society fm. man at all, and not rather fm. books. As for the female Cambridge society, I incline to the impression that it is provincial, common and inelegant. Certain it is that the young women whom I have seen are not of the species that appeal to my fancy. But perhaps I am grossly insensible. I had a visit at commencement fm. your friend Jno. Curtis,[3] who struck me as an interesting fellow, prevented by diffidence fm. doing himself justice. Prof. Gurney[4] I occasionally see, but he seems retiring, diffident and inaccessible. Next winter I expect to see more of him. W. J. Sedgwick is truly barren and unavailable. But he does his civil and social duties, works hard in a lawyer's office, and maintains a genial bearing.—Wilky has been spending the summer at home. He saw Tiffany at Newport, who spoke of you. You see I haven't paid my annual visit to that place (the first summer I have missed since we left it) or I should have made a point of seeing him. —So much for small talk. Pray do write, as you say, once a month. I don't forget you. I feel always that you exist.—You told me not whither you were bound; so I can't follow you in fancy; nor whether you had your ladies with you; so I can't send them my respects. But of course you are in some heart stirring spot. My dearest love to it and the assurance that it may one of the days expect me.—I say I still remember you—but your sensations and emotions must have somewhat transformed you. I feel that I have in the last year become much transformed, without any. Do you keep a copious journal? Do you feel the promptings of Genius before what you see? At all events God bless you.—You ask me to send my tales.—I will send what are printed in the future, if any. Those published aren't worth it.—American literature is at a dreadful pass.—Nothing decent comes to the light.—Farewell—

Yours always dear S.

H. James Jr.

1. Moorfield Storey (1845–1929), later a lawyer and publicist.
2. Fairly obviously HJ's speedwriting—"from him this morning."
3. John G. Curtis (1844–1913).
4. E. W. Gurney (1829–1886), professor of history at Harvard.

To Charles Eliot Norton

Ms Harvard

Cambridge. Sept. 5*th* [1867]

Dear Mr. Norton—

Here is my little account of *Jason*[1]—after I hope not too long a
delay. I thank you very much for having asked me to review the
book, because it forced me to read it and saved me the loss of a real
pleasure. But I am not in a very critical mood or even a very literary
one, and I beg you to excuse on this ground the various shortcom-
ings of my work.

Arthur Sedgwick in giving you my reply to your request will
have also given you my messages of remembrance, as well as to
Mrs. Norton and your mother and sisters. I expect to see him before
long and to get news of you in return. Of news, indeed, he can have
brought you very little from Cambridge. At least I have been here
all summer long and haven't been able to detect any—unless indeed
that to spend the summer in Cambridge is not so bad as it sounds.
Nevertheless I shall be very glad to see the winter coming and
bringing you back.

Let me recommend you not to trouble yourself to answer my
note, as I shall take for granted that you have received my package.
I should like very much to hear from you, but not at the cost of any
unwelcome exertion to yourself.

With renewed regards to all your circle, believe me most truly
yours

H. James Jr.

1. William Morris, *The Life and Death of Jason, A Poem* (Boston 1867).
Unsigned review in the *North American Review* CV (October 1867), 688–692.

To Francis P. Church

Ms N.Y. Public Library

Cambridge, Oct. 23*d* [1867]

My dear sir:[1]—

I recd. your note and the inclosed cheque—for which many
thanks.—I am sorry the story is not a little shorter but I am very

glad that you are to print all at once. As for adding a paragraph I should strongly object to it. It doesn't seem to me necessary. Silence on the subject will prove to the reader, I think, that the marriage *did* come off.[2] I have little fear that the reader will miss a positive statement to that effect and the story closes in a more dramatic manner, to my apprehension, just as I have left it. Yours most truly

H. James Jr.

P.S. Let me reiterate my request that I may see a proof. This I should particularly like to do.

H. J. Jr.

1. Francis P. Church and his brother W. C. Church owned and edited the *Galaxy* (1866–1878) a monthly literary magazine published in New York as a metropolitan counterpart to Boston's *Atlantic Monthly*.
2. The allusion here appears to be to "The Story of a Masterpiece," *Galaxy*, V (Jan.–Feb. 1868), 5–12, 133–143.

To Thomas Sergeant Perry

Ms Colby

Cambridge, Sept. 20*th* [1867]

Mon cher vieux Thomas:—

J'ai là sous les yeux depuis hier ta gentille lettre du 4 7bre. Je fus bien aisé de te savoir de retour a Paris, que tu n'as sans doute pas quitté. Je crois que tu ne regretteras jamais d'y avoir passé une grosse partie de ton temps; car enfin, quoiqu'on en dise, c'est une des merveilles de l'univers. On y apprend a connaître les hommes et les choses, et pour peu qu'on soit parvenu à y attraper le sentiment du *chez soi,* quelque genre de vie que l'on mène plus tard, on ne sera jamais un ignorant, un ermite—enfin un *provincial.*—Tu as depensé toute une page de ta lettre à me parler de l'Exposition.— Que le diable l'emporte, cette maudite baraque! Nous en avons bien assez, même ici à Cambridge. J'aurais bien mieux aimé que tu m'eusses parlé de toi, que tu m'eusses donné de tes nouvelles intimes. (En voilà, des imparfaits du subjonctif! Après cela dira qui voudras que je ne sais pas le Français!) Je me suis donné hier le plaisir d'aller chez tes camarades, Storey et Stratton, recueillir de tes nouvelles.

Ces messieurs ont été bien bien aimables, ils m'ont fait part des lettres qu' ils ont reçues de toi pendant l'été. J'en ai beaucoup ri, de ces lettres folles et charmantes. On ne peut avoir plus d'esprit, ni une gaillardise de meilleur ton. Ah mon cher, que je t'en porte envie, de tes courses et de tes aventures, et de ton humeur Rabelaisiaque!—Decidément, je plante là mon français: ou plutôt c'est lui qui me plante.—As I say, Storey and Stratton read me and lent me a large portion of your recent letters, beginning with a long one from Venice to the former. Many of your gibes of course I didn't understand, the context being absent. But I understood enough to enjoy the letters very much and to be able to congratulate you on your charming humour. (How detestable this *you* seems after using the Gallic *toi*!) Let me repeat in intelligible terms that I'm very glad to think of you as being as much as possible in Paris—city of my dreams! I feel as if it would count to my advantage in our future talks (and perhaps walks.) When a man has seen Paris somewhat attentively, he has seen (I suppose) the biggest achievement of civilization in a certain direction and he will always carry with him a certain little *reflet* of its splendour.—I had just been reading, when your letter came, Taine's *Graindorge,*[1] of which you speak. It seems to me a truly remarkable book in the way of *writing* and description, but to lack very much the deeper sort of observation. As a writer— a man with a language, a vocabulary and a style, I enjoy Taine more almost than I do any one; but his philosophy of things strikes me as essentially superficial and as if subsisting in the most undignified subservience to his passion for description.—I have also read the last new Mondays of Ste.B., and always with increasing pleasure.[2] Read in the 7th (I think) if you haven't already, an account of A. de Vigny. Truly, exquisite criticism can't further go.—Have you read *M. de Camours,* by Octave Feuillet?[3]—a sweet little story! Read by all means if you haven't, (I assume that you have the time,) *Prosper Randoce,* by V. Cherbuliez.[4] It's a work of extraordinary skill and power and I think takes the rag off all the French Romancers, save the illustrious G. Sand, *facile princeps.* I read recently, by the way, this lady's *Memoirs* a compact little work in ten volumes. It's all charming (if you are not too particular about the exact truth) but especially the two 1st volumes, containing a series of letters from her father, written during Napoleon's campaigns. I think they are the best letters I ever read. But you doubtless know the book.—In English I have read nothing new, except M. Arnold's *New Poems,* which of course you will see or have seen.—For real and exquisite pleasure read Morris's *Life & Death of Jason.* It's long but fascinating, and replete with genuine beauty.—There is nothing new of course in the universe of American letters—except the projected resuscitation of Putnam's Magazine.[5] Great news, you see! We live over here in a thrilling atmosphere.—Well, I suppose there *are* thrills here; but they dont come from the booksellers—not even from Ticknor and Fields, publishers of *Every Saturday.* I applaud your high resolves with regard to work, when you get home. You will always have my sympathy and co-operation.—Have you in view a *particular office* here at Harvard, for which you are particularly fitting yourself, or meaning so to do?—Upon this point, on which I have long felt a natural curiosity I have as yet failed to obtain satisfaction. Tell me all about it and unfold your mind to your devoted H. J.—I should think that by the time you get home you will have become tolerably well saturated with the French language and spirit; and if you contrive to do as much by the German, you will be a pretty wise man. There will remain the classical and the English. On the 1st I say nothing. *That* you will take care of; and I suppose you will study Latin and Greek by the aid of German and *vice-versa.* But the English literature and spirit is a thing which we tacitly assume that we know much more of than we actually do. Don't you think so? Our vast literature and literary history is to most of us an unexplored field—especially when we compare it to what the French is to the French.—Deep in the timorous recesses of my being is a vague desire to do for our dear old English letters and writers *something* of what Ste. Beuve and the best French critics have done for theirs. For one of my calibre it is an arrogant hope. *Aussi* I don't talk about it.—To enter upon any such career I should hold it invaluable to spend two or three years on English soil—face to face with the English landscape, English monuments and English men and women.—At the thought of a study of this kind, on a serious scale, and of possibly having the health and time to pursue it, my eyes fill with heavenly tears and my heart throbs with a divine courage.—But men don't accomplish valuable results alone, dear Sarge, and there will be nothing so useful to me as the thought of having companions and a laborer with whom I may exchange feelings and ideas. It is by this constant exchange and comparison, by the wear and tear of living and talking and observing that works of art shape themselves into completeness; and as artists and workers, we owe most to those who bring to us most of human life.—When I say that I should like to do as Ste. Beuve has done, I don't mean that I should like to imitate him, or reproduce him in English: but only that I should like to acquire something of his intelligence and his patience and vigour. One feels—I feel at least, that he is a man of the past, of a dead generation; and that we young Americans are (without cant) men of the future. I feel that my only chance for success as a critic is to let all the breezes of the west blow through me at their will. We are Americans born—*il faut en prendre son parti.* I look upon it as a great blessing; and I think that to be an American is an excellent preparation for culture. We have exquisite qualities as a race, and it seems to me that we are ahead of the European races in the fact that more than either of them we can deal freely with forms of civilization not our own, can pick and choose and assimilate and in short (aesthetically etc.) claim our property wherever we find it. To have no national stamp has hitherto been a defect and a drawback, but I think it not unlikely that American writers may yet indicate that a vast intellectual fusion and synthesis of the various National tendencies of the world is the condition of more important achievements than any we have seen. We must of course have something of our own—something distinctive and homogeneous—and I take it that we shall find it in our moral consciousness, our unprecedented spiritual lightness and vigour. In this sense at least we shall have a national *cachet.*—I expect nothing great during your lifetime or mine perhaps: but my instincts quite agree with yours in looking to see something original and beautiful disengage itself from our ceaseless fermentation and turmoil. You see I am willing to leave it a matter of instinct. God speed the day.—But enough of "abstract speculation", marked as it is by a very concrete stupidity. I haven't a spark of your wit and humor, my boy, and I can't write amusing letters. Let me say, now while I think of it, that I was quite unaware until I heard it the other evening from Ben Peirce, of how serious your accident had been on Mt. Vesuvius. In writing to you after 1st hearing of it, I believe I didn't even speak of it. A 1000 pardons for my neglect. My poor dear fellow: accept all my retrospective commiseration. It must have been the very devil of an exasperation. And you carry a classic wound—a Vesuvian scar!—Ah why was I not there (i.e. at the hotel) to sponge your gory face, and to change your poultices?—Well, thank the Lord it was no worse, I always said so when we used to walk on the hanging rock at Newport.—I have used up my letter with nonentities, and have no space nor strength for sweet familiar talk. No news. The summer (like a civil young man in the horse car) is giving its seat to the mellow Autumn—the glorious, the grave, the divine. We are having October weather in September: *pourvu que ca dure*. This is *American* weather—worth all the asphaltic breezes of Paris.—I have been all summer in Cambridge—*sans découcher une seule nuit*. Tiens! mon francais qui me retrouve!—It has been quite cool and comfortable, but "stiller than chiselled marble"—Vide Tennyson. I have a pleasant room with a big soft bed and good chairs, and with books and shirtsleeves I found the time pass rapidly enough.—I'm sorry to hear you say that your plans may not agree with Willie's for the winter. I hope you may adjust them. You'll of course find it pleasant enough to be together; but I hope neither of you will sacrifice any thing to your serious interests. I should suppose of course that *you* will prefer Berlin. We are expecting daily to hear from W. He wrote 8 weeks ago that he was feeling much better: news which gladded my heart.—I haven't seen John all summer; but I heard from him yesterday.—Your sister is again a mother: a little girl, and doing well. But this you will have heard. I draw to a close. My letter is long but not brilliant. I can't make 'em brilliant until some one or something makes me brilliant. A 100 thanks for the photos. About has a capital, clever face;[6] and Sardou a highly refined and Parisian

one.[7]—By all means send your own and others. Write punctually.—
Farewell, *mon vieux*. tout à toi

H. J.

1. Hippolyte Taine, *Notes sur Paris, Vie et opinions de M. Frédéric-Thomas Graindorge* (1868) a series of ironical studies of Parisian life.

2. An allusion to the *Nouveaux lundis* in Sainte-Beuve's first series of *Causeries de Lundi* published in the newspaper *Constitutional*. The new series of his weekly essays was published in 13 volumes between 1863 and 1870.

3. A novel reminiscent of *Les Liaisons Dangereuses*.

4. The French novelist of Swiss origin was a great favorite of the young Henry James.

5. *Putnam's Monthly Magazine*, founded in 1853, suspended in 1857, was revived in 1868 as *Putnam's Magazine*, but lasted only two years.

6. Edmond About (1828–1885) journalist and novelist. For an account of HJ's early impressions of About see his *William Wetmore Story and his Friends*, I, 359.

7. Victorien Sardou (1831–1908), the technique of whose "well-made" plays was greatly admired by HJ.

To William James

Ms Harvard

Cambridge Nov. 22*d* [1867]

Dear Willy—

I haven't written to you for some time, because the others seemed to be doing so. We at last got some little news about your health. Praised be the Lord that you are comfortable and in the way of improvement!—I recd. about a fortnight ago—your letter with the review of Grimm's novel[1]—after a delay of nearly a month on the road, occasioned by I know not what. I am very sorry for the delay as it must have kept you in suspense, and even yet I am unable to give you a satisfactory reply. I liked your article very much and was delighted to find you attempting something of the kind. It struck me as neither dull nor flat, but very readable. I copied it forthwith and sent it to the *Nation*. I received no answer—which I take to be an affirmative. I expected it to appear in yesterday's paper; but I see it is absent, crowded out I suppose by other matter. I confess to a dismal apprehension that something may have happened to it on the road to New York and have just written to Godkin[2] to tell me whether he actually received it. But I have little doubt he has done so and that it is waiting, and will appear next week.—Were it not for the steamer I would keep your letter till I get his answer.—I hope you will try your hand again. I assure you it is quite worth your while. I see you scoffing from the top of your arid philosophical dust-heap and comission T. S. Perry to tell you (in his own inimitable way) that you are a d--d fool. I very much enjoy your Berlin letters. Don't try to make out that America and Germany are identical and that it is as good to be here as there. It can't be done. Only let me go to Berlin and I will say as much. Life here in Cambridge—or in this house, at least, is about as lively as the inner sepulchre. You have already heard of Wilky's illness—chills and fever. It finally became so bad that he had to come home. He arrived some 10 days ago and is now much better; but he must have had a fearfully hard time of it. He eats, sleeps and receives his friends; but still looks very poorly and will not be able to return for some time. Bob went a few days ago out to his old railroad place at Burlington. He was very impatient to get something to do, but nothing else turned up, altho' he moved heaven and earth, *more suo*. I have no news for you. Aunt Kate is in N. Y., attending "Em" Walsh's wedding. The rest of us are as usual—whatever that may be called. I myself, I am sorry to say, am not so well as I was some time since. That is I am no worse but my health has ceased to improve so steadily, as it did during the summer. It is plain that I shall have a very long row to hoe before I am fit for anything—for either work or play. I mention this not to discourage you—for you have no right to be discouraged, when I am not myself—but because it occurs to me that I may have given you an exaggerated notion of the extent of my improvement during the past six months. An important element in my recovery, I believe, is to strike a happy medium between reading etc and "social relaxation." The latter is not to be obtained in Cambridge—or only a ghastly simulacrum of it. There are no "distractions" here. How in Boston, when the evening arrives, and I am tired of reading and know it would be better to do something else, can I go to the theatre? I have tried it *ad nauseam*. Likewise *"calling"*. Upon whom?—Sedgwicks, Nortons, Dixwells, Feltons. I can't possibly call at such places oftener than two or three times in six months; and they are the best in Cambridge. Going into town on the winter nights puts a chill on larger enterprizes. I say this not in a querulous spirit, for in spite of these things I wouldn't for the present leave Cambridge, but in order that you may not let distance falsify your reminiscences of this excellent place. Tonight for example, I am going into town to see the French actors who are there for a week, give Mme. Aubray.[8] Dickens has arrived for his readings. It is impossible to get tickets. At 7 o'clock A.M. on the first day of the sale there were two or three hundred at the office, and at 9, when I strolled up, nearly a thousand. So I don't expect to hear him. Tell Sargy I got his little note, enclosed by you, and am anxiously awaiting his letter. I *hope* (for his sake) he will be able to extend his absence. If not and he comes in March, I shall be first to welcome him. I haven't a creature to talk to. Farewell. I wanted to say more about yourself, personally, but I can't. I will write next week. *Je t'embrasse.*

H. J. Jr

1. Herman Grimm, *Unüberwundliche Machte*.
2. Edwin Lawrence Godkin (1831–1902) founder of the *Nation* in 1865 and later editor of the *New York Evening Post* published the young HJ consistently and remained a devoted friend in later years.
3. *Les Idées de Madame Aubray,* a play by Alexandre Dumas *fils* (1867).

To Thomas Sergeant Perry

Ms Colby

Cambridge, March 27, 1868

Dear Sarge:—

I have long meant to answer your last letter, but somehow the pen wouldn't move. At last I push it along, but I know not what will come of it. I think of you as getting half a dozen letters a week from your various young friends in these parts, who must give you all the general news that turns up. Of particular news I, individually turn out but little—tho' to that little you are welcome. Until Willy left Berlin, he generally in his letters made some mention of you, so that I was not entirely in the dark as to your doings and intentions. On the other hand, your friends Storey and Stratton have vanished out of Cambridge and I have lost the privilege of reading your letters. The latter having gone abroad I suppose you will have seen him, or are likely to see him. There was a moment, you will remember, when I expected to see you at home by this time and thought much of it, until you had deferred your return to next autumn. On the whole I am glad you did so, both on your own account and on mine. On your own, because you will have time as it were to *clinch* the profit, or pleasure (or whatever it is you're getting) of your stay in Europe; and on mine because I have conceived an abject dread and terror of your character and conversation as developed by European influences, and shall have time to fortify myself and pluck up courage against our encounter. *Vrai,* are you not another T. S. Perry than the "boy Sargy" of bygone days—a languid, florid cosmopolite, clad in black velvet, knowing in French wines, actors, actresses and sich—knowing well thy Paris—thy Figaro—thy Poisson du Terrail? I shall clasp thy hand in friendship, *tout de meme* and I shall study thy nature and thy manners with humble and reverential affection. I have a vague impression that you didn't grow quite to love Berlin—is it not so? By this time I suppose you are nevertheless on speaking terms with the Berlin tongue. Yet you love better Paris and you are going there for the spring and summer. I suppose you might do better and worse. I fancy you will be there when this reaches you, for which reason, I shall send it Rue de la Paix. If a hundred things were precisely a hundred other things—guess a little what I would in fain do. I would take ship for Havre—disembark—train for Paris, *via* Rouen —arrive, see thee in station—embrace thee with effusion—spend summer, too, in Paris. I know not why, I can't lay the ghost, but Paris, vulgarized as it has become, haunts my imagination. It may be that it is better so, and that in the very interest of joy, I had best never go there. I wish very much at any rate that, while you are there, Sarge, you could manage to write me a few letters.

We shall spend the prime of summer far—far—asunder—thou sniffing the asphalte of the Boulevards, I the primeval odors of (I hope) some mountain lake in New Hampshire. What a vast and terrible thing is human experience—life—in fine, the world. Excuse this sublime platitude. I was struck by a momentary sense of the diversity of our prospective destinies and of the power of "culture" to reduce it to naught—comparatively. I received yesterday a letter from Willy from Teplitz, March 4th, which cost me a great deal of deep regret and pain. His "cure" had turned out a failure and he was worse than before. He spoke of coming home. But I wrote him a long letter and I can't bear to talk about it. I suppose you hear from him and write to him. This frigid, rigid town is gradually melting and moistening springwards; but departing winter has kicked off its shift in its flight and smothered us all in a snow storm. I hear little of Cambridge things and see little of Cambridge people. I see none indeed but the Nortons and Howells. Once in a while I see Gurney, who I believe is suffering a good deal with his head. The Nortons are going to Europe and there is I believe a chance of Gurney taking the *North American Review*. The Longfellows are also going. I don't know, when you get back, who or what you'll find for your delectation. There is a Men's Club on foot in Cambridge, but it hangs fire wofully for want of rooms. It may die still. But I hope not; for I think it would be a pleasant thing. There is likewise a new Theatre in Boston—a very good one, as such things go here. But 'twill be nothing to you after Sardou, Augier, the Favart and the Fargueil. Have you seen— shall you see—*Paul Forestier*? A charming *donnée*. What next? You see I keep up with the novelities. There are none here, as you may imagine, in literature or in art. The last thing is a swarm of new magazines, *plus bêtes les uns que les autres*. Read, if you haven't, in the *Revue des Deux Mondes,* two articles on *Lessing* by V. Cherbuliez. It is an admirable piece. I do adore that man—I mean V. C. Could you find his photog? or that of *Taine,* or that of Flaubert—or any other one of G. Sand than the common one I have. It would be a kindness to slip one into a letter. But go to no trouble.—I went a month ago to spend a Sunday at Newport and saw your sister. The place struck me with a chill and horror which would have been fatal but for her sweet and charming influence. John was in New York; but his wife showed me some extremely promising beginnings of large pictures.—I read more or less, of course, but nothing noteworthy. A good deal of French, of which, at times, I get very sick. Nevertheless I hope you will bring all the French books you have picked up—so that I can beg, borrow and steal 'em. I write little and only tales, which I think it likely I shall continue to manufacture in a hackish manner, for that which is bread. They *cannot* of necessity be very good; but they *shall not* be very bad. What are your own literary views and tendencies? How many languages are you perfect master of? But I sink to the horizon. I glow, dear Sarge, with good will, affection and desire to see. Do be kind—you who are strong—and write.

Farewell
perpetually thine
H. J. Jr

3
The Grand Tour

1869-1870

3
The Grand Tour

William James went to Germany in 1867–68 to pursue his studies and perfect his knowledge of German. Henry James's friend T. S. Perry had made a tour of Europe during 1866–67; Wendell Holmes, future justice of the Supreme Court, at this time also took his turn abroad—and during these journeyings of his brother and his friends the future novelist remained in Cambridge, enviously reading their letters, listening to reports from the parents of the voyagers, and experiencing a nostalgic longing to be with them. He traveled vicariously in each letter received from abroad. Even moderately prosperous parents of the period felt that Europe—"our old home" as Hawthorne had called England—was required to provide the polish, the cachet, the learning, the air and spirit of the great wide world, before the young could settle into their careers. The Civil War, moreover, had sharpened a desire in young Americans for new scenes, foreign places, an escape from the guilt of fratricidal war.

In 1869 Henry James's turn came. William had returned to the familiar horizons of Cambridge, still in doubt about his future. The James family provided funds for Henry's journey and expected him to follow his brother's path. They wanted Henry to go to Germany. He was already fluent in French; they felt he needed German speech and German philosophers: and in this were strongly supported by William. Henry James decided on his own itinerary once he was abroad. His crucial decision, after England, France, and Switzerland, was to go to Italy, a country never visited by his parents during the period when they had wandered abroad. Henry walked into Italy in a memorable descent from the Simplon, and it was as if he walked into his future. His exposure to the cities, the people, the galleries and the ancient ruins, affected him as it had his illustrious literary predecessors. For him it was a journey not only into the Italy of actuality, to a meeting of the contemporary Italians as he saw them in the street life and in their parks and cafes, but a step by step progress through the renaissance and the Italy of the romantics. "Oh Italy—the Italy *of* Italy!" he would exclaim a quarter of a century later in a letter to Gosse, meaning the Italy of his prime as against the Italy of romantic novels. He traveled in 1869, reading Goethe, Stendhal, the Président de Brosses and Hawthorne. Although he felt then that he would always see Italy "from without" —he was totally at home only in England—he nevertheless got to know Florence and Rome, and ultimately Venice, with an intimacy rare among American travelers and observers. We discover him in Rome "reeling and moaning" as he put it, through the ancient streets, in that bravura passage describing his first day in the Holy City, but we see also a mature and artistic young American singularly conscious of himself and his destiny. He recognized his grand tour as the moment when his impressions would have a freshness they could never again have: as he wrote, this was the time to have them; the future would be something else again. His family seems to have been worried by what seemed to them a tendency to idleness: they little understood what Henry James was acquiring—the cultural capital which would inform all his future writings.

He avoided Germany. That territory belonged to his brother. He had an antipathy for it. In England he was fortunate to have the guidance and friendship of Charles Eliot Norton, then abroad, and through him he met Ruskin, Darwin, Rossetti; he renewed an acquaintance with Leslie Stephen; he was enabled to call on George Eliot and would draw an unforgettable portrait of her in one of his early letters to his father. But even these meetings, so important to him, faded before his immersion in Italy's past, its paintings, its palaces and villas, its literature. He seems to have acquired the language with some ease, and a number of Italian books purchased during this journey remained on his shelves through later years. The letters preserved from his grand tour—kept by his family as if they were a diary—show with what feeling he visited England first as a "passionate pilgrim" looking at its green landscapes and buildings, capturing old literary associations, particularly with the eyes of his predecessor Hawthorne, and then with his own eyes—as if to bring to the earlier American traveler the corrections, the refocusing, of an artist of the new generation.

His journey was a liberation, a grand ecstasy, a period of acute observation and also of ill-health. His illness, from all evidence, was largely "functional." He suffered from a debilitating costiveness. It would be idle to speculate about the symptoms which were bothersome and in reality temporary, the consequence perhaps of continental regimen or psychological anxieties. Its direct effect was to make him interrupt his sightseeing and to visit health spas; and his euphemistic letters on the subject, largely to his medical brother, convey a sense of his discomfort and his reluctant leave-taking of the sights so indispensable to his artistic well-being. But his state of unwellness did not prevent him from seeing Rome and attaching himself to the single country to which he returned again and again from his future residence in England to find refreshment of spirit and the cultural nourishment that fed his work. He did finally have to tear himself away—and he journeyed by way of the Riviera in midwinter (relishing the warmth and the sun while remembering the blizzards of New England) back to damp and foggy England, and thence crossed the ocean to parochial Cambridge in Massachusetts. The climax of his journey, as the letters eloquently attest, was the death of his beloved cousin Minny Temple. He later spoke of it as the end of his youth. The year abroad did that as well. It completed his education. And while further years of toil lay ahead, he knew, once he had made his "grand tour," that he wanted above all to be "just literary." That wish sufficed for all time.

To Alice James

Ms Harvard

London 7 Half-Moon St. W.
March 10 [1869]

Ma soeur cherie[1]—

I have half an hour before dinner-time. Why shouldn't I begin a letter for Saturday's steamer. You will by this time have received my letter from Liverpool—or rather will just be receiving it. Mercy on us! What an age it seems to me since that letter was written and yet to think that it's only now finishing its dreary homeward voyage! On Friday last I despatched an immensely copious effusion to mother, which she will get in due time, and yet it seems to me that I now have matter for another chronicle on quite as large a scale. But I see you turn pale; *rassure toi*; I shall not yet repeat the infliction. I have now been in London some ten days and actually feel very much at home here—feel domesticated and naturalized in fact, to quite a disgusting extent. I feel that in proportion as I cease to be perpetually thrilled surprised and delighted, I am being cheated out of my fun. I really feel as if I had lived—I don't say a lifetime—but a year in this murky metropolis. I actually believe that this feeling is owing to the singular permanence of the impressions of childhood, to which my present experience joins itself on, without a broken link in the chain of sensation. Nevertheless, I may say that up to this time I have been crushed under a sense of the mere magnitude of London—its inconceivable immensity—in such a way as to paralyse my mind for any appreciation of details. This is gradually subsiding; but what does it leave behind it? An extraordinary intellectual depression, as I may say, and an indefineable flatness of mind. The place sits on you, broods on you, stamps on you with the feet of its myriad bipeds and quadrupeds. In fine, it is anything but a cheerful or a charming city. Yet it is a very splendid one. It gives you, here at the West End and in the city proper, a vast impression of opulence and prosperity. But you don't want a dissertation of commonplaces on London and you would like me to touch on my own individual experience. Well, my dear, since last week, it has [been] sufficient, altho' by no means immense. On Saturday I received a visit from Mr. Leslie Stephen[2] (blessed man) who came unsolicited and with the utmost civility in the world invited me to dine with him (early) the next day. This I did in company with Miss Jane Norton.[3] His wife made me very welcome and they both appear to much better effect on their own premises than they did in America. After dinner he conducted us by the underground railway to see the beasts in the Regent's Park, to which as member of the Zoological Society he has admittance "Sundays." This same underground railway, by the way, is a marvellous phenomenon—ploughing along in a vast circle thro' the bowels of London, and giving you egress to the upper earth in magnificent stations, at a number of convenient points. The trains are the same as above ground. As for cheapness, I went on Monday from the Nortons, in Kensington, to the Barings[4] in the heart of the city, first class, for sixpence. As for speed, owing to the frequent stoppages, I should have gone faster in a Hansom; but I should have paid several shillings. Of course at each end I had a little walk to the station.

12th A.M.

After we had seen the beasts I went back with Stephen to his house and had some tea and a little talk, after which I departed to my own residence. On Monday morning I breakfasted at the Nortons, "to meet" two gentlemen friends of theirs—Dr. Bridges a famous Comtist,[5] of the *Fortnightly Review* group and Mr. Simon[6] (pronounced *à la Francaise*) a very witty man, and occupying some high medical post in government. He politely asked me to dine at his house to meet Mr. and Mrs. Tom Taylor,[7] but I declined. (I forgot to say just now by the way, *apropos* of the Stephens, that Miss Thackeray[8] is absent on the Continent—gone to Rome to to stay with the Storys[9]—else I should have seen her. Two other other persons I have missed seeing are Mr. and Mrs. G. H. Lewes,[10] whom under the Norton's auspices I should have met: they have seen much of the former and something of the latter.) On Tuesday I breakfasted with Rutson,[11] my neighbor above stairs, Charles Norton's friend, who initiated me here. He is private secretary to Mr. Bruce,[12] the Home Secretary, and he had invited a young member of Parliament to meet me. The banquet was not an immense success. The two gentlemen were oppressively political and high-toned; I had been invited only as a matter of grim duty by Rutson; I knew and cared nothing for my hosts and their interests; in short 'twas decidedly flat. Rutson must have loathed me for being thus rudely thrust into his existence. After breakfast I received another visit from Leslie Stephen, with renewed offers of service. He is evidently an excellent fellow and will make me adore him prostrate before he gets thro', if he goes on at this rate. Then remembering father's injunction to call on Mr. White,[13] I proceeded forth to Hampstead to perform the ceremony. He opened his door in person—received my name with blushes and "friendly greetings" and did his best to make me comfortable. His notion of hospitality however, seemed to be to get me out of the house as soon as possible, first under the pretext of calling on Father's old friend Mrs. Welford, who lives near him, and whom we didn't see, owing to her being laid up with "a bad face" (White says, by the way, that she has grown so fat she can't walk) and then for the purpose of walking me to death over the hills and dales of Hampstead. This I resisted, but he nevertheless showed me a good bit of it. It's a charming old town, nestling under oaks and ivied walls and sprawling over the deep misty verdure of its undulous heath. Mr. White is a little short-legged Scot with a vast bald head, a broad brogue and a red face—a shrewd little North British vulgarian. He asked many questions about Father. On my way home I called at the Wilkin-sons[14] (to apologise for not having come on the Sunday, as I had partially agreed to do) and saw Mrs. W. alone, Mary to my sorrow having gone to Brighton to spend a month with Florence. Mrs. W. is very clever. I think however under the above circumstances that I shall not see much more of them, save, probably to dine there again. The Dr. is extremely busy. In the evening I dined with the invaluable Nortons and went with Charles and Madame, Miss S. and Miss Jane (via underground railway) to hear Ruskin lecture at University College on Greek Myths.[15] I enjoyed it much in spite of fatigue; but as I am to meet him someday thro' the N's, I will reserve comments. On Wednseday evening I dined at the N.'s (*toujours* Nortons you see) in company with Miss Dickens[16]— Dickens's only unmarried daughter—plain-faced, ladylike, (in black silk and black lace) and the image of her father. I exchanged but 10 words with her. But yesterday, my dear old sister, was my crowning day—seeing as how I spent the greater part of it in the home of Mr. William Morris, Poet. Fitly to tell the tale, I should need a fresh pen, paper and spirits. A few hints must suffice. To begin with, I breakfasted, by way of a change, with the Nortons, along with Mr. Sam Ward,[17] who has just arrived and Mr. Aubrey

De Vere, *tu sais*, the Catholic poet, a pleasant honest old man and very much less high-flown than his name. He tells good stories in a light natural way. After a space I came home and remained until 4.30 P.M. when I had given rendezvous to C. N. and ladies at Mr. Morris's door, they going by appointment to see his shop and C. having written to say he would bring me. Morris lives on the same premises as his shop, in Queen's Square, Bloomsbury, an antiquated ex-fashionable region, smelling strong of the last century, with a hoary effigy of Queen Anne in the middle. Morris's poetry you must know, is only his sub-trade. To begin with, he is a manufacturer of stained glass windows, tiles, ecclesiastical and mediaeval tapestry altar-cloths, and in fine everything quaint, archaic, pre-Raphaelite—and I may add exquisite. Of course his business is small and may be carried on in his house: the things he makes are so handsome, rich and expensive (besides being articles of the very last luxury) that his *fabrique* can't be on a very large scale. But everything he has and does is superb and beautiful. But more curious than anything is himself. He designs with his own head and hands all the figures and patterns used in his glass and tapestry and furthermore works the latter, stitch by stitch with his own fingers—aided by those of his wife and little girls. Ah, *ma chère*, such a wife![18] *Je n'en reviens pas*—she haunts me still. A figure cut out of a missal—out of one of Rossetti's or Hunt's pictures—to say this gives but a faint idea of her, because when such an image puts on flesh and blood, it is an apparition of fearful and wonderful intensity. It's hard to say [whether] she's a grand synthesis of all the pre-Raphaelite pictures ever made—or they a "keen analysis" of her—whether she's an original or a copy. In either case she is a wonder. Imagine a tall lean woman in a long dress of some dead purple stuff, guiltless of hoops (or of anything else, I should say,) with a mass of crisp black hair heaped into great wavy projections on each of her temples, a thin pale face, a pair of strange sad, deep, dark Swinburnish eyes, with great thick black oblique brows, joined in the middle and tucking themselves away under her hair, a mouth like the "Oriana" in our illustrated Tennyson, a long neck, without any collar, and in lieu thereof some dozen strings of outlandish beads—in fine Complete. On the wall was a large nearly full-length portrait of her by Rossetti, so strange and unreal that if you hadn't seen her, you'd pronounce it a distempered vision, but in fact an extremely good likeness. After dinner (we stayed to dinner, Miss Grace, Miss S. S.[19] and I,) Morris read us one of his unpublished poems, from the second series of his un-'Earthly Paradise,' and his wife having a bad toothache, lay on the sofa, with her handkerchief to her face. There was something very quaint and remote from our actual life, it seemed to me, in the whole scene: Morris reading in his flowing antique numbers a legend of prodigies and terrors (the story of Bellerophon, it was), around us all the picturesque bric-a-brac of the apartment (every article of furniture literally a 'specimen' of something or other,) and in the corner this dark silent medieval woman with her medieval toothache. Morris himself is extremely pleasant and quite different from his wife. He impressed me most agreeably. He is short, burly and corpulent, very careless and unfinished in his dress, and looks a little like B. G. Hosmer, if you can imagine B. G. infinitely magnified and fortified. He has a very loud voice and a nervous restless manner and a perfectly unaffected and business-like address. His talk indeed is wonderfully to the point and remarkable for clear good sense. He said no one thing that I remember, but I was struck with the very good judgment shewn in everything he uttered. He's an extraordinary example, in short, of a delicate sensitive genius and taste, served by a perfectly healthy body and temper. All his designs are quite as good (or rather nearly so) as his poetry: altogether it was a long rich sort of visit, with a strong peculiar flavour of its own. You will have had enough, my dear, of this descriptive stuff by this time and I stay my ruthless hand. When I stopped writing this morning I went out and travelled over to the British Museum, with regard to which I wish to stick in a pin. I found it a less formidable process, going there, than I supposed. That is, there is only one region, the three or four Greek or Roman rooms, that I can pretend to look at properly and these I shall hope to pay a couple more visits. One may say indeed that the only thing to look at are the Elgin Marbles; they vulgarize everything else so, that you are fain to rest content with them. Of their wondrous beauty, my dear, I can say nothing. Had I the pen of an immortal bard I would comment with a Sonnet;[20] but failing this I must hold my tongue. I didn't say, I believe, that I have been once to the great Kensington Museum—a vast store house of art treasures. It's a marvel of richness and arrangement. I hope to get a couple of hours there again. When I add that I have done St. Paul's—I and Miss J. Norton together—and that to my infinite disgust the National Gallery is closed—I shall have finished the tale of my pleasures and pains.—Ouf! What a repulsively long letter! This sort of thing won't do. A few general reflections, a burst of affection (say another sheet and I must close.)—You can see for yourself that I see a great deal of the Nortons and I need hardly say that it is everything to me, to have them here. But for their presence I should have gone off (somewhere!) a week ago. In London you must have one of two things (money being assumed)—friends or work. If I were able to work (either at home or in the way of poking about and sightseeing *ad libitum*) I might successfully contend with the loneliness and gloom which is the necessary lot of a stranger here. As it is, the only basis on which I can remain any time (save finish my month) is on the easy social one furnished by the N's. I should have said instead of saying that they are as pleasant as ever, that they are much improved. They are decidedly more joyous, wild and free than before and are so kind and friendly to me that if I did as they would have me, I would in their house feel absolutely at home. So much for myself and my own affairs.—How I long to know something of thine, lovely child and of all the rest of your's—if that isn't grammar, it's love. Last Monday (I have waited till now to say it) I went over to Barings in quest of a letter and found mother's note of the 23rd. Woe, woe if I had found none. Of course the time seems so much shorter to you than to me and you don't feel as if you had anything to say; but for these first weeks, till I get used to the confounded thing, do try and send me some little scrap by each steamer and you will confer favour on a most de-serving creature. On Monday next I shall skurry over to Barings on the wings of the wind—or rather the wheels of a Hansom —or most probably, economically on the top of a "bus." Perhaps, sweet maid, there will be a little note from you. Perhaps there will be one from Mother—from Father—from Bill. I hardly hope to hear from you all; I'm curious to see how you will arrange it. Meanwhile I thank Mother *de profundis* of my soul for her last: it was sweet. Even as the draught given by the Jewess of old to her little son in the Wilderness. What wilderness is equal to this tremendous London?—What Jewess to my Mother. I needn't say how I long to hear the the sanitary record of the household—beginning with thine, dear child, *cette bonne petite sauté à toi*. Has Willie felt my absence in any poignant—or rather any practical degree: if so—if he misses me "round the room" he mustn't scruple to send for me to return. I only want a pretext. My last letter was full of drivelling homesickness; do not think that I have not slain the enemy. A mild melancholy, at most, enshrouds my being. I know not why or what it is—whether I've come too late or grown too old, owlish and stupid, but I don't anticipate any rapturous emotions on this alien soil.—It must be confessed, however, that London is hardly the place for romances and raptures, and that when I leave it, they may attack me in earnest. The point I wish to make is simply that I am not homesick. I wouldn't go any further if I could.—On the chapter of bodily vigour, you see what has been the scale and programme of my performances, and that may imply a goodly share of it. The best thing I can say is that I'm *thoroughly* satisfied with my progress and condition. My venture is taking just the course I counted upon. There is no sudden change, no magic alleviation; but a gradual and orderly recurrence of certain phenomena which betray slow development of such soundness as may ultimately be my earthly lot. In short my life agrees and directly tends and administers to my recovery and will do so more and more as I get properly "attuned," as I may say to it. This is positive. I haven't felt better in I don't know when, than I felt last night when I reached home at the close of my busy day—breakfast at the Nortons and the long afternoon and evening at the Morris's. I have recovered my sleep, my appetite is enormous, especially for beer of which I drink largely. The climate creates and stimulates the taste. (I had torn off that leaf to make a ditch, as it were, for my run away pen to pull up at; but you see, it leaps the gulf.) I'm at my old trick of growing repulsively fat. If I only get as good news from Bill and you, I shall feel that I haven't lived in vain. You will receive in 10 days (or at least see advertised, whereupon pray buy it) the *Galaxy* for April, with something of mine in it, which you will read.[21] It's sure to be badly printed. I came very near seeing a proof in New York but the man disappointed me at the last moment—confound him! Has anything more been heard from Youmans?—But I must pull in. I blush for the hideous magnitude of this letter. Don't read it, if it bores you. I want very much to know how Wilk and Bob took my departure. You will have heard and of course reported. Do give the dear fellows a brother's love and greetings. Tell T. S. Perry, with my love, that I await on this further shore the answer to that farewell note of mine. Give my love to Howells and tell him that I feel I owe him a letter in return for his last note. Is Aunt Kate at home? Farewell. Tell Arthur Sedgwick that I have in mind that promised letter. Farewell, dear girl and dear incomparable all—

your
H.

1. Some of the feelings expressed in this letter were incorporated in HJ's later essay on "London," reprinted in *Essays in London and Elsewhere* (1893).

2. Leslie Stephen and his wife Minnie, Thackeray's daughter, had met the Jameses during a journey to America. Stephen at this time was a literary critic in London.

3. Jane Norton (1824–1877), sister of Charles Eliot Norton.

4. HJ's bankers.

5. Dr. John Henry Bridges (1832–1906) translated Comte into English.

6. Sir John Simon (1816–1894) sanitary reformer, pathologist, and a friend of Ruskin.

7. Tom Taylor (1817–1880) author of *Still Waters Run Deep*, a play seen by HJ during his childhood, and other stage successes.

8. Anne Isabella Thackeray (1837–1919), later Lady Ritchie, eldest daughter of the novelist and herself a writer of fiction.

9. William Wetmore Story (1819–1895) American sculptor who lived in Rome for many years and whose biography HJ wrote in 1903.

10. Mary Ann Evans (George Eliot) (1819–1880) who had lived for years out of wedlock with George Henry Lewes (1817–1878).

11. Albert Rutson figures in HJ's account of his early days in London in his posthumous autobiographical fragment *The Middle Years* (1918).

12. Henry Austin Bruce, First Baron Aberdare (1815–1895), Home Secretary in Gladstone's first government of 1868.

13. William White, English Swedenborgian, wrote a two volume life of Swedenborg published in 1868.

14. J. J. Garth Wilkinson (1812–1890) an eminent Swedenborgian, friend of HJ Sr. The James and Wilkinson families had formed a close friendship during the Jameses' stay abroad in 1843.

15. Ruskin's lectures on March 8 and 15, 1869, dealt with Greek myths of storm, later published as *The Queen of the Air*.

16. Kate MacCready Dickens (b. 1839), later Mrs. Perugini.

17. Sam Ward (1814–1884), banker.

18. Jane Burden Morris (1839–1914) sat for many of the paintings of the pre-Raphaelites.

19. Grace Norton (1834–1926) sister of C. E. Norton and Mrs. Norton's sister Sara Sedgwick (1864–1922).

20. An allusion to Keat's sonnets "On Seeing the Elgin Marbles."

21. The April *Galaxy*, VII, 538–549 published one of HJ's early experiments in the dramatic form, a sketch called "Pyramus and Thisbe" reprinted in *Collected Plays*, ed. Edel (1949).

To William James

Ms Harvard

London March 19*th* [1869]
7 Half-Moon St. W.

Dear Bill—

As I have written three very long letters home without as yet anything like a sufficient equivalent, I won't trouble you this time with more than a few lines. You must be very much startled, by the way, by my charming prolixity; I suppose my impressions have been too many for me and that I shall gradually acquire greater self-control. You see, I'm still in London but without a great deal of news beyond that simple fact—if simple it can in any sense be called. Or rather I have a piece of news which ought to interest you very nearly as much as myself—which is two words that my experiment is turning out a perfect success and taking in all essentials the course that I had counted upon. I go thro' everything that comes up, feeling the better and better for it; I feel every day less and less fatigue. I made these long recitals of my adventures in my former letters only that you might appreciate how much I am able to do with impunity. You mustn't think of course that I am literally on the gallop from morning till night: far from it. I mentioned all the people and things I saw, without speaking of the corresponding intervals of rest, which of course have been numerous and salutary. But I may say that I can do all that I care to—all I should care to, if I were in perfect order. I wouldn't go in if I could, for perpetual and promiscuous pleasure. It cheapens and vulgarizes enjoyment. But when a man is able to breakfast out, to spend a couple of hours at the British Museum and then to dine out and go to the play, and feel none the worse for it, he may cease to be oppressed by a sense of his physical wretchedness. Such is my programme for today—the first item of which has been executed. (You can interpolate this letter, by the way, into the list of my achievements.) I have been breakfasting with my neighbor Rutson, of whom I have spoken, who seems to take a most magnanimous view of his obligations towards me. He entertained me this morning with a certain Hon. George Broderick (a son of Lord Middleton, you know)—an extremely pleasant and intelligent man. (Rutson has just stopped in to ask me again for Sunday. He is indeed as my landlord describes him—"wrapped up in goodness and kindness.") The dinner this evening is to be at the Stephen's. It will have been however, except at the Nortons and Wilkinsons, the only house at which I've dined. I've really of course seen no people on my own basis. I breakfasted yesterday at the Nortons along with Frederic Harrison[1] and Professor Beesly—the political-economists of the *Fortnightly Review*. It's very pleasant meeting people at the Nortons as thanks to their large numbers, you are lost in the crowd and can see and hear them without having to talk yourself. The gents in question were very agreeable—altho' I felt of course no special vocation for "meeting" political economists. I shall have gone off without seeing any literary folk, I suppose, save Leslie Stephen—who in spite of his good nature seems mortally untalkative. I was asked to dine today at the N's with Ruskin and John Morley,[2] editor of the *Fortnightly* but this dinner prevents. Also to go with C. N. to Lord Houghton's[3] to see his collection of Blakes, but for various reasons I have declined. I spent a very pleasant morning the other day by going out to Ruskin's at Denmark Hill, near Sydenham, with C. N. I didn't see the *grand homme*, in person, as he was shut up with some very urgent writing; but I saw what was as good, his pictures—a splendid lot of

Turners (the famous *Slaver* among others) a beautiful Tintoret and an ineffably handsome Titian—a portrait. I enjoyed very much too the sight of a quiet opulent long-established suburban English home. Tell Alice the house was fundamentally just like Miss Austen's novels. I shall perhaps (or probably) dine there next week. I went out the other morning, by rail, to Dulwich to see the gallery and spent an hour there very pleasantly. One long gallery, lit from an old fashioned ceiling, paved with brick tile and lined with very fair specimens of most of the great masters. A pale English light from the rainy sky—a cold half-musty atmosphere and solitude complete save for a red nosed spinster at the end of the vista copying a Gainsborough—the scene had quite a flavor of its own. Only these indifferent Rubenses and Rembrandts make me long for the good ones. The National Gallery is still closed.—I dined yesterday with the Wilkinsons. Mary is away. Madame is agreeable and the Doctor excellent. He is a great admirer of Swinburne and said some very good things about him. In fact he said nothing but good things. Father will know what I mean by his peculiar broad rich felicity of diction. I doubt whether I should see in England a better talker in a certain way. But my "few lines" are losing their fewness. I leave as usual to the end to say that on Monday I received father's little note of March 2 enclosing Nelly's which I have answered. I was thankful for this small favor, but woefully disappointed at getting nothing else. I live in the expectation of the next mail. Next week I will have matured and will communicate my plans ahead. I shall not outstay April 1st in this place. Of course I shall go to Malvern, as I intended. I needn't say how much I hope to get from you as good news as I have given. I am in the most superior spirits— and very anxious to get some news from the boys or, at least, of them. *Beaucoup d'amour!*

H. J. Jr

1. Frederic Harrison (1831–1923) English Positivist, writer, editor.
2. John Morley (1838–1923), later first Viscount Morley of Blackburn, statesman, historian, and editor of the "English Men of Letters" series.
3. Richard Monckton Milnes (1809–1885), first Baron Houghton biographer of Keats, bibliophile, intimate of many Victorian writers.

Mrs. Henry James Sr.

To Mrs. Henry James Sr.

Ms Harvard

London
7 Half Moon St.
March 20 [1869]

My dearest Mother—

I got last Monday your letter of March 9th—and a woeful thing it would have been all round if I hadn't! What did Willy mean by his *hideous* suggestion that you shouldn't write? I assure you I am quite guiltless of the indifference of which, by analogy with his own base character, he accuses me. "So soon," forsooth! I feel as if I had been away a year at the very least—I find it very hard to believe that at your last writing you shouldn't even have received my first letter—written ages ago. By the time you next write it will have reached you and such as it is I hope it will stimulate and quicken your languid pens. Your letter was most delectable, dear mamma, and so was Wilky's verily a prophet does get a little honor in his own country. I will write to him before long. This will have been my fifth weekly bundle since my arrival, and I can't promise—or rather I forbear to threaten—that it shall be as hugely copious as the others. But there's no telling where my pen may take me.—You see I am still in what my old landlord never speaks of but as 'this great metropolis'; and I hope you will believe me when I add, moreover, that I am in the best of health and spirits. During the last week I have been knocking about in a quiet way and have deeply enjoyed my little adventures. The last few days in particular have been extremely pleasant. You have perhaps fancied that I have been rather stingy-minded towards this wondrous England, and that I was [not] taking things in quite the magnanimous intellectual manner that befits a youth of my birth and breeding. The truth is that the face of things here throws a sensitive American back on himself—back on his prejudices and national passions, and benumbs for a while the faculty of appreciation and the sense of justice. But with time, if he is worth a copper, the characteristic beauty of the land dawns upon him (just as certain

102

vicious chilblains are now dawning upon my poor feet) and he feels that he would fain plant his restless feet into the rich old soil and absorb the burden of the misty air. If I were in anything like working order now, I should be very sorry to leave England. I should like to settle down for a year and expose my body to the English climate and my mind to English institutions.—But a truce to this cheap discursive stuff. I date the moment from which my mind rose erect in impartial might to a little sail I took on the Thames the other day in one of the little penny steamers which shoot along its dirty bosom. It was a grey, raw English day, and the banks of the river as far as I went, hideous. Nevertheless I enjoyed it. It was too cold to go up to Greenwich. (The weather, by the way since my arrival has been horribly damp and bleak, and no more [like] spring than in a Boston January.) The next day I went with several of the Nortons to dine at Ruskin's, out of town. This too was extremely pleasant. Ruskin, himself, is a very simple matter. In face, in manner, in talk, in mind, he is weakness pure and simple. I use the word, not invidously, but scientifically. He has the beauties of his defects; but to see him only confirms the impression given by his writing, that he has been scared back by the grim face of reality into the world of unreason and illusion, and that he wanders there without a compass and a guide—or any light save the fitful flashes of his beautiful genius. The dinner was very nice and easy, owing in a great manner to Ruskin's two charming young nieces who live with him—one a lovely young Irish girl with a rich virginal brogue—a creature of a truly delightful British maidenly simplicity—and the other a nice Scottish lass, who keeps house for him. But I confess, cold-blooded villain that I am, that what I most enjoyed was a portrait by Titian—an old doge, a work of transcendent beauty and elegance, such as to give one a new sense of the meaning of art.—The next day, dearest mother, to proceed with my simple catalogue, I went off alone to Hampton Court and spent the afternoon there in a most gladsome spirit. Visits to these dreadfully [*word illegible*] are apt to be rather flat and vulgar but on this particular occasion I assure you I made a very good thing of it. Of course you remember the place well; I found I did. It's of a sufficient and comfortable antiquity; it doesn't assault the mind like the old abbey here, but gently titillates the fancy. It was a chilly sombre afternoon—a proper day to wander thro' an old deserted palace, to tread the terraces of an ancient garden and survey generally the haunts of departed and mortalized royalty. I took a short stroll in Bushey Park—of which I remember often to have heard you and Father speak. The old vistas and alleys and hollows were curtained and choked with mist; the whole prospect was immense, spectral and delightful. The trees here at present are quite as undeveloped as with us, but the grass is rich with the deepest darkest dampest green. Yesterday, I plucked up a spirit of adventure and went down to Brighton (a couple of hours by rail-slow train) to see Florence Matthews and Mary Wilkinson. I had an extremely nice day of it and am very glad I paid them this little attention, for I think it was much appreciated. Moreover (if that is anything) I have seen Brighton the famous. The latter is simply London-on-the-sea—a great city planted along the top of a cliff for some four miles, looking straight out to the ocean. Florence M. occupies a very pleasant little lodging, quite on the sands, at the base of the said cliffs and inserted as it were into the body thereof. She and Mary were extremely gracious and amiable. Florence is a pale dark eyed person of five and twenty with decided pretentions to elegance and even to beauty—both quite *a l'anglaise*. She is a little greasy and "Jewish" in her style, but very bright, graceful and good.—Mary, however, is the flower of the household—the sweetest and fairest of English maidens of the old, simple type. I must make a point of telling you that she is just engaged to be married to a Mr. Frank Matthews (a cousin of Florence's husband—who by the way was absent.) He came down to see his beloved just as I was leaving and seems a very good fellow, with a witty face and a very handsome voice. He's a lawyer. I think if on the occasion, you could drop your God-daughter a little note it would be appreciated. She is a very simple affectionate girl and spoke of meaning to send you a painting of her handiwork. It appears that Jamie W. has made a very unhappy marriage. His wife drinks horribly and is a general reprobate, tho' a lady by birth. I am going out tomorrow to Mr. Darwin's,[1] somewhere down in Kent, to lunch with Mrs. Norton the younger and will give you news thereof. I see the N's constantly; they are invaluable. I don't find myself much *en rapport* with Charles —altho' he is very kind; but I lounge and gossip with the ladies, who are one and all charming.—Reading over my letter it seems to exhale such a potent breath of salubrity that explicit statements seem superfluous. I will say nevertheless that I am every inch as well as my most reasonable hopes depicted me. I am able to do not only with impunity, but with benefit, everything that turns up. I left for Brighton yesterday (left my rooms that is) at 11.30 A.M. and got back to them at 10.30 P.M. and I don't know when I felt better than at the latter moment. Likewise today. Until I say the contrary, therefore, think of me as in good order. I mean to leave London on Tuesday (31st) for Malvern, where I think I shall grow stronger and better still—especially in a certain department of my organism on which it's needless to dilate, but which has proved rather more recalcitrant than I hoped. My digestion in other words continues decidedly bad—owing in a measure to a fact that being (thanks to change of climate and active habits) perpetually ravenous for food, I give it too much work. At all events as I say, I shall next write from Malvern.—I have asked so many questions in my other letters, that I will wait till a few of them are answered before going further. I thought it would be a neat thing the other day to drop a line of farewell to Aunt M. Tweedy which I did—as well as to Nelly Grymes.[2] I am of course especially anxious to hear from Willy—as I hope he has by this time understood. Who in the world does his share and runs his errands and me over here? It's terrible to think of.—But dearest Manny, I must pull up. Pile in scraps of news. Osculate my sister most passionately. Likewise my aunt. Be assured of my sentiments and present them to my father and brother—thy

Henry Jr.

1. This was James's sole encounter with Charles Darwin.
2. Mary Helen James (1840–1881), a cousin, had married Dr. Charles Alfred Grymes (1829–1905) of New York.

To Grace Norton

Ms Harvard

Great Malvern
Apr. *6th* [1869]

Dear Miss Grace—

Your painfully reproachful (tho' exquisitely delightful) letter has come fortunately just too late—too late, that is, for its reproaches to be deserved—by no means for its delights to be relished. Your brother will by this time have received my note of Sunday morning and have been able to assure you that I am in quite as good health and spirits as he supposed. I am very sorry to put all you good ladies for once in the wrong—but it will give you a chance to see how it feels.—I have remained silent from—from what?—from a vulgar fear, partly, of suggesting that you were not so well rid of me as you might have hoped—and more particularly I confess because my first impressions of this remarkable spot were not quite so deeply rose-tinted as they have since become and I felt that there was a certain sort of good taste in sparing you a letter of darksome blue. In plain English, Malvern on acquaintance turns out so charming that I wonder I could even for a moment have fancied it anything less than the lovely region it is. Since you were so aggravating as to withold those "narrative" pages for which you said you had been during the past week so fast gathering material, it's no more than fair that I on my side should decline the descriptive— which I assure you (I have been so intoxicated in my various walks by the delicious beauties of the country) that I could do in a thoroughly superior manner.—The fact of the matter is simply that I have at my command (we all of us have who can walk at all) the various shoulders and summits of a great range of hills which soar into the purest mid-air from a mighty expanse of rich teeming plain and that you can hardly walk five minutes from the house without feeling that you have the whole of gentle England stretched out at your feet. The view is literally immense—and immensely beautiful. Knowing the usual features of English country scenery from your summer in Kent, you can fill in the details—only do it lavishly and don't omit one.—As for indoors, it's of course not so pleasant as this staring at the hills and valleys (especially now that the April rains have set in and a certain amount of unwilling confinement is inevitable) but it is entertaining enough in another way and altho' experience tells me that I might be in better company—imagination (to say the least) suggests that I might be in worse. The house is about half full of people—chiefly men—some of whom have not yet exhibited features of startling interest. Most of them have indeed extended me as a stranger—twice a stranger—a sort of vague inarticulate welcome which has been duly appreciated. They are mostly a plain, civil, amiable lot—addicted to reading the *Telegraph* and *Standard*—by day and to playing interminable rubbers by night. We have a number of Indian officers with yellow faces and declining livers—a high conservative and radically stupid fox-hunting clergyman—a very gentlemanly and indifferent young squire from the next county—and a great variety of other specimens of the British world. We are all on the best terms with each other and with things in general and we do nothing but bathe and walk and feed and read the papers and gossip from morning till night. The baths are ingeniously delicious: the doctor (in spite of a black velvet coat and a somewhat oleaginous beard) inspires confidence; the house is extremely comfortable, the table grimly plain (*tant mieux*) and the air delightfully fresh and bracing. In this last respect coming here from London, is like transmigrating to another planet and I can't help wondering whether three or four weeks of it wouldn't do you good. (The second clause of that sentence is somewhat ambiguously related to the first; but excuse logic in favor of enthusiasm.) There are lots of charming villas and lodges here advertising apartments and lots of donkeys and poney-chaises and bath-chairs to carry you over the hills and along the lovely terraced roads which survey the plain—in short everything that a Christian gentlewoman in imperfect health could possibly desire. Do think of it.—But I quite agree with Miss Armstrong: what a big fool am I!—to think you capable of wantonly foregoing those breakfasts and lunches and dinners which are made memorable by the first minds of the age. Decidedly, after a week in Malvern, I agree

with you: I go in for genius and fame even at breakfast and lunch.—
Do drop a hint of your recent adventures: I can hear it—with the aid
of the cold baths. I am very glad to know of your hearing from
home. I too got a letter—quite an empty one from my brother
William. My plans remain indefinite. I am rent in twain by a
simultaneous sense of delight at being in this sweet old England and
a horribly fascinating vision of starting off to the sour old Continent. But I vaguely foresee that I shall spend sometime on this
spot. For the present I doubt that I can do better. That mighty
northern tour that we talked of the last evening is fading away
into the future. I doubt that with my actual sentiments I shall
execute it at present. Still, I live from day to day and don't pretend to answer for the emotions of the morrow.—Excuse this
blatant egotism and tell me everything that has happened since
my departure. Give my particular and especial love to your mother
—as well as to your sister—to Mrs. Norton, Miss Sedgwick,
the Messrs. Norton (*père et fils*) and the Misses Norton *cadettes*.
Think of me as united to the world of intelligence only by means of
your letters. Let them be proportionately long and copious and you
may be sure that you will lay up heavy treasures in the affections of
your tout devoué.

Henry James Jr

Address Care Dr. Rayner
Great Malvern Worcestershire

To William James

Ms Harvard

Oxford April 26th [1869]
Randolph Hotel.

Dearest Bill—

I found here today on my arrival your letter of April 9th which I
was mighty glad to get. It seemed strange, foul and unnatural to
have heard from you only once in all these weeks. What you
say of yourself and your prospects and humor interested me deeply

and half pleased, half distressed me. I thoroughly agree with you
that to exonerate your mind in the manner you speak of will of itself conduce to your recovery, and I fancy that the result of such a
decision will be to smooth the way to convalescence in such a
manner that much sooner than you seem inclined to believe you
will be able to redeem your pledges and find that you have been
even too much reconciled. For heavens sake don't doubt of your
recovery. It would seem that on this point I ought to need to say
nothing. My example is proof enough of what a man can get over.
Whenever you feel downish, think of me and my present adventures and spurn the azure demon from your side. At all events I am
heartily glad that your reflections have cleared up your spirits and
determined you to take things easy. *À la bonne heure!*—Altho' it
lacks some days of mail-time I can't resist putting pen to paper for a
few minutes this evening and getting the start of any possible
pressure of engagements or fatigue later in the week. I feel as if I
should like to make a note of certain recent impressions before they
quite fade out of my mind. You know, by the way, that I must
economise and concentrate my scribblements and write my diary
and letters all in one. You must take the evil with the good. These
same impressions date from no earlier than this evening and from
an hour and a half stroll which I took before dinner thro' the streets
of this incomparable town. I came hither from Leamington early
this morning, after a decidedly dull three days in the latter place. I
know not why—probably in a measure from a sort of reaction
against the constant delight—the tension of perception—during my
three days run from Malvern—but the Leamington lions were
decidedly tame. I visited them all faithfully. Warwick Castle is
simply a showy modern house with nothing to interest save a
lot of admirable portraits, which I couldn't look at, owing to my
being dragged about by a hard alcoholic old housekeeper, in the
train of a dozen poking, prying, dowdy female visitants. Kenil-
worth, for situation and grandeur, reminded me forcibly of the
old stone-mill, and at Stratford, too, my enthusiasm hung fire
in the most humiliating manner. Yesterday afternoon I drove
over to Coventry. I enjoyed the drive but the place disappointed

me. It would seem decidedly odder if it didn't seem quite so new. But I investigated a beautiful old church, alone worth the price of the drive. These English Abbeys have quite gone to my head. They are quite the greatest works of art I've ever seen. I little knew what meaning and suggestion could reside in the curve of an arch or the spring of a column—in proportions, and relative sizes. The Warwickshire scenery is incredibly rich and pastoral. The land is one teeming garden. It is in fact too monotonously sweet and smooth—too comfortable, too ovine, too bovine,[1] too English, in a word. But in its way its the last word of human toil. It seems like a vast show region kept up at the expense of the poor.—You know, as you pass along, you feel, that it's not poor man's property but rich man's. *Apropos* of Leamington, tell Alice that I found at the hotel her friend the late Julia Bryant and family. I called and had a pleasant visit. I don't find in myself as yet any tendency to flee the society of Americans. I never had enough of it in America to have been satiated and indeed, from appearance, the only society I shall get here will be theirs.—

27th A.M. I turned in last evening without arriving at the famous "impressions". Nrs. Norton gave me a letter to A. Vernon Harcourt Esq.[2] fellow of Christ Church and at about five P.M. I strolled forth to deliver it. Having left it at his college with my card I walked along, thro' the lovely Christ Church meadow, by the river side and back through the town. It was a perfect evening and in the interminable British twilight the beauty of the whole place came forth with magical power. There are no words for these colleges. As I stood last evening within the precincts of mighty Magdalen, gazed at its great serene tower and uncapped my throbbing brow in the wild dimness of its courts, I thought that the heart of me would crack with the fulness of satisfied desire. It is, as I say, satisfied desire that you feel here; it is your tribute to the place. You ask nothing more; you have imagined only a quarter as much. The whole place gives me a deeper sense of English life than anything yet. As I walked along the river I saw hundreds of the mighty lads of England, clad in white flannel and blue, immense, fair-haired, magnificent in their youth, lounging down the stream in their punts or pulling in straining crews and rejoicing in their godlike strength. When along with this you think of their haunts in the grey-green quadrangles, you esteem them as elect among men.[3] I received last evening when I came in a note from Harcourt, telling me he would call this morning and asking me to dine at his college commons in the evening. I have also from Jane Norton a note to Mrs. Pattison, rectoress of Lincoln College which may shew me something good. As this letter promises to become long, I will here interpolate a word about my physics, *en attendant* Harcourt, whose hour is up. I gave you at Leamington, a list of my *haut faits* in Monmouthshire. What I then said about my unblighted vigor is more true than ever. I felt my improvement in the midst of my fatigue; I feel it doubly now. There is no humbug nor illusion about it and no word for it but good honest *better*. If my doings at Oxford have the same result I shall feel as if I have quite established a precedent.

29th. Harcourt turns out to be simply angel no. 2. He is tutor of chemistry in Christ Church and a very modest pleasant and thoroughly obliging fellow. He came for me the other morning and we started together on our rounds. It is certainly no small favor for a man to trudge about bodily for three hours in the noon-day sun with a creature thus rudely hurled into his existence from over the sea, whom he neither knows nor cares for. His reward will be in heaven. He took me first to Convocation—a lot of grizzled and toga'd old dons, debating of University matters in an ancient hall and concluding with much Latin from one of them. Thence to lunch with the rector of Lincoln's—Harcourt having kindly arranged with Mrs. Pattison[4] beforehand to bring me there. The Rector is a dessicated old scholar, torpid even to incivility with too much learning; but his wife is of quite another fashion—very young (about 28) very pretty, very clever, very charming and very conscious of it all. She is I believe highly emancipated and I defy an English-woman to be emancipated except coldly and wantonly. As a spectacle the thing had its points: the dark rich, scholastic old dining room in the college court—the lanquid old rector and his pretty little wife in a riding-habit, talking slang. Otherwise it was slow. I then went about with Harcourt to various colleges, halls, and gardens—he doing his duty most bravely—and I mine for that matter. At four I parted from him and at 6 rejoined him and dined with him in Hall at Christ Church. This was a great adventure. The Hall is magnificient: an immense area, a great timbered and vaulted roof and a 100 former worthies looking down from the walls between the high stained windows. I sat at the tutors' table on a platform, at the upper end of the Hall, in the place of honor, at the right of the Carver. The students poured in; I sat amid learned chat and quaffed strong ale from a silver tankard. The dinner and the service, by the way, were quite elaborate and elegant. On rising *we tutors* adjourned to the Common-room across the court, to dessert and precious wines. In the evening I went to a debating club, and to a soirée at Dr. Acland's[5] (I've quite forgotten who and what he is) where I saw your physiological friend Mr. Charles Robin. 'Twas mortal flat. All this was well enough for one day. Yesterday I kindly left Harcourt alone and drove in the morning out to Blenheim, which was highly satisfactory. The palace is vast cold and pretentious but the park is truly ducal. As far as you can see, it encircles and fills the horizon—"immense, ombreux, seigneurial." (T. Gautier) *Enfin,* I could talk a week about the park. But the great matter is the pictures. It was with the imperfect view at Warwick, the other day, my first glimpse (save Ruskin's Titian and the poorish things at Dulwich) of the great masters: thank the Lord it is not to be the last. There is a single magnificient Raphael and two great Rembrandts, but the strength of the collection is in the Rubenses and Vandykes. Seeing a mass of Rubenses together commands you to believe that he was the first of painters—of *painters,* in fact, I believe he was[6] A lot of his pictures together is a most healthy spectacle—fit to cure one of any woes. And then the noble, admirable modern Vandyke! His great portrait of Charles I on horse-back is a thing of infinite beauty—I strolled slowly away thro' the park, watching the great groves and avenues, murmuring and trembling in the sunny breeze and feeling very serious with it all. On my return I went out alone and spent the afternoon in various college gardens. These same gardens are the fairest things in Oxford. Locked in their own ancient verdure, behind their own ancient walls, filled with shade and music and perfumes and privacy—with lounging students and charming children—with the rich old college windows keeping guard from above—they are places to lie down on the grass in forever, in the happy belief that the world is all an English garden and time a fine old English afternoon. At 6 o'clock, I dined in hall at Oriel with Mr. Pearson[7] (the author of the early English History who was in America while you were away.) It was Christ Church over again on a reduced scale. I stole away betimes to get a little walk in Magdalen Gardens —where by way of doing things handsomely they have, in the heart of the city—an immense old park or Chase filled with deer— with deer, *pas davantage. Ce detail,* it seems to me, gives, as well as anything, a notion of the scale of things here. Today I am to lunch with Harcourt but shall take things quietly. Tomorrow I shall depart. I received yesterday a note from Frank Washburn saying he had just arrived in England *en route* for home, May 11th. We shall probably meet. If I feel as well tomorrow as today I shall satisfy my desire for seeing a little more in the Cathedral line by going to London (roundabout) *via* Salisbury and Winchester. My present notion is to stay a fortnight in London in lodgings and then make for Geneva. There is much in and about London that I want still to see. My letter has been long and I fear, boresome.—Do in writing give more details gossip etc. I am glad you've been seeing Howells: give him my love and tell him to expect a letter. Tell T. S. Perry *I* expect one. Do tell me something about Wendell Holmes. One would think he was dead. Give him my compliments and tell him I'm sadly afraid that one of these days I shall have to write to him.—I suppose all is well within doors, from your silence. What demon prompts Father to direct the letters he doesn't write? It is really cruel. If he only would write a few lines I'd as lief Isabella should direct them. You must have received my message about the *Nation*: I miss it sadly. I repeat I heartily applaud your resolution to lie at your length and abolish study. As one who has sounded the *replis* of the human back, I apprise that with such a course you cannot fail to amend. Love to Mother and Alice, to Wilk and Bob.

Aunt Kate will have sailed. Regards to Ellen and Isabella. Is Eliza's successor a success?—Another piece of mine will have appeared in the *Galaxy*[8]—probably very ill printed. You will of course have sent it. Howells will send Father a proof to correct. I am haunted with the impression that it contains an imperfect quotation of a Scripture text to the effect that out of the lips of babes and sucklings cometh knowledge.[9] If there is such a text or anything like it ask him to establish it; if not suppress it. But farewell—

yours
H. J. Jr

1. HJ used this description in his essay "Lichfield and Warwick," *Nation* (25 July 1872) republished in *Transatlantic Sketches* (1875) and much later in *English Hours* (1905).
2. A. Vernon Harcourt (1840–1919), a distinguished chemist.
3. A portion of this passage was used by HJ in "A Passionate Pilgrim."
4. Mark Pattison (1813–1884), rector of Lincoln from 1861, believed by some critics to have been George Eliot's model for Casaubon in *Middlemarch*. His widow, Frances Amelia Strong (1840–1904), later married Sir Charles Dilke.
5. Henry Wentworth Acland (baronet 1890) Regius Professor of Medicine at Oxford 1858–1894.
6. Later HJ changed his mind and described Rubens as reigning with magnificent supremacy among the "coarse" painters.
7. Charles Henry Pearson.
8. "Pyramus and Thisbe," *Galaxy*, VII (April), 538–549.
9. An allusion to the forthcoming "Gabrielle de Bergerac." The Biblical line appears in the tale paraphrased "The truth comes out of the mouths of children."

To Henry James Sr.

Ms Harvard

23 Sackville Street
Monday May 10*th* [1869]

Dear father—

It is a rare satisfaction at last to hear from you—which I did this morning per date of April 29, as well as from Mother and Willy. I am much obliged to you all for your good advice—altho' I confess that I have been acting somewhat against the spirit of it. You will by this time have received my letters written *en voyage* and have perceived that I was executing a little tour. To have you think that I am extravagant with these truly sacred funds sickens me to the heart, and I hasten in so far as I may to reassure you. When I left Malvern, I found myself so exacerbated by immobility and confinement that I felt it to be absolutely due to myself to test the impression which had been maturing in my mind, that a certain amount of regular lively travel would do me more good than any further treatment or further repose. As I came abroad to try and get better, it seemed inexcusable to neglect a course which I believed for various reasons to have so much in its favor. After lying awake therefore as usual on the subject, I grimly started and proceeded. You know what I did and where I went. I am sufficiently justified I think by success. I have now an impression amounting almost to a conviction that if I were to travel steadily for a year I would be a good part of a well man. With such a conviction ahead of me, you will cease to wonder that I should have been tempted to put forth a feeler. As to the expense of my journey, in telling that tale about the £60. I acted on gross misinformation. I was circulated for nearly three weeks and spent less than £25.00, seeing a very great deal on it. I am obliged of course, on account of the seats, to travel first class. My constant aim is to economise and make my funds minister, not to my enjoyment,—which may take care of itself— it wasn't assuredly for that I came hither—but to my plain physical improvement, for which alone I live and move. I think I have moved for it to some purpose. I have got quite my £25's worth of flexibility in the back, of experience and insight into my condition. I may declare, in fact, that when I started on my journey it seemed to me an absolute necessity to do so. I indulge in this somewhat diffuse elucidation, dear Father, because I attach not only so much value to the money you have given but so much respect and gratitude to the temper in which you gave it and I can't bear to have you fancy I may make light of your generosity. I incline I think to take my responsibilities to my little fortune too hard rather than too easy and there have been moments when I have feared that my satisfaction here was going to be very seriously diminished by a habit of constant self-torturing as to expense. You will perhaps think that the fear is superfluous when I tell you that during my eleven weeks in England I shall have spent about 120£. The sum sounds large but on investigation, it will scarcely turn out to be excessive, distributed as it is among five weeks in London, three at an expensive water-cure and three in travelling. It covers the purchase of considerable clothing and other articles of permanent use—or such as will last me during much of my stay here. It covers on the other hand very little trivial, careless or random expenditure—altho' it indicates perhaps some inexperience, which I am rapidly getting over. It involves for one thing a large amount of cab-hire. I have treated you to this financial budget as a satisfaction to myself rather than because I suppose you expect it. I leave London on Friday 14th inst. the day my week is up in these lodgings. I proceed to Geneva *via* Paris, arriving there if possible Saturday evening. What Geneva will bring forth for my amelioration remains to be seen. You shall hear. I should have gone on immediately but that I thought it best to rest here a few days on my return from Lincolnshire, before undertaking so long a journey, and as you can't take a lodging for less than a week, I'm in for that period. The one marvel as yet, of my stay, is having finally seen Mrs. Lewes,[1] tho' under sadly in-felicitous circumstances. I called on her yesterday (Sunday) after-noon, with Grace Norton and Sara Sedgwick—the only way in which it seemed possible to do it, as she is much hedged about with sanctity and a stranger can go only [under] cover of a received friend. I was immensely impressed, interested and pleased. To begin with she is magnificently ugly—deliciously hideous. She has a low forehead, a dull grey eye, a vast pendulous nose, a huge mouth, full of uneven teeth and a chin and jaw-bone *qui n'en finessent pas*. By far the best description of her is to say that she is an ugly image of Mrs. Sam Ward.[2] The likeness is most strange. The whole air, the dress, the pose of the head, the smile, the motion, recall Mrs. W. Now in this vast ugliness resides a most powerful beauty which, in a very few minutes steals forth and charms the mind, so that you end as I ended, in falling in love with her. Yes behold me literally in love with this great horse-faced blue-stocking. I don't know in what the charm lies, but it is thoroughly potent. An admirable physiognomy —a delightful expression, a voice soft and rich as that of a counselling angel—a mingled sagacity and sweetness—a broad hint of a agreat underlying world of reserve, knowledge, pride and power—a great feminine dignity and character in these massively plain features—¡a hundred conflicting shades of consciousness and simpleness—shyness and frankness—graciousness and remote indifference—these are some of the more definite elements of her personality. Her manner is extremely good tho' rather too intense and her speech, in the way of accent and syntax peculiarly agreeable. Altogether, she has a larger circumference than any woman I have ever seen. The sadness of our visit was in the fact that Mrs. Lewes's second son, an extremely pleasant looking young fellow of about twenty four, lay on the drawing-room floor, writhing in agony from an attack of pain in the spine to which he is subject. We of course beat a hasty retreat, in time to have seen G. H. Lewes come in himself in all *his* ugliness, with a dose of morphine from the chemists.

Wednesday, 12th. I have had no adventures since Monday and am chiefly engrossed in thinking of those that are in store for me in Switzerland. I leave as I think I have said, Friday A.M. I have seen the Nortons again several times. They have finally concluded to go to the Lake of Geneva for the summer which may make us neighbors again, for a time—a circumstance wh. I regard philosophically. In very sooth I have had enough of them—and all of my own seeking, too,—to last me for ever and ever. In fact I shouldn't mind seeing the ladies again repeatedly—but Charles inspires me with a terrible lack of sympathy and unfortunately, there's a popular delusion between us that he is my guide philosopher and bosom friend. I must be an arrant hypocrite. But I must do Charles the justice to say that he has come out strong since he has been in England and is very much of a man. I was to have gone to Queen's Gate Terrace this evening to meet Mr. Arthur Helps,[3] who has been dining there; but on coming in late from dinner, after spending three hours steady in the National Gallery, and then taking a walk in St. James's park, then working hard at my eating house as interpreter to a terribly obscure Frenchman who turned up in my neighborhood—

after all this, coming up to my room in a certain languor of spirit with a fresh copy of the Pall-Mall in my pocket—the idea of thrusting myself into my finery and travelling faraway to Kensington in a costly cab in order to grin away half an hour in the Norton's drawingroom quite frowned me out of countenance. So here I am in dressing gown and slippers conversing with my Papa. Part of the fun of seeing Mr. Helps was to have been, by the way, in conversing about this same Papa; inasmuch as Charles Norton tells me that he is (by his own account) a great reader of Swedenborg and carries a richly annotated copy of it about his person—or very near it. If I had seen him, therefore, I might have had something to tell you; but you will probably value my not having gone, against my bodily inclination more than his compliments. I dined yesterday at the Wilkinsons' rather stupidly. The Doctor seems pre-occupied and lacking in light conversation. Mary spoke with very real pleasure, evidently, of having got a letter from Mother. Her young man was present and after dinner they sang duets together. He seems a very nice fellow and a truly fine singer. He has a noble and delicious voice.—I was very glad to hear from Mother of Bob's being at home and in such good spirits and health. Do give him a brother's love and benison. I wish he would drop me a line. To Wilky too when he comes up, commend me most affectionately. I wish I could once more improve his elastic abdomen. It does my soul good to hear that he is in any way up to time with his crops. I'm mighty glad Alice is dropping her elegant invalidity; I think she will find a proper state of health so becoming that she will decide to stick to it. I send a kiss or so, to encourage her in the path of propriety. To Willy I enclose a short note: to Mother I enclose everything that my letter contains. The great subject here is the American quarrel. It is evident that the English have pronounced their *ultimatum.* Sumner's speech has produced a great irritation: I observed it greatly in Dr. W. If we want war we shall be served to our taste. But heaven forbid that we should want it. If Sumner's speech seems half as unreasonable at home as it does here, there is little danger.[4]— At next writing let something be said about your summer plans.—I am watching for Aunt Kate's arrival but I don't expect to see her in some time. Farewell. Now that you've begun to write, dear Father, do continue. What of your *Swedenborg?*[5] Of course I shall hear of it.

With much love
your ancient child
H. James Jr

1. George Eliot. James describes this visit in his unfinished volume of autobiography, *The Middle Years,* posthumously published (1918).

2. The former Medora Grymes.

3. Sir Arthur Helps (1813–1875), historian, who wrote a series of popular works on ethical and aesthetic questions. HJ reviewed his *Social Pressure* in the *Nation,* XX (18 March 1875), 193–194.

4. Charles Sumner (1811–1874), the senator, had attacked Britain's concessions to the Confederate States and demanded satisfaction for the United States "national claims."

5. The elder HJ had just completed his book *The Secret of Swedenborg* which was to be published in this same year.

To John LaFarge

Ms New York Historical

Hotel du Righi-Vaudois
Glion, Lake of Geneva
June 20th [1869]

My very dear John—

Your letter of June 3d was handed me last night, just at a moment when I was recording a silent oath that today and not a day later, I should execute my long designed and oft-deferred letter to you. Truly, I have most earnestly been meaning to write to you. I felt the need of so doing: our parting in New York was so hurried and unsatisfactory that I wished to affix some sort of supplement or correction. Happily now, what I write may be a greeting rather than a farewell.

I am deeply delighted to hear that there is a prospect of your getting abroad this summer. Don't let it slip out of your hands. That your health has continued bad, I greatly regret; but I can't consider it an unmitigated curse, if it brings you to these parts. You must have pretty well satisfied yourself that home-life is not a remedy for your troubles, and the presumption is strong that a certain amount of Europe may be.—As you see I am already in Switzerland: in fact I have been here for the past five weeks. I came directly to Geneva (giving but a day to Paris, and that to the Salon) and spent a month there; and then came up to this place which is at the other extreme of the lake, beyond Vevey, perched aloft on the mountain side, just above the Castle of Chillon. It is what they call a *hotel-pension:* a number of people, capital air, admirable scenery. Unhappily the weather is bad and seems determined to continue so. Heaven defend us from a rainy summer—no uncommon occurrence here. My actual plans are vague; they are simply to continue in Switzerland as long as I can, but as I am not a regular tourist, I shall distribute my time between two or three places.—I enjoyed most acutely my stay in England. If you can only touch there, I think you will find it pay. Of people I saw very few, of course: and of places no vast number, but such of the latter as I did get a glimpse of, were awfully charming. I did see Rossetti, Charles Norton having conducted me to his studio—in the most delicious melancholy old house at Chelsea on the river. When I think what Englishmen *ought* to be, with such homes and haunts! Rossetti however, does not shame his advantages. Personally, he struck me as unattractive, poor man. I suppose he was horribly bored!—but his pictures, as I saw them in his room, I think decidedly strong. They were all large, fanciful portraits of women, of the type *que vous savez,* narrow, special, monotonous, but with lots of beauty and power. His chief inspiration and constant model is Mrs. William Morris (wife of the poet) whom I had seen, a woman of extraordinary beauty of a certain sort—a face, in fact quite made to his hand. He has painted a dozen portraits of her—one, in particular, in a blue gown, with her hair down, pressing a lot of lilies against her breast—an almost great work. I told him I was your intimate friend and he spoke very admiringly of three of your drawings he had seen.—I saw also some things of another man (tho' not himself), one Burne Jones, a water-colorist and friend of Charles Norton. They are very literary &c; but they have great merit. He does Circe preparing for the arrival of Ulysses—squeezing poison into a cauldron, with strange black beasts *dans les jambes:* thro' the openings of a sort of cloister you see the green salt ocean, with the Greek galleys blowing up to land. This last part is admirably painted. I enjoyed vastly in London the National Gallery, which is a much finer collection than I supposed. They have just acquired a new Michael Angelo—Entombment of Christ—unfinished, but most interesting, as you may imagine. Then they have their great Titian— the Bacchus and Ariadne—a thing to go barefoot to see; as likewise his portrait of Ariosto. Ah, John! What a painter. For him, methinks, I'd give you all the rest. I saw in the country (i.e. at Blenheim near Oxford and at Wilton House near Salisbury) some magnificent Vandykes. The great Wilton Vandyke (the Earl of Pembroke and family—an immense canvas) is I think worth a journey to contemplate. *A propos* of such things, I oughtn't to omit to say that I dined at Ruskin's, with the Nortons. R. was very amiable and shewed his Turners. The latter is assuredly great: but if you wish to hold your own against exaggeration, go to see him at the National Gallery, where some thirty of his things stand adjoining the old Masters. I think I prefer Claude. He had better taste, at any rate.—In England I saw a lot of Cathedrals—which are good things to see; tho' to enjoy them properly, you mustn't take them quite as wholesale as I was obliged to do.—You ask my intentions for next winter. They are as yet indefinite, and are not firmly fixed upon Paris. That is, I am thinking a little of Italy. If I give up Italy, however, of course I shall take up Paris. But I do most earnestly hope we shall be able to talk it over face-to-face. Of course, if you decide to come, you will lose no time. I wish greatly that your wife were to come with you; short of that, I must hope that your visit if it takes place, will really pave the way for her. Give her my love and tell her, persuasively, that if Europe does not wholly solve the problem of existence, it at least helps the flight of time—or beguiles its duration. You give me no local or personal news, beyond that of your illness. I hope other matters are of a more cheerful complexion. I can hear nothing better than that you have sailed. If you determine to do so, write to me (Lombard, Odier & Cie, Genève) and give your own address. Meanwhile, till further news, farewell. *Portez vous mieux,* at least.

Regards to J. Bancroft, if you see him. Most affectionate messages to your wife and youngsters and a *bon voyage*, if any, to yourself.

Yours, always

H. James jr.

To Mrs. Henry James Sr.

Ms Harvard

Glion sur Montreux

Hotel du Righi. Vaudois.

June 28*th* [1869]

My dearest Mother—

Glion last week and Glion, as you see, still. Glion has produced however, in the interval, your most amiable letter of June 7th or 8th (I conjecture: it has no date.) Besides this, it has brought forth nothing so wonderful as to be particularly described or related. Nevertheless, I can't help writing, at the risk (I persist in suspecting) of boring you by my importunity. It is a warm Sunday afternoon: I have come up to my room from dinner, and after lying down snoozingly on the sofa for half an hour find a thousand thoughts and memories of home invade my languid mind with such pertinacity that there is nothing for it but to seize the pen and work off my emotions. Since I last wrote, the situation has changed very much for the better. The weather has cleared up and we have had nearly a week of fine warm days. I have found it possible to profit by them to my very great satisfaction. Every afternoon I have taken a long lonely lovely ramble of some three or four hours. The walks hereabouts are extremely numerous and singularly beautiful. It is true that they are all more or less on the perpendicular; nevertheless I have learned them almost all. Judge of my improvement since leaving Malvern, where I found the little hills a burden and a nuisance. Now I think nothing, so to speak, of a mountain, and climb one, at least, on an average every afternoon. I should extremely like to be able to depict the nature of this enchanting country; but to do so requires the pen of a Ruskin or a G. Sand.

Back from the lake, at Montreux, stretches the wide deep gorge or ravine, on one side of which, on a little plateau, this hotel is planted. Into this gorge, above, below, horizontally, you can plunge to your heart's content. Along its bottom rolls the furious course of a little mountain river, hurrying down to the lake. Leaving the hotel and striking into the fields, a winding footpath, wandering up and down thro' meadows and copses and orchards, leads down to a heavenly spot where a little wooden bridge spans this tremendous little torrent. It is smothered in the wilderness; above your head tangled verdure shuts out the hillsides; beneath, the racketing stream roars and plunges far down in its channel of rocks. From here you can cross up and ascend the opposite side of the gorge, pursue it along its edge, to its innermost extremity, where the great mountain walls close sheer about it and make it lonely, awful and Alpine. There you can again cross the river and return thro' the woods to Glion. This is one walk in a dozen. I enjoy them all: I relish keenly the freedom of movement, the propulsion of curiosity, the largeness and abundance of the scenery—and for that matter its richness and gentleness too. Crossing the bridge aforesaid and turning out toward the lake and along the hillsides above you can walk to Vevey thro' a region of shady meadows and slanting orchards as tranquil and pastoral as an English park.—Nevertheless this is not yet real Switzerland and I am preparing to take myself thither. I want to get into genuine alpine air and scenery. I went over to Vevey by train a few days since and paid a second visit to the Nortons. I have made up my mind on leaving this place to go and spend a week in the farm-house adjoining their premises. They are so utterly buried and lonely that I think they would be somewhat grateful for my society and I can thereby do something to pay off their hospitalities to me in London and cancel a possibly onerous obligation.

They enjoy extremely their seclusion and rusticity and find it a very pleasant relief after England. It is well they do, for it is absolute and without appeal. In this house I shall probably remain a week longer. It is a little more expensive than what I expect to find elsewhere, but it affords a number of comforts which I am glad to have at this stage of my initiation into mountain habits. A fortnight hence I shall be better able to rough it. With this view I shall proceed to the Lake of Lucerne, seek out an abode and remain there probably to the 1st of September. I have about given up the idea of going to St. Moritz. I am deterred by the stories I hear about the extreme cold and the severity of the climate. I want the air of some great altitude, but enough is as good as a feast; I want the summer too. But of all this, you will hear when it takes place. I duly noted your injunction to spend the summer quietly and economically. I hope to do both— or that is, to circulate in so far as I do, by the inexpensive vehicle of my own legs. You will by this time have received a letter written nearly a month ago in Geneva on this matter of travelling and expenditure containing propositions somewhat at variance with the spirit—or rather with the letter of the above advice. I don't know in what manner you have replied to it; exactly as you felt you ought, of course. When you speak of your own increased expenses etc. I feel very guilty and selfish in entertaining any projects which look in the least like extravagance. My beloved mother, if you but knew the purity of my motives! Reflection assures me, as it will assure you, that the only economy for me is to get thoroughly well and into such a state as that I can work. For this consummation, I will accept everything—even the appearance of mere pleasure-seeking. A winter in Italy (if I feel two months hence as I do now) enabling me to spend my time in a certain way, will help me on further than anything else I know of—more than a winter in Paris and of course, so long as the very semblance of application is denied me—than one in Germany. But it will by so much hasten (so I reason) the moment when I can spend a winter or some months at any rate, in Germany without damage and with positive profit. If before I left home I had been as certain as I have now become, that to *pay,* my visit here must at present be a real change—a real active taking hold of the matter—we could have talked over the subject far better than we can do in this way. In effect when I consider how *completely,* during the three or four months before I sailed I was obliged to give up all reading and writing (Willy can tell you) I see that it was a very absurd extension of my hopes to fancy that mere change of place would enable me to take them up again—or that I could lead the old life with impunity in Paris more than in Cambridge. Having lost all the time I have, you see I naturally wish to economise what is left. When I think that a winter in Italy is not as you call it a winter of "recreation" but an occasion not only of physical regeneration, but of serious culture too (culture of the kind which alone I have now at twenty-six any time left for) I find the courage to maintain my proposition even in the face of your allusions to the need of economy at home. It takes a very honest conviction thus to plead the cause of apparently gross idleness against such grave and touching facts. I have trifled so long with my trouble that I feel as if I could afford now to be a little brutal. My lovely mother, if ever I am restored to you sound and serviceable you will find that you have not cast the pearls of your charity before a senseless beast, but before a creature with a soul to be grateful and a will to act.—There are two things which I hardly need add. 1st, that of course you will be guided in your rejoinder simply by the necessities of the case, and will quite put aside any wish to please or any fear to displease me; and 2d that whether I go to Italy or to Paris I shall be as economical as possible. After all, there are two months yet; so much discussion of protestation will strike you as premature. I may find that by the 1st of September I am quite strong enough to face the *dulness* of Paris. *Wednesday* 30th I left my letter standing and shall add but a few words before closing it. I have had an adventure worth mentioning. On Monday evening (night before last) I agreed with three gentlemen here (two Englishmen and a German) to make with them the ascent of a certain mountain hard-bye, by name the Roche de Neige. (For the various localities hereabouts, by the way, tell Willy to shew you M. Arnold's two poems on *Obermann*). We started accordingly at midnight, in order to be on the summit to see the sunrise. W reached the top after four hours steady walking—the last part by moonlight. The sunrise was rather a failure owing to an excess of clouds: still, the red ball shot up with the usual splendid suddenness. The summit was extremely cold—tho' we had brought a guide with overcoats etc. We descended in about half the time and reached the hotel by 7 A.M. in time for a bath and breakfast. I was of course tired but not to excess and today finds me alright again. The expedition was a stupid one, however, and I shall undertake no more night feats. They don't pay. But the rocks of Naye are about as high as Mt. Washington. What would you have thought last summer of my starting off at midnight to scale the latter? As far as impunity is concerned I feel perfectly disposed to start off tomorrow, with a pleasant companion, by daylight, on the same errand.—I have just received with gratitude, the July *Atlantic*. My story strikes me as the product of a former state of being.[1] The second part, I fancy, is better. I heard recently from John La Farge to the effect that he would probably come out to Switzerland this summer. I hope much he may, but I doubt it. Minny Temple writes me that she *may* appear in Rome next winter. This too I hope somewhat faintly. I hear often from Aunt Kate who evidently is enjoying things hugely. You must be on the point of starting for Pomfret. Write me all about it. Address me until I give you a more permanent address to the Nortons, *la Pacotte, Vevey*. Farewell, my dearest Mother. Tell Willy I shall speedily answer his last. My blessings upon Father and Alice. Make Wilky write. Your devoted son

H. James jr

1. The first installment of "Gabrielle de Bergerac," XXIV (July-Sept.), 55–71, 231–241, 352–361.

To Alice James

Ms Harvard

Hotel Belle-Vue
Cadenabbia
(August 31*st*)
Lago di Como [1869]

My dearest old sister—

Your wonderment and anxiety as to my fate has perhaps by this time reached the stage of perfect indifference. I confess I have well-nigh given it time to do so. My excuse is the very best—and one that will quite reconcile you to my guilt:—I have been roaming and rambling—walking and scrambling so hard and so constantly that I have not had time to sit down and write such a letter as I deemed consonant to the situation. *Voyons: où en étais-je* when I last wrote? Great heavens, since that dim and distant day what an age has elapsed? I was at Gersau, if I mistake not, on my return from the Oberland, waiting for the rain to stop and for my letters to come. Well finally the rain did go—and one blissful evening my letters did come and flattened me out beneath the weight of my joy—one from Father, one from Mother, and from you. One delightful long one too from Howells—as well as an *Atlantic* with No. 2 of my story. I read and re-read them—groaned and moaned and howled over them all the evening and took them to bed with me and renewed the scene at intervals during the night. Mother's was especially delicious: but I can't stand such another. I shall shuffle off this stale old tourist-coil and go leaping home in the simple spirit of childhood. Since then another dreary blank has elapsed but I count most devoutly upon finding treasures laid up for me in Venice, thro' Jane Norton's charitable hands. At the same moment I got your letters came one also, long delayed from Aunt Kate. Her announcement of her party's projected movements led me to go up to Lucerne in the hope of meeting them—where I spent two days in the vain expectation of their arrival, and then, the wretches having settled fair, despatched my luggage to Milan, shouldered my knapsack, took the steamer down the lake to Fluelen and began to trudge over the St. Gotthard. At Lucerne, by the way, I met Dana Horton[1] (who used to be at Cambridge, you know and to frequent the Sedgwick's tea-fights—he is now in Europe, having his headquarter with G. P. Marsh American Minister at Florence) (I mustn't forget to mention that I also met that very sweet Mrs. Otto Dresa with her stupid husband and that she sent especial messages to Father and Mother.) I partially agreed with Horton to meet him and some cousins of his at Bel-Alp (or rather *on* it—'tis in the clouds) in the higher Valais and proceed with them to Zermatt. I walked in two days from Fluelen to Hospenthal—the greater part of the Swiss descent of the St. Gotthard

—a most lovely journey with glorious weather. At the latter place I diverged to the right and crossed the Furka Pass to the Rhône Glacier—a wondrous silent cataract of snow framed clean in the rocks and rolling down straight out of the blue of heaven and expiring at your feet, at the inn door. Here having dined I started to cross the Grimsel and proceed thence to the Asggishorn and Bel-Alp: excuse all these stupid names: I give as few as possible. But about an hour up the Grimsel, I suddenly collapsed and was obliged to return. I didn't just then quite understand the *rationale* of it, but I did later. 'Twas partly (*excusez ce detail*) a disordered stomach and partly that I had exhausted myself by carrying my knapsack from Lucerne. At all events I renounced the idea of meeting Horton and that afternoon took the diligence (5 hours) for Brieq—the foot of the Simplon Pass. Here of course I slept and the next morning rose in my might at 4.30, and having procured an individual to carry my sack (which by the way a little forethought, tho' at some inconvenience, would have enabled me to send by the diligence) began to streak away over this famous road. This day was somehow on the whole the pleasantest I have known in Switzerland. The superb weather—the clean unclouded views—the rapture of finding my strength returned to me with interest—the rest and dinner at the Hospice on the summit, with a dozen mild picturesque priests—and above all the sense of going down into Italy—the delight of seeing the north melt slowly into the south—of seeing Italy gradually crop up in bits and vaguely latently betray itself—until finally at the little frontier Village of Isella[2] where I spent the night, it lay before me warm and living and palpable (*warm,* especially)—all these fine things bestowed upon the journey a delightful flavor of romance. It was moreover, a great day's work—about thirty-three miles from Brieq to Isella. I will not pretend to conceal that I was slightly fatigued. Nevertheless I was up betimes the next morning to catch the diligence on its way to the Domo d'Ossola (the terminus of the pass) and thence to the Lago Maggiore. I had a ride of six hours to Baveno on the shore of the Lake. Down, down—on, on into Italy we went—a rapturous progress thro' a wild luxuriance of corn and vines and olives and figs and mulberries and chestnuts and frescoed villages and clamorous beggars and all the good old Italianisms of tradition. At Baveno is a vast, cool, dim delicious hotel, with a great orange-haunted terrace on the lake. I had a cold bath in a great marble tank, I dined and touched up my toilet, and then as the afternoon began to wane, took a little boat at the terrace-stairs, lay out at my length beneath the striped awning and had myself pulled out to these delicious absurd old Barromean Islands—the Isola Madre and the Isola Bella. I'll not treat you to a graphic description or a keen analysis. They're a quaint mixture of tawdry flummery and genuine beauty—a sort of tropical half-splendid, half slovenly Little Trianon and Hampton Court. The most striking feature of Italian scenery seems to be this same odd mingling of tawdriness and splendor—a generous profuse luxuriance of nature and the ludicrous gingerbread accessories of human contrivance. But I shall develop this pregnant theme hereafter. I think of beginning a series of desultory letters to the *Nation* and I shall touch off this region[3]. At Baveno I felt in the first place so relaxed by the heat and in the second, so fortified and excited by my few days walking in Switzerland that I resolved again to cross the Alps—and simply do what I could from day to day—nourishing a vague hope however of being able to proceed thro' the Engadine and Tyrol and recross into Italy by the great Italvio Pass. So having slept at Baveno I took the early boat to Magadino at the head of the lake and thence walked (a sweltering ten miles) to Bellinzona, a charming dirty suffocating old town, where the St. Gotthard and San Bernardino roads converge. Next morning I chose the latter—with a companion of course for my knapsack. The Bernardine is a lovely pass—but it turned out an awful grind. Partly thro' misinformation and miscalculation I had underestimated the length of the ascent and mistimed my feeding-hour—and the result was a day of truly heroic fatigue. There is something strange and wild and curious in the sensation of great weariness in the midst of the lonely silent irridescent beauty of these Italian Alps and now that it's all over I'm not sorry to have known it. I lay that night—(I unfortunately can't say I slept) at San Bernardino, a village on the Italian slope just below the summit and the next morning pursued my way (less than four hours) to the village of

Splügen, where I was glad to halt and rest and where I diverted myself the rest of the day, as I lay, supine, with Mrs. Stowe's *Old Town Folks,* which I found kicking about, and which struck me under the circumstances as a work of singular and delicious perfection. From Splügen next morning I went bravely thro' the famous *Via Mala*—a fine bit, in its way, to Thusis, (a good fine hour's trudge) where I stopped at the inn and communed with my soul—to say nothing of my body. We all three had a little breakfast together and unanimously agreed that our poor old legs were very tired and had become conscious of an obstinate chronic aching. We noted with immense satisfaction however that it was simply our legs and that our much-tried back was holding out bravely. In fact this was the case. These poor long-suffering limbs have been worked so hard all summer in the service of their weaker brother that they have finally begun to cry mercy and to suggest that they too are mortal. So I gave up the Engadine, the Tyrol and all the rest of it and sadly took a vehicle back to Splügen. The next morning I entrusted my knapsack to the diligence and started off over the Splügen pass to Chiavenna—which I reached at about the end of eight hours. Toward the end of the walk my legs betrayed such a tendency of actually *se dérober sans moi* that I was glad to think I hadn't counted on them for further service. At Chiavenna where I spent the night I was again in Italy—and met Italian beauty heat and dirt. I took the following morning the diligence to Colico—a woefully hot and dusty drive. Thence the steamer for two hours to this delicious spot, where I have been since 4 P.M. yesterday. *Non*—it's too rapturous. Nothing is wanting but to feel fluttering at my side in the soft Italian breeze, some light muslin drapery of the sister of my soul. It's the place of places to enjoy *à deux* and it's a shame to be here in gross melancholy solitude. In its general presentment and contour the Lake of Como strikes me as hardly superior to the finest Swiss lakes—but it's when you come to the details—the swarming shimmering prodigality of the landscape—that you stand convinced and enchanted before Italy and summer. I may find it too hot here to stay, but I shall be glad to have had at least this glimpse of a potent southern August. I took yesterday after my arrival as the sun began to sink, a fine mile's stroll along the shore of the lake—following a broad foot-road that leads thro' the most enchanting variety of scenes—past the fantastic, iron gates of idle, pretentious villas, dozing in a perpetual *siesta* amid the grey-green boskage of their parks—between vineyard walls all hedged and overtopped with the flaunting wealth of their vinery—thro' the arcades of dirty little villages with houses of pink and blue and orange, where at a fruit stall you may buy for six cents as many luscious peaches, pears, grapes and ambrosial figs as you can possibly, as ArtemusWard says, conceal about your person.—The only blot upon the scene is the excessive heat which quite forbids moving about and leads me to apprehend that—a considerable amount of locomotion being needful to my welfare—I may have come hither too early in the season. In fact I already feel a good deal of my stout Swiss starch taken out of me. I shall tomorrow go on to Milan to get my luggage and shall then see how I feel and how things look. I have laid in such a capital stock of strength and satisfaction in Switzerland that I shall be sorry to be compelled to see it diminished and if I find it is melting away beneath the southern sun I shall not scruple to quietly execute a little scheme which all your combined affection and sagacity will not pronounce unwise and which Father's and Mother's last letters make me feel I may do, if needful, with an easy conscience: *i.e.* cross over from Verona into southern Germany and make a tour thro' Trent, Innsbruck, Vienna, Salzburg, Augsburg, Nuremburg, and Munich—all well worth seeing. I can then come back to Italy a month hence and begin my winter. Address your letters still, as before enjoined to *MM. Schielin Ferers, Venice*. Even if I take another route I shall find means to get them. I shall then look upon this dip into Italy as simply the little run southward which the walker in Switzerland usually winds up with. My pedestrian developments have more or less modified my prospects and projects. I hope to be able, in walking, to get so much diversion and to save so much money that I may strike out freely at certain times and places. I already have distant visions of doing England in bits, next summer on foot. But I'll not bother you with these greedy shadows and ghosts of my egotism: you have listened to a long enough tale.—And now for your dear old domestic selves. I lack *affreusement* a letter from Willie; *pourvu* that there only be one in Venice! I enjoyed immensely your and Mother's account of that blessed Pomfret. Every little bit of tittle-tattle seems written like the words on Belshazzar's wall. Today I suppose you are moving back to Cambridge—rested, I devoutly hope, healed and comforted. What the summer has done for Willy, I can only conjecture. And this I'm afraid to do too freely. At least, I trust, as much as he hoped. Then never, night and day, forget to reflect how wretched a being I once was. To do this and as little else as possible—this is best counsel I can give him at present.—It is very jolly to hear of Wilky's and Bob's getting up their muscle for rowing. Heaven reward them. Just now I believe only in muscle. I read yesterday in the *Times* the news of the defeat of the Harvard crew on the Thames. I had expected nothing else. When I was in London I saw the stupendous crowd of spectators come surging along Piccadilly on its return from the Oxford and Cambridge match—and I have since felt in my bones that the land which produced that awful host would certainly produce a proportionate crew—a crew of immeasurable British "go", such as would outdo our gallant meagre Yankees.—I don't see why Bob shouldn't make a capital oarsman: he's so "splendidly formed" about the chest etc.—I shall find in your next letters I suppose some news of the cotton crops—good news I beseech you.—I am much obliged to you for your compliments and to Mother for hers, about my story[4]. I'm more obliged still to Father, for the decent figure, which thanks to his revision, it makes in print. It all strikes me as amusingly thin and watery—I means as regards its treatment of the Past. Since coming abroad and seeing relics, monuments, etc I've got a strong sense of what a grim old deathly reality it was, and how little worth one's while it is to approach it with a pen unless your mind is *bourré* with facts on the subject—how little indeed it is worth-while at all to treat it imaginatively. You can *imagine* nothing so impressive as Queen's Elizabeth's battered old tomb in Westminister. The present and the immediate future seem to me the best province of fiction—the latter especially—the future to which all our actual modern tendencies and leanings seem to build a sort of material pathway. But excuse all these bad images and crude notions. This is a long letter for one sitting—another San Bernardino.—Farewell. It's hideous to have so much family and yet to be here alone in all this beauty. I'm too tired to write another word, except my love to all—and especially to my sweet little sister.

H James jr

1. Samuel Dana Horton (1844–1895), bi-metallist and briefly a diplomat, attached to the American minister in Florence before the unification of Italy. HJ to Grace Norton, 12 Sept. 1896 "the brave, remarkable but tragically frustrated and sadly extinguished Dana."
2. HJ incorporated some of his memories of this journey into the tale "At Isella," *Galaxy*, XII (August 1871), 241–255.
3. HJ did not write this paper, but later, after a further trip, wrote "From Chambéry to Milan," unsigned, *Nation*, XV (21 November 1872), 332–334.
4. "Gabrielle de Bergerac."

To John LaFarge

Ms New York Historical

Venice, Hotel Barbesi
September 21, [1869]

My dear John—

Tho' I am tired with much writing I must answer your letter of Aug. 26th without loss of time—in the hope that I may be able to say something to accelerate your coming abroad. I was very sorry your original plan had to be abandoned and sorry again that your wife and children are not to come. I can't but agree with you tho', that if you are to come with full benefit, you should come without care. I can't help thinking that a six-months' or a year's stay here would do you great good. I speak from my own daily experience. As regards expense, I consider it on my own part as a species of investment, destined to yield later in life sufficient returns in the way of work to repay me. Can't you do the same? Of course the point is to raise ready money; and certainly it is better not to come than to come on such slender means that you have to be constantly preoccupied, to the detriment of a free appreciation of things, with the money question. You are right I think in not particularly caring to see any special country, and in longing generally for something European. Even if you only saw a portion of England, you would be richly rewarded. The more I see of the Continent, the more I value England. It is striking how as a mere place for sight-seeing—a home of the picturesque—she holds her own against Italy. It may be that I think so chiefly because my first stay was there and my enjoyment enchanced by novelty. Nevertheless the only very violent wish I entertain with regard to my travels is that I may get three more months of England before my return.—Not, however, that Italy is not unspeakably fair and interesting—and Venice perfectly *Italianissima*. I extremely wish we were likely to meet and see some things together. Here, especially, one needs a companion and intellectual sympathy. Properly to see things you need to talk about them, and we should do much talking and seeing. I hope to be in Italy five or six months more: you might still get here. I have already eaten a good dish of the feast. I came over the Alps by Maggiore and Como, Milan, Pavia, Brescia, Verona and Vicenza; and I have been a week among these happy isles. I have seen a vast number of paintings, palaces and churches and received far more "impressions" than I know what to do with. One needs a companion to help him to dispose of this troublesome baggage. Venice is quite the Venice of one's dreams, but it remains strangely the Venice of dreams, more than of any appreciable reality. The mind is bothered with a constant sense of the exceptional character of the city: you can't quite reconcile it with common civilization. It's awfully sad too in its inexorable decay. Newport by the way is extremely like it in atmosphere and color; and the other afternoon, on the sands at the Lido, looking out over the dazzling Adriatic, I fancied I was standing on Easton's beach. Its treasures of course are innumerable, and I have seen but a small fraction. I have been haunting chiefly the ducal palace and the Academy and putting off the churches. Tintoretto is omnipresent and well-nigh omnipotent. Titian I like less here than in London and elsewhere. He is strangely unequal. P. Veronese is great and J. Bellini greater. Perfect felicity

I find nowhere but in the manner of the ducal palace, and bits of other palaces on the Grand Canal. One thing strangely strikes me; viz. that if I were an *"artist"* all these immortal daubers would have anything but a directly discouraging effect upon me. On the contrary: they are full of their own peculiar compromises, poverties and *bêtises,* and are as far off from the absolute as Miss Jane Stuart. —I go hence to Florence, *via* Bologna, in about ten days. I hope to remain some time at F., to see Rome and Naples and possibly have a glimpse of Sicily. I must stay my hand just now. I only wanted to let you know that if you find it possible to come within a short time, I should like well to do some travelling in your company. Offering counsel is repugnant to the discreet mind; yet I can't but say that I should predict serious good of your coming. Steady sight seeing is *extremely* fatiguing, but there is a way of taking it easy—such as I—theoretically—practice. I think of spending from March 15th to May 15th in France—(Paris, Normandy and Brittany;) going during the next two months thro' Belgium, Holland and the Rhine, and then going for three months to England.—I shall then either make up my mind to return (I shall have been abroad about a year and eight months) or if I feel up to any serious reading shall make straight back to Dresden and spend the winter.[1] There you have my "line of march" as far as 'tis defined. But it's not in the least fixed.—I hope your wife and young ones are well and that you've been having a decently entertaining and comfortable summer. I wish I were hereditary possessor of one of these old palazzi. I would make it over to you for a year's occupancy. The gondola by the way is a thing divine. Did you ever get my letter from Glion, in June? You don't mention it. Thank Sargy for his good intentions in regard to writing to me—infernal asphalti. Farewell. Let me hear from you hopefully and believe me yours always

H. James, jr.

The Nortons are to spend this winter in Florence.

1. HJ did not carry out this plan. Illness forced him to return to the United States the following spring.

To William James

Ms Harvard

Venise Hotel Barbesi Sept. 25*th* [1869]

My dear Bill—

I wrote to father as soon as I arrived here and mentioned my intention of sending you some copious account of my impressions of Venice. I have since then written to J. La Farge (briefly) and to Howells and worked off in some degree the *éblouissement* of the first few days. I have a vague idea that I may write some notes for the *Atlantic* or the *Nation;* but at the risk of knocking the bottom out of them, I feel that I must despatch you a few choice remarks— although I'm too tired to plunge deeply into things.—Among the letters which I found here on my arrival was a most valuable one from you, of the last of July, which made me ache to my spirit's core for half an hour's talk with you. I was unutterably gladdened by your statement of your improvement. Three days since however came a letter from Mother of Sept. 6th speaking of a slight decline, hence your return home. As she also mentions, however, your meaning to go to Newport and Lennox I trust you have not lost courage. I hope next to hear that you have made your visits and are the better for them. Give Mother unutterable thanks for her letter: my only complaint is that I don't get one like it everyday. But I can't be at home and abroad both. I have now been here nearly two weeks and have experienced that inevitable reconciliation to things which six months of Europe cause to operate so rapidly and smoothly, no matter what the strangeness of things may be. A little stare—a little thrill—a little curiosity, and then all is over. You subside into the plodding *blasé,* homesick "doer" of cities. Venice is magnificently fair and quite, to my perception, the Venice of romance and fancy. Taine, I remember, somewhere speaks of "Venice and Oxford—the two most picturesque cities in Europe." I personally prefer Oxford; it told me deeper and richer things than any I have learned here.[1] It's as if I had been born in Boston: I can't for my life frankly surrender myself to the Genius of Italy, or the Spirit of the South—or whatever one may call the confounded thing; but I nevertheless *feel* it in all my pulses. If I could only write as I might talk I should have no end of things to tell you about my last days in Switzerland, and especially my descent of the Alps— that mighty summer's day upon the Simplon when I communed with immensity and sniffed Italy from afar. This Italian tone of things which I then detected, lies richly on my soul and gathers increasing weight, but it lies as a cold and foreign mass—never to be absorbed and appropriated. The meaning of this superb image is that I feel I shall never look at Italy—at Venice, for instance —but from without; whereas it seemed to me at Oxford and in England generally that I was breathing the air of home. Ruskin recommends the traveller to frequent and linger in a certain glorious room at the Ducal Palace, where Paolo Veronese revels on the ceilings and Tintoret rages on the walls, because he "nowhere else will enter so deeply into the heart of Venice."[2] But I feel as if I might sit there forever (as I sat there a long time this morning) and only feel more and more my inexorable Yankeehood. As a puling pining Yankee, however, I enjoy things deeply. What you will care most to hear about is the painters; so I shall not feel bound to inflict upon you any tall writing about the canals and palaces; the more especially as with regard the them, photographs are worth something; but with regard to the pictures comparatively nothing— *rapport à la couleur*—which is quite half of Venetian painting. The first thing that strikes you, when you come to sum up after you've been to the Ducal Palace and the Academy, is that you have not half so much been seeing paintings as *painters*. The accumulated mass of works by a few men drive each man home to your senses with extraordinary force. This is especially the case with the greatest of them all—Tintoretto—so much so that he ends by becoming an immense perpetual moral presence, brooding over the scene and worrying the mind into some species of response and acknowledgement. I have had more eyes and more thoughts for him than for anything else in Venice; and in future, I fancy, when I recall the place, I shall remember chiefly the full-streaming, dazzling light of the heavens, and Tintoretto's dark range of colour. Ruskin truly says that it is well to devote yourself here solely to three men— Paolo Veronese, Tintoretto and Jacopo Bellini, inasmuch as you can see sufficient specimens of the rest (including Italian) amply elsewhere but must come here for even a notion of these. This is true of the three, but especially of Tintoretto—whom I finally see there is nothing for me to do but to admit (and have done with it) to be the biggest genius (as far as I yet know) who ever wielded a brush. Once do this, and you can make your abatements; but if Shakespeare is the greatest of poets Tintoretto is assuredly the greatest of painters. He belongs to the same family and produces very much the same effect. He seems to me to have seen into painting to a distance unsuspected by any of his fellows. I don't mean into its sentimental virtues or didactic properties, but into its simple pictorial capacity. Imagine Doré a thousand times refined in quality and then as many times multiplied in quantity and you may have a sort of notion of him. But you must see him here at work like a great wholesale decorator to form an idea of his boundless invention and his passionate energy and the extraordinary possibilities of color—for he begins by striking you as the poorest and ends by impressing you as the greatest of colorists. Beside him the others are the simplest fellows in the world. For the present I give up Titian altogether. He is not adequately represented here. His *Assumption* strikes me as a magnificent second-rate picture; his presentation of the Virgin is utterly killed by another of Tintoretto's. I fancy you must see him in England, Madrid etc. P. Veronese is really great, in a very simple fashion. He seems to have had in his head a perfect realization of a world in which all things were interfused with a sort of silvery splendor delicious to look upon. He is thoroughly undramatic and "impersonal". A splendid scene in the concrete was enough for him and when he paints anything of a story the whole action seems to rest suspended in order to look handsome and *be* painted. If I weren't a base Anglo-Saxon and a coward slave, I should ask nothing better than his *Rape of Europa* in the Doge's Palace where a great rosy blond, gorgeous with brocade and pearls and bouncing with salubrity and a great mellow splendor of sea and sky and nymphs and flowers do their best to demoralize the world into a herd of Théophile Gautiers.[3] The great beauty of P. Veronese is the perfect unity and placidity of his talent. There is not a whit of struggle, nor fever, nor longing for the unobtainable, simply a glorious sense of the look of things out of doors—of heads and columns against the sky, of the lustre of satin and of the beauty of looking up and seeing things lifted into the light above you. He is here chiefly found in the ceilings, where he is perfectly at home, and delights to force you to break your back to look at him—and wonder what sort of a back *he* must have had. John Bellini, a painter of whom I had no conception—one of the early Venetians—is equally great and simple in his own far-different way. He has everything on a great scale—knowledge color and expression. He is the first "religious" painter I have yet seen who has made me understand that there can be—or that there once was at least, such a thing as pure religious art. I always fancied it more or less an illusion of the critics. But Bellini puts me to the blush. How to define his "religious" quality I know not; but he really makes you believe that his genius was essentially consecrated to heaven and that each of his pictures was a genuine act of worship. This is the more interesting because his piety prevails not the least against his science and his pictorial energy. There is not a ray in his works of debility or vagueness of conception. In vigor, breadth and richness he is a thorough Venetian. His best pictures here possess an extraordinary perfection. Everything is equal—the full deep beauty of the expression—the masterly—the more than masterly firmness and purity of the drawing—and the dimmed, unfathomed lucidity and richness of the coloring. And then over it all the sort of pious deference has passed and hushed and smoothed and polished till the effect is one of unspeakable purity. He has hardly more than one subject—the Virgin and Child, alone, or enthroned and attended with Saints and cherubs; but you will be slow to tire of him, for long after you've had enough of his piety there is food for delight in the secret marvels of his handling. It gives me a strong sense of the vastness and strangeness of art, to compare these two men, Bellini and Tintoretto—to reflect upon their almost equal greatness and yet their immense dissimilarity, so that the great merit of each seems to have been that he possesses just these qualities the absence of which, apparently, ensures his high place to the other. But to return to Tintoretto. I'd give a great deal to be able to fling down a dozen of his pictures into prose of corresponding force and color. I strongly urge you to look up in vol. 3d of Ruskin's *Stones* (last appendix) a number of magnificent descriptive pages touching his principal pictures. The whole appendix by the way, with all its exasperating points is invaluable to the visitor here and I have profited much by it. I should be sadly at a loss to make you understand in what his great power consists—the more especially as he offers a hundred superficial points of repulsion to the well-regulated mind. In a certain occasional imbecility and crudity and imperfection of drawing Delacroix is nothing to him. And then you see him at a vast disadvantage inasmuch as with hardly an exception his pictures are atrociously hung and lighted. When you reflect that he was willing to go on covering canvas to be hidden out of sight or falsely shown, you get some idea of the prodigality of his genius. Most of his pictures are immense and swarming with figures; all have suffered grievously from abuse and neglect. But there are all sorts; you can never feel that you have seen the last; and each new one throws a new light on his resources. Besides this, they are extremely unequal and it would be an easy task I fancy to collect a dozen pieces which would conclusively establish him an unmitigated bore. His especial greatness, I should be tempted to say lies in that fact that more than any painter yet, he habitually conceived his subject as an *actual scene* which could not possibly have happened otherwise; not as a mere subject and fiction—but as a great fragment wrenched out of life and history, with all its natural details clinging to it and testifying to its reality. You seem not only to look *at* his pictures, but *into* them,—and this in spite of his not hesitating to open the clouds and shower down the deities and mix up heaven and earth as freely as his purpose demands. His *Miracle of St. Mark* is a tremendous work, with life enough in it to animate a planet. They can all paint a crowd and this is as much Venetian as individual. A better specimen of his peculiar power is a simple *Adam and Eve,* in the same room as a *Cain and Abel,* its mate, both atrociously hung—away aloft in the air. Adam sits on a bank with his back to you; Eve facing you, with one arm wound round a tree leans forward and holds out the apple. The composition is so simple that it hardly exists and yet the painting is so rich and expressive that it seems as if the *natural*, the real, could go no further—unless indeed in the other, where Cain assaults Abel[4] with an intent to kill more murderous and tragical than words can describe it. One of his works that has much struck me is a large *Annunciation*, immensely characteristic of this unlikeness to other painters. To the right sits the Virgin, starting back from her angelic visitant with magnificent surprise and terror. The Angel swoops down into the picture, leading a swarm of cherubs, not as in most cases where the subject is treated, as if he had come to pay her a pretty compliment but with a fury characteristic of his tremendous message. The greatest of all though—the greatest picture it seemed to me as I looked at it I ever saw—is a *Crucifixion* in a small church. (He has treated the same subject elsewhere on a stupendous scale; but on the whole I prefer this.) Here, as usual, all is original and unconventional. Ruskin describes it far better than I can do.

Monday 26th Having written so much last evening I succumbed to slumber, and this evening I hardly feel like resuming the feeble thread of my discourse. I have been abroad all day bidding farewell to Venice, for I think of leaving tomorrow or next day. I began the day with several churches and saw two new and magnificent Tintorets and a beautiful Titian. Then I paid a farewell visit to the Academy, which I have got pretty well by heart—and where I saw Mr. and Mrs. Bronson of Newport who knew me not—the latter very haggard and pale.[5] After which I took a gondola over to the Lido to look my last at the Adriatic. It was a glorious afternoon and I wandered for nearly two hours by the side of the murmuring sea. I was more than ever struck with the resemblance of Venice— especially that part of it—to Newport. The same atmosphere, the same luminosity. Standing looking out at the Adriatic with the low-lying linked islands on the horizon was just like looking out to sea from one of the Newport beaches, with Narragansett afar. I have seen the Atlantic as blue and smooth and musical—almost! If words were not so stupid and colorless, *fratello mio*, and sentences so interminable and chirography so difficult, I should like to treat you to a dozen pages more about this watery paradise. Read Théophile

Gautier's *Italia;* it's chiefly about Venice. I'm curious to know how this enchanted fortnight will strike me, in memory eleven years hence—for altho' I've got absurdly used to it all, yet there is a palpable sub-current of deep delight. Gondolas spoil you for a return to common life. To begin with, in themselves they afford the perfection of indolent pleasure. The seat is so soft and deep and slumberous and the motion so mild elastic and unbroken that even if they bore you through miles of stupid darkness you'd think it the most delectable fun. But when they lift you thro' this rosy air, along these liquid paths, beneath the balconies of palaces as lovely in design and fancy as they are pathetic in their loneliness and decay—you may imagine that it's better than walking down Broadway. I should never have forgiven myself had I come to Venice any later in the season. The mosquitoes are perfectly infernal—and you can't say more for Venice than that you are willing, at this moment, for the sake of the days she bestows to endure the nights she inflicts. But, bating this, all else is in perfection—the weather, the temperature and the aspect of the canals. The Venetian population, on the water, is immensely picturesque. In the narrow streets, the people are far too squalid and offensive to the nostrils, but with a good breadth of canals to set them off and a heavy stream of sunshine to light them up as they go pushing and paddling and screaming—bare-chested, bare-legged, magnificently tanned and muscular—the men at least are a very effective lot. Besides lolling in my gondola I have spent a good deal of time in poking thro' the alleys which serve as streets and staring about in the *Campos*—the little squares formed about every church—some of them most sunnily desolate, the most grass-grown, the most cheerfully sad little reliquaries of a splendid past that you can imagine. Every one knows that the Grand Canal is a wonder; but really to feel in your heart the ancient wealth of Venice, you must have frequented these canalettos and campos and seen the number and splendor of the palaces that stand rotting and crumbling and abandoned to paupers.—If I might talk of these things I would talk of more and tell you in glowing accents how beautiful a thing this month in Italy has been and how my brain swarms with pictures and my bosom aches with memories. I should like in some neat formula to give you the *Italian feeling*—and tell you just how it is that one is conscious here of the aesthetic presence of the past. But you'll learn one day for yourself. You'll go to that admirable Verona and get your fill of it.—I wanted not only to say a hundred things about Tintoretto which I've left unsaid (indeed I've said nothing) but to gossip a bit about the other painters. Whether it is that the three great ones I've mentioned practically include all the rest or not, I can't say; but (with the exception of two or three primitive members of the school, especially Carpaccio, who seemed to have learned laboriously for themselves,) there flows from the great mass of the secondary fellows no very powerful emanation of genius. Immense aptitude and capital teaching—vigorous talent, in fine—seems to be the amount of the matter. In them the school trenches on vulgarity. Bonifazio, Caligiari, the two Palmas, Paris Bordini etc have all an immense amount of ability, (often of a very exquisite kind) to a comparatively small amount of originality. Nevertheless I'm very willing to believe—in fact I'm quite sure— that seen in other places, in detached examples each of them would impress and charm you very much as their betters do here. All of them know endless things about color: in this they are indeed exquisite. Bonifazio is a somewhat coarser Titian—a perfect Monarch of the mellow and glowing and richly darksome. Paris Bordoni equals him, on a slightly different range. C. Caligiari (son of P. Veronese) is a very handsome imitation of his father—and if the latter's works were destroyed, we'd vote him a great master. But what has fascinated me most here after Tintoretto and Co. are the two great buildings—the Ducal Palace and St. Mark's church. You have a general notion of what they amount to; it's all you can have, until you see them. St. Marks, within, is a great hoary shadowy tabernacle of mosaic and marble, entrancing you with its remoteness, its picturesqueness and its chiaroscuro—an immense piece of Romanticism. But the Ducal Palace is as pure and perpetual as the facade of the Parthenon—and I think of all things in Venice, it's the one I should have been gladdest to achieve the one most worthy of civic affection and gratitude. When you're heated and weary to death with Tintoretto and his feverish Bible Stories, you can come out on the great Piazetta, between the marble columns, and grow comparatively cool and comfortable with gazing on this work of

143

art which has so little to do with *persons!* But I too am weary and hot—tho' I expect to find on my couch but little of coolness or comfort. I have the delightful choices of sleeping with my window open and being *devoured*—maddened, poisoned—or closing it, in spite of the heat, and being stifled!—I have made no allusion to the contents of Mother's letter, which I none the less prize. I have written to Minny Temple about her sisters. Elly's marriage strikes me as absolutely *sad.* I care not how good a fellow T. Emmet may be: Elly deserved a younger man.[6] Mother says nothing about Wilky's crops. I hope no news is good news. I am not surprised to hear of Dr. Wilkinson's being at hand. When I was in England he was evidently all ready for a chance to sail. I'm very curious to know the impression he made. I'm not to meet Aunt Kate. They come at present no further South than the Lakes.—But I *must* say good-night. I mean to write you again in a few days—*Not* about painters. À toi

H. James jr.

1. HJ later changed his mind and preferred Venice.
2. *Modern Painters.*
3. HJ alludes here to Gautier's "éclat, solidité, couleur," his love of the palpable and the visual.
4. In *Roderick Hudson* HJ would impart to his young American sculptor a desire to carve these very subjects.
5. Katherine deKay Bronson of New York and Newport was destined to become one of HJ's closest friends in ensuing years when she made her home in Venice.
6. Elly Temple Emmet, elder sister of Minny.

To Alice James

Ms Harvard

Hotel de l'Europe, Florence
October 6*th* (?)[1] [1869]

Carissima Sorella—

I have before me the fragment of a letter begun yesterday at Parma, while I waited for the train, but it looks so flat and stale that I shall choose a clean sheet and begin afresh. The last news you will have got of me is contained in a letter to Willy—despatched if I mistake not the day before I left Venice. Yes, Venice too has become a figment of the past—she lies like a great dazzling spot of yellow paint upon the backward path of my destiny. Now that I behold her no more I feel sadly as if I had done her wrong—as if I had been cold and insensible—that my eyes scowled and blinked at her brightness and that with more of self-oblivion I might have known her better and loved her more. Wherever we go we carry with us this heavy burden of our personal consciousness and wherever we stop we open it out over our heads like a great baleful cotton umbrella, to obstruct the prospect and obscure the light of heaven. Apparently it's in the nature of things. To come away vaguely dissatisfied with my Venetian sojourn is only one chapter in the lesson which this hardened old Europe is forever teaching—that you must rest content with the flimsiest knowledge of her treasures and the most superficial insight into her character. I feel sadly the lack of that intellectual outfit which is needful for seeing Italy properly and speaking of her in words which shall be more than empty sounds— the lack of facts of all sort—chiefly historical and architectural. A mind unprepared by the infusion of a certain amount of knowledge of this kind, languishes so beneath the weight of its impressions, light as they might necessarily be—that it is ready at times to give up the game as lost. Your only consolation is in the hope that you may be able by hook or by crook to retain a few of the impressions and confront them with the facts in the leisure of subsequent years.— Well, Venice has gone, but Florence treads fast on her heels. I have a good deal to recount however before the inexorable logic of my story brings me hither. Since leaving Venice I've transformed Padua, Ferrara, Bologna and Parma from names into places—and most interesting places too. At Padua I spent twenty-four hours of immense felicity—for at Padua are many charming things. I will speak neither of the Caffè Pedrocchi, nor of the delightful old court of the University, nor of the Church of San Antonio, nor even of that of the Eremitani. The great central treasure of Padua is a certain edifice known unto men and angels as *Giotto's Chapel*. Padua like many other Italian towns has perforce its Roman arena—a vast oval enclosure, quite disfurnished of its ancient fixings. The interior has been turnèd in a great cornfield and orchard, save that at one extremity stands a little medieval chapel—a mere empty shell—lined with a series of decorative frescoes by the great hand of Giotto. I say the "great" hand advisedly; no sooner have you crossed the threshold than you perceive with whom you have to deal. I have seen nothing yet in Italy which has caused me so to long for the penetrating judgment and genial sympathy of my accomplished William. I have always fancied that to say anything about Giotto was to make more or less a fool of one's self and that he was the especial property of the mere sentimentalists of criticism. But he is a real complete painter of the very strongest sort. In one respect he has never been surpassed—in the faculty of telling a story—the mastery of dramatic presentation. The amount of dramatic expression pressed into these quaint little squares would equip a hundred later masters. And then the simplicity—the purity—the grace! The whole exhibition suggests more reflections than I have time for. Happy, happy art, you say to yourself as you seem to see it, beneath Giotto's hand, tremble and thrill with a presentiment of its immense career —for the next two hundred years. What a prodigiously "good time" you are going to have! At Ferrara I spent some fine memorable hours walking about the streets and tasting the exquisite quality of Ferrarese desolation and decay. The city is immense in extent (like all these lesser Italian towns—there's no end to their length and breadth) and peopled, I should say, to the tune of one individual to a dozen houses. The streets are lined with mighty palaces and all coated and muffled in silent grass. I got in particular a walk at sunset upon the old ruined ramparts that enclose the town and melt away in most pacific verdure into the great murmuring plain of the Po. It was unique: I can't render it. Some old steel engraving, seen in childhood and re-discovered in future years, comes as near to it as anything else. To Bologna I devoted three good days—Bologna being, if you please, "quite a place." Bologna is rich in all great gifts. A mighty public square, with the Middle Ages and the Renaissance all frowning and smiling together about its margin—no end of fine churches and palaces—a remarkable gallery of pictures (to say nothing of a capital hotel—unhoped for blessing!)—such is Bologna. The physiognomy of the city is most grand, gloomy and peculiar owing to its being wholly built upon arches, like the Rue de Rivoli! The Gallery of course is the organ of the so-called Bolognese School—to which, however, I should send no boy of mine whom I wished to train up in the way he should paint. There you [*word illegible*] the exact reversion of the spectacle you witness at Padua—art having played itself out and living on memories, precepts, and ambitions—Guido, Domenichino, the Carracci etc. As a most delightful old Frenchman whom I met at Padua said to me, "they have neither the *couleur Vénitienne ni la belle ligne romaine*". The gallery contains a Rafael (his *St. Cecilia* —we have a small photo of Marc Antonio's engraving of it) in which the *belle ligne Romaine* makes all things else look tipsy. *Après cela,* Guido and all the rest are very clever painters. From Bologna I made a pilgrimmage to Parma (where I spent the night) in order to see what there is to be seen of Coreggio. Parma was his lifelong residence and possesses some of his best works—tho' they are very few in number. He had a most divine touch—and seems to have been a sort of *sentimental* Leonardo—setting Leonardo down as "intellectual." A couple of his masterpieces at Parma perfectly reek with loveliness. A little infant Christ in one of them diffuses a holiness fit to convince unbelievers and confound blasphemers. I reached Florence last evening—after a long journey thro' a glorious country —the bosom of the Appenines. I have been spending the day strolling about, thro' the streets and the two Great Galleries—the Uffizi and the Pitti Palace. They are *incroyables*—and will give me work for many days. Florence strikes me very pleasantly and I should like to settle down here for a series of weeks. I am just now wrestling with the problem of exactly how I shall live. I shall not go into a *Pension* tho' I believe there are several good ones because it's of the last necessity that I should escape public tables. An "apartment" looks lonesome and would not be especially cheap. I therefore think I shall remain at this hotel or go to another. Dining at a restaurant, and paying here for my room, solid breakfast and service I can live for 10 frs. a day, which is about as much as I should pay at the best

Pension here (the only one I should be willing to go to)—tho' of course considerably more than if I were to hunt up a small room and concentrate my energies on economy. I am very sorry to say (if you'll allow me to mention the topic) that in spite of the most religious prudence (and I have learned many things) my digestive organs are the bane of my existence and so long as this state of things continues I must ensure myself the best conditions in the way of food and lodging. But I shall look about me and consult simply my genuine needs. I went this morning to my bankers, dreaming wildly of letters. But all was cold and dark—or would have been but for a very pretty letter from Miss Peabody and one from Sara Sedgwick. The Nortons are to reach here about the 22d. Mrs. Huntington and her daughter (formerly of Cambridge) and Mrs. Horatio Greenough and daughter (ditto) are here for the winter. I fancy there is quite a little group of Americans. J. Lorimer Graham jr of New York is Consul. I hope for letters tomorrow and shall keep this over *Friday*. I found this morning at my bankers' with feelings that may be [more] easily imagined than described Mother's blessed letter of Sept. 21st. telling of Dr. Wilkinson's visit etc. Also a most characteristic and amusing one from Bob Temple.[2] I was very sorry to hear of Father's having been so long in trouble with his boil. I hope by this time it's well over, for ever. Mother speaks of his book being out, but says nothing of any plan of sending it to me. This will not be neglected at least. She likewise says nothing more of Bob's (*our* Bob's) Texan plans tho' Bob Temple mentions his being in New York "negotiating" on the subject. Let me hear all about it. Not a word either about Wilky's crops, tho' she speaks of his having gone back to Florida.[3] I don't know whether to infer from her silence that they are good bad or indifferent. Most sweet it is to get all your Cambridge news. Bob Temple expresses great disgust with Elly's marriage. I must say I can't help in some degree feeling with him. There is that remarkable charm and loveliness about Elly which seems to have marked her for fresher destiny. At the same time she is a very old little person and I hope she'll not feel the weight of her husband's years. Do write me yourself, beloved girl, and tell me your impressions of all things—Dr. Wilkinson, Bob

Temple, Kitty Prince etc. Mother says you are doing nicely: I shall believe it far better if I hear from you.—Florence pleases me passing well. I have never seen a city which took my fancy so fully and speedily. *C'est une ville sympathique.* I took a long long walk this morning, as I didn't feel in the need for the Galleries. I went out to Fiesole—"*my* Fiesole"—Mrs. Browning's, of course that is,—and thence away into the hills beyond it. A lovely country—all pale olives and dark cypress—with beautiful views of Florence lying in her circle of hills like—like what?—like a chiselled jewel in a case of violet velvet! Farewell *ton frère qui t'adore*

H. J. jr

1. HJ's question mark.
2. Robert Temple (b. 1840) eldest brother of HJ's Temple cousins, described in *Notes of a Son and Brother*, p. 142 *et seq.*
3. The younger James sons, Garth Wilkinson and Robertson were engaged in their costly experiment of conducting a plantation with dangerous disregard of their status as "Northerners."

To Mrs. Henry James Sr.

Ms Harvard

Florence Hotel de l'Europe, Oct. 13*th* [1869]

My darling Mammy—

I wrote to Alice only a week ago and tho' in the interval nothing has occurred to interrupt the monotony of my career, such is the weakness of the human heart that I must again fall a-scribbling and prattling to my dearest Mamma. At the moment I wrote to Alice I received a lovely letter from you, of Sept. 21st—telling of Dr. Wilkinson's visit etc. You had begun to worry (as I feared you might) over the long suspension of my letters in Switzerland: but by this time your doubts will have been replaced by better feeling. I have told of my journey hither and of my first impressions of Florence. My later ones are quite as pleasant, and if I should ever feel like living awhile in Italy I fancy I should choose this place. Not that it strikes me as a particularly cheerful city; its aspect—thanks to the narrowness of many of the streets and the vast cyclopean structure of many of the buildings is rather gloomy than otherwise. But it has the gaiety of plenty of business (apparently), plenty of comfort and of strangers and of an unsurpassed collection of art treasures; and then it has on all sides the loveliest *échappés* into the beautiful hills among which it lies deposited, like an egg in a nest. I have been spending my days in a regular philosophical appreciation of things. I've gone each morning to the great Uffizi Gallery to commune with the immortals and in the afternoon I have taken a good walk out into the country. I have not yet opened the chapter of churches, having been recently rather over-churched—save to stare with the proper and inevitable feeling at the magnificent many-colored, marble-plated walls and dome of the Cathedral. I have not even been to see M. Angelo's Medicean statues at St. Lorenzo. I take a rare satisfaction in keeping this adventure in reserve, till my appetite is of just that temper to relish the *Haut Gout* of the affair. A journey in Italy moreover, is a great killer of impatience. You learn not only to wait—but in a degree, to like to wait. So as yet I have only done the Uffizi—and that incompletely. There is so much more to say about it that I can begin to even hint at, that it were easier to let talking alone altogether. The great things on the whole, I suppose, are the Rafaels—which give one a feeling distinct from the works of any other painter. More, far more, than any others, he seems to have been a genius pure and simple, unalloyed and un-modified by the struggles of development and the teachings of experience. The succession of his famous "three manners" is ap-parently nothing more than the order of youth, manhood and maturity. How interesting this is, at once, and how uninteresting, you must see his pictures to understand. But until you have seen them, I fancy, you lack an adequate conception of the beauty of Genius—of simple intellectual spontaneity—*per se*. I say its beauty— I mean its exquisite unutterable beauty. As regards meaning and character, religious feeling etc I don't believe there is much more in his work than the spectator himself infuses under the inspiration of the moment—the influence that descends from them and lifts him from the level of his common point of view. What they con-tain is a sort of general formal indifferent beauty. But we poor vulgarians, catalogue in hand, find it hard to conceive a man working in such magnificent freedom and in order to get a purchase on the works we furnish them provisionally with this spiritual element by which in this high superiority, they neither gain nor lose. This beauty seems a direct result of the fact that to Rafael apparently, the world was clear, tranquil and serene—he looked at things and they pleased him. You don't in the least feel about his figures as about many others—M. Angelo's especially—that they *might* have been ugly—that they have escaped it by so much more or less.—I suppose it's in the nature of the mind to rebel against the violent dominence of even delightful sensations. At any rate, half out of spite to the Italian painters, two of the other things that I most enjoy at the Uffizi are a magnificent Albert Dürer and a most celestial Memling or Hemling—or whatever it may be. I enjoy immensely standing before them and murmuring invidiously "Ah que c'est bien Allemande—que c'est bien Flamand!" But you'll not care, beloved Mammy for more of this dreary stuff. And yet to what else shall I treat you? Except pictures and churches I see but little. For the past six weeks that I have been in Italy I've hardly until within a day or two exchanged five minutes' talk with any one but the servants in the hotels and the custodians in the churches. As far as meeting people is concerned, I've not as yet had in Europe a very brilliant record. Yesterday I met at the Uffizi Miss Anna Vernon of Newport and her friend Mrs. Carter, with whom I had some discourse; and on the same morning I fell in with a somewhat seedy and sickly American, who seemed to be doing the gallery with an awful minuteness, and who after some conversation proposed to come and see me. He called this morning and has just left; but he seems a vague and feeble brother and I anticipate no wondrous joy from his acquaintance. The 'hardly' in the clause above is meant to admit two or three Englishmen with whom I have been thrown for a few hours. One especially, whom I met at Verona, won my affections so rapidly that I was really sad at losing him. But he has vanished, leaving only a delightful impression and not even a name—a man of about thirty-eight, with a sort of quiet perfection of English virtue about him, such as I have rarely found in another. Willy asked me in one of his recent letters for an 'opinion' of the English, which I haven't yet had time to give—tho' at times I have felt as if it were a theme on which I could write from a full mind. In fact, however, I have very little right to have any opinion on the matter. I've seen far too few specimens and those too superficially. The only thing I'm certain about is that I like them—like them heartily. W. asked if as individuals they 'kill' the individual American. To this I would say that the Englishmen I have met not only kill, but bury in unfathomable depths, the Americans I have met. A set of people less framed to provoke national self-complacency than the latter it would be hard to imagine. There is but one word to use in regard to them—vulgar; vulgar, vulgar. Their ignorance—their stingy, grudging, defiant, attitude towards everything European—their perpetual reference of all things to some American standard or precedent which exists only in their own unscrupulous wind-bags—and then our unhappy poverty of voice, of speech and of physiognomy—these things glare at you hideously. On the other hand, we seem a people of *character,* we seem to have energy, capacity and intellectual stuff in ample measure. What I have pointed at as our vices are the elements of the modern man with *culture* quite left out. It's the absolute and incredible lack of *culture* that strikes you in common travelling Americans. The pleasantness of the English, on the other side, comes in a great measure from the fact of their each having been dipped into the crucible, which gives them a sort of coating of comely varnish and color. They have been smoothed and polished by mutual social attrition. They have manners and a language. We lack both, but particularly the latter. I have seen very 'nasty' Britons, certainly, but as a rule they are such as to cause your heart to warm to them. The women are at once better and worse than the men. Occasionally they are hard, flat, and greasy and dowdy to downright repulsiveness; but frequently they have a modest, matronly charm which is the perfection of womanishness and which makes Italian and Frenchwomen—and to a certain extent even our own—seem like a species of feverish highly-developed invalids. You see Englishmen, here in Italy, to a particularly good advantage. In the midst of these false and beautiful Italians they glow with the light of the great fact, that after all they love a bath-tub and they hate a lie.

16th, Sunday. I *have* seen some nice Americans and I still love my country. I have called upon Mrs. Huntington and her two daughters —late of Cambridge—whom I met in Switzerland and who have an apartment here. The daughters more than reconcile me to the shrill-voiced sirens of New England's rock-bound coast. The youngest is delightfully beautiful and sweet—and the elder delightfully sweet and plain—with a plainness *qui vaut bien des beautés.* I'm to go there this evening to meet certain Perkinses who live here—or nearby. With the H's is a Miss Gray. I know not who she is—save that she's concentrated Brookline. The Nortons are to arrive here about a week hence. I have just got a letter from Jane. I have not heard from Aunt Kate in a month. I owe her however a letter. I don't know when we shall meet—perhaps not till the spring when we may be together in Paris. *Maman de mon âme,* farewell. I have kept my letter three days, hoping for news from home. I hope you're not paying me back for that silence of six weeks ago. Blessings on your universal heads. Thy lone and loving exile—

H. J. jr

To Henry James Sr.

Ms Harvard

[Florence 26 Oct. 1869]

My dearest Daddy—

I feel as if I should write a very dismal letter; nevertheless, write I must, tho' it be but three lines. There are moments when I feel more keenly than ever the cheerlessness of solitude and the bitterness of exile. Such a one is the present. The weather has turned fearfully bleak and cold, and gloomy skies and piercing winds are the order of the day. The dusk has fallen upon my small and frigid apartment and I have lit my candle to warm my fingers—as I begin this letter to warm my thoughts. Happy Florence is going to dine *en famille* and to enjoy the delights of mutual conversation.—Well; so be it. Well

153

it's something to have a *famille* to write to if not to dine and converse with.—I have recently come in from a long walk in the *Cascine*—the great Bois de Boulogne of Florence—a lovely verdurous park, skirting the Arno, with no end of charming outlooks into the violet-bosomed hills. The Florentine *beau-monde* and *bourgeoisie* were there in force—a remarkably good looking set of people they are: the latter—the pedestrians—especially. I've been vastly struck throughout with the beauty of the Italian race, especially in the men. After the hideous population of German Switzerland, they are most delightful to behold; and when hand in hand with their charming smiles come flowing the liquid waves of their glorious speech, you feel positively ashamed of your Anglo-Saxon blood. Never in my life as since I've been in Florence have I seen so many young men of princely aspect. The charm of it all too is that it's the beauty of intelligence and animation quite as much as of form and feature.—Their beauty, however, consoles me little in my sorrow—my sorrow at the cold silence of my home—owing to which I have had no letter—no sign or sound of life, of love—for nearly three weeks. I got a letter from Mother on my arrival here; but I've waited in vain for further news.—I seek not to complain; but I feel lonely and weak minded and if I mention the fact cannot pretend to be indifferent. I devoutly trust the stillness will soon be broken.—I set you all a good example by writing even tho' I've very little to tell. My life in Florence is very quiet and monotonous and unless I go in for a *catalogue raisonné* of the two great galleries, my letter must perforce be brief. Such a catalogue indeed would be as good an account of my time as anything I could give; inasmuch as I have spent it chiefly in looking at pictures. I feel able to say now with a certain amount of truth that I *know* the Uffizi—and the Pitti. How much the wiser I am for my knowledge I hope one of these days to learn—if not to teach. These two Galleries are unutterably rich and I hope before I leave Florence to transmit to William a few glittering generalities on their contents.

Monday evening. 25th. I was obliged to give up writing yesterday because my room was too cold to abide. A fierce *tramonta* has been blowing for several days and Florence is like Boston in January. I adjourned for warmth and cheer to a very good English reading-room near at hand; and there, having spent an hour, I made my way across the river to call upon Mrs. Huntington and daughters, whom I have already mentioned. I found them seated with Mrs. Horatio Greenough and daughter, round a jolly fire which it was a joy to behold. In the centre of this rich group of my fair country-women, I spent a very pleasant evening. Today too I have tasted of society. Charles Norton arrived here this morning from Pisa, where he had left his family, in quest of an apartment. I went about the city with him and parted with him in the afternoon, he returning to Pisa. We saw two good places—a large handsome apartment in town in the same house as the Huntingtons and a most delightful old Villa, a good bit out of the city gates. Charles inclines to the latter—and indeed with friends and books it would be hard to contrive a brighter lovelier home: the house capacious, elderly, Italian—and the garden and all the outside prospect Italianissimi—Florence lying at your feet and the violet snow-tipped Appenines ornamenting the distance. In one way or another I suppose they will settle themselves within a week. I am very glad to have looked at that Villa, at all events. It gave me a most penetrating sense of the peculiar charm of Florence—of the general charm indeed of Italy—a charm inexpressible, indefineable, which must be observed in its native air, but which, once deeply felt, leaves forever its mark upon the sensitive mind and fastens it to Italian soil thro' all its future wanderings by a delicate chain of longings and regrets. I wish I could get you and Mother and Alice implanted for a while in some such habitation—feeding on its picturesqueness and drinking the autumn sunshine—which like everything about Florence seems to be colored with a mild violet, like diluted wine. But it's a very silly wish. You would die of loneliness and you'd curse your antique privacy.—I have placed myself half under a promise to go down to Pisa within a day or two, to see the Nortons 'ere they come to Florence. I hesitate somewhat to do it because if I turn my back upon Florence now, I'm afraid I shall turn it upon Italy altogether. I'm very sorry to say that I am anything but well. Not that I have any new and startling affliction, but an old trouble which I had most confidently hoped by this time to have got the mastery of, has settled down upon me during the last six weeks with a most inexorable weight. Willy will tell you what it is: I wrote him on the subject soon after I came to Florence. I fought a hard battle all summer with it in Switzerland; but I left the country with a painful sense that I hadn't gained an inch of ground. Ever since I have been in Italy I have been rapidly losing ground and now I have scarcely a square inch to stand on. During my stay in Venice my journey hither and the three weeks of my being here I have been in a very bad way. Shortly after getting here I was so knocked up that I had to take to my bed and have the doctor and I have since then been in his hands. He plies me with drugs, but to no purpose: I only seem to get worse. But I'll not treat you to a string of details: I recommend you to Willy for information. I don't know whether to think that Italian air has anything to do with the matter: I'm utterly unable to explain so violent an aggravation of my state, in the very face of a mode of life magnificently calculated (as one would say) to ensure a steady improvement. But the fact remains and I must come to some sort of terms with it. I feel as if I couldn't live on a week longer in my present pernicious condition. I'm not impatient: I have given the thing a fair chance and my present condition, which is all that has come of my patience, is quite unendurable. I would give a vast deal to be able to believe that all I have to do is to hang on in Italy and change will come. Experience assures me that I have no reason whatever to look for a change on these terms and without a change I absolutely can't remain. It makes a sad trouble of what ought to be a great pleasure. My malady has done a great deal towards spoiling Florence for me: I should be sorry to have it meddle with other places. The question is of course what to do, inasmuch as I've pretty nearly exhausted expedience. I have almost made up my mind to depart straight from Italy and take refuge at Malvern again. The sole period of relief that I have enjoyed since I've been abroad came to me during the last part of my stay there and the subsequent month of my travels in England. On leaving England I immediately relapsed. I therefore feel justified in hoping that if I buckle down to a good two months at Malvern (or whatever shorter time may seem sufficient) I may gain a solid benefit. I have come to this decision with much cogitation and infinite regret. In leaving Italy now I shall be doing I think, the hardest thing I ever did. But I don't see that any other way is open to me. To be at the very gates of Rome and to turn away requires certainly a strong muscular effort. A very faint ray of light ahead would make me advance with a rush. But I cannot undertake to see Rome as I have seen Florence: the sooner I do it the better. This will be a great disappointment to your dear sympathetic souls at home, just as it is to my own: place on the other side the chance of my recovery by going to M. There will be no Rome and no Italy like the Rome and Naples of my getting really relieved of this dismal burden. They will be utterly vulgar in comparison. You may measure the *need* of my bolting thus out of Italy, by the simple fact of things having reached that point that it's easier to go than to stay.

Tuesday morning. I was driven to bed last night by the cold and before going out this morning I take up my shaky pen to finish my letter. It's such a dismal effusion that the sooner I bring it to a close the better. Don't revile me and above all don't pity me. Simply be as comfortable and jolly as you can yourselves and I shall get along very well. Don't wholly give up writing to me, however; such an extravagance of jollity I should wholly deprecate.—Dear Father, if once I can get rid of this ancient sorrow I shall be many parts of a well man. Remember this and give me your good wishes. This trouble now is the only rock in my path: if I remove it I shall march straight ahead, I think, to health and work.—I spent a good portion of last night wondering whether I *can* manage not to go to Rome. *Nous verrons:* I shall go to Pisa for a couple of days and may there with a change of circumstances and a little society receive an impulse for the better, on which I shall perhaps try Rome for a couple of weeks. I shall drop you a line from there saying whether I am to move North or South, so that you may know where to write. Meanwhile farewell. *Je vous embrasse*—I *squeeze* you all.—I have invented for my comfort a theory that this degenerescence of mine

157

is the result of Alice and Willy getting better and locating some of their diseases on me—so as to propitiate the fates by not turning the poor homeless infirmities out of the family. Isn't it so? I forgive them and bless them.

Your ever affectionate young one
H. James Jr.

To William James

Ms Harvard

Florence Hotel de l'Europe
October 26th [1869]

Dear Bill—

I wrote you the enclosed long letter some ten days ago, but abstained from sending it, on account of its darksome purport and in the hope that by waiting I might have better news. But I haven't. My condition has become so intolerable that I am well nigh made up my mind to leave Italy and fly to England—for the reason and with the purpose mentioned in my letter. For the past ten days I have been in the very depths of discomfort. If it wasn't as great as it I can imagine it being, I should say it was getting worse. I haven't the shadow of a reason left I think, after my long experience, for supposing that I shall encounter any change, on this footing. Moreover, my back as I have related in my letter, is so chronically affected by my constipated state that there are times when I can hardly drag myself about. Half the week I can eat not a single meal a day; I can't possibly find room for more—and this in spite of getting very tired and passably hungry with all my poking about. I mean therefore to return to England in a very short time. Just at the present moment, I am undecided as to whether I shall push on to Rome for a fortnight or depart straightway *via* Leghorn and Marseilles. I shall advise you a couple of days hence. I have just written to Father. I have heard nothing from home in three weeks. Excuse brutal brevity.

Yours in haste
H.J. jr

To William James

Ms Harvard

Rome Hotel d'Angleterre, Oct. 30*th* [1869]

My dearest William—

Some four days since I despatched to you and Father respectively, from Florence, two very doleful epistles, which you will in course of time receive. No sooner had I posted them, however than my spirits were revived by the arrival of a most blessed brotherly letter from you of October 8th, which had been detained either by my banker or the porter of the hotel and a little scrap from Father of a later date, enclosing your review of Mill and a paper of Howells— as well as a couple of *Nations*. Verily, it is worthwhile pining for letters for three weeks to know the exquisite joy of final relief. I took yours with me to the theatre whither I went to see a comedy of Goldoni most delightfully played and read and re-read it between the acts.—But of this anon.—I went as I proposed down to Pisa and spent two very pleasant days with the Nortons. It is a very fine dull old town—and the great Square with its four big treasures is quite the biggest thing I have seen in Italy—or rather was, until my arrival at this well-known locality.—I went about a whole morning with Charles Norton and profited vastly by his excellent knowledge of Italian history and art. I wish I had a small fraction of it. But my visit wouldn't have been complete unless I had got a ramble *solus,* which I did in perfection. On my return to Florence I determined to start immediately for Rome. The afternoon after I had posted those two letters I took a walk out of Florence to an enchanting old Chartreuse—an ancient monastery, perched up on top of a hill and turreted with little cells like a feudal castle.[1] I attacked it and carried it by storm—i.e. obtained admission and went over it. On coming out I swore to myself that while I had life in my body I wouldn't leave a country where adventures of that complexion are the common incidents of your daily constitutional: but that I would hurl myself upon Rome and fight it out on this line at the peril of my existence. Here I am then in the Eternal City. It was easy to leave Florence; the cold had become intolerable and the rain perpetual.

I started last night, and at 10½ o'clock and after a bleak and fatiguing journey of twelve hours found myself here with the morning light. There are several places on the *route* I should have been glad to see; but the weather and my own condition made a direct journey imperative. I rushed to this hotel (a very slow and obstructed rush it was, I confess, thanks to the longueurs and lenteurs of the Papal dispensation) and after a wash and a breakfast let myself loose on the city. From midday to dusk I have been roaming the streets. *Que vous en dirai-je?* At last—for the first time—I live! It beats everything: it leaves the Rome of your fancy—your education— nowhere. It makes Venice—Florence—Oxford—London—seem like little cities of pasteboard. I went reeling and moaning thro' the streets, in a fever of enjoyment. In the course of four or five hours I traversed almost the whole of Rome and got a glimpse of every-thing—the Forum, the Coliseum (stupendissimo!), the Pantheon, the Capitol, St. Peter's, the Column of Trajan, the Castle of St. Angelo—all the Piazzas and ruins and monuments. The effect is something indescribable. For the first time I know what the pic-turesque is.—In St. Peter's I stayed some time. It's even beyond its reputation. It was filled with foreign ecclesiastics—great armies encamped in prayer on the marble plains of its pavement—an inexhaustible physiognomical study. To crown my day, on my way home, I met his Holiness in person[2]—driving in prodigious purple state—sitting dim within the shadows of his coach with two uplifted benedictory fingers—like some dusky Hindoo idol in the depths of its shrine. Even if I should leave Rome tonight I should feel that I have caught the keynote of its operation on the senses. I have looked along the grassy vista of the Appian Way and seen the topmost stone-work of the Coliseum sitting shrouded in the light of heaven, like the edge of an Alpine chain. I've trod the Forum and I have scaled the Capitol. I've seen the Tiber hurrying along, as swift and dirty as history! From the high tribune of a great chapel of St. Peter's I have heard in the papal choir a strange old man sing in a shrill unpleasant soprano. I've seen troops of little tonsured neophytes clad in scarlet, marching and countermarching and duck-ing and flopping, like poor little raw recruits for the heavenly host.

In fine I've seen Rome, and I shall go to bed a wiser man than I last rose—yesterday morning.—It was a great relief to me to have you at last give me some news of your health. I thank the Lord it's no worse. With all my heart I rejoice that you're going to try loafing and visiting. I discern the "inexorable logic" of the affair; courage, and you'll work out your redemption. I'm delighted with your good report of John La Farge's pictures. I've seen them all save the sleeping woman. I have given up expecting him here. If he does come, *tant mieux.* Your notice of Mill and Bushnell seemed to me (save the opening lines which savored faintly of Eugene Benson) very well and fluently written. Thank Father for his ten lines: may they increase and multiply!—Of course I don't know how long I shall be here. I would give my head to be able to remain three months: it would be a liberal education. As it is, I shall stay, if possible, simply from week to week. My "condition" remains the same. I am living on some medicine (aloes and sulphuric acid) given me by my Florentine doctor. I shall write again very shortly. Kisses to Alice and Mother. Blessings on yourself. Address me *Spada, Flamine* and Cie. Banquiers, Rome. Heaven grant I may be here when your letters come. Love to Father.

À *toi*

H.J. jr

1. The visit to the Carthusian monastery outside the Porta Romana is described in *Italian Hours* in the Florentine Notes, pp. 299–302.

2. Pope Pius IX. The glimpse of the Pope would be mentioned in *Roderick Hudson*.

To Alice James

Ms Harvard

Rome Hotel de Rome

Nov. 7*th* Sunday [1869]

Beloved sister—

A week ago, on my arrival here I despatched a hasty note to Willie, telling of my few first impressions. Since then, with time, and (I am most happy to say, an improved physical state—thanks to my good Florentine doctor) I have largely added to the stock—in many cases for your especial benefit. The excitement of the first hour has passed away and I have recovered the healthy mental equilibrium of the sober practical tourist. Nevertheless Rome is still Rome at the end of a week or rather is more thoroughly Rome than ever. But before I proceed with Rome, let me say that I feel frequently that I have quite failed of justice to that delightful admirable Florence—the very *sweetest* among cities. In spite of being so poorly, I saw more and enjoyed more while there than I managed to tell you of. I had planned in particular to write to William a high-toned letter on the two Great Galleries—wherein I should have spoken with infinite wisdom of certain sublime portraits by Rafael, Titian and Leonardo. I had likewise arranged a brilliant discourse on Michael Angelo's Medicean tombs—the last word of Romantic Art—and had collected some notes on the characteristics of Florentine scenery. I hope to stop again in the lovely city on my way out of Italy and I shall then perhaps be inspired. *En attendant,* tell my brother not to cherish the fond illusion that in seeing the photos of M. Angelo's statues he has *même entrevu* the originals. Their beauty far surpasses my prior conception. As they sit brooding in their dim-lighted chapel, exhaling silence and thought, they form, I imagine, the most impressive work of art in the world. The warrior with the cavernous visage is absolutely terrible: he seems to shed an amount of inarticulate sorrow sufficient to infest the Universe.—And now as for this Rome, it seems a sadly vain ambition to attempt to give you any idea of its affect upon the mind. It's so vast, so heavy, so multitudinous that you seem to require all your energy simply to bear up against it. Your foremost feeling is that of your own ignorance. In a certain way the *premier venu* can enjoy the place as much as another: its immense superficial picturesqueness appeals to the elementary sentiments of your common nature. But at every step you feel that in the line of a sort of sympathetic comprehension you are losing something thro' your want of knowledge. It's a place in which you needn't in the least feel ashamed of a perpetual reference to *Murray:* a place in which you feel emphatically the value of "culture". At every step in some guise or other History confronts you and the mind must make some response: the more intelligent the better. I have buckled down to my work with a fair amount of resolution. In the morning I have regularly gone to the Vatican, and in the afternoon have strolled about at hazard, seeking what I might devour, and devouring (frequently with something of the languor of fatigue) whatever I have found. I have seen tolerably well—i.e. got the feeling of—some half dozen special localities, besides absorbing incidentally a sufficiently ample sense of the general physiognomy of Rome. The Vatican, the Museum of the Capitol, the Colisium and the Baths of Caraculla, the Pantheon, the forum, and the churches of the Lateran and Sta. Maria Maggiore —such are my special acquisitions. In spite of an immense deal of dove-tailing and intermingling, Pagan and Christian Rome keeps tolerably distinct and the ancient city is a fact that you can appreciate more or less in its purity. Appreciate, but not express! No words can reproduce the eloquence of a Roman block of blunted marble or a mass of eternal brickwork—let alone the crowded majesty of an original inscription. Last Sunday, the Vatican being closed, I went down and had a long lounge in the Coliseum. The day was magnificent and the sun seemed to shine on purpose to illumine its crevices and set off its immensity. I climbed over the accessible portions of the summit and communed with the genius of the spot—in the person of a heavy-souled German whom I met and whom I had formerly encountered on the Rigi. The Coliseum is a thing about which it's useless to talk: it must be seen and felt. But as a piece of the picturesque—a province of it—it is thoroughly and simply delightful. The grassy arena with its circle of tarnished shrines and praying strollers[1]—the sky between the arches and above the oval— the weeds and flowers against the sky etc.—are as charming as anything in Rome. The next day in the afternoon I betook myself to the almost equal ruins of the Baths of Caracalla. It was the hour of sunset and I had them all to myself. They are a collection of perfectly mountainous masses of brickwork, to the right of the Appian Way. Even more than the Coloseum I think they give you a notion of the Roman *scale*. Imagine a good second class mountain in reduced circumstances—perforated and honeycombed by some terrestrial cataclysm—and you'll have an idea of these terrific ruins. Through a modern staircase in one of the columns I ascended to the roof (or what remains of it) and saw the Campagna bathed in the sunset. At this giddy elevation the effect is more mountainous than ever. The aged masonry seems all compacted and condensed into natural stratifications and a great wilderness of trees and thickets sits blooming over the abyss.—By far the most beautiful piece of ancientry in Rome is that simple and unutterable Pantheon to which I repeated my devotions yesterday afternoon. It makes you profoundly regret that you are not a pagan suckled in the creed outworn that produced it. It's the most conclusive example I have yet seen of the simple sublime. Imagine simply a vast cupola with its drum, set directly on the earth and fronted with a porch of columns and a triangular summit: the interior lighted by a hole in the apex of the cupola and the circumference furnished with a series of altars. The effect within is the very *delicacy* of grandeur—and more worshipful to my perception than the most mysterious and aspiring Gothic. St. Peter's, beside it, is absurdly vulgar. Taken absolutely however St. Peter's is extremely interesting—not quite so much so as it pretends to be—but quite enough so to give you a first class sensation. Its pretention, I take it, is to be the very synthesis and summit of all sensations and emotions. I can't dispose of it in three words. As a whole it's immensely picturesque. As you journey thro' its various latitudes, moreover, you really feel that you stand at the heart and centre of modern ecclesiasticism: you are watching the heart-beats of the church. The past week has been a season of great performances; but the combined absence of a dress-suit and an aversion to a crowd has prevented my going to the Sistine Chapel, where the best of the fun has been going on. Before I leave Rome, however, I mean to get a glimpse. A glimpse indeed I had some three days since, when the Pope came in state to say mass at a church opposite this hotel. I made no attempt to enter the church: but I saw tolerably well the arrival of the cardinals and ambassadors etc and finally of the Grand Llama in person. The whole spectacle was very handsome, but it was precisely like a leaf out of the Middle-Ages—or even more out of the last century—pre-revolutionary times. It's a "merciful providence" that the spectators of all this Papistry has at hand so vast a magazine of antiquity to appeal to for purgation and relief. When you have seen that flaccid old woman waving his ridiculous fingers over the prostrate multitude and have duly felt the picturesqueness of the scene—and then turn away sickened by its absolute *obscenity*—you may climb the steps of the Capitol and contemplate the equestrian statue of Marcus Aurelius. This work, by the way, is one of the things I have most enjoyed in Rome. It is totally admirable—the very model of the *genre:*—so large and monumental and yet so full of a sweet human dignity—stretching out a long thin arm in the act of mild persuasive command—that affects you like an audible personal voice out of that stony Roman past. As you revert to that poor sexless old Pope enthroned upon his cushions—and then glance at those imperial legs swinging in their immortal bronze, you cry out that here at least was a *man*! But the mention of this statue brings me to the Museum of the Vatican. Here I have had great satisfactions. Before plunging into the antiques however I took a look at Rafael, as the Vatican shows him. It contains his *Transfiguration* and his famous *Stanze*—a series of ravens painted in frescoe—the *School of Athens, Heliodorus* etc. Whether I have completed my "evolution" in the enjoyment of painting or—terrible fate!—have got stuck fast in the middle of it—I know not: but in truth my uppermost feeling before these works was one of the most irresponsive sort. In a word, I was disappointed. Before Rafael's great portraits in Florence there was nothing I wouldn't have conceeded to him: but as I looked at these heroic compositions I begrudged him even his proper dues. The more I see of painting and scultpure, the more I value a good portrait. In proportion to the subject, difficulties seem to me more boldly faced and more honestly solved than in "compositions." The inventive—the would-be creative faculty, left to itself, seems sadly inclined to wander and stumble—sadly fallible. There is at the Vatican a statue of Demosthenes—you may see a cast of it at the Athenaeum—a fine wise old man with his head bent and his hands dropped, holding a scroll—so perfect and noble and beautiful that it amply satisfies my desire for the ideal. Great are the Venetians:

these things of Rafael make me feel it: they stick to the real, though in so doing they missed the *belle ligne romaine*. Without going into metaphysics, it is easy to say that the great works of Rafael are vitiated by their affected classicism—their elegance and coldness. I sat staring stupidly at the *Transfiguration* and actually *surprised* at its thinness—asking myself whether *this* was the pretended greatest of pictures. Not so had I sat before the great *Crucifixion* of Tintoret. It's very foolish to lay down any rules or form by theories in advance. In painting you must deal with accomplished facts. There is hardly any painter who has fairly earned the name in whom I *don't* feel capable on occasion and on certain special grounds of taking a critical interest: but I find the number of those who afford me genuine spontaneous delight sifted down to a few. One. The best Venetians —Bellini, Tintoret, Titian, Veronese and the rich Giorgione—who is entirely unrepresented in his native city and whom I learned to know in Florence. Two. Giotto and a small number of the early Italians—notably the great Orcagna in the Campo Santo at Pisa. In these primitive men, when thro' their stiffness and ignorance a ray of genius breaks forth, it has a *quality*—a freshness and directness— which makes it leap home to the mind like a winged arrow. Three. The portraits of Leonardo and Rafael. Here, while their education has made them free, their subjects have kept them honest. What Leonardo's education has enabled him to put—or to keep—in the physiognomy of a certain clever young woman at Florence—it would take a Leonardo of the pen to relate. Four. After this, *for pleasure*, give me any amount of good Dutch realism.—But with my good Dutch realism *me voilà loin du Vatican*!—From the Apollo Belvedere and the Laocoön. These clever pieces don't err on the side of realism. My first movement at the Vatican was to run to the Belvedere and get them off my conscience. On the whole they quite deserve their fame: famous things always do, I find: even the *Transfiguration* is no exception. But there are some other things on the premises which deserve their delicious (comparative) obscurity. The Apollo is really a magnificent youth—with far more of solid dignity than I fancied. The Laocoön on the other hand, strikes me as a decidedly made up affair and much less complete and successful embodiment of human anguish than that sublime *Niobe* at Florence—a perfect image of maternity on the rack.—I don't of course mean, beloved child, to enumerate the contents of the Vatican. Broadly, until you've trod these glorious halls you don't know what sculpture is. They are immense in content and crowded with different specimens: even the really interesting things, of course, being of various degrees of merit. Among them, the innumerable busts and statues of the Roman emperor hold a foremost place. I find a particular fascination in a magnificent statue of Augustus, excavated only some five years since, in a marvelous state of preservation. Also in a ravishing little bust of Augustus as a boy, as clear and fresh in quality as if it dated from yesterday. He may have been an arrant knave but he had a sweet most interesting intellectual visage. I saw yesterday at the Capitol the dying Gladiator, the Lydian Apollo, the Amazon etc—all of them unspeakably simple and noble and eloquent of the breadth of human genius. There's little to say or do about them, save to sit and enjoy them and let them act upon your nerves and confirm your esteem for completeness, purity and perfection. After two crowded months of pictures this effect is delightfully cooling and reassuring. All the Roman portraits give me a deep desire to plunge into Roman history—so that yesterday I narrowly escaped paying 22 frs. for an English publication on the subject. But to approach it, you must have a Roman will.—Out of the high windows of the Vatican you get glimpses of all kinds of delicious Italian courts and gardens. You even surprise the secrets of the papal household. I am sure I saw one of the pontifical petticoats hanging out to dry. In the corridors and stairways you likewise see the Swiss Guard—glorious medieval warriors clad in splendid fantastic trappings of red and yellow. Indeed the human picturesque in Rome is quite as rich as the architectural. The peasantry are in a decided minority and to get a proper notion of them I suppose one must leave the city and plunge into the Campagna which I hope in some small way to do. I have hoped to have a good deal to do with the Campagna (in the way of afternoon walks etc) but it is at a much greater distance from any given point than I supposed. Besides there is far more than enough to do within the walls.—The human picturesque as I say is visible in the innumerable host of soldiers and priests—of whom there is about an equal swarm. You may meet in any half hour's walk a dozen as genuine squalid friars of the early church—or a dozen pale ascetics of as good a quality—as the imagination could possibly desire.—

Monday 8th. So much I wrote yesterday and then in mercy stayed my hand. It must suffice for the present. I have made in the above no mention of letters because since leaving Florence I have received none. The next I fondly hope may be from you. In his last note Father mentioned your having gone with Miss Theodora Sedgwick to spend the day at Milton. It would be a little more becoming I think if instead of to *livrer à ces folles jouissances* you should *once in a while* spend a morning in your room, writing to your poor old brother.—I am very sorry to hear of Addy Watson's bad state. I always liked her. She had a certain graceful way with her which I suppose her gradual extinction doesn't diminish. If I could invent a message proper to her condition I would send it. But I can't. Jane Norton read me last summer a remarkably good and singularly *pathetic* letter from Silvia W., which made me resolve at the time to write to her: but the flesh is weak.—Of *intime* and personal news I have little to give beyond the fact that for the present, as I have said, I am vastly better in body. If I can only manage to keep so I shall feel that a brighter day has dawned.—Since sending my last letter I have changed my hotel—much for the better. I suffered so from the cold in Florence that I made a point of taking a room *with sun,* which I have found here very fairly. If I were surer of my health and the duration of my stay I would take a private room or a couple of them. Prices, this winter, however are so high in Rome, that I fancy I should pay as much for good quarters as I do here and from my lack of friends and of the language be more lonely and less comfortable. I made a rapid and feverish excursion into a *pension* of good repute—but what with high terms, poor room and a vicious *table d'hôte* concluded I had not changed for the better and backed out. I should have paid seventy-five francs a week; here, I live for about eighty—dining to suit myself at a very good restaurant. It's not cheap—but for Rome, apparently (and for comfort) it's not dear. I have of course no company but my own, but in the intervals of sightseeing find a rare satisfaction in the long-denied perusal of a book. I have been reading Stendhal—a capital observer and a good deal of a thinker. He really knows Italy. I have no plans. There are moments when I feel as if I should like to establish myself for the winter in Rome: at others I feel as if (sightseeing apart) I should prefer another course. A whole winter of sight-seeing were too much of a good thing. If I were in good working order I have little doubt of my movements. I should (at the end of a brief sojourn here and a fortnight at Naples) betake myself to Florence and settle there for the winter. There, with books and photos, in a sunny room on that divine *Lung'Arno,* I should study Italian art and history. Concerning my actual course I have this vague prevision:—that I shall remain in Rome until about the 10th of December (just after the opening of the Council)[2] and then go down to Naples for three weeks; return northward on Jan'y 1st and stop for a fortnight at Florence. I shall have then spent five months in Italy. I should leave for France *via* Genoa and Marseilles and travel up to Paris by way of Avignon, Nîmes, and Arles. In Paris I should abide for three months: *i.e.* till May 1st. Here ceases this shadow of a scheme. If I had a *compagnon de voyage* I should prattle to him in some such strain: as I have none, I must exhale my unrest in your sympathetic ear. By May 1st *j'aime à croire* that I shall be able to pronounce as to my going to Germany. I have a glimmering hope that I may then and there embark upon the Rhine—the stream of study.[3] Putting Germany aside and thinking only of travel, I am conscious only of these definite desires. ONE. To get a couple of months of Paris. Willy will scoff at this but I have good reasons forsooth. TWO. See the Flemish and Dutch painters. THREE. To get another glimpse of England.

Evening. I had kept my letter all day—happily: for I have the receipt of a celestial missive from Mother to announce. Language cannot reveal the deep still tremulous joy with which I possessed myself of its contents. I have been out all day—since I laid away my letter after breakfast; dusk had fallen and I came home tolerably done up with my work. Going into the porter's lodge for my key, my first glance was at the little case where the letters are exposed. There stood my joy, in legible black and white! I brought it up to my lofty 4th *piano* and—laid it carefully on the bed. I then proceeded to cleanse myself of all evils and stains, and not before I was duly washed brushed and refreshed did I address myself to its perusal. It contained the very essence of my lovely Mammy.—The news of Ellen's departure give me a real pang. You *must* get her back before I return. She has been among the foremost objects which on that happy day I have often dreamed of folding in my arms. I can't believe but that she is destined to re-enter the family. She seems the very keystone of the arch. All Mother's little facts were most delicious: especially the sale of "your Father's" immortal work. Has he yet made any money on it, or merely covered his expenses?—Poor Wilky's caterpillar (of which I have at last got explicit mention) can hardly be called delicious: I am sure I don't know what to think about it. I hope Miss Mason yields him some compensation: he rarely deserves it. I shall be glad to hear that Minny *has* gone to San Francisco. I wrote her a long letter from Venice and suppose I shall soon have an answer. I take an awful interest in your English hat. Thereby hangs a tale! It reminds me of a visit I paid to Mrs. Brown, Bond St. London—and of a most lovely young shopwoman who shewed me a most lovely young hat—which I came *so* near buying! and would have utterly bought (you'll be gratified to hear) had I not bethought myself to inquire the extra cost of shipping it to America: on learning which I feared that your delicate pate might ache beneath the weight of so costly a monument. Describe it in your next. If it's not of green felt peaked at the summit and decked with a little eagle's feather and with a long streaming veil, wound about your throat—*ça ne vaut rien.* Tell me all about your *neu things.* How do you wear your hair? in those long drooping braids I hope: they are very pretty. If I could only get you to do it in the manner of some of the busts of the Roman Empresses!—I have meant a thousand times in the intervals of writing to send some message to poor dear Mrs. Lombard, which Mother adjures me to do, but have always forgotten it in the decisive act.—Tell her then that I adore her! or rather, give her my love and tell her that I'm extremely glad to hear of her having really fixed herself in Cambridge. I have always included her among those missing friends who make the sadness of absence and exile and should be very sorry not to find her on my return still within reach, to make the satisfaction of home. Ask her to give my especial regards to Miss Fanny and my best hopes for her uninterrupted recovery.— Let me beg you once for all to keep giving my love, regards etc in all proper quarters.*—Mother says no more about Bob's Texan appointment; so I suppose it is extinct.—I met Miss Bessy Ward lately in the street, attended by her maid. She looked old and fat and didn't know me: but I mean shortly to call upon them.—In the same enclosure with Mother's letter, I get a note from Aunt Kate announcing her arrival in Venice for the 8th. They will therefore not reach Rome before December 1st. I hope I shall still be here— for A. K's sake at any rate, and Helen Ripley's. Indeed I shall receive A. K. with the wildest enthusiasm. It will at last be someone to talk to. We shall gossip mightily about home. I can easily understand that she suffers from the insensibility of her companions. I have seen specimens of unregenerate American stolidity which (if her fellow travelers are gifted with it) make me feel for her.—But my letter is of a perfectly barbarous length.—I'm glad Howells shewed you what I wrote him from Venice. Goad him on to answer me. They take the Daily Adv. at this hotel and I have just read of Mr. Eliot's installation.[4]—I enclose a note to W. Farewell.—Love to Father and Mother. I close my eyes and fancy you going into Dr. Butler's (blessed man)—tossing your beautiful hat—the pride of the horse-car!—and of your devoted brother

H. J. jr

*N.B. Especially to the Gurneys.

1. HJ is describing the Colosseum—as he did in *Roderick Hudson*—in its earth-filled overgrown state, prior to the excavations instituted after Rome was secularized. His inconsistent spellings of Colosseum are retained.
2. Pius IX had convened the Ecumenical Council to solidify the papacy on the eve of the unification of Italy.
3. HJ keeps referring to Germany because it was the country to which William James had gone in preparation for his work as philosopher and psychologist.
4. Charles W. Eliot (1834–1926) had just been installed as President of Harvard.

To Mrs. Henry James Sr.

Ms Harvard

Rome Hotel de Rome Nov. 21*st* [1869]
Sunday evening.

My dearest Mother—

In consideration of my last letter having been a terrifically long one, I have let two whole weeks slip away without writing again. I find here so many uses for my time that except in the evening it is hard to find a moment for letters, and in the evening I am apt to be rather too jaded with my day's exploits to take up my pen with much energy. I had hoped to succeed in devoting this blessed Sunday morning to a long homeward scribble; but I spent a large part of it in going with Mrs. Ward to a famous Musical Mass at St. Cecilia's: this being the eve of that holy virgin and martyr. But of this anon. I mentioned in my last the receipt of your dearest and sweetest of letters. A week later I received an excellent communication from Willy in answer to my first letter from Florence—written as it seems to me, so long ago. I now, insatiable wretch as I am, begin to crave and expect some heavenly missive from Father or Alice: and even to count the days until the revolving month shall bring me another letter from you. Heaven speed the time!—Meanwhile I am up to my neck in Rome and have today begun the fourth week of my stay. In spite of the dense fulness of the days the time has passed most rapidly. I have seen, in some cases repeatedly, most of the important shows and wonders. Would that I could give you a twentieth part—a select condensed twentieth—of my swarming impressions and emotions. Most happily, I have been very decently well, and if the same blissful condition will outlast my stay and accompany me to Naples I shall be immensely thankful. Soon after writing last I called upon Mrs. Ward, but learning that she was feasting an Archbishop I modestly withdrew. The next day, however, I received a very kind note from her, bidding me to dinner, which I of course accepted. She turned out as usual to be laid up with one of her ancient attacks. But we were largely entertained by the loquacious Miss Lily and the adorable Miss Bessy—"we" being

172

beside myself, Mrs. Charles Strong[1] of New York—a very sweet and agreeable woman whose "conversion," chiefly I believe thro' Mrs. Ward's agency, made some noise here last winter—and her youthful and precocious daughter Miss "Pussy" Strong. Bessy Ward spoke very joyfully of having received a letter from Alice, asked many questions about her and sent her her love. She has grown up into a most charming creature—pretty, intelligent, gracious and elegant—a most noble and delightful maiden—as nice a girl as you often see. Her poor sister looked very feeble and jaded, but conversed as fluently as ever. One day last week Mrs. Ward called for me to drive, but I was absent. Last evening I again went to see her and had the benefit of her precious discourse for a couple of hours. Her garrulity is something stupendous—and the best that you can say of her is that she makes such garrulity graceful—which she certainly does, extremely. She was very sweet and kind and obliging in her offers and sent her love to you and Father. She arranged with me to accompany her today to the Vesper Service (3 o'clock) at the little Church of St. Cecelia away over in the Trastevere. She duly called for me in company with Miss Ripley, an ancient virgin of the Faith, established in Rome. The music and singing on this occasion draws great crowds and is most divinely beautiful. Much of it was immensely florid and profane in tone—as far as least as I could judge; but in spite of the crowded and fetid church and the revolt provoked in my mind by the spectacular catholicism (for if you don't love it, here in Rome you must hate it: there is no middle path) I truly enjoyed the performance. On our way home, in the carriage, Mrs. Ward, who had become highly excited and *exaltée,* recited with a great deal of color and warmth the history of her conversion and blessedness of her state. At all points apparently she bravely takes the bull by the horns. For a Catholic as thoroughly *lancée* and active as she, this must be a truly *délicieux séjour.* I don't at all agree with the people who assume that Rome is the place to discuss and disenchant you with the Church. On the contrary, a faint impulse once received (an essential premise) Rome makes the rest of the journey all down-hill work. The sense you get here of the great collective Church must be far more potent than elsewhere to swallow up and efface all the vile and flagrant minor offenses to the soul and the senses. Once *in* the Church you can be perfectly indifferent to the debased and stultified priests and the grovelling peasantry: out of it you certainly can't. But enough on this chapter. There is a better Rome than all this—a Rome in the lingering emanation of whose genius and energy I have spent many a memorable hour. It makes all this modern ecclesiasticism, to my perception, seem sadly hollow and vulgar. The ruins and relics and chance wayside reminders of this ancient strength are far more numerous and absorbing than I supposed. You come upon them in some form at every step and when once encountered, they fix and fascinate the mind. All the old Roman fragments that I've seen, of whatever nature or dimensions, have a character and dignity that makes it salutary to handle and frequent them. I wish I could knock off with stroke of the pen a clear impression of one of my days here and make you feel the interest of two or three of the choicest spots. It's hard to say, however, what are the choicest spots. Each one at the moment seems richer in suggestion, more eloquent and thought-provoking than the last and you surrender yourself to the absolute spell of its melancholy charm. I betook myself one glorious morning a number of days since to the mighty Baths of Caracalla (of which I spoke in my last) and spent a long time alternately quaking among their damp cold shadows and roasting in the sunshine which floods their crumbling summits, as they gaze out across the Campagna. From there I went to certain *Columbaria* in the same quarter—a series of subterranean vaults recently discovered, in which the Romans *pigeon-holed* or deposited on small concave shelves the vases containing the ashes of their dead. They stand in a great sunny rubbishy Italian vineyard, whence you descend into the dead moist air and the dim mildewed light of these strange funeral wells. Few things transport you so forcibly into the past. Their perfection is almost unimpaired. Tier upon tier the little pigeon holes sit yawning upon you, each subscribed with its original Latin statement. From here, at the invitation of a solitary Englishman whom I encountered on the premises, I took a drive along the Appian Way, as far as the tomb of Cecelia Metella—or rather some distance beyond it. "Who was this lady?—Was she chaste and fair?" I'm sure I don't know; but her tomb at any rate is one of the effective objects of the world. The great violet Campagna, at this point, stretching its idle breadth to the horizon known of Roman eyes—a wilderness of sunny decay and vacancy—must be seen to be appreciated. Another day of the same tender color I had more recently when I drove out to the glorious restored Basilica of St. Paul's without the walls—and came home by the Pyramid of Caius Cestius—(whose mighty Roman mortality was deemed worthy of entombment in the heart of that solid mountain of masonry—I went into the little sepulchral chamber and saw the jaded frescoes and measured the thickness of the walls)—and that divine little protestant Cemetary where Shelley and Keats lie buried—a place most lovely and solemn and exquisitely full of the traditional Roman quality[2]—with a vast grey pyramid inserted into the sky on one side and the dark cold cypresses on the other, and the light bursting out between them and the whole surrounding landscape swooning away for very picturesquenness. Another morning I spent at the Palace of the Caesars, a vast enclosure covering a large portion of the Palatine Hill, in which great excavations are being carried on by the Emperor of the French— and mighty mansions and temples and theatres restored to the sight of day and to some faint semblance of their primitive shape. It's a most enchanting spot. You have a view of all Rome and you wander at your will through a wilderness of evergreen shrubbery and eternal Roman basements and partitions. One afternoon recently towards dusk, after a day spent I don't quite remember how, I found myself standing in a little hollow between the foot of the Palatine and the Tiber and gazing at the massive, battered and ugly Arch of Janus Quadrifrons. A man sallied forth from the neighboring shades with an enormous key and whispered the soul-stirring name of the *Cloaca Maxima*. I joyfully assented and he led me apart under a series of half-buried arches into a deeper hollow, where the great mouth of a tunnel seemed to brood over the scene and thence introduced me into a little covered enclosure, whence we might survey a small section of the ancient sewer. It gave me the deepest and grimmest impression of antiquity I have ever received. He lit a long torch and plunged it down into the blackness. It threw a red glare on a mass of dead black travertine and I was assured that I was gazing upon the masonry of Tarquinius Prisens. If it wasn't I'm sure it ought to have been. A few days since I went to see the strange old church of *San Clementi*, which has long passed for one of the most curious and interesting of the early Roman basilicas. You may judge whether its reputation was increased by the recent discovery of a complete subterranean church, upon whose walls as on a foundation, the later edifice was reared. Thro' the now wholly excavated labyrinth of this primitive tabernacle, taper in hand, I was *promené* by an old Irish monk, who told me stories of all the blessed saints whose adventures you may yet decipher in the most rudimentary frescoes on the walls. But he ended by conducting me down into a still deeper and darker and narrower compartment and in this triply buried sanctuary laid my hand upon an enormous block of granite (or what-not) and pronounced in a magnificent brogue the name of Servius Tullius. To the non-antiquarian mind these are quite first class sensations. Another emotion of equal value was the fruit some three nights since of a moonlight visit to the Coliseum. I started off by myself on foot, about 8 o'clock, beneath a radiant evening sky. The Coliseum itself was all very well; but it was not that that repaid me, but my halt in the square before the Capitol, beneath the great transfigured statue of M. Aurelius.[3] I like this grand old effigy better every time I see it. It commands the sympathies somehow more than any work of art I know. If to directly impress the soul, the heart, the affections, to stir up by some ineffable magic the sense of all one's human relations and of the warm surrounding frames of human life—if this is the sign of a great work of art—this statue is one of the very greatest. It massed itself up before me in the magical moonlight with a truly appalling reality.— Of course I go a great deal to the Vatican—and never without feeling somewhat the wiser for it. The really good statues there would gain by being looked at every day of your life, so manly and definite and strong are they. They have no pretention, affectation, subtlety etc. But one can't talk about them. I am buying no photos.; but if I were, should like to send you about a hundred. In my last letter,

I remember I let out rather savagely on Rafael. Since then I have been back to his [illegible] in the Vatican and feel rather more philosophical about the matter. I don't think him more interesting; but I mind less his being as he is. Evidently there are two moods for looking at pictures. One in which the mind demands simple unqualified pleasure and exaltation: the other critical considerate and questioning. The first is really much the more fastidious of the two and I fancy it to be well that it should find only occasional satisfaction. When the second is uppermost almost any gallery is a very pleasant place. I have seen almost all the Roman collections. Half their merit to my taste is in their being in their delightful princely shabby old palaces—with their great names—Borghese, Farnese, Colonna, Corsini, Doria. Among them all I don't know that I have seen anything very noteworthy. In the Borghese collection is a Correggio of heavenly merit—and a Titian of earthly. In the magnificent Dorian halls is the famous portrait by Velasquez of Innocent X, of which Taine speaks rather memorably—and a most memorable portrait it is—one of those works which by its heavy drain on your faculty of respect seem absolutely to exhaust it and get to leave you only the richer for the loss. At the Corsini Palace the other day I got myself let into the Gardens where I spent a delicious hour. I did the same at the Vatican and went strolling about the sunny terraces like a wicked old Cardinal. But this is gossip enough. We are each rather tired. I wanted to say something about the Sistine Chapel, the Moses etc— and about a rapturous little fresco of the cunning Leonardo, which I chanced upon, during a delicious random stroll, in a convent on the top of the Janiculum. But they'll keep—they be kept thus far.—This by the way is no longer last night but Monday afternoon.—I have just got—a richer fate than I expected, your and Willy's letter of November 1st. They are full of sympathy and advice with regard to the burden of my letters from Florence. You will by this time have learned that I've derived invaluable relief from the use of sulfuric acid, prescribed by my Florentine doctor. How long this is going to last I can't foresee; but the medicine has done me at any rate, the immense service of letting me see Rome. As yet its effect continues very fairly; tho'

I fancy that I see signs of its gradual diminution. If it will only carry me thro' a fortnight at Naples! In my last letter I remember I prattled away in fine style about my "plans." I have really no right to have any beyond the morrow: I should like to remain here another fortnight and then make the trip to Naples. If a month hence I am as well as I am now I shall rather feel that I am better—tho' I'm not sure how far it is just to regard as an improvement a condition wholly dependent on medicine. I have been awfully tempted to "settle" in Rome for the winter; but I have lacked (I don't know what to call it) the rashness or the courage. I have amused myself by looking at a dozen lodgings—all repulsive. They consist either of a single room in the bosom of an Italian family—or of an independent group. The latter for obvious reasons—i.e. expense—are unsuitable —and the former on grounds nonetheless valid, for one obliged to exact certain comforts. Altogether, on reflection I have shrunk from binding myself here in any way. If, after Naples, I still feel like remaining in Italy, I shall have Florence to turn to—Florence the lovely (and the comfortable.) If not I shall make for Paris, where my ulterior plans may freely develop themselves. I shall there be equidistant from England and Germany and during any period of suspense shall feel that it's no loss to have a month of Paris. Tell Willy that I mean to answer his two letters fully in a day or so. I meant to inclose herewith a reply to the 1st, but am rather tired of writing.—Your own letter, my dearest Mother, was an excellent thing in letters, and very welcome your news of Father Alice and the boys. The two former I see, have tipped each other the wink to neglect and ignore me.— With such conduct they will never prosper. I'm extremely glad to hear of Minny's journey. Aunt Kate will probably arrive here a week hence. I should much enjoy going about here, a little, with her; but I fear I shan't find much sympathy in her party.—Farewell. This is the home-sick hour—twilight. Be sure I keep it religiously. —Love to all. Your son of sons—

H. James Jr.

1. Mrs. Charles E. Strong, the former Eleanor Fearing, had married George Templeton Strong's cousin, but was estranged from him and lived abroad. For an allusion to her Roman Catholicism and her being "jaded with

French novels" see *The Diary of George Templeton Strong*, IV, 232 (25 Nov. 1868).

2. This was James's first visit to the cemetery called by the Italians "Protestant" though actually simply "non-Catholic" where later he would bury the Daisy Miller of his fiction and where he would visit the grave of his devoted friend, Constance Fenimore Woolson.

3. Alluded to several times by James in both his fiction and travel sketches. James called it "transfigured" in the light of Hawthorne's description of its pagan qualities foreshadowing Christian feeling.

To William James

Ms Harvard

Rome [Dec.] 27 [1869]

Beloved Bill,—

I have just found at my bankers a long letter from you (Dec. 5th) which has gratified me so inexpressibly that altho' I despatched home a document only a couple of days since, I feel powerfully moved to write to you directly,—the more especially as my letter contained a promise that I would. Your letter fills me with a divine desire to occupy for an hour that old cane-bottomed chair before your bedroom fire. One of these days it will hold me for many hours. I am extremely glad you like my letters—and terrifically agitated by the thought that Emerson likes them.[1] I never manage to write but a very small fraction of what has originally occurred to me. What you call the "animal heat" of contemplation is sure to evaporate within half an hour. I went this morning to bid farewell to M. Angelo's *Moses* at San Pietro in Vincoli, and was so tremendously impressed with its sublimity that on the spot my intellect gushed forth a torrent of wisdom and eloquence; but where is that torrent now? I *have* managed tolerably well however, which is the great thing, to *soak* myself in the various scenes and phenomena. Conclusions occasionally leap full-armed from my Jovine brain, bringing with them an immensely restful sense of their finality. This morning I think I definitively settled the matter with regard to Michael Angelo. I believe, by the way, I never explicitly assured you of the greatness of the "Moses."—or of the vileness of that calumnious photograph. It is a work of magnificent beauty,—beauty very nearly equal to that of the statue of Lorenzo d'Medici. I now feel as if I could judge of Michael Angelo's merits in tolerably complete *connaissance de cause*. I have seen the Great Greek things; I have seen Raphael and I have seen all his own works. He has something—he retains something, after all experience—which belongs only to himself. This transcendent "something" invested the *Moses* this morning with a more melting, exalting power than I have ever perceived in a work of art. It was a great sensation—the greatest a work can give. I sat enthralled and fascinated by that serene *Aristides* at Naples; but I stood agitated this morning by all the forces of my soul. The beauty of such a thing as the Aristides is in the effect achieved; that of the *Moses*, the *Lorenzo*, the figures on the Sistine roof in the absence of a limited effect. The first take no account of the imagination; the others the largest. They have a soul. Alack! 'tis poor work talking of them; *je tenais seulement* to work off something of the tremor in which they have left me, and to gratify myself by writing down in black and white and, if need be, taking my stand on it against the world, the assertion that Michel Angelo is the greatest of artists. The question remained solely as between him and the Greeks; but this morning settled it. The *Moses* alone perhaps wouldn't have done it; but it did it in combination with the vision of Lorenzo's tomb—which I had it with the deepest distinctness. It's the triumph of feeling: the Greeks deny it—poor stupid old Michel proclaims its sovereign air a regenerated world:— and affords a magnificent pretext for making a stand against it *en suite*. It's the victorious cause: the other will never be so well pleaded. It behoves therefore the generous mind to take up the latter. It was worth the trouble going, afterwards, as we did this morning, to San Agostino and Sta. Maria della Pace to look upon Raphael's two wretchedly decayed frescoes of Isaiah and the Sybils, in which *il a voulu faire du Michel Ange*. There was in him none but the very smallest Michel Angelesque elements.—I fancy that I have found after much fumbling and worrying—much of the deepest enjoyment and of equal dissatisfaction—the secret of his incontestable thinness and weakness. He was incapable of energy of statement.

This may seem to be but another name for the fault and not an explication of it. But *enfin* this energy—positiveness—courage,—call it what you will—is a simple, fundamental, primordial quality in the supremely superior genius. Alone it makes the real man of action in art and disjoins him effectually from the critic. I felt this morning irresistibly how that Michel Angelo's greatness lay above all in the fact that he *was* this man of action—the greatest, almost, considering the temptation he had to be otherwise, considering how his imagination embarrassed and charmed and bewildered him—the greatest perhaps, I say, that the race has produced. So far from perfection, so finite, so full of errors, so broadly a target for criticism as it sits there, the *Moses* nevertheless by the vigor with which it utters its idea, the eloquence with which it tells the tale of the author's passionate abjuration of the inaction of fancy and contemplation—his willingness to let it stand, in the interest of life and health and movement as his *best* and his only possible,—by this high transcendent spirit, it redeems itself from subjection to its details, and appeals most forcibly to the generosity and sympathy of the mind. Raphael is undecided, slack and unconvinced—I have seen little else since my return from Naples. I have been staying on from day to day—partly from the general difficulty there is in leaving Rome, partly from the Christmas doings, and partly because it's a certain comfort to Aunt Kate and Helen Ripley. My departure however is fixed for tomorrow. You will have heard from Aunt K. of the steady hideousness of the weather. It tells sadly upon her party and reduces to a very small amount the utmost that can be done in a day. I have seen very little of the Christmas ceremonies. I got my fill so completely at the Council of a crowd and a struggle that I made no attempt to go out on Christmas Eve. On Christmas Day I roamed about St. Peter's. I saw nothing of the Mass or the Pope—but the crowd there is immensely picturesque and well worth seeing. Aunt K. and Helen R. (cousin Henry having been laid up for a week with a violent cold) went with their Courier, got beautiful places and saw to perfection. I'm sick unto death of priests and churches. Their "picturesqueness" ends by making you want to go strongly into political economy or the New England school system. I conceived at Naples a tenfold deeper loathing than ever of the hideous heritage of the past—and felt for a moment as if I should like to devote my life to laying rail-roads and erecting blocks of stores on the most classic and romantic sites. The age has a long row to hoe.—Your letter was full of delightful things. I can't too heartily congratulate you on your plan of visiting. *Vous allez bien voir.* You will live to do great things yet.

Assisi. Tuesday, Dec. 28th.—Since writing the above I have been taking a deep delicious bath of mediaevalism. I left Rome this morning by the 6.40 A.M. train and under a villainous cloudy sky, and came along in a mortally slow train (all the better to see from) thro' the great romantic country which leads up to Florence. Anything *more* romantic—more deeply and darkly dyed with the picturesque and all the happy chiaroscuro of song and story, it would be impossible to conceive. Perpetual alternations of the landscape of Claude and that of Salvator Rosa—an unending repetition of old steel engravings—raised to the 100th power. Oh! *Narni*—oh! *Spoleto!* who shall describe your unutterable picturesqueness?—What words can shadow forth your happy positions aloft on sinking mountain spurs,—girt with your time-fretted crumbling bastions—incrusted with the rich deposit of history? I've seen such passages of color and composition—such bits—such effects—as can only be reproduced by a moan of joy. It's *dramatic* landscape. The towns are all built alike, perched on a mountain summit and huddled together within the dark-belted circuit of their walls. At 2.30, after a long morning of delight (despite occasional grievous showers) I arrived at this famous little spot—famous as the birthplace of St. Francis and the seat of that vast wondrous double church of which you, perhaps, remember the description in Taine. The town lies away up on the mountain and the church is built sheer upon its side. I got the one little *carriole* at the station to convey me thither, and found to my delight that I had time to see it tolerably well and get a hasty ramble through the terrific little city before dark. I have made a magnificent afternoon of it, and I am now scribbling this in the strangers' room of the *Leone d'Oro,* having just risen from an indigestibilissimo little repast.—The church is a vast and curious edifice of a great deal of beauty and even more picturesqueness—a dark cavernous solemn sanctuary below—and above it another, high, aspiring and filled with light—and with various sadly decayed frescoes of Giotto. The position is glorious. A great aerial portico winds about it and commands a tremendous view. The whole thing is intensely mediaeval, and the vocabulary of Michelet alone could furnish a proper characterization of it.[2] And if such is the church—what are the strange, tortuous, hill-scaling little streets of the city? Never have I seen the local color laid on so thick. They reek with antiquity. The whole place is like a little miniature museum of the *genre*—a condensation of the elements of mediaevalism—or the effect it produces at least, a condensation of one's impressions of them.

I am to go on this evening by the 8.30 train to Perugia. The man who brought me up has promised me to return with his vehicle and convey me down the mountain and across the plain to the station. Meanwhile however, the wind howls wofully, the storm seems to be rousing itself, and our transit may perhaps be uncomfortable. But I am bent on reaching Florence tomorrow night, and I wish to see Perugia in the morning. I am haunted with the apprehension that the host has bribed the little driver *not* to return, so that I may be kept over night.—I have vilely calumniated the establishment: the *padrona,* with the loveliest and most beaming Italian face I have ever seen, has just come in, to herald the approach of the *vetturino. Buona sera!* I shall add a word at Florence.

Florence. Jan. 1st 1870. A happy new-year! I have been here nearly three days but have been unable until now to get at my letter. I made with success the transit from Assisi to Perugia and now feel as if I had [laid] up a store of thrilling little memories which will last for many a year and witness many a recurrence of this would-be festive day. I spent at Perugia (which I found decorated with a snow-storm which would have done no discredit to the clime of obstructed horse-cars) a morning of unalloyed enjoyment. I put myself for the first time in Italy in the hands of a valet-de-place and found him a capital investment. So if there is one spot in Europe I know it's Perugia—Perugia the antique, the high-created—the

Etruscan-walled, the nobly-palaced—the deeply darkly densely curious. It's the centre of that fine old Umbrian school of art, of which Perugius and he of Urbino were the brightest efflorescence and I saw there a number of noble specimens of the former painter which almost reconciled me to his eternal monotony and insipid sweetness. What a summer could be spent in a long slow journey of long lingering days between Florence and Rome—every town stopped at—every landscape stared at—and lofty grim old Roman Cortona not whizzed by in the pitiless train near the Lake of Thrasymene barely glanced at through a gust of cinders. With these reflections and under these annoyances I arrived in Florence. But the sweetness of Florence restores me to perfect equanimity. I feel once more its delicate charm—I find it the same rounded pearl of cities—cheerful, compact, complete—full of a delicious mixture of beauty and convenience. There is for the moment at least a return of fine weather, but the cold is simply devilish. The streets, the hotels, the churches and galleries all strive to out-freeze each other. I begin to appreciate now the mildness of Rome and Naples. Yesterday, however, the sun was glorious and I got a good warming up in a sweet lone walk all beside the rapid Arno to the uttermost end of the charming Cascine, where, sheltered from the north by a magnificent wall of perpetual verdure and basking full in the long-sealed smile of the South, all happy graceful Florence was watching the old year decline into its death-shroud of yellow and pink. I have spent a long day with the Nortons who are established in a cold capacious Villa not too far from one of the city gates, to their apparent perfect contentment. They made me as welcome as ever and we talked about Rome and Naples. Charles seems sufficiently well and is working in a way it does one good to see so many-burdened a man work, on Italian history and art. The rest are excellent and pleasant, *comme toujours*. I took a turn yesterday thro' the Uffizi and the Pitti. All my old friends there stood forth and greeted me with a splendid good-grace. The lustrissimo Tiziano in especial gave me a glorious Venetian welcome. I spent half an hour too in Michel Angelo's chapel at the San Lorenzo. Great Lorenzo sits there none the less, above that weary giantess who reclines at his feet, gazing at the future with affrighted eyes and revolving the destinies of humanity. He has not yet guessed his riddle or broken his awful stillness. Such lines were never conceived in other vision as Michel Angelo has there wrung out of his marble. For the notion of real grandeur we must knock at that door.—

But I am scribbling on without remembering that before I close I must thank you for your further counsel upon what you term so happily my moving intestinal drama. I wrote you before I went to Naples that I had consulted Dr. Gould, the "popular" American physician at Rome. He recommended me a mineral water, which I tried without the least success. Meanwhile, however Dr. Duffy's pills began to resume their action and at Naples (owing I think to the concurrent influence of many oranges) became decidedly efficacious. They are slacking up once more, but I continue to take them, wear a sort [of] bandage and get along very decently. Dr. Gould recommended fluid extract of senna, of which I procured a supply but have as yet held off from going into it. I am extremely glad to hear that you tested on yourself the virtues of the sulfuric acid. It has evidently an especial application to this matter. I don't know where Dr. D. got hold of it. I mean to see him again and will ask him.—Meanwhile I am gravitating northward. You bid me not hope to escape wholly the bore of Malvern. I don't in the least. I am determined to get rid of this thing before my return home, if not without Malvern, then with it. I wish to put off my visit there till such a moment as that when I leave, the season will be advanced enough for me to remain in England without disadvantage. I shall try and hold off therefore till the 1st of March. But you will be hearing from me again before I leave Florence. I don't know that there is anything more to say upon this solemn theme.—In reading over what I have written it occurs to me that you will reproach me with brevity and paucity of *data* regarding Aunt Kate. But there is nothing very startling to communicate. The three ladies apparently found my presence a useful distraction from the unbroken scrutiny of each other's characters. I think they are a little bit tired of each other and owing partly to the presence of an insane[3] and partly to the absence of a sane, gentleman among them, have not introduced a "foreign element" into their circumstances to the degree they would have liked. Aunt Kate's energy, buoyancy,

185

and activity are magnificent. With a male companion and without a courier (a very stupefying as well as a very convenient appendage) she would have had a better chance to exercise them. Helen Rogers is very observant and very American (both for better and worse). She regrets somewhat, I fancy, the "good time" which she might have had under different circumstances. Cousin Henry seems mild and gentle and patient of her adventures rather than actively interested in them. I did what I could for them all but was very sorry I couldn't do more.—But I must bring this interminable scrawl to a close.—I am perpetually and deliciously preoccupied with home— as little as I can help to the detriment of European emotions—but to a degree which condemns me decidedly of being less in the intellect than the affections. But my intellect has a hand in it too. When you tell me of the noble working life that certain of our friends are leading in that clear American air, I hanker wofully to wind up these straggling threads of loafing and lounging and drifting and to toss my ball with the rest. But having waited so long I can wait a little longer.—I rejoice in the felicity of Minny Temple's visit— and deplore her disappointment with regard to California. But I mean to write her. The *Nation* has ceased to come to me; but I felt a most refreshing blast of paternity, the other day in reading Father's reply to a "Swedenborgian," in a number I saw at the bankers. But was there ever so cruel a father? He writes to the newspapers but not to his exiled child. I have not yet got his letter to England. I saw Ripley and Mrs. R. on my return to Rome. The former sent his love to Father: the latter looked very pretty and related an "audience" she had had of the Queen of Wurtemburg, who was living at the same hotel.—But a truce to my gossip. *Addio.* A torrent of love and longing to my parents and sister. Your brother

H.

P.S. Since T. S. Perry is so hard at work on philology, ask him the Persian for a faceless and perjured friend!—

1. HJ's father had been lending his son's travel letters to his friends.
2. Jules Michelet, the French historian, wrote in a high romantic style.
3. HJ wrote the name Henry, crossed it out, and substituted the words "an insane." The reference is to his cousin Henry, who was in the ladies' party.

To Henry James Sr.

Ms Harvard

Genoa Hotel Feder Jan. 14*th* 1870

Dearest father—

I drew from my bankers in Florence the day before I left your excellent and most welcome letter of Dec. 22d. You speak of having written me along with Mother and Willy, on the receipt of my bad news from Florence. Your letter is probably destined soon to come to hand. I imagine it to be the document I am now in treaty for with the P. O. at Naples—it having gone there after I had left the place thro' the carelessness of my Roman bankers, and various complexities since having clustered about its fate. When I next write I hope to be able to announce its arrival. Meanwhile, for the present, your last is good enough to content me—tho' it pleases you to call it a sermon. For heaven's sake don't fear to write exactly as the spirit moves you. I should be as sorry to have you delay any injunction on your natural humor as to have you not write at all. Be very sure that as I live more I care none the less for these wise human reflections of yours. I turn with great satisfaction to any profession of interest in the fate of collective humanity—turn with immense relief from this wearisome European world of idlers and starers and self-absorbed pleasure seekers. I am not prepared perhaps to measure the value of your notions with regard to the amelioration of society, but I certainly have not travelled a year in this quarter of the globe without coming to a very deep sense of the absurdly clumsy and transitory organization of the actual social body. The only respectable state of mind, indeed, is to constantly express one's perfect dissatisfaction with it—and your letter was one of the most respectable things I have seen in a long time. So don't be afraid of treating me to a little philosophy. I treat myself to lots. With your letter came two *Nations,* with your Swedenborgian letters, which I had already seen and I think mentioned. I read at the same time in an *Atlantic* borrowed from the Nortons, your article on the woman business[1]—so you see I have had quite a heavy blow of your genius. Your *Atlantic* article I decidedly liked—

I mean for matter. I am very glad to see someone not Dr. Bushnell and all that genus insist upon the distinction of sexes. As a mere piece of writing moreover I enjoyed it immensely:—I had been hoping before I left Florence to write a good long "descriptive" letter to Willy; but between my various cares it never came to the light. But it's only adjourned. Florence is the one thing I mean to talk about when I reach home. Talk alone can deal with it—talk as light and delicate and many shaded as its own inestimable genius. At present I feel as if I could hardly speak of it: all my instincts are sunk in the one dull dismal sensation of having left it—of its holding me no more. I sit here and wonder how my departure effected itself. The better man within me—the man of sympathies and ideas—soul and spirit and intellect, had certainly not the least little finger in the business. The whole affair was brutally and doggedly carried through by a certain base creature called Prudence, acting in the interest of a certain base organ which shall be nameless. The angel within me sate by with trembling fluttering wings watching these two brutes at their work. And oh! how that angel longs to spread these wings into the celestial blue of freedom and waft himself back to the city of his heart. All day yesterday, in the train as it dragged me along I could hardly believe that I was doing the hideous thing I was. Last night I spent—so to speak, in tears. Today I have been *more meo* trudging over Genoa, trying hard to make it do service, as an humble step-sister—a poor fifth cousin, of my Florence. But it's wretched work. The divine little city has no mortal relationships. She has neither father nor mother, nor brother nor child. She sits alone in the great earth with nothing but a lover—and that lover *moi!*—I was there about a fortnight—making six weeks in all. Day by day my fondness ripened into this unhappy passion. I have left my heart there and I shall be but half a man until I go back to claim it.—I should be now however in some degree a con- soled and comforted man, dear father if I could give you some sufficient statement—some faithful account, of this delightful object of my choice. But in truth no mere account of Florence—no cata- logue of her treasures or colloquy of her charms—can bring you to a knowledge of her benignant influence. It isn't this that or the other thing; her pictures, her streets or her hills—it's the lovely genius of the place—its ineffable spirit—its incalculable felicity. It's the most feminine of cities. It speaks to you with that same soft low voice which is such an excellent thing in women. Other cities beside it, are great swearing shuffling rowdies. Other cities are mere things of men and women and bricks and mortar. But Florence has an immortal soul. You look into her deep grey eyes—the Florentines have great cheap brown eyes, but the spiritual city has orbs of liquid grey—and read the history of her early sympathies and her questing youth—so studious, so sensitive, so human. Verily, of the history of Florence I as yet know the very smallest amount. I should be sorry to establish my passion on deeper foundations than really belong to it. No—Florence is friendly to all men and her beauty is equal to her wisdom. I spent a couple of days before I came away in going about to take a farewell look at the places I had more or less haunted. It was then that my heart was wrung with its deepest pain. To know all this and yet to forswear it—is there any sense in life, on such a basis? In point of fact, after all, there are very few individual objects in Florence of transcendent excellence. Michel Angelo's tombs stand first—then the Raphael's and Titian's portraits in the Uffizi and Pitti and then the Fra Angelicos at the Marco and half a dozen specimens of the early Florentine masters (Ghirlandaio, Lippo Lippi, Botticelli etc.) in various places. There is no great church; no great palace (a dozen capital *fine* ones) and save Leonardo, there was no great Florentine painter—(counting M.A. as a Roman.)—Which he wasn't!

Mentone. H. de Gde. Bretagne. Jan. 17th P.M. I stayed my hand three nights ago at Genoa—since when I haven't had time to add a word. Tonight finds me on French soil—too tired with four days' of constant exertion to hope to finish my letter; which I must keep till I get to Nice and rest my bones and my mind. But I don't want to fail to make a note of my impressions at the close of this memorable journey—the famous drive along the upper Riviera—the so-called Cornice Road. I had the good luck—the most blessed good fortune indeed I must call it—to find at Genoa a return carriage to Nice—the proprietor whereof was glad to take me at about a fourth of the rate of the regular journey—but little more than I should have had to pay for my *coupe* in the diligence. I left

Genoa yesterday morning at five A.M. by train for *Savona* (two hours) where I met my carriage, which turned out thoroughly comfortable. How can I tell you what followed? how can words express it or minds conceive it? The naked facts are that I started from Savona at eight o'clock, halted and lunched at the little sea-side village of *Loano* and slept at *Onegha*: that I started this morning again at the same hour, lunched at *San Remo* and reached Mentone this evening at five: that tomorrow finally I am to take the short remnant of the drive (four hours) to Nice. Amid all that I have seen and done and felt in Europe, this journey stands forth triumphant. I have been *too, too* happy—and at the same time too utterly miserable—the latter to think that some parent or brother or sister was not at my side to help to dispose of such overwhelming impressions. The weather has been simply perfect—which in this particular region means a good deal.

Nice, Grand Hotel. Jan. 18th. P.M. I have carried out my programme. I spent this morning at Mentone and established myself in my carriage at about one. We reached this place at five. The drive is said to be the most beautiful part of the Riviera. Beautiful indeed it is. It leaves the shore and climbs and winds aloft among the mountains, giving you on one side a succession of the grandest masses of hill-scenery, all clad in purple and spotted and streaked with broken lights—and on the other, seen thro' the open portals of shady seaward gorges, the vast blue glitter of the Mediterranean. But it lacks the lovely swarming detail—the lingering clinging *Italianism* of the earlier portions of the road. Mentone is delicious and I am *tout desolé* to find myself in this ugly pretentious sprawling Nice. I speak on the evidence of half an hour's stroll I got before dinner. Here Italy quite gives it up and Imperial France reigns supreme—France which I used to love—but somehow love no more. That passion is dead and buried.—But what *shall* I tell you of this transcendent journey? Great heavens! That while he has breath in his body and a brain in his head a man should leave that land of the immortal gods! Never never never have I got such a sense of the essential enchantment—the incomparable "distinction" of Italy. Happy, thrice happy, the man who enters the country along that road! Proportionately deep and serious the melancholy of one who leaves it. No, one has not *lived* unless one has left Italy by the Cornice, in the full mid-glow of enjoyment, in the divinest weather that ever illumined the planet!—I have been journeying, as I suppose you know, thro' a belt of eternal spring. It has been a revelation of the possible kindness of nature. And that such a power should be the power of storm and darkness and cold! The country is a land of universal olive—a foliage as gentle and tender as the feathers on the breast of a dove—of olives and lusty cacti and fierce fantastic date-palms, perfect debauches of light and heat. Two moments stand out beyond the rest in my memory of the last three days—the night I spent at Oneghi—and the two sweet morning hours I passed at San Remo, yesterday. The first had a peculiar sanctity from the fact that it was my last night on Italian soil. I still had a good long hour of day-light after arriving and well I used it to roam thro' the little sea-side town. But it was the moon-light which set its stamp on the event—the biggest brightest highest moon I ever beheld—a few pale stars looking on and the Mediterranean beneath, a sheet of murmurous silver. At San Remo, as the Italian coast draws to a close it gathers up on its lovely bosom the scattered elements of its beauty and heart-broken at ceasing to be that land of lands, it exhales towards the blind insensate heavens a rapturous smile, more poignant than any reproach. There is something hideous in having at such a place to get back into one's carriage. The color of the Mediterranean there is something unutterable—as blue as one has dreamed the skies of heaven—as one's seen the Rhone at Geneva. There, too, the last sweet remnant of the beautiful Italian race looks at you with kindly dark eyed wonder as you take your way to the stupid unlovely North. I made a hundred notes of things I wanted to describe to you but I give it all up. The details overwhelm me. I can only bid you come and see it for yourself—come and see what you feel as you drive thro' a wide low plantation of olives, with their little tender sparkling leaves all interwoven overhead into a filter of grey-green light and their little slender twisted stems and trunks forming on the grassy hill-side an upper and lower horizon, and a foot-path trodden in the grass making a vista to shew in the distance two young Italians strolling arm in arm.—I made one note, tho', which I shan't forebear to dwell upon—a note relating to the deep gratitude I feel to the beloved parents to whom I owe all the rich acquisitions of these inestimable days. My second thought is always of them. *19th.* I was so tired last night that I knocked off just after the above little spurt of filial affection. Tho' I had nominally driven from Mentone, yet so much of the way was up the mountains that I walked for miles together, to ease the horses: I was consequently a bit jaded by ten o'clock. Meanwhile however, the days are treading on each other's heels and you will have been an age without hearing from me. I don't forgive myself for not having managed to write in Florence: it was a rare occasion lost. I did however write three long letters, the two first of which you had better get hold of: one to Mr. Boott[2] (thro' Father) one to A.G. Sedgwick and one to M. Temple.—Tonight again I am rather tired and in view of this and of your probable impatience will make short work of what I have left to say. I oughtn't to abuse Nice, she has given me a charming day—charming, that is, by getting away from her. I plucked up my energies after breakfast and walked over to the beautiful little adjoining bay and town of Villefranche—where my heart beat proudly at seeing a noble American Man of War riding alone and glorious in the still blue basin of the harbor. Once at Villefranche I walked about promiscuously for hours (as I may say) among the loveliest conceivable olive-shaded paths, beside the sweet blue coves that look across the outer sea toward the bosky cliffs of Italy. I took a little carriage home, just in time for dinner. I have never seen anything so unmitigatedly innocent and sweet as all this coast region. It but—Italy's England. I mean to hang on as many days as I think I can afford to get some more walks. —Woe betide me! All this time I see I have told you nothing about Genoa. I was there but two days but I saw it tolerably well, and be-walked it, I fancy, as few mortals have ever done before. It's an extremely curious and interesting place—a sort of prosaic Naples; full moreover of a magnificent second-rate architectural picturesqueness. Lots of tremendous ornate palaces whose rusty cornices take the afternoon light, as the sun descends to the ocean, with a grand glaring melancholy. Of especial sights the one chiefly worth mentioning is the beautiful collection of paintings at the Brignole-Sale Palace: four tremendous Vandykes. I can't write of them. Before their immortal elegance I lay aside my plebeian pen. I enclose a poorish photo. of the greatest (one of the early marquises of B.S.) for Alice. It's not Rafael—it's not Titian; it's not an Italian. But it *is* Vandyke—transcendent Dutchman!—I have already hinted of my probable course on leaving this place. I shall *filer sur Paris*, stopping en route at three or four places—chiefly Avignon Arles and Nîmes and be settled in Paris by Feb. 1st.—settled for three or four weeks. To this has fizzled down my youthful dream of spending *years* in the brilliant capital! No: If I had any extra years on hand I should have given them to Florence. By the first week in March I hope to have reached Malvern. But enough of projects.—These are dreary days in respect of letters. You will have been directing I suppose to Bowles frères, as I asked you. I hope to find at least a dozen, teeming with news and health and happiness. Farewell. I read in the last *Atlantic* Lowell's poem and Howells's Article.[3] I admire them both largely—especially the latter. Tell H. I haven't been waiting for him to write, to write again myself, but simply for the convenient moment. It will soon come. *Addio.* Unsuchliche Liebe.—

Your H.

1. "Is Marriage Holy?" *Atlantic*, XXV (1870), 360–368.
2. Francis Boott (1813–1904) an old friend of the James family who spent many years in Florence where he reared his daughter Elizabeth (1846–1888).
3. Howell's article, "A Pedestrian Tour," appeared in the November 1869 issue of the *Atlantic*, pp. 591–603.

To Mrs. Henry James Sr.

Ms Harvard

London. Charing Cross Hotel.
Feb. 5. [1870]

My own dear Mother.

I despatched home a letter about a week ago which will in some degree have prepared you for this superscription of the present. I left Paris yesterday morning and after a fairly good passage of the

Channel (*via* Boulogne) (during which however I only just managed to escape the last tribulation) arrived at seven P.M. in this brilliant metropolis. I have been poking about the streets all day, doing several needful errands; I have dined in the coffee room off the inevitable *régale* of a cut of roast beef, brussel sprouts and a pint of beer, and now I find myself in the reading room, having appropriated the public blotting-book, up to my neck in British local color and hankering by the same token woefully after my dear old Yankee kith and kin. I found at my bankers just before leaving Paris a second letter apiece from Willy and you, of I forget what date—the letters are up in my room. Most joyful was I to get them. I have had since leaving Florence such a plentiful lack of society that for nearly a month I have hardly exchanged ten words with a human creature—and to get a couple of letters reminds one agreeably that I am not quite the isolated human particle that I am tempted to fancy. Your letter, dearest Mother, was most delightful—full of succulent gossip about all the *bonnes gens* in Cambridge. Willy alludes scornfully in his letter to my habitual "jaunty promises" to write to him in a day or two—so at present I'll indulge in no promises: but I'm much obliged to him for his letter and as soon as I reach Malvern I *won't* answer it. It had the inestimable merit of containing tolerably good news about his health, which has put me in so good a humor that I don't mind his incriminations. I made as you see a shorter stay in Paris than I expected; a much shorter one than I should have liked. So, when I came to prepare to go, I found that I immensely liked the old city—the new city rather. And what do I say to it now, after a day in this *beastly* London. Its darkness and grim and grime and filth and misery are doubtless overwhelming and Paris shines from afar with the lustre of the New Jerusalem. When I first arrived there, still haunted with the memory of Florence I was oppressed and irritated by its pretentious splendor and its pedantic neatness and symmetry: but gradually its immense merits began to impress me and now I have quite succumbed to it as the perfect model of a mighty capital. And the excellent little Hotel de l'Amirauté in the Rue Neuve St. Augustin (recommended me on I know not whose authority by Willy) to which I removed (economically) from the Louvre and which just as I had got to know it well and to love it, I was obliged to leave. To live at the H. de l'Amirauté, to spend the morning at the Louvre, to dine modestly (but none the less well) at some restaurant on the Boulevards and to go in the evening to the Théâtre Français—or equally good—to come back in the evening to your well appointed little room and put your feet into your slippers and touch a match to the little edifice of logs on your hearth, and in the frequent pauses of your book lend an ear to the whisper of a maternal voice in the fizzing of the burning wood—such—such are the elements of a decently happy life—a life which I glanced at and passed. I found it every day more needful that I should get to Malvern without further delay; so I broke short off and started. I left a good deal in Paris unseen and undone: but I had a very pleasant ten days—and three prime emotions. I saw Nôtre-Dame—a far finer edifice than I supposed— a most glorious one, indeed; I saw, after a fashion, the Louvre and I went (four times) to the Théâtre Français. I feel almost like ranking these three exhibitions on a line. The Louvre is even more rich and wonderful than I supposed. I should have liked to give a month to it. I should have learned *bien des choses* at the Théâtre Français. I of course had immense pleasure—a real feast of the intellect. Two nights I saw Molière done more delectablly and deliciously than words can say. You know nothing about Molière till you have seen him acted by Regnier, Got and Coquelin;[1] nor about Émile Augier till you have seen Mlle. Favart[2]—the no longer young and the never beautiful, but the supremely elegant and exquisitely dramatic Mlle. Favart.—But here I am scribbling along without coming to what I want chiefly to say. In the first of your two last letters you touch upon a theme on which I was myself just on the point of opening up—viz: my "plans" and my expenses. I have been careering along, drawing money which has seemed furnished by some mysterious magic on which I have been almost afraid to reflect—but in follow- ing the golden stream to its source I should find it flowed from the great parental lap in obedience to something of a cruel pressure. But it has been gushing forth in noble abundance and still it gushes. I have been feeling for some time that I owed you a report of the situation and here it is:—I have drawn from Barings up to the present moment £379 [$1,895] and have £621 [$3,105] left in his hands. I have been abroad eleven months and have spent (or rather have drawn, for I have £30 [$150] in my pocket 1,895$ in gold. You say that Father has sent to Barings the sum of $3,000. I don't know whether you mean in gold or in paper. In the former case, it will furnish 1110$ to carry me on into next year: in the latter it little more than covers I suppose (I don't know the actual price of gold) my expenditure for the present one. This expenditure is exclusive of what Father paid for my passage and of 10 sovereigns he gave me before I started. I may be considered therefore to have cost you in a year about 400£ [$2,000]. This is certainly a good round sum and as I consider it I feel a most palpable weight of responsibility and gratitude. I know thoroughly well at the same time that any difficulty on your own part must have melted away in your sense of the great good the money was doing. Have I on the whole spent the money not wisely but too well? I feel unable to pronounce. At moments I have seemed to myself to be spending very moderately considering always what I was doing—and at others very largely. One thing I have become sensible of—that I am not a good economist, in the proper sense of the word. I can dispense with things with comparative ease and alacrity—but I can't get them and do them cheap. I have for instance a strong sense of having gone about constantly giving excessive fees and paying extra carriage-fares. On the other hand I have frittered away no money and spent none vainly or at random. Except a few clothes and half a dozen books I have literally bought nothing. My grand abstention and the one that has told most (in favor of my purse and against my "culture"— or at least my pleasure) has been in the matter of photographs. On your arrival in Italy it very soon becomes apparent that you must take some firm ground in this respect. I immediately took that of leaving them wholly alone. If I had got any it would have been largely for the sake of the rapacious Willy and the voracious Alice— but I hereby notify them that I shall come home quite empty-handed. Two facts have conspired to increase my expenses: viz: my being unwell, and my travelling alone. A companion reduces one's expenditure by at least a third (this tells especially in carriage-hires.) My being unwell has kept me constantly from attempting in any degree to rough it. I have lived at the best hotels and done things in the most comfortable way. Ah me, stubborn fact never-theless remains that I shall have spent £400! I might have spent less. One always might have spent less. I think on the whole I may claim this:—that I have spent little more than was needful for the full and proper fruition of my enterprise. To have kept myself on a materially narrower financial basis would have been to lay up a store of bitter memories and regrets for the future—memories of a stingy timid spirit, lagging behind their great opportunities. As it is, (believe it as you can) I have a certain number of such ignoble memories. There are certain glorious extra-mural drives at Rome in regard to which when in future I hear folks descant upon them I must silently hang my head. The more fool you, you'll say, to have spent so much and have got so little. But really I have got a great deal. Wait till I get home and you behold the glittering treasures of my conversation—my fund of anecdote—my brilliant descriptive powers. I assure you, I'll keep the table in a roar. Your guests will forget to eat—and thus you'll get back your money.—To say nothing of my making your universal fortunes by the great impetus with which I shall have been launched into literature. Consider therefore what you know me to have done and what you believe me to have gained and try to think that my return will not be altogether that of the prodigal—altho' perhaps not quite either that of the prodigy.—As for my plans I shall wait to hear what you think of the situation before I indulge in any: wait also until I see what Malvern does for me. Unless I get thoroughly started towards a cure I frankly confess that I shall be in no state to form any project—save that of immediate return to America—where at least I shall not be on the footing of striving towards a gain—a gain of enjoyment, I mean—which is perpetually defeated. If Malvern fails to do for me what I hope I shall therefore turn my face homeward. But my hopes are strong. They are perhaps in some degree a simple "sentiment"—but senti-ments propel one forward and give one a grip of a chance. If Malvern does for me I shall stay there eight or ten weeks. This will cost money. I shall be living there at an expense of about 4£ per week. If at the end of my stay I am veritably better I shall be able to discuss my subsequent movements. Even in that case I fancy I shall still be inclined to go home in the autumn. If I do spend a second winter abroad I think I shall renounce the idea of going to Germany. I declared to myself when I was last in Florence that in case of my being in Europe next winter, there and there only should I spend it. But next autumn is six months away and when these have elapsed I can't but think I shall feel it best to return home and leave a residence in Italy to some future day and some new basis. You will as soon as possible let me know what money you shall be able with *perfect comfort*, to let me have and I will shape my programme accordingly. One thing I beg you to believe, that no disappointment worth taking account of is possible to me. I have now been abroad a good round year and have had a most magnificent holiday and if you should be obliged to bid me desist immediately I should feel as if I had at least bitten the fruit to the core if not wholly devoured it. If I remain abroad the coming summer I should like to spend a month or six weeks of it in Switzerland. I had little idea six months ago that I should really care to go back there: but I now feel strongly that if I go home in the Autumn a few weeks walking in the Alps would be a valuable preparation for getting at some sort of work on my return. On economical grounds (even allowing for the journey) to go to Switzerland would be decidedly less expensive than to stay here. But let me without reserve and without passion reveal to you my utmost lurking thought. To go to Switzerland means in this brief synopsis more than it seems to mean. Say I fix my return for the 20th October. If I leave Malvern towards the middle of April I shall have between then and July 1st some ten weeks to dispose of in England. If I travel a little I shall have small difficulty in disposing of them happily. I should like to go to Switzerland via Paris and Geneva—there being several things on the road and within a day's excursion from Paris which I had hoped recently to see but was obliged to pass by—i.e. notably the cathedrals of Amiens, Abbeville, Rheims, Chartres and Sens. Once in Switzerland I should make no bones of walking over to the Italian lakes. Now Milan is but an hour by rail from the town of Como and Venice but a

September morning's journey from Milan. Oh blissful vision—to spend another week at Venice—a well man instead of the poor disease-haunted being that I was last autumn! From Verona (an hour this side of Venice,) a railway crosses the Brenner pass into Southern Germany—thro' which via Augsburg Nuremberg etc, one may make a very pretty journey to the Rhineland and thence to Holland and Belgium and thence down to Brest in time to take the French steamer for New York. *Ma foi*, I like this scheme! It has a certain breadth and nobleness which pleases me! On the ground that the past year has cost me 400£, the ensuing six months including return so spent would cost me £200. *Allons:* the really economical way of spending my time would be to remain in England as quietly as possible to July 1st. To repair then to Switzerland for two months. To spend September in Paris and sail from Brest October 1st. Consult above all things your first own necessities and conveniences. I know they must drain you most heavily. Say but the word and I'll sail for home the next day. This is not bravado but truth. Otherwise name the sum you can allow me and I'll try and get the utmost out of it. The summer is the summer wherever I spend it and that is the great thing.—But I have written a tremendous letter. Farewell, without more words. I shall duly report from Malvern. Tell Father that last letter of his persists in not turning up. Between Naples, Rome and Florence heaven knows what has become of it—I was so stupid in my last as *not* to tell you to direct to *Dr. Rayner Great Malvern.* I have been hoping you will have done so. Farewell. Tell Father to send me all his magazineisms. No end of things to everyone —and of kisses to Alice and you.

H. James jr.

P.S. The figure above of the sum in Baring's hands is: *£621.*
P.P.S. By talking about money in B's hands I simply allude to the nominal figure of my original credit viz: £1000—purely nominal as of course I know. If father has sent him $300 in gold he holds £200 to my credit—the sum which, used properly, would enable me to carry out the programme sketched above.

1. Francois Joseph Regnier (1807–1885); Francois Jules Edmond Got (1822–1901); Benoit-Constant Coquelin (1841–1909). The latter had been a

school friend ot HJ's during the James family's sojourn at Boulogne-sur-mer in 1857.

2. Guillaume Victor Emile Augier (1820–1889), French playwright; Marie Favart (1833–1908), stage name for Pierette Ignace Pingaud. HJ calls her "no longer young"—she was actually thirty-seven when James saw her during this visit: From this period at the Théâtre Français HJ dated his fascination with the formal French theater. See *The Scenic Art*, ed. Wade, (1947).

To William James

Ms Harvard

Great Malvern, Sunday—February 13, [1870]

Beloved Brother—

I have before me two letters from you—one of Dec. 27th of that dead and gone old year which will have been so heavily weighted a one in my mortal career (to say nothing of yours)—the other of the 19th January in this lusty young '70. They were both received in Paris in those all too rich and rapid days that I tarried there on that memorable—that tragical pilgrimage from Florence—from Naples, I may say—across the breadth of Europe to the actual British Malvern. A week ago I wrote to Mother from London and on the following day, Monday last, came up to this place. Here I am, then, up to my neck in cold water and the old scenes and sensations of ten months ago. It's a horrible afternoon—a piercing blast, a driving snow storm and my spirits *à l'avenant*. I have had a cheery British fire made up in my dingy British bedroom and have thus sate me down to this ghastly mockery of a fraternal talk. My heart reverts across the awful leagues of wintry ocean to that blessed library in Quincy Street, and to the image of the gathering dusk, the assembled family, the possible guest, the impending—oh! the impending—American *tea!* In fine, if I wanted I could be as homesick as you please. All the conditions are present: *rien n'y manque*. But I'll steep myself in action lest I perish with despair. I'll drive the heavy-footed pen and brush away the importunate tear.—Your last letter was a real blessing and a most indispensable supplement to the previous one. It contained, in your statement of your slowly dawning capacity for increased action, just the news that I had been expecting

—that I had counted on as on the rising of tomorrow's sun. I have no doubt whatever that you have really entered upon the "second stage". You'll find it a happier one than the first. Perhaps when I get home, six months hence (heaven forbid that at the present moment I should entertain any other hypothesis) I shall be able gently to usher you into the third and ultimate period of the malady. It does me good to think of you no longer leading that dreary lonely prison life. Before long I hope to hear of your trying Dr. Butler. I can assure you, it will be a great day when, having lifted, you find you're no worse, and then, having lifted again, you find you are visibly better. This experience sets the seal, in the very sanctity of truth, to your still timid and shrinking assumption that you *can* afford—that you must attempt, to indulge in action: and I almost think (as I look back hence to those blessed two months that I practised it) that the trouble is almost worth having for the joy of hugging to your heart that deep and solid conviction which you wring from those iron weights. Yet, just as I did, possibly you may find that having brought you to a certain point the lifting will take you no further. What I gained I gained in two months. But the gain was immense. God speed you! I see you booked indelibly for the ringing grooves of change.—I believe that I haven't written to you since my last days in Rome, and any reflections on my subsequent adventures will have reached you thro' father, mother and Alice. Nevertheless I have had many a fancy and feeling in the course of that extraordinary achievement—the deliberate, cold-blooded, conscious turning of my back on Italy—the gradual fatal relentless progression from Florence to Malvern—many a keen emotion and many a deep impression which I should have been glad to submit to your genial appreciation. Altogether, it has been a rather serious matter. I mean simply that you feel the interest of Italy with redoubled force when you begin to turn away from it and seek for the rare and beautiful in other lands. Brave old bonny England of ten short months ago—where are you now? Where are the old thrills of fancy—the old heart-beats, the loving lingering gaze—the charm, the fever, the desire of those innocent days? Oh but I'll find them again. They lie nestling away with the blossom of the hedges

—they sit waiting in the lap of the longer twilights, and they'll burst forth once more in the green explosion of April. This I firmly count upon. Meanwhile I sit shuddering up to my chin in a "running sitz" and think of the olive groves at San Remo—of the view of Florence from San Miniato—of the Nortons at the Villa d'Elsi—of Aunt Kate looking across the Neapolitan bay to Capri. I got a letter from her yesterday. I haven't read it properly—I'm afraid to. I only know that it tells of a drive to Sorrento—of a drive [to] Baise—of a projected day at Perugia on the way to Florence. When Aunt Kate gets back make much of her! She's not the common clay you parted with. She has trod the perfumed meadows of Elysium—she has tasted of the magic of the south and listened to the echoes of the past!—I was very much disappointed in not being able to write to you at Florence, about which I fancied I had a good deal to say. Perhaps, however, this was an illusion, and that of definite statements I should not have found many rise to my pen. One definite statement, however, I do feel warranted in making, namely, that I became interested in the place and attached to it to a degree that makes me feel that it has really entered into my life and is destined to operate there as a motive, a prompter, an inspirer of some sort.—By which I suppose I mean nothing more pregnant or sapient than that one of these days I shall be very glad to return there and spend a couple of years. I doubt that I shall ever undertake— shall ever care—to study Italian art—Italian history—for themselves or with a view to discoveries or contributions—or otherwise than as an irradiating focus of light on some other matters. *Ecco!* that I hope is sapient enough for one sitting!—I hope you managed to wring from my torpid pages some living hint of the luminous warmth and glory of my two days at Genoa and the following three days' journey to Nice. These latter were not surpassed by anything in my whole Italian record; for beside their own essential divineness of beauty and purity they borrowed a fine spiritual glow from the needful heroics of the occasion. They're a precious possession of memory, at all events and even Malvern douches can't wash them out. At Nice the charm of that happy journey began to fade: at Marseilles I found it dead in my bosom—dead of cold and inanition.

I tried to stop and do a little sight-seeing in the South of France: but between being half paralysed by the *mistral* and half-sickened by the base insufficiency of the spectacle I was glad enough to push rapidly on to Paris.

At first glance I found Paris strangely hollow and vulgar; but after the lapse of a few days, as soon as I had placed myself on a clean fresh basis I began to enjoy it—to admire it—and lo! before I left, to esteem it. I should be sorry to think that for a little paltry prettiness that confounded Italy had left me with a warped and shrunken mind. Let us be just to all men! (I'm coming to England presently.) From Nice to Boulogne I was deeply struck with the magnificent order and method and decency and prosperity of France—with the felicity of *manner* in all things—the completeness of form. There was a certain *table d'hôte* breakfast at Dijon where the whole cargo of the express train piled out and fed leisurely, comfortably, to perfection, *qui en disait* on the subject more than I can repeat. And the excellence of the little hotel de l'Amirauté where I spent a week—and the universal merit and sagacity of the cookery—and above all the splendors of arrangement—quite apart from the spendors of material—in the Louvre! The latter by the way are wondrous—a glorious synthesis of Italy. Altogether, as I say, I enjoyed Paris deeply. Beautiful weather came to my aid. A fortnight ago this afternoon—amazing thought!—I climbed the towers of Notre Dame. She is really great. Great too is the Théâtre Français where I saw Molière and Émile Augier most rarely played. *En voilà, de l'Art!* We talk about it and write about it and criticize and dogmatize and analyse to the end of time: but those brave players stand forth and exemplify it and act—create—produce—! It's a most quickening and health giving spectacle!—with a strange expression of simplicity and breadth and dignity which I wouldn't have gone there to find. I also went to the Palais Royal to see a famous four act Farce of the latest fashion: but I confess seeing Got as Sganarelle had spoiled me for it. Molière is every inch as droll and so much more beside! I saw little else. I needn't tell you how one feels and leaving Paris half-seen, half-felt, you have only to remember how you left it a year and a half ago. I have now been some ten days in England. In one of your last letters you very wisely assure me that England, like every other place, would seem very flat on a second visit. For this contingency I made the most ample and providential preparation, and in this way I have eluded serious disappointments. But on the whole I don't much pretend or expect now, at best, to be ravished and charmed. I've been to my rope's length and had my great sensations. In spite of decidedly unpropitious circumstances I find I like England still, and I expect her (if I get better) to yield me many an hour of profit and many a visible delight. I have come upon very fierce hard weather and of course I feel it keenly for this plunge into cold water. We have had a week of grim winter that would do honor to Boston. I find this house all that I remember it—most comfortable—most admirably and irreproachably conducted. There are some eighteen persons here at present—from whom however (without misanthropy) I expect little and gain less—such a group of worthy, second-rate Britons as invests with new meaning and illuminates with a supernatural glow—the term common-place. But as if we Americans were any better! I can't affirm it to my knowledge! I find in Malvern itself even at this dark season, all the promise of that beauty which delighted me last spring. The winter indeed here strips the landscape far less than with us or in the south. Literally (save for the orange trees) the country hereabouts looks less naked and out of season than that about Naples. The fields are all vivid with their rain-deepened green,—the hedges all dark and dense and damp with immediate possibilities of verdure,—the trees so multitudinously twigged that as they rise against the watery sky a field's length away, you can fancy them touched with early leafage. And ah! that watery sky—greatest of England's glories!—so high and vast and various, so many-lighted and many-shadowed, so full of poetry and motion and of a strange affinity with the swarming detail of scenery beneath! Indeed what I have most enjoyed in England since my return—what has most struck me—is the light—or rather, if you please, the darkness: that of Du Maurier's drawings. Elsewhere 'tis but a garish world. If I can only get started to feeling better (of which I have good hopes) I shall get my fill of old England yet. I have had a long walk every day of the past week. The *detail* of the scenery is the great point. Beside it even Italy is vague and general. I walked this morning six miles—half of them in the teeth of the snow sharpened blast—down this Newlands to Maddersfield Court —a most delightful old curated manor-house, the seat of Earl Beauchamp. In spite of the snow it was still gentle England. English mutton was grazing in the lee of the hedges and English smoke rolling from the chimneys in low-latticed, steep-thatched cottages. *À propos* of mutton I wish I could enclose herewith one of those unutterable joints which daily figure on our board. You don't *eat* it—you devoutly ecstatically appropriate it: you put a bit into your mouth and for the moment *il n'y a que ça*. It beats the beef. The beef varies—it has degrees, but the mutton is absolute, infallible, impeccable. With plenty of mutton and a good many walks and a few books I hope to thrive and prosper. I am able thus to walk and read much more than when I was here before and I am quite amused at having then objected to the place on the ground of its giving you so much up-hill. I shall probably do no very serious reading, but I hope at least to win back the habit. I received your *Atlantic* with Lowell's poem, which I enjoyed largely, tho' it seems to me to be lacking in the real poetic element through excess of cleverness—the old story. I enjoyed unmitigatedly Howells' little paper. I have enjoyed all his things more even since being abroad than at home. They are really American. I'm glad you've been liking Hawthorne. But I mean to write as good a novel one of these days (perhaps) as the House of the Seven Gables.

Monday, 14th. With the above thrilling prophecy I last night laid down my pen. I see nothing left but to close my letter. When I began I had a vague intention of treating you to a grand summing up on the subject of Italy. But it won't be summed up, happily for you. I'm much obliged to you for your regret that I didn't achieve any notes for the *Nation*. I have a vague dream, if I get started towards a cure, of attempting a few retrospective ones here. Oh, no words can tell of the delicious romantic look it now suits my Italian journey to put on!—I have my heart constantly burdened with messages to all my friends at home which I never manage to discharge. Keep me in the memories of my brothers. Give my love to T. S. Perry to whom I have the best will to write. I wrote lately to A. G. Sedgwick. Tell me anything that comes up about J. La Farge and O. W. Holmes. I am in daily hope of a letter from Howells. Aunt Kate mentions that Mrs. Post has asked Minny to go abroad with her. Is it even so? But I must be getting up a "pre-action" for that d–d running sitz. I calculate while here to walk from eight to ten—or from ten to twelve miles daily. Farewell. Think of me as most comfortable hopeful and happy. I *may* not write for a fortnight, until I have some results to announce. But I'll not promise silence. Farewell. Love to all. Yours most fraternally,

H. James, Jr.

P.S. An Anecdote. You spoke recently of having read with pleasure Lecky's *History of Morals*. I found at Florence that for a fortnight at Rome I had been sitting at breakfast opposite or next to the elegant author. We never spoke. He is very young and lanky and blond and soft-looking—but most pleasant of face: with quite the look of a better-class Cambridge divinity student. I have been sorry ever since that I never addressed him: but he always came in to his breakfast about as I was finishing—*à propos*—one of these days I'll tell you my little tale of "The Little Frenchman of Padua"—just such a one as F. J. Child likes to tell.

1. W. E. H. Lecky (1838–1903); his *History of European Morals from Augustus to Charlemagne* had recently been published.
2. Francis James Child (1825–1896), professor of English at Harvard and collector and editor of *English and Scottish Popular Ballads* (1883–1898).

To William James

Ms Harvard

Great Malvern
March 8*th* '70

Beloved Bill—

You ask me in your last letter so "cordially" to write home every week, if it's only a line, that altho' I have very little to say on this windy Sunday March afternoon, I can't resist the homeward tendency of my thoughts. I wrote to Alice some eight days ago—raving largely about the beauty of Malvern, in the absence of a better theme: so I haven't even that topic to make talk of. But as I say, my thoughts are facing squarely homeward and that is enough. The fact that I have been here a month today, I am sorry to say, doesn't even furnish me with a bundle of important tidings. My stay as yet is attended with very slight results—powerful testimony to the obstinacy of my case. Nevertheless I have most unmistakeably made a beginning—or at least the beginning of one and in this matter it is chiefly a *premier pas qui coût*. On the whole I am not disappointed. When I think of from what a distance I have to return. It is unfortunate here that the monotony and gross plainess of the diet (mutton, potatoes and bread being its chief elements) are rather calculated in this particular trouble to combat the effect of the baths. Ye powers immortal! How I do find myself longing for a great succulent swash of American vegetables—for tomatoes and apples and Indian meal! The narrowness of English diet is something absolutely ludicrous. Breakfast cold mutton (or chop) toast and tea: dinner leg or shoulder, potatoes and rice pudding; tea cold mutton again (or chop) toast and tea. I sometimes think that I shall never get well until I get a chance for a year at a pure vegetable diet—at unlimited tomatoes and beans and peas and squash and turnips and carrots and corn—I enjoy merely writing the words. I have a deep delicious dream of someday uniting such a regimen with a daily ride on horseback—walking having proved inefficient. So you see I have something ahead of me to live for. But I have something better too than these vain impalpable dreams—the firm resolve to recover on my present basis—to fight it out on this line if it takes all summer—etc! It would be too absurd not to! A fortnight hence I count upon being able to give you some definite good news—to which period let us relegate the further discussion of the topic. It constantly becomes more patent to me that the better I get of this—the more I shall be able to read—up to a certain point. During the past month I have been tasting lightly of the pleasure—reading among other things Browning's Ring and Book,[1] in honor of Italy, the President de Brosse's delightful letters,[2]

Crabbe Robinson's memoirs[3] and the new vol. of Ste Beuve. Browning decidedly gains in interest tho' he loses in a certain mystery and (so to speak) infinitude, after a visit to Italy. C. Robinson is disappointing I think—from the thinness of his individuality, the superficial character of his perception and his lack of descriptive power. One of your letters contains something to make me think you have been reading him. I have quite given up the idea of making a few retrospective sketches of Italy. To begin with I shall not be well enough (I foresee) while here; and in the second place I had far rather let Italy slumber in my mind untouched as a perpetual capital, whereof for my literary needs I shall draw simply the income—let it lie warm and nutritive at the base of my mind, manuring and enriching its roots. I remember by the way that you recently expressed the confident belief that I had made a series of notes for my own use. I am sorry to say that I did nothing of the sort. Mere bald indications (in this I was very wrong) seem to me useless, and for copious memoranda I was always too tired. I expect however to find that I have appropriated a good deal from mere "soaking": i.e. often when I *might* have been scribbling in my room I was still sauntering and re-sauntering and looking and "assimilating." —But now that I am in England you'd rather have me talk of the present than of pluperfect Italy. But life furnishes so few incidents here that I cudgel my brain in vain. Plenty of gentle emotions from the scenery etc: but only man is vile. Among my fellow-patients here I find no intellectual companionship. Never from a single English man of them all have I heard the first word of appreciation or enjoyment of the things here that I find delightful. To a certain extent this is natural: but not to the extent to which they carry it. As for the women I give 'em up: in advance. I am tired of their plainness and stiffness and tastelessness—their dowdy beads, their dirty collars and their linsey woolsey trains. Nay, this is peevish and brutal. Personally (with all their faults) they are well enough. I revolt from their dreary deathly want of—what shall I call it?—Clover Hooper[4] has it—intellectual grace—Minny Temple[5] has it—moral spontaneity. They live wholly in the realm of the cut and dried. "Have you ever been to Florence?" "Oh yes." "Isn't it a most peculiarly interesting city?" "Oh yes, I think it's so very nice." "Have you read *Romola?*" "Oh yes." "I suppose you admire it." "Oh yes I think it's so very clever." The English have such a mortal mistrust of anything like criticism or "keen analysis" (which they seem to regard as a kind of maudlin foreign flummery) that I rarely remember to have heard on English lips any other intellectual verdict (no matter under what provocation) than this broad synthesis—"So immensely clever." What exasperates you is not that they can't say more, but that they wouldn't if they could. Ah, but they are a great people, for all that. Nevertheless I should vastly enjoy half an hour's talk with an "intelligent American." I find myself reflecting with peculiar complacency on American women. When I think of their frequent beauty and grace and elegance and alertness, their cleverness and self assistance (if it be simply in the matter of toilet) and compare them with English girls, living up to their necks among comforts and influences and advantages which have no place with us, my bosom swells with affection and pride. Look at my lovely friend Mrs. Winslow. To find in England such beauty, such delicacy, such exquisite taste, such graceful ease and laxity and freedom, you would have to look among the duchesses —*et encore!*, judging from their photos. in the shop windows. Not that Mrs. Winslow hasn't her little vulgarities, but taking one thing with another they are so far more innocent than those of common English women. But it's a graceless task, abusing women of any clime or country. I can't help it tho', if American women have something which gives them a lift!—Since my return here there is one thing that I have often wished for strongly—i.e. that poor John La Farge were with me sharing my enjoyment of this English scenery—enjoying it that is, on his own hook, with an intensity beside which I suppose, mine would be feeble indeed. I never catch one of the perpetual magical little "effects" of my walks without adverting to him. I feel sorry at moments that a couple of months ago I didn't write to him proposing a rendezvous at Malvern, March 1st, where he could stay and be doctored too, and whence we might subsequently roam deliciously forth in search of the picturesque. If I were at all sure of my condition a couple of months hence and of the manner I shall spend the spring and summer I would write to him and ask him if it is at all in his power to take a three or four months holiday. We might spend it together and return together in the Autumn. I feel sure that as a painter he would enjoy England most intensely. You may be a little surprised at my thus embracing for a whole summer the prospect of his undivided society. But for one thing I feel as if I could endure his peculiarities much better now than formerly; and then I feel too as if in any further travelling I may do here—I should find it a great gain to have a really good companion: and for observation what better companion than he? The lack of such a companion was in Italy a serious loss. I shall not write to him (if at all) with any such idea until I see myself fairly on the way to be better; but meanwhile, you, if you see him, might make some tentative enquiry and transmit me the result. I have no doubt that he would vastly like the scheme; but little hope of his finding it practicable. —Of Wendell Holmes I get very much less news than I should like to have. I heard recently from Arthur Sedgwick who mentioned his being appointed at Harvard College instructor in Constitutional Law. This has a very big sound; but I never doubted of his having big destinies.—Do speak of him in your next. Nor of Gray[6] do I hear anything. Do you often see him and how does he wear? I am very nervous about a letter from Howells which Mother some months ago mentioned his being on the point of sending. It hasn't yet turned up and I am utterly sickened at the idea of its being lost. Do ascertain from him whether it was ever sent. His letters are really things of value and I should find it a great feast to get one. Heaven speed it and guard it!—I received a few days since thro' Father a letter from Bob: very pleasant but with a strangely quaint and formal tone about it. But I was very glad to hear from him. It fills me with wonder and sadness that he should be off in that Western desolation while I am revelling in England and Italy. I should like extremely to get a line out of Wilky: but fate seems adverse. I very much wish by the way, that someone would let me know *who and what* is William Robeson, his partner. I simply know that he is not Andrew R. A propos of the family property, you've bought the house—an event I don't quarrel with. Since I began my letter the afternoon has waned into dusk and by my firelight and candles Cambridge looks like the sweetest place on earth. And it's a good old house too and I'm not ashamed of it. This reminds me of what you said in your last about getting photos, and books. I sometime since sent home a statement of my complete non-purchase of the former, save four very handsome statues I got for Alice in Rome which Aunt Kate will bring her, viz. the great Augustus, the boy Augustus, the Demosthenes and the so called "Genius of the Vatican" (Praxitiles). As soon as I arrived in Italy I saw that I must either buy more than I believed I had means for or leave them quite alone. The mere going into shops to buy an occasional one would have been fatal: besides you can't carry a few; if you get many, you provide a particular receptacle. Oh then! The delicious things I left unbought. If I return to the Continent I will do what I can to repair discreetly my abstinence. I very much regret now that I didn't immediately demand of Father and Mother a commission of purchase. But I seem condemned to do things in a small way. I am sure that as notes for future reference photos. are unapproached and indispensable.—As for books you rather amuse me by your assumption that in Italy I went in for a certain number of *vellum bindings*. Not for one. To get books seemed to me at that stage of my adventures to needlessly multiply my cares: and I felt like waiting till I had read a few of the vast accumulation on my hands before swelling the number. I shall probably pick up a few before going home; I fancy not many. If you want any particular ones you'll of course let me know. A very good way to get books in England—modern ones—is to buy them off Mudies' Surplus Catalogue—frequently great bargains.—But I must put an end to my stupid letter. I have been shut up all day and the greater part of yesterday with a bad sore throat and feel rather muddled and stultified. In a couple of days or so I hope again to be hearing from home. I look very soon for a letter from you correcting that last account of your relapse. I re-echo with all my heart your impatience for the moment of our meeting again. I should despair of ever making you know how your conversation *m'a manqué* or how when rejoined, I shall enjoy it. All I ask for is that I may spend the interval to the best advantage—and you too. The more we shall have to say to each other the better. Your last letter spoke of Father and Mother having "shocking colds." I hope they have melted away. Among the things I have recently read is Father's *Marriage* paper in the *Atlantic*—with great enjoyment of its manner and approval of its matter. I see he is becoming one of our prominent magazinists. He will send me the thing from *Old and New*. A young Scotchman here gets the *Nation*, sent him by his brother from New York. Whose are the three female papers on Woman? They are "so very clever." *À propos*—I retract all those brutalities about the Englanderinnen. They are the mellow mothers and daughters of a mighty race.—I expect daily a letter from Aunt Kate announcing her arrival in Paris. She has been having the inappreciable sorrow of a rainy fortnight in Florence. I hope very much to hear tho' that she has had a journey along the Riviera divinely fair enough to make up for it. But I must pull in. I have still lots of unsatisfied curiosity and unexpressed affection, but they must stand over. I never hear anything about the Tweedies. Give them my love when you see them. T. S. Perry I suppose grows in wisdom and virtue. Tell him I would give a great deal for a humorous line from him. Farewell. Salute my parents and sister and believe me your brother of brothers

H. James jr.

1. *The Ring and the Book* had been published during the preceding year.
2. Charles de Brosses (1709–1777), a magistrate of the *parlement* of Burgundy whose *Lettres familières écrites d'Italie en 1739 et 1740* remained permanently in HJ's library.
3. Henry Crabbe Robinson (1775–1867), journalist, barrister, friend of many literary personalities, whose diaries had just been published.
4. Marion (Clover) Hooper (1843–1883), later Mrs. Henry Adams.
5. Minny Temple, HJ's cousin, died on the day this was written.
6. John Chipman Gray (1839–1915), friend of Minny Temple, later professor of law at Harvard.

To Henry James Sr.

Ms Harvard

Malvern March 19*th* '70.
Saturday.

Dear father—

I received yesterday with immense satisfaction your letter of March 3d and by its 2 weeks journey was made to feel very near you. To get letters at this place is the only comfort—or at least the only solid delight—in life. I think you would be what the English call extremely "diverted" to see how I handle yours—how I hoard and treasure them and flatten them out into the entertainment of two or three days. Shortly before, I had got Mother's of Feb. 25th—and together with it a long one from Aunt Kate, from Paris, describing her journey from Geneva: so you see I had an ample feast of the affections—to say nothing of the intellect. I have written you so often since my arrival here that I feel as if I have nothing left to talk about and I take up my pen merely to thank you for your letter and to enjoy the sensation of looking homeward. To Willy I wrote, stupidly enough, only a week ago; and as neither of these last letters contain any particular news of him I am keenly impatient to hear from him. If good wishes could help me to a recovery I ought to be wafted on the breath of yours straight to a *terra firma* of everlasting health. Out of much tribulation I fancy it finally will come. I am pursuing my "cure" here with unfailing energy and unabated hope. I have taken a start, I think, and whatever I gain, I shall keep. I was glad to receive from Mother an acknowledgement of my financial statement of six weeks ago. Your view of the future is one in which I gladly coincide. I had already quite renounced the project of travelling in England—travelling that is in a regular way. One or two bits of the country I still cherish the hope of seeing on foot. I have now been here nearly six weeks, and expect to remain a month longer, when I mean to go up to London and meet Aunt Kate. A fortnight in London—a couple of days at Oxford on my way thither—and a little pedestrian turn in Devonshire and round the Isle of Wight:

this is the amount of what I should like to accomplish. I shall then depart for the Continent—*i.e.* for Switzerland *via* Paris. Everything however will depend upon my condition at the end of my ten weeks here; so it's useless at present to worry you with details.— I was of course deeply interested in your news about poor Minny. It is a wondrous thing to think of the possible extinction of that immense little spirit.[1] But what a wretched business too that her nerves should be trifled with by the false information of unwise physicians. Mother says that she asks for letters—which I'm glad to know of. Writing a dozen pages is easy term for lightening such a miserable sorrow. But something tells me that there is somehow too much Minny to disappear for some time yet—more life than she has yet lived out. At any rate I mean to write her immediately.— Your letter was full of things that I don't know how to answer —beginning with your ingenious excuse for not having written before. Your letter however was worthy of your silence. You hit it perhaps more happily than you fancied when you speak of *dull Albion.* Dull indeed it is beside that bright immortal Italy. I feel at moments as if it were only now that I am beginning to enjoy my Italian journey. My memory, at any rate, is a storehouse of treasures. I keenly envy Alice and Willy—happy mortals!—not having been to Italy. To think of having it all before one—of knowing for the first time that first month on Italian soil! I wish very much I could exorcise this Italian ghost that haunts me. If I were feeling in better order physically I would sit me down and never rest from scribbling until I had written the life out of him. It may be that in reality I never shall see Italy again: it may be that if I do see it, half its glory will have faded: but I feel just now as if I should be greatly disappointed if my recent visit shall have turned out to be anything less than a beginning, a "reconnaissance" of the ground. Your little sketch of home affairs went to my heart. I feel a little less mean and shabby in thinking that Mother and Alice and Willy have been tasting of aesthetic joys in Fechter's[2] acting. I had an immense revelation of the power of good acting at the Théâtre Français. The French are certainly a great people. So long as the Théâtre Français subsists on its present basis—there will be overwhelming testimony of this. I was deeply moved, too, by your mention of your glorious wintery weather—such weather as Europe knows not. But now that the spring is coming, this grey-green old England reminds us from time to time that she has a small reserve of beautiful days. On the whole, since coming to Malvern, I have been very happy in the absence of rain, which would have made a dismal thing of life. The absence of rain however is rather a negative merit: but half a dozen times the day has plucked up a spirit and burst out in positive exquisite beauty—a beauty tempered and chastened by the memory of former gloom and by the foresight of gloom to come—but wonderfully delicate and perfect. The English skies still remain my especial admiration—the more so that from these hillsides we have a capital stand-point for watching them. When the immense misty plain of hedges-checkered Worcestershire lies steeped in the beautiful verdurous shades which seem to rise as an emanation from its meadows and farm-steads and parks, and the sky expands above it, tremendous and Turneresque, a chaos of rolling grey—a rain of silver, a heaven of tender distant blue—there is something to my eyes in a sight so wonderfully characteristic and national so eloquent of the English spirit and the English past that I half expect to hear from a thousand throats a murmur of sympathy and delight. But as a general thing all the people I see here are utterly indifferent or densely insensible to the beauty of their country. When I'm fairly at home again I expect to enjoy a pleasure I have never known before—to speak of—that of long walks in the country; but I'm sorely afraid that these long walks on English highways and lanes will have wrought such work on my taste that the fairest American scenery will seem wofully tame and cold. The other afternoon I trudged over to Worcester—thro' a region so thick-sown with good old English 'effects'—with elm-scattered meadows and sheep-cropped commons and the ivy-smothered dwellings of small gentility, and high-gabled, heavy-timbered, broken-plastered farm-houses, and stiles leading to delicious meadow footpaths and lodge-gates leading to far-off manors—with all things suggestive of the opening chapters of half-remembered novels, devoured in infancy—that I felt as if I were pressing all England to my soul. As I neared the good old town I saw the great Cathedral tower, high and square, rise far

215

into the cloud-dappled blue. And as I came nearer still I stopped on the bridge and viewed the great ecclesiastical pile cast downward into the yellow Severn. And going further yet I entered the town and lounged about the close and gazed my fill at that most soul-soothing sight—the waning afternoon, far aloft on the broad perpendicular field of the Cathedral spire—tasted too, as deeply, of the peculiar stillness and repose of the close—saw a ruddy English lad come out and lock the door of the old foundation school which marries its heavy Gothic walls to the basement of the Church, and carry the vast big key into one of the still canonical houses—and stood wondering as to the effect of a man's mind of having in one's boyhood haunted the Cathedral shade as a King's scholar and yet kept ruddy with much cricket in misty meadows by the Severn. —This is a sample of the meditations suggested in my daily walks. Envy me—if you can without hating! I wish I could describe them all—Colwell Green especially, where, weather favoring, I expect to drag myself this afternoon—where each square yard of ground lies verdantly brimming with the deepest British picturesque, and half begging, half deprecating a sketch. You should see how a certain stile-broken footpath here winds through the meadows to a little grey rook-haunted church. Another region fertile in walks is the great line of hills. Half an hour's climb will bring you to the top of the Beacon—the highest of the range—and here is a breezy world of bounding turf with twenty counties at your feet—and when the mist is thick something immensely English in the situation (as if you were wandering on some mighty seaward cliffs or downs, haunted by vague traditions of an early battle). You may wander for hours—delighting in the great green landscape as it responds forever to the cloudy movements of heaven—scaring the sheep—wishing horribly that your mother and sister were—I can't say *mounted*—on a couple of little white-aproned donkeys, climbing comfortably at your side.—But at this rate I shall tire you out with my walks as effectually as I sometimes tire myself. The feast of roast mutton approaches. The mutton is good, but where are those rarer delights of my native larder?—The amber-tinted surface of the scalloped oysters—the crimson dye of the tomatoes—the golden lustre of the Indian pudding—the deep dark manes of the charlotte of apple and of peach?—You say that you have been having all winter "plenty of society"—delightful fact! Keep at it—the more the better. You have my complete adherence, by the way, to the purchase of the house. It seemed to have proved itself a residence appointed of heaven and I will do what I can in the way of getting photos; to contribute to its adornment. I could have done this better at Venice, Florence and Rome than elsewhere—but I didn't feel as if I could afford to: and I can still do well. I take great pleasure in all mention of home people and things. How is J. T. Fields? Do you see anything of Longfellow and Lowell? Do you go to the Club?[3]—Have you begun to agitate the summer question again? Write me of all your debates and hopes and fears. I have lately received three *Nations,* for which thanks. The notice of your *Marriage* paper[4] seemed to me rather flippant. I heard some time since that the great Drouet[5] had left the *Nation* and come to Cambridge; but I still detect his hand. Have you got him among you? —But the roast mutton impends: Farewell.—I have written a very dull letter—the less excuseable as before beginning I fancied myself full of material. If I knew just a little more about the English I wouldn't hesitate to offer my "views" on British character. They're a doggedly conservative lot. You come bump up against it, in what you have innocently fancied to be friendly sympathetic discourse, as against a Chinese Wall of cotton-bales. But their virtues are of goodly use to the world. Kiss Mother for her letter—and for that villainous cold. I enfold you all in an immense embrace.

Your faithful son
H.

P.S. You all attack me about Dr. Gully. I wish that, if you have any special facts about him, you had communicated them. I didn't go to him because what I had learned about his place deterred me. He has little or nothing to do with it the thing being in the hands of another man.[6] When I was here before he was wintering in Italy. Some time since I went to see him, for an opinion, but he was absent for the whole spring. He has but a few people—only men. The other day a gentleman left his place to come here, he being the only patient. This seemed too lonely and gloomy.—By the way, you had better address your next letter to *Barings* again. I will give you any ensuing permanent address.[7]

1. Minny Temple, suffering from tuberculosis, had been warned that her illness might prove fatal.

2. Charles Albert Fechter (1824–1879), "realistic" actor, who was playing Hugo's *Ruy Blas*.

3. The Saturday Club of Boston, founded in 1855, a dining club whose members included the city's intellectual elite.

4. The elder HJ had published an article "The Woman Thou Gavest Me" in the January 1870 *Atlantic,* which the *Nation* criticized for its idealism.

5. The "great" is a euphemism; Drouet was a minor member of the *Nation* staff.

6. James Manby Gully (1808–1883), British specialist in hydropathy, had increasingly turned over the direction of his establishment to others.

7. The bottom of the letter has been cut off, either by an autograph collector or perhaps HJ's executor who on occasion destroyed passages in which family ailments were described.

To Mrs. Henry James Sr.

Ms Harvard

Great Malvern, March 26, 1870.

Dearest Mother,

I received this morning your letter with father's note, telling me of Minny's death—news more strong and painful that I can find words to express. Your last mention of her condition had been very far from preparing me for this. The event suggests such a host of thoughts—that it seems vain to attempt to utter them. You can imagine all I feel. Minny seemed such a breathing immortal reality that the mere statement of her death conveys little meaning; really to comprehend it I must wait—we must all wait—till time brings with it the poignant sense of loss and irremediable absence. I have been spending the morning letting the awakened swarm of old recollections and associations flow into my mind—almost *enjoying* the exquisite pain they provoke. Wherever I turn in all the recent years of my life I find Minny somehow present, directly or indirectly—and with all that wonderful ethereal brightness of presence which was so peculiarly her own. And now to sit down to the idea of her *death!* As much as a human creature may, I fancy, she will survive in the unspeakably tender memory of her friends. No attitude of the heart seems tender and generous enough not to do her some unwilling hurt—now that she has melted away into such a dimmer image of sweetness and weakness! Oh dearest Mother! oh poor struggling suffering *dying* creature! But who complains that she's gone or would have her back to die more painfully? She certainly never seemed to have come into this world for her own happiness—as that of others—or as anything but as a sort of divine reminder and quickness—a transcendent protest against our acquiescence in its grossness. To have known her is certainly an immense gain, but who would have wished her to live longer on such a footing—unless he had felt within him (what I felt little enough!) some irresistible mission to reconcile her to a world to which she was essentially hostile. There is absolute balm in the thought of poor Minny and *rest*—rest and immortal absence!

But viewed in a simple human light, by the eager spirit that insists upon its own—her death is full of overflowing sadness. It comes home to me with irresistible power, the sense of how much I knew her and how much I loved her. As I look back upon the past, from the time I was old enough to feel and perceive, her friendship seems literally to fill it—with proportions magnified doubtless by the mist of tears. I am very glad to have seen so little of her suffering and decline—but nevertheless every word in which you allude to the pleasantness of that last visit has a kind of heartbreaking force. "Dear bright little Minny" as you most happily say: what an impulse one feels to sum up her rich little life in some simple compound of tenderness and awe. Time for you at home will have begun to melt away the hardness of the thought of her being in future a simple memory of the mind—a mere pulsation of the heart: to me as yet it seems perfectly inadmissible. I wish I were at home to hear and talk about her: I feel immensely curious for all the small facts and details of her last week. Write me any gossip that comes to your head. By the time it reaches me it will be very cheerful reading. Try and remember anything she may have said and done. I have been raking up all my recent memories of her

Minny Temple

and her rare personality seems to shine out with absolute defiant reality. Immortal peace to her memory! I think of her gladly as unchained from suffering and embalmed forever in all our hearts and lives. Twenty years hence what a pure eloquent vision she will be.

But I revert in spite of myself to the hard truth that she is *dead*—silent—absent forever—she the very heroine of our common scene. If you remember any talk of hers about me—any kind of reference or message—pray let me know of it. I wish very much father were able to write me a little more in detail concerning the funeral and anything he heard there. I feel absolutely *vulgarly* eager for any fact whatever. Dear bright little Minny—God bless you dear Mother, for the words. What a pregnant reference in future years—what a secret from those who never knew her! In her last letter to me she spoke of having had a very good photograph taken, which she would send. It has never come. Can you get one—or if you have only the house copy can you have it repeated or copied? I should very much like to have it—for the day when to think of her will be nothing but pure blessedness. Pray, as far as possible, attend to this. Farewell. I am melted down to such an ocean of love that you may be sure you all come in for your share.

Evening. I have had a long walk this afternoon and feel already strangely familiar with the idea of Minny's death. But I can't help wishing that I had been in closer relation with her during her last hours—and find a solid comfort at all events in thinking of that long never-to-be-answered letter I wrote to her from Florence. If ever my good genius prompted me, it was then. It is no surprise to me to find that I felt for her an affection as deep as the foundations of my being, for I always knew it; but I now become sensible how her image, softened and sweetened by suffering and sitting patient and yet expectant, so far away from the great world with which so many of her old dreams and impulses were associated, has operated in my mind as a gentle incentive to action and enterprise. There have been so many things I have thought of telling her, so many stories by which I had a fancy to make up her lack to her,—

as if she were going to linger on as a graceful invalid to listen to my stories! It was only the other day, however, that I dreamed of meeting her somewhere this summer with Mrs. Post. Poor Minny! how much she was not to see! It's hard to believe that she is not seeing greater things now. On the dramatic fitness—as one may call it—of her early death it seems almost idle to dwell. No one who ever knew her can have failed to look at her future as a sadly insoluble problem—and we almost all had imagination enough to say, to murmur at least, that life—poor narrow life—contained no place for her. How all her conduct and character seem to have pointed to this conclusion—how profoundly inconsequential, in her history, continued life would have been! Every happy pleasant hour in all the long course of our friendship seems to return to me, vivid and eloquent with the light of the present. I think of Newport as with its air vocal with her accents, alive with her movements. But I have written quite enough—more than I expected. I couldn't help thinking this afternoon how strange it is for me to be pondering her death in the midst of this vast indifferent England which she fancied she would have liked. Perhaps! There was no answering in the cold bright landscape for the loss of her liking. Let me think that her eyes are resting on greener pastures than even England's. But how much—how long—we have got to live without her! It's no more than a just penalty to pay, though, for the privilege of having been young with her. It will count in old age, when we live more than now, in reflection, to have had such a figure in our youth.

But I must say farewell. Let me beg you once more to send me any possible talk of reminiscences—no matter how commonplace. I only want to make up for not having seen her—I resent their having buried her in New Rochelle. She ought to be among her own people.[1] Good night. My letter doesn't read over-wise, but I have written off my unreason. You promise me soon a letter from Alice— the sooner the better. Willy I trust will also be writing. Good night, dearest Mother,

Your loving son,
H. James

Write me who was at the funeral and I shall write next from here
—then possibly from London.

1. Minny Temple was ultimately buried in Albany Rural Cemetery near
her parents.

To William James

Ms Harvard

Great Malvern, March 29, 1870

Dear Willy—

My mind is so full of poor Minny's death that altho' I immediately
wrote in answer to mother's letter, I find it easier to take up my pen
again than to leave it alone. A few short hours have amply sufficed to
more than reconcile me to the event and to make it seem the most
natural—the happiest, fact, almost in her whole career. So it seems, at
least, on reflection: to the eye of feeling there is something immensely moving in the sudden and complete extinction of a vitality
so exquisite and so apparently infinite as Minny's. But what most
occupies me, as it will have done all of you at home, is the thought
of how her whole life seemed to tend and hasten, visibly, audibly,
sensibly, to this consummation. Her character may be almost literally
said to have been without practical application to life. She seems a
sort of experiment of nature—an attempt, a specimen or example—a
mere subject without an object. She was at any rate the helpless
victim and toy of her own intelligence—so that there is positive
relief in thinking of her being removed from her own heroic
treatment and placed in kinder hands. What a vast amount of truth
appears now in all the common-places that she used to provoke—
that she was restless—that she was helpless—that she was unpractical.
How far she may have been considered up to the time of her illness
to have achieved a tolerable happiness, I don't know: hardly at all,
I should say, for her happiness like her unhappiness remained wholly
incomplete: but what strikes me above all is how great and rare a
benefit her life has been to those with whom she was associated. I
feel as if a very fair portion of my sense of the reach and quality

223

and capacity of human nature rested upon my experience of her character: certainly a large portion of my admiration of it. She was a case of pure generosity—she had more even than she ever had use for—inasmuch as she could hardly have suffered at the hands of others nearly as keenly as she did at her own. Upon her limitations, now, it seems idle to dwell; the list of her virtues is so much longer than her life. My own personal relations with her were always of the happiest. Every one was supposed I believe to be more or less in love with her: others may answer for themselves: I never was, and yet I had the great satisfaction that I enjoyed *pleasing* her almost as much as if I had been. I cared more to please her perhaps than she ever cared to be pleased. Looking back upon the past half-dozen years, it seems as if she *represented,* in a manner, in my life several of the elements or phases of life at large—her own sex, to begin with, but even more *Youth*, with which owing to my invalidism,[1] I always felt in rather indirect relation.

Poor Minny—what a cold thankless part it seems for her to have played—an actor and setter-forth of things in which she had so little permanent interest! Among the sad reflections that her death provokes for me, there is none sadder than this view of the gradual change and reversal of our relations: I slowly crawling from weakness and inaction and suffering into strength and health and hope: she sinking out of brightness and youth into decline and death. It's almost as if she had passed away—as far as I am concerned—from having served her purpose, that of standing well within the world, inviting and inviting me onward by all the bright intensity of her example. She never knew how sick and disordered a creature I was and I always felt that she knew me at my worst. I always looked forward with a certain eagerness to the day when I should have regained my natural lead, and one friendship on my part at least might become more active and masculine. This I have especially felt during the powerful experience of the past year. In a measure I had worked away from the old ground of my relations with her, without having quite taken possession of the new: but I had it constantly in my eyes. But here I am, plucking all the sweetest fruits of this Europe which was a dream among her many dreams—

William James at twenty-one

while she has "gone abroad" in another sense! Every thought of her is a singular mixture of pleasure and pain. The thought of what either she has lost or won, comes to one as if only to enforce the idea of *her* gain in eternal freedom and rest and ours in the sense of it. Freedom and rest! one must have known poor Minny to feel their value—to know what they may contain—if one can measure, that is, the balm by the ache. I have been hearing all my life of the sense of loss which death leaves behind it—now for the first time I have a chance to learn what it amounts to. The whole past—all times and places—seems full of her. Newport especially—to my mind—she seems the very genius of the place. I could shed tears of joy far more copious than any tears of sorrow when I think of her feverish earthly lot exchanged for this serene promotion into pure fellowship with our memories, thoughts and fancies. I had imagined many a happy talk with her in years to come—many a cunning device for cheering and consoling her illness—many a feast on the ripened fruits of our friendship: but this on the whole surpasses anything I had conceived. You will all have felt by this time the novel delight of thinking of Minny without the lurking impulse of fond regret and uneasy conjecture so familiar to the minds of her friends. She has gone where there is neither marrying nor giving in marriage! no illusions and no disillusions—no sleepless nights and no ebbing strength. The more I think of her the more perfectly satisfied I am to have her translated from this changing realm of fact to the steady realm of thought. There she may bloom into a beauty more radiant than our dull eyes will avail to contemplate.

My first feeling was an immense regret that I had been separated from her last days by so great a distance of time and space; but this has been of brief duration. I'm really not sorry not to have seen her materially changed and thoroughly thankful to have been spared the sight of her suffering. Of this you must all have had a keen realization. There is nevertheless something so appealing in the pathos of her final weakness and decline that my heart keeps returning again and again to the scene, regardless of its pain. When I went to bid Minny farewell at Pelham before I sailed, I asked her about her sleep. "Sleep," she said, "Oh, I don't sleep. *I've given it up.*"

And I well remember the laugh with which she made this sad attempt at humor. And so she went on, sleeping less and less, waking wider and wider, until she awaked absolutely!

I asked mother to tell me what she could about her last weeks and to repeat me any of her talk or any chance incidents, no matter how trivial. This is a request easier to make than to comply with, and really to talk about Minny we must wait till we meet. But I *should* like one of her last photos, if you can get one. You will have felt for yourself I suppose how little is the utmost one can *do*, in a positive sense, as regards her memory. Her presence was so much, so intent—so strenuous—so full of human exaction: her absence is so modest, content with so little. A little decent passionless grief—a little rummage in our little store of wisdom—a sigh of relief—and we begin to live for ourselves again. If we can imagine the departed spirit cognizant of our action in the matter, we may suppose it much better pleased by our perfect acceptance of the void it has left than by our quarreling with it and wishing it filled up again. What once was life is always life, in one form or another, and speaking simply of this world I feel as if in effect and influence Minny had lost very little by her change of state. She lives as a steady unfaltering luminary in the mind rather than as a flickering wasting earth-stifled lamp. Among all my thoughts and conceptions I am sure I shall never have one of greater sereneness and purity: her image will preside in my intellect, in fact, as a sort of measure and standard of brightness and repose.

But I have scribbled enough. While I sit spinning my sentences she is *dead*: and I suppose it is partly to defend myself from too direct a sense of her death that I indulge in this fruitless attempt to transmute it from a hard fact into a soft idea. Time, of course, will bring almost even-handedly the inevitable pain and the inexorable cure. I am willing to leave life to answer for life; but meanwhile, thinking how small at greatest is our change as compared with her change and how vast an apathy goes to our little measure of sympathy, I take a certain satisfaction in having simply written twelve pages.—

I have been reading over the three or four letters I have got from her since I have been abroad: they are full of herself—or at least of a fraction of herself: they would say little to strangers.[2] Poor living Minny! No letters would hold you. It's the *living* ones that die; the writing ones that survive.

One thought there is that moves me much—that I should be here delving into this alien England in which it was one of her fancies that she had a kind of property. It was not, I think, one of the happiest. Every time that I have been out during the last three days, the aspect of things has perpetually seemed to enforce her image by simple contrast and difference. The landscape assents stolidly enough to her death: it would have ministered but scantily to her life. She was a breathing protest against English grossness, English compromises and conventions—a plant of pure American growth. None the less tho' I had a dream of telling her of England and of her immensely enjoying my stories. But it's only a half change: instead of my discoursing to her, I shall have her forever talking to me. Amen, Amen to all she may say! Farewell to all that she was! How much this was, and how sweet it was! How it comes back to one, the charm and essential grace of her early years. We shall all have known something! How it teaches, absolutely, tenderness and wonder to the mind. But it's all locked away, incorruptibly, within the crystal walls of the past. And there is my youth—and anything of yours you please and welcome! turning to gold in her bright keeping. In exchange, for you, dearest Minny, we'll all keep your future. Don't fancy that your task is done. Twenty years hence we shall be loving with your love and longing with your eagerness and suffering with your patience.

30th P.M. So much I wrote last evening: but it has left me little to add, incomplete as it is. In fact it is too soon to talk of Minny's death or to pretend to feel it. This I shall not do till I get home. Every now and then the thought of it stops me short, but it's from the life of home that I shall really miss her. With this European world of associations and art and studies, she has nothing to do: she belongs to the deep domestic moral affectional realm. I can't put away the thought that just as I am beginning life, she has ended it. But her rare death is an answer to all the regrets it provokes. You remember how largely she dealt in the future—how she considered and planned and arranged. Now it's to haunt and trouble her no longer. She has her present and future in one.

To you, I suppose, her death must have been an unmitigated relief—you must have suffered keenly from the knowledge of her sufferings. Thank heaven they lasted no longer. When I first heard of her death I could think only of them: now I can't think of them even when I try.

I have not heard from you for a long time: I am impatiently expecting a letter from you. With this long effusion you will all have been getting of late an ample share *de mes nouvelles*. From Alice too I daily expect to hear. Yesterday came to me a very welcome and pleasantly turned note from Mr. Boott.—I hope I haven't hitherto expressed myself in a way to leave room for excursive disappointment when I say that after now nearly eight weeks of this place, I have made materially less progress than I hoped. I shall be here about ten days longer. In town I shall immediately go to see a couple of as good and *special* physicians as I can hear of. Unhappily my sources of knowledge are few.[3]

1. "Invalidism" is perhaps too strong a word to describe HJ's recurrent back-ache, the result of a strain suffered while serving as a volunteer fireman in Newport, or the constipation which troubled him during these early years. There is abundant evidence that HJ thought himself in his youth more sickly than he was—much of his illness was a state of melancholy induced by the war. He himself describes in *Notes of a Son and Brother* how quickly he revived when the war was ended (Chap. IX) and thereafter he led a strenuous life of travel and work for many years until beset by the infirmities of old age.
2. These letters survived HJ's burning of his personal papers late in life.
3. The remainder of this letter is missing.

To Grace Norton

Ms Harvard

Malvern April 1st 1870

Dear Grace—

If I possessed in anything like such perfection as yourself the noble art of *printing*, I would assure you forthwith, in the very largest and fairest capitals, that I received no longer than an hour ago, with "unfeigned delight," your good gracious graphic letter of—a certain "Monday evening." I say a truce to all incriminations and explanations. What matters a wave more or less in the ocean?—A letter more or less in the fathomless floods of affection and sympathy which discharge their equal tides on English and Italian shores? In the letter, as in the spirit, let me believe that we are "square." Let me nonetheless thank you for this last note with as much *effusion* as if it were a fruit of pure generosity (which indeed, I strongly suspect.) And no remote response to any appealing utterance of mine.—Inexpressibly sweet it is to hear from you and Florence—from Florence in you. How shall I tell you what a strange look of contradictory nearness and distance overlies all that you remind me of? so near is it all in time—so incalculably remote in character from the medium in which I here live and move. I could treat you to five pages of the flattest platitudes about Italy as she dwells in my mind *entre coeur et jardin*—between memory and hope. But with the infinite reality before you what need have you for the poor literary counterfeit? "Oh how the March-sun feels like May!"—exquisite truth! And what does the April sun feel like? and what do the April hills look like? And what does the lengthening April twilight put into one's heart—down in the city piazzas, in front of the churches? For all your mention of your various household facts I am duly grateful—tho' hardly for the facts themselves. I sincerely hope that by this time the colds have melted away before the breath of the older and kindlier spring— the real Florentine season. Of Charles's and Susan's projected visit to Rome I am delighted to hear. If Rome will only do a little in the way of health-giving to Charles I will freely forgive it all its sins and follies. For Susan—she can dispense with even the most pious adjurations—and going to Rome for the first time can easily snap a scornful finger and thumb at poor me who have in the vague future but the prospect of a poor second.—But in what utterly ungracious and unlikely attitudes am I thus fantastically treating Susan? Since I have done her a wrong, let me profit by it to do her the right (the fullest I know) of begging of her a favour—that once in a while—at St. Peter's—at the Vatican, in the Coliseum, in the Campagna—out of a dozen long glances that she takes for herself and you in Florence, she will take one short one for me in England; and that into a hundred deep thoughts which she bestows upon the ancient Romans, she will insinuate one little heart-beat of regret that a luckless modern American was able to see only half as much *de tout cela* as he wanted.—Of immediately personal news I have none to give you; save that in repeating to you the tidings which I had a week ago from home, I shall tell you of what has been for me a great personal sorrow. You will possibly have learned them by your own Cambridge letter. My cousin Minny Temple died most suddenly some three weeks ago. I am not sure that you ever knew her well enough to understand how great a sense of loss this fact brings with it to those who really knew her—as *I* did. I knew her well and her friendship had always been for me one of the happiest certainties of the future. So much for *certainties!* But already, after the lapse of a week, I am strangely—most serenely—familiar with the idea of her death. The more I think of it, the more what there is to accept—almost with thanks—gains upon and effaces what there is to deplore and quarrel with. She is one about whom there would be much to say—much which I know, as the lapse of time tends to clarify and simplify, as it were, her memory, will seem to me so much more and more that one of these days I shall surely say to you a large part of it. She was a divinely restless spirit —essentially one of the "irreconcilables;" and if she had lived to great age, I think it would have been as the victim and plaything of her constant generous dreams and dissatisfactions. During the last year moreover it had become obvious that her life would be one of immense suffering—suffering far harder to think of than (to me at least) even the death which has cut short the sweetness of her youth. A fortnight before she died she had her lungs examined by some great New York authority, who told her point blank that she had less than two years to live. From this moment she sank. Other physicians offered her far more cheerful hopes and her family (on the testimony of Dr. Metcalf) had made up their minds that she would even recover. But she had never been afraid of the truth: and it seemed as if she had no care to accept the respite which had been granted her in charity. She died apparently from simple exhaustion. Her memory will be full of interest and delight to all her friends. I feel not only much the wiser for having known her, but—I find—really the happier for knowing her at absolute peace and rest. Her life was a strenuous, almost passionate *question,* which *my* mind, at least, lacked the energy to offer the elements of an answer for. It would be really a great spirit that should contain a power to affirm and illumine and satisfy, equal to her exquisite energy of wonder, conjecture and unrest.—Her peculiar personal charm and grace you will doubtless remember. This had never been greater, I am told, during the year before her death. She was to have come abroad this next summer—but one little dream the more in a life which was so eminently a life of the spirit—one satisfied curiosity the less in a career so essentially incomplete on its positive side—these seem to make her image only more eloquent and vivid and purely youthful and appealing. She had a great fancy for knowing England.—Meanwhile here I sit stupidly scanning it with these dull human eyes!—But in speaking of her one must return to what one begins with—her rare simple superficial charm of physiognomy and presence. Amen! Her absence, too, has its sweetness.—But I am scribbling all this my dear Grace, in a wretchedly cold room—made tolerable only by the thought that I am writing to a very warm heart.—For the moment farewell. I can talk of *moments*: I feel as if I were going to write so soon again. I am full of wonder and sympathy and interest in all your coming days of spring and summer. It's a great boon to my imagination to have you there on duty for me in Italy. To Baron Mackay, if he comes, you might venture, tentatively, to present my warm regards. To your mother—abruptly, recklessly—my love. The same to Susan, Charles and Jane—as opportunity—of time and humour, seems to favor. To Jane I will write *not*—when inclined—which she is not to confound with "when *not* inclined." Happy Spain-faring Sara! *Addio.* Get well of everything—save a lingering kindness for

Yours most faithfully
H. James jr.

Address me next please to *Barings*. I shall be in London 10 days hence. "The rest is *silence*."

232

To Grace Norton

Ms Harvard

London Bath Hotel
Piccadilly
April 28*th* [1870]

Dear Grace—

I have time only for a single word—a sad sad word: farewell. I received your blessed birth-day letter. Many many thanks. I have been a week in London; I sail on Saturday April 30th in the *Scotia*. Many reasons combine. I'm not altogether well—that's one: and hope to mend rapidly at home—that's another. But I have no heart to dilate on it. It's a good deal like dying. Farewell, beloved survivors. My heart's affection to one and all. I shall write you dear Grace, in some calmer transatlantic hour. Meanwhile this kind office with Sara. Thank her warmly for a certain note she lately sent me; assure her it was deeply appreciated and beg her to wait for a Cambridge answer. I trust she is really enjoying Spain. Have Charles and Susan come back? But I can't ask Italian questions. I can only think of you dear Grace mournfully, joyfully and in all friendship and shake your hand all across Europe. Say for me the very tenderest things to your mother and to Jane and to Charles and Susan if they are there. All health and peace! Kiss the children. On the whole I am very well disposed toward going—!

Yours ever—more than ever
H. James jr.

P.S. I am to have on the *Scotia* the excellent company and kindness of my Aunt.

4
A Season in Cambridge

1870–1872

4
A Season in Cambridge

In later years Henry James would say that his return to Cambridge in 1870 was a kind of death: he had to be reborn again. He had had his year of wayfaring, his *wanderjahr*, and discovered that he could be a comfortable and self-reliant traveler; and he had glimpsed his future—the sustenance that Europe offered his art. But in "our dear detestable common Cambridge" he had to suffer the painful nostalgia and malaise which is described in a memorable passage in one of his prefaces—the preface in which he discusses the writing of "A Passionate Pilgrim"—and images Europe as having inflicted a fatal wound, not mortal by any means, but one which gave him a permanent ache, as if the head of an arrow or a bullet were buried within his flesh. The ache was simply a continuing melancholy, a sense of estrangement, a sense too of participation in the trans-Atlantic world he had absorbed so intensely during his twelvemonth abroad.

We depend for our principal record of this period on a small sheaf of letters, those written to the members of the Norton family, who had remained abroad, and with whom James had visited the studios and literary homes of London. The other record is written into his story of the passionate pilgrim, who makes his way to England in quest of his past, and feels as if he is a "claimant," that the land and its culture belongs to him. It was the one tale of this time that James reprinted in his Definitive Edition. For a young writer as fastidious and complex—and as ruminative—as Henry James, he found in America a dearth of the history, manners, rituals, customs, which made the art of the novel rich in "documentation." But if James went through a depression which we can read, in his wistful letters to Grace Norton, he did not divorce himself from reality. He traveled to Saratoga and to various historical places in

Vermont and wrote sketches for the *Nation*; he kept at his writing of tales and he began a novel. There is a refreshing candor as he gossips about his Cambridge life—"Mr. J. T. Fields lectured here on *Cheerfulness* lately (as who should say 'I know I'm a humbug and a fount of depression but grin and bear it,') and Mr. Longfellow feasted him afterwards at supper . . . Lowell seems to write nothing. I believe he is given over to the study of Low French—I use the term in a historic and not a moral sense."

His tales continued to appear. To Charles Eliot Norton he announced, "To write a series of good little tales I deem ample work for a life-time." The modesty was simulated. He had larger plans. And his short novel, *Watch and Ward*, about a Boston bachelor and his ward, was also written during these months of "exile." Before the end of two years Europe once again became a possibility. The rescue occurred at a crucial moment, when he was ready to seek— and to find—new opportunities for his career.

To Grace Norton

Ms Harvard

Cambridge May 20*th* 1870

My dear Grace.

Nothing more was needed to make me feel utterly at home— utterly *revenu* and awake from my dream again—than to get your letter of May 2d. Hearty thanks for it! Here I am—here I have been for the last ten days—the last ten years. It's very hot! the window is open before me: opposite thro' the thin trees I see the scarlet walls of the president's *palazzo*.[1] Beyond, the noble grey mass—the lovely outlines, of the library: and above this the soaring *campanile* of the wooden church on the *piazza*. In the distance I hear the carpenters hammering at the great edifice in process of erection in the college yard—and in sweet accordance the tinkle of the horse-cars. Oh how the May-wind feels like August. But never mind: I am to go into town this P.M. and I shall get a charming breeze in the cars crossing the bridge.—Nay, *do* excuse me: I should be sorry wilfully to make you homesick. I could find in my heart to dwell considerately only on the drawbacks of Cambridge life: but really I know of none: or at least I have only to look at that light elegant *campanile*—that simple devout Gothic of the library—or indeed at that dear quaint old fence of wood, of stone (which is it most?) before the houses opposite—to melt away in ecstasy and rapture.—My voyage I am happy to say, was as prosperous as if I had received your good wishes at its beginning instead of its close. We made it in nine days and a half, without storms or serious discomforts. I will agree with you in any abuse of the cabins and state-rooms of the Scotia: but the deck is excellent and there I chiefly spent my time. I find all things here prosperous, apparently, and all people decently happy. My own family may be well reported of. My sister is in strength and activity quite an altered person and my brother inspires me with confident hopes. My parents are particularly well. I lately spent an evening in Kirkland Street where of course I found many questions to answer; and boasted hugely of all your favors. Miss Theodora[2] is a most delightful young lady: I say it because I don't believe you adequately know it. Arthur I have seen several times: we enjoy very much reminding each other of you. The Gurneys too I have seen and the Howells—all very well. Howells is lecturing very pleasantly on Italian literature. I go to the lecture room in Boylston hall; and sit with my eyes closed, listening to the sweet Italian names and allusions and trying to fancy that the window behind me opens out into Florence. But Florence is within and not without. When I'm hopeful of seeing Florence again not ten years hence—that *is* Florence!—all that you tell me is delightful. I can fancy what a game Florence and May are playing between them. Poor May just here has rather an irresponsible playmate. But when May is a month older she will amuse herself alone.—I congratulate you on Charles and Susan having returned from Rome. When I think that in this latter season they have made that journey thro' the very vitals of Italy, I feel almost as if it were a merry world. Indeed when I hear that you really think of summering (not simmering) in Venice, I pronounce it altogether a mad world —using the term in no invidious sense. Thrice happy thought! I

239

could say horrible things—invent the fiercest calumnies, about Siena, to drive you to Venice. If you write to me not from Venice—I shall—I shall almost delay to answer your letter. Siena would be all very well if you had never thought of Venice—but having done this I don't see how you can escape going there. There are things the immortal gods don't forgive. Beware them.—I wish I were able to tell you where I am going to outlast the genial season—or what, now that I have got America again, I am going to do with it. Like it enormously *sans doute*: they say there is nothing like beginning with a little aversion. My only fear is that mine is too old to end in a grand passion. But America is American: that is incontestable, and consistency is a jewel. I wish I could tell you how characteristic every thing strikes me as being—everything from the vast white distant sky—to the stiff sparse individual blades of grass.

22d. A.M. I went yesterday to lunch at Shady Hill.[3] Don't think me very cruel when I tell you how lovely it was—in the very sweetest mood of the year—the fullness of the foliage just all but complete and the freshness of the verdure all undimmed. The grass was all golden with buttercups—the trees all silver with apple blossoms, the sky a glorious storm of light, the air a perfect hurricane of zephyrs. We sat (Miss C. Hooper, Miss Boott[4] &c) on a verandah a long time immensely enjoying the fun. But oh my dear Grace it was ghostly. For me the breeze was heavy with whispering spirits. Down in that glade to the right three women were wading thro' the long grass and a child picking the buttercups. One of them was you, the others Jane and Susan—the child Eliot. Mesdemoiselles Hooper and Boott talked of Boston, I thought of Florence. I wanted to go down to you in the glade and we should play it was the Villa Landor. Susan would enact Miss Landor. But the genius of my beloved country—in the person of Miss Hooper—detained me. I don't know indeed whether I most wanted you to be there or to be myself in Florence. Or rather I do very well know and I am quite ashamed of my fancy of robbing that delightful scene of its simple American beauty. I wished you all there for an hour, enjoying your own.—But my intended note is turning into a very poor letter. One of these days I shall intend a letter.—I ought to tell you by the way, that my having taken a turn for the worse in England, was

240

partly concerned in my return home. I was wise in doing as I did apparently: for I am already vastly better. At all events, economy had begun to make my return necessary. I don't feel very much further from you here than I was in England. I may safely assume —mayn't I?—that you are to be abroad two or three years yet. Largely within that time we shall meet again. When I next go to Italy it will be not for months but years. These are harmless visions, but I utter them only to you.—Wherever you go this summer, remember that—*I* care most about hearing the whole story. This is not modest, but I maintain it. Live, look, enjoy, write a little for me. Tell all your companions how fondly I esteem them. I implore your mother to exert her maternal authority in favor of Venice. I perceived no bad smells there: and as for mosquitoes, I imagine that a private house properly furnished with curtains needn't in the least fear them. Howells tells me *they* never suffered. Wherever you go, however, I shall be happy in your contentment and shall believe you blessed with peace and prosperity. Farewell. Love to one and all. Believe me dear Grace your's most faithfully

Henry James jr.

I don't ask about Sara because I have just written to her and have hopes of an answer if she has time before her return.

1. The residence of President Eliot of Harvard was located opposite the home of the Jameses.
2. Maria Theodora Sedgwick (1851–1916).
3. Shady Hill, the Phillips-Ware-Norton house, northwest of the Harvard Yard, accessible from Irving Street, had been the home of Andrews Norton, father of C. E. Norton.
4. Elizabeth, daughter of Francis Boott, then visiting Cambridge from her home in Florence.

To J. T. Fields

Ts Harvard

Cambridge, Sept. 24th [1870?]

My dear Mr. Fields:[1]

The *Atlantic* was so good, a couple of months ago, as to accept the m.s. of a story from my pen. May I take the liberty of suggesting through you, that Messrs. F. and F. should send me a cheque in payment at their earliest convenience, instead of awaiting the publication of the story?—I should be much obliged to you for your intercession.—

Yours very truly
H. James Jr.

1. James Thomas Fields (1817–1881) was editor of the *Atlantic Monthly* from 1861 to 1871.

To Grace Norton

Ms Harvard

Cambridge September 26<i>th</i> [1870]

My dear Grace—

I have before me two letters: your long and most delectable one of last June and eighteen pages of an answer written to it a few weeks later at Saratoga. Nay, I have three—Jane's being the third, received just after I had written the pages above mentioned. Why I never finished these pages I am quite unable to say—nor exactly why I am unwilling to send them now. In truth, they are pervaded by an unutterable staleness. I speak of them because I want you to know that I haven't been quite so silent as you think. It is many many weeks since I got your letter; but not too long ago yet for me to recall, my dear Grace, the deep delightful pleasure it gave me. I have vaguely felt, I think, that to such an utterance neither my nature nor my circumstances could furnish an adequate or pertinent answer. You put me in possession, thus, at the beginning of the summer, of a picture, which thro' much of its fierce discomfort and barren *ennui*, remains suspended in the line of my bitterly yearning vision, to cool my fever and illuminate my mind. Now that I have really and vitally *used* your letter, I can formally reply to it. I wrote to you from Saratoga[1] where I spent a month, taking the waters, but somehow I felt that Saratoga had no vocation to commune with Sienna, and I left my letter unfinished. While I was in this state of mind came Jane's benignant missive—all the perfumes of whose Araby couldn't make me feel near to you. But now I am back in Cambridge—our dear detestable common Cambridge and I have seen Sara arrive from the Villa Spanocchi and Theodora depart into it—and I have grown able a little to believe that I may pitch my voice to your Italianized ear.—Yes I have seen Sara and I have bidden God-speed to her sister. I spent with Sara a week ago a goodly private afternoon, discoursing of the priceless possessions of memory. She seems to me as well and prosperous as you would like to have her, and kindly disposed to the mysteries of re-initiation here. May they be gentle to her—even as they have been to me!—She brought with her a number of Siennese photos, which I have literally devoured. My brother says that to him, for several days, they have been as meat and drink. Be thus assured that your pictures, verbal and other, have been duly appreciated. By this time your summer is over, I suppose, but Sienna must continue to please—the more, doubtless that you can be more in the open air. With your five or six months in that rare old city you will have had a rich experience—how rich Shady Hill one of these days will tell you.—But you had rather I talked of home at first hand than of Siena at second. Of distinctly home-news there is little to tell you; we are all living in these days on your side of the Atlantic. The war is wonderfully present to us,[2] thanks to the abundance and immediacy of our telegraphic. And then, in heart and mind during these later days, we have been living in Italy as well as France. Heaven reward the Italians, amid this hideous tumult of carnage, for their silent and bloodless revolution.[3] Its other merits—whatever they are—seem just now as nothing beside the consoling fact of its peacefulness. You have felt at Siena of course, a ripple of that particular wave. If I imagine rightly, you apprehend as yet nothing more. The fortune of the French Republic, it seems to me, has not as yet been so brilliant as to offer a very enticing example to latent Republicanism elsewhere. I rather doubt of its duration in France. But my very moderate intelligence of current events is wholly merged into the single strenuous desire that slaughter should cease. It seems to me not over-fastidious now to demand it. But who is to demand? You have been feeling, I suppose, very much as we (*we*,

I mean of this immediate family)—feeling, that is, strongly with the Germans. The war up to this time, has to my perception effected such a prodigious unmasking of French depravity and folly that it has been in a measure blessed and sanctified, in spite of its horrors, by this illuminating and disillusioning force. All the French utterances I read, seem to me, almost unexceptionally, those of barbarians and madmen. As yet it has brought out little but the virtues of Germany. If it is further prolonged, however, though I don't apprehend, that French character and intelligence will rise in the scale, that of Germany may decline. You know the Italians better than I do and can better establish the proportion of their virtues and vices; but for myself, I take a private sentimental satisfaction in the simple fact that while France and Germany, those great pretentious lands, were fiercely cutting each other's throats, the lovely country of my heart was Italianizing Rome with barely a gunshot. As regards the occupation I have chiefly been busy thanking my stars that they have not denied me a glimpse of Rome Roman and Papal. One reflection slightly consoles me against this heart-thrust at the picturesque: viz: that Rome being of its nature a city of relics and memories, perhaps it may gain (ALMOST!) as much as it will lose by this reduplication within its walls of the pure melancholy memorial reminiscential element! Another reflection I have also ventured upon: to the purpose that the departure of the capitol from Florence may reconvert it in some degree into the Florence of old and arrest the rank modernization which we used to deplore. But I stand aghast at these crude ratiocinations on a Cambridge basis: especially as on coming to consult a couple of newspapers, I find that there *was* a goodly amount of shelling and shooting on the occupation of Rome. I have followed your fortunes of late as much in detail as I have been able to;—having heard with particular sympathy of your mother's illness and of her convalescence. Do not fail to assure her of my most affectionate remembrance. I don't know that there is anything of weight to tell you either regarding Cambridge or myself. We are still up to our necks in obstinate, implacable fine weather—a monotony of blue sky which has lasted upwards of four months.

During the summer our *beau temps* took the shape of the most hideous and infernal heat—heat which enlarged one's conception of the range and reach of nature. But of this you must have heard. I spent the summer agreeably enough in spite of having been a month at Saratoga. Even there however, I cunningly noted many of the idiosyncrasies of American civilization. I was a week at Lake George—a fortnight with my family at Pomfret—the lovely—the *quasi* Italian! and a fortnight at Newport, where nature was perhaps more attractive and man rather less so, than ever. I was recently down at Beverly, where I saw, among other folk, the serene and conjugal Gurneys. All *ce monde-là* seems invested with a steady prosperous immobility. I have seen no strangers of importance. I spent lately a couple of days with Mr. Emerson at Concord—pleasantly, but with slender profit. J. R. Lowell I haven't seen since my return. Howells I frequently see and find prosperous and fairly contented. He has just come into possession of a new domicile, opposite Richard H. Dana's former one. He is to deliver a dozen of Lowell lectures this winter on Italian poetry. Arthur Sedgwick I often see: our principal theme of discussion is a plan of going abroad together in the spring of 1873—from which you may infer that our domestic and contemporary interests are not thrilling. *Que faire en un gîte à moins que l'on ne songe?* My own household is not prolific of news. My brother's health has small flunctuations of better and worse, but maintains steadily a rather lowly level. My parents and sister are fairly well. Publicly, the time is so interesting that I think we none of us feel that life is void of meaning or promise. (The last of that sentence is desperately cynical but not its spirit.) I take so much satisfaction in reading the papers that I largely manage to forget that I am doing no work of consequence and that the time when I shall be able to do it seems indefinitely postponed. What I best succeed in doing is looking flagrantly well and wantonly idle. If others could see us as we see ourselves!—My year in Europe is fading more and more into the incredible past. The continuity of life and routine and sensation has long since so effectually re-established itself here; that I feel my Europeans gains sinking gradually out of sight and sound and American experience closing *bunchily* together over them, as flesh over a bullet—the simile is *àpropos!* But I have only to probe a little to hear the golden ring of that precious projectile. I am thoroughly content to have returned just when I did—it was a wise act. When I go abroad again it will be on a better basis. I enjoy America with a poignancy that perpetually surprises me; and have become "reconciled" to it so many times since the first tribulations of my return that by this time, I ought to be a formidable rival to the most popular fourth of July lecturers. I will not deny however that I am constantly beset by the vision of my return to Europe. A large part of this desire I set down as morbid; for I am very sure that I should be very much less subject to it, if I were engaged here in some regular and absorbing work. It is the simple feeling that idleness in Europe is so much more graceful and profitable than here.—The rest of it, however, stands firm as a definite and religious intention. I think time has fairly tested the quality of my Italian sympathies. I feel that they have not been found wanting. The wish—the absolute sense of need—to see Italy and especially Florence again increases in force every week that I live. I dream therefore of going forth before the chill of age has completely settled upon me, and spending a long series of months in that world of my choice. Since my next stay in Europe however, (if nothing disturbs my plans) will be a long one, I shall undertake it without precipitancy and give my purpose ample time to mature and accumulate beneath this Western sky. Meanwhile I shall see all I can of America and *rub it in*, with unfaltering zeal. I know that if I ever go abroad for a long residence, I shall at best be haunted and wracked, whenever I hear an American sound, by the fantasy of thankless ignorance and neglect of my native land—and I wish in self defence to make up a little list of accomplished devotions and emotions, which may somewhat abbreviate that sentimental purgatory.—I decline to entertain the idea of your coming home in two years. If you should however, I fear my own departure would be still further shoved along into the future, for I should, with affectionate economy, insist on draining you dry of *your* Europe before I began the process of direct absorption.—There! dear Grace: I think I have treated you to a very pretty piece of egotism. Let me once more become objective. But I cast about in vain for objects. We are smashing and hammering with great fury in our lower domiciliary regions, with a view to removing the kitchen from beneath my bedroom, as I am beginning to be a little over-done.— Do you know Henry Adams?—Son of C. F. A.[4] He has just been appointed professor of History in College, and is I believe a youth of genius and enthusiasm—or at least of talent and energy. If you were interested in collegiate matters and I knew anything about them, I fancy that I might tale unfold which would excite you to a lofty pitch. I believe the university is just now very lively; but I am uninitiated. The Professorship of History was (I believe it's no secret) offered to Godkin, who declined. I am glad to have him stick to the *Nation:* which, by the way, has been (as you will have observed) excellent in its treatment of the war.—I should like to hear what you think and what Charles thinks of the present political temper of Italy what is to follow this last move. You must observe much. I suppose much will depend on the stability of the Republic in France. If it should fall, it will probably be a great positive gain to monarchy elsewhere. Poor dispapalized—dis-aestheticized Rome! I can't get over it. But I selfishly exult in having had a glance at the old regime.—I learn from Sara that you are probably to return to Florence for the winter and to go in the spring to Venice. A very neat arrangement!—Of your present life and *mise en scène.* dear Grace your picture was as vivid as it was masterly. What an admirable spot must be that great concave piazza, with the Palazzo Publico! The tower of the latter, seems to me finer than any I saw in Italy. I noted with sympathy Jane's account of Mr. Ruskin's visit. It must be rather a spectacle to have Ruskin in juxtaposition with his subjects.—I want vastly to hear from Charles; but of course he is not to believe this till he receives a direct demand for a letter. I will not do Jane the injustice to add anything herein to the mention of her received letter. Occasion shall yet wait upon her. I feel as if it were half impertinent to send my sentiments to Susan; such a richly sentient envoy is even now on the way to her. But ask her to remember me a little till her sister comes. I have asked you no questions about yourself. I have only set you an example of the most effusive confidence. Show me it's not lost upon you; write me that you are well and happy. Repeat to your mother my most favoring wishes and offer them also to Charles. Greet the children all round—and Jane—all round too. Answer my letter but not my silence and believe me dear Grace—

yours most faithfully
H. James jr.

1. HJ had gone there to drink its medicinal waters shortly after returning from Europe; he subsequently visited Vermont and Rhode Island and wrote a series of travel sketches for the *Nation*.

2. The Franco-Prussian war had begun in the latter part of July.

3. The unification of Italy was being completed and Rome had been occupied by the Italian army six days earlier when the French garrison was withdrawn. The secular power of the Pope was abolished and this paved the way for his withdrawal into Vatican City.

4. Charles Francis Adams (1807–1886), son of John Quincy Adams, and father of Henry (1838–1913).

To J. T. Fields

Ts Harvard

Cambridge, Nov. 15*th* [1870]

[Dear Mr. Fields.]

I told Howells this morning, on his mention of your proposal to defer for a couple of months the publication of my story, that my own preference was for immediate publication—and this he said he would communicate to you. I find, however, on reflection that if it suits you better to delay it, I shall be well pleased to have it lie over. My wish to have it appear in the January number was prompted by the desire to "realize" upon it without delay. If, as it is, you can enable me to do so, I shall not regret your keeping back the work—to do so, of course, I mean, on the three parts already in your hands. The two others then will have been joined with them before publication begins—which probably will turn out to be a relief to my own mind. There is only one drawback: if you wish to take cognition of the tale, you lose the comfort of doing so in the proof: the m.s. I can recommend to no man's tolerance.

Perhaps you will content yourself with my assurance that the story is one of the greatest works of "this or any age."[1]

> Yours very truly
> H. James Jr.

P.S. I should like Mrs. Fields to know that I last night heard our friend Nillson.[2] What a pity she is not the heroine of a tale, and I didn't make her!

1. HJ's first novel *Watch and Ward* which he later repudiated (dating his start with *Roderick Hudson*, 1875) was serialized in the *Atlantic* during 1871, XXVIII (August–December), 232–246, 320–339, 415–431, 577–596, 689–710. It was published in a much-revised form in 1878 to protect its copyright, but HJ never reprinted it thereafter.
2. Christine Nillson, Swedish opera singer, was visiting Boston. James had met her at the home of the Fields' in Charles Street.

To Charles Eliot Norton

Ms Harvard

> Cambridge
> Jan. 16, '71

My dear Charles,

If I had needed any reminder and quickener of a very old-time intention to take some morning and put into most indifferent words my very frequent thoughts of you, I should have found one very much to the purpose in a most lovely letter from Grace, for which pray thank her, both as from a devoted friend and from an emulous fellow-artist in literature received some ten days ago. But really I needed no deeper consciousness of my great desire to punch a hole in the massive silence which has grown up between us. There have been moments indeed when I have felt not ill at ease in this roomy interval of speech, because of a firm conviction that it was, after all, but the hollow in a larger wave of gathering utterance and reattested sympathies. But I have felt more than this that the long run in human affairs is not so very long that one may be careless of tolerable occasion—such as this cold hard long-deferred rainy morning seems to furnish—when the more common world being forbidden to our feet, we sit and make fireside pictures of the far-off worlds of memory and desire. It is something more than a year today, I think, since I bade you farewell at Florence at the outset of that reluctant northern and western pilgrimage. Then commenced for us a great divergence—or for me, rather; for I hold that you, in your subsequent Italian days and scenes, have but adhered to the normal medium of the man of expressive sense. The recurrence of the precise season of my last stay in Florence brings all the time and place back to me with irresistible vividness. It was but a few days ago that I sat on that little knee-high parapet of your Bellosguardo gazing-place and saw beneath me the ample hollow of the mountain circle filled with Florence and beauty, like an alms-giving hand with gold. The day before I stood on the terrace of San Miniato and saw the landscape steaming with iridescent vapors—as if on every hillside I had kindled a fire of sacrificial thanks for Italy. But you will be amused at receiving instructions in Florentine landscape from Cambridge! Of what you have done and how you have done it, all this while, I have a deeper sense than I can expound just the method of my getting. I was one of you, all last summer at Siena. The cunning of Jane's and Grace's pens was assuredly for much in my metaphysical presence there; but let me claim credit, too, for a willing mind! If you had listened hard, you might have heard in the noon-day stillness of your August hours the parting flutter of its hovering wings.—But in that noon-day stillness, I take it, you were listening to the echoes of French battle-fields. What a cloud of battle-smoke there is between us! And how I wish I were on your side of it, to guess with you and hope with you at all the chances and changes it conceals. Grace hinted in her letter most vividly at the way you felt the overwhelming presence of the war, so that it seemed to form a background sombre enough to absorb the cares and trials of your mother's illness and her own. I confess I am light-minded enough to feel how, in a way, this very gloominess may have deepened (to the distant observer at least) the romantic color of your situation—made it seem more medieval and intensely Italian. To live in a Sienese palace, with the sense of a sombre and perturbed world outside, with the monotonous echo, in the air, of battle-sounds and death-blows and public suffering—must have given you a glimpse of a really antique state of mind. A glimpse however was probably more than enough. To talk of the war seriously requires one to take up a great many threads. I have a strange impression that the history of your sympathies has been very much that of our own. Every day, at least, confirms my impression that the upshot of the matter will have been to leave the French completely and deservedly beaten, with a large range of possibilities of recuperation and self-redemption; and the Germans thoroughly and deservedly victorious, with a considerable share of actual and a vast amount of possible demoralization and disorder. But the Germans will have grown a vastly bigger people through it all and the bigger body and bigger life must of necessity bring with them more chances for evil as well as for good. If you still have any plan of spending some months in Germany you will perhaps find it a different Germany from the one you used to talk of with such moderate enthusiasm—a less local and provincial one and therefore the less picturesque but on the whole a milder dose of pure Teutonism.—Italian affairs, I suppose, give you plenty to reflect and moralize upon—there being little more morality in them than what one supplies. As regards the occupation of Rome, I confess, my most definite feeling has been one of gratitude that my own particular occupation preceded it. What Rome loses in its dreadful old aesthetic interest by the extinction of its temporal sanctity, I think Italy gains in the same line by the completion of her ideal unity. There is a picturesqueness in that, too. But perhaps I don't sufficiently allow for your having got tired of picturesqueness. Call it by some other name then—there are names which more fairly express it! But don't deny it's a primordial passion of the human, or at any rate of the American, heart. We could, each of us, be ill occupied just now, in so horribly blaspheming; inasmuch as the keenest of my recent pleasures has been in looking over, with my brother William (and with the most reverent care) several portfolios of photographs and prints, the fruits of your previous journey, to Italy, which Arthur Sedgwick has very kindly lent us. Let your wit, who collected them, and ours who now enjoy them, attest the dignity of Italianism in the aspect of things—and in the sympathies of mankind! I don't know when you last looked at the portfolios in question; but the photos (among the earliest taken I suppose) have the most lovely old-time mellowness and softness. The technique is better now but the effect harsh in proportion. We have spent over them the most deeply agreeable hours.—Of what more I see and do and enjoy there are no great things to tell. Cambridge and Boston society still rejoices in that imposing fixedness of outline which is ever so inspiring to contemplate. In Cambridge I see Arthur Sedgwick and Howells; but little of anyone else. Arthur seems not perhaps an enthusiastic, but a well-occupied man, and talks much in a wholesome way of meaning to go abroad. Howells edits, and observes and produces—the latter in his own particular line with more and more perfection. His recent sketches in the *Atlantic*, collected into a volume, belong, I think, by the wondrous cunning of their manner, to very good literature. He seems to have resolved himself, however, into one who can write solely of what his fleshly eyes have seen; and for this reason I wish he were "located" where they would rest upon richer and fairer things than this immediate landscape. Looking about for myself, I conclude that the face of nature and civilization in this our country is to a certain point a very sufficient literary field. But it will yield its secrets only to a really *grasping* imagination. This I think Howells lacks. (Of course *I* don't!) To write well and worthily of American things one needs even more than elsewhere to be a *master*. But unfortunately one is less! You have heard, I suppose, how Henry Adams has taken the *North American Review* and feel a grandfatherly interest in the matter. Your grandson promises extremely well. The *Nation* throughout the war has been excellent and has written of matters in a far better-instructed way than any of our papers. But it has been good to notice that having to deal with the war has been to some of them, (the *Tribune* e.g.) a rather useful education. They have had to pitch their tone to a certain gravity and this has reacted on their general manner. When I say that Bayard Taylor[1] has published a very good (I believe) translation in verse of Faust and that Lowell is to republish more of his delectable essays (with, I believe, a title no more to your taste than his last—title that babbles of J. T. Fields)[2] I shall have mentioned the only serious literary facts of our hemisphere. I myself have been scribbling some little tales which in the course of time you will have a chance to read. To write a series of good little tales I deem ample work for a life-time. I dream that my lifetime shall have done it. It's at least a relief to have arranged one's life-time!—All this time, my dear Charles, my soul is full of impatient questions and protesting desires as to your own work, your own humor, health, and occupations, opinions and prospects. What are you making out of Italy and Italy out of you? Do you find yourself able to do any manner of work? Even with the *minimum* of regular occupation you must have learned many things, absorbed innumerable impressions and assimilated much Italian matter. These things can be but narrowly expressed in a letter; but I look hopefully forward to the day when, by the library fire at Shady Hill, you may utter them in gentle streams of discourse. The actual state of public affairs is of such commanding interest that I can imagine it in a measure to dwarf the attraction of remoter times and questions; but on the other hand it is so largely fraught with the tragical and insoluble that one may readily turn for relief to the contemplation of issues from which we catch no side-wind of responsibility. Do you continue to hear from any of your English friends? There is an immensity of stupid feeling and brutal writing prevalent here about recent English conduct and attitude (innocuous to some extent I think from its very stupidity) but I confess there are now to my mind, few things of a more appealing interest than the various problems with which England finds herself confronted: and this owing to the fact that, on the whole, the country is so deeply—so tragically—charged with a consciousness of her responsibilities, dangers and duties. She presents in this respect a wondrous contrast to ourselves. We, retarding our healthy progress by all the gross weight of our massive contempt of the refined idea: England striving vainly to compel her lumbersome carcass by the straining wings of conscience and desire. Of course I speak of the better spirits there and the worse here. But the former are just now uppermost in my mind through my just having read in the *Fortnightly* for December last two articles by your two friends F. Harrison and J. Morley, on Bismark and Byron respectively. They are red-radical and intemperate, each; but they have a great tone: and I can't despair of the situation of a country in which that tone is so positively represented. Morley's article (if you've not read it) is really remarkable. It's a view of Byron from the quasi-political standpoint and reveals in the writer (more, decidedly, than his previous things) a broad critical genius and most admirable style. We have over here the high natural light of chance and space and prosperity; but at moments dark things seem to be almost more blessed by the dimmer radiance shed by impassioned thought. (This is a pretty tribute to Jno. Morley; but of course arrant nonsense.)— But I must stay my gossiping hand. Methinks I could inflict upon you a world of questions and of fond assurances. Do kindly imagine my curiosity and affection. Does Florence wear well? Oh vulgar demand! I see you coming down along that winding channel, between garden walls, from Bellosguardo and stopping on mid-bridge to look once more at the Arno, and passing at the base of those mosaic mountain-walls of the Duomo. Grace gave me so vivid a sketch of your household *mise en scène* that I almost feel as if I had yesterday been dining with you. Do you still go to the galleries and churches? Do you see any Florentines?—This letter of mine such as it is, is none the less addressed equally to Susan because I have not specifically invoked her gracious presence. The interests of life must be so deepening and multiplying for her in the growth of her children that is seems hardly worth while to wish her any great realization of the interest of Italy in particular: but I have no doubt she finds means to combine them and conjures a great united contentment out of both. The last definite fact with regard to your mother of which we have heard was her gradual recovery from her summer's illness: but she is altogether a very definite fact to me and I beg you, by that token, to define to her the very affectionate nature of my sentiments. I wish her all strength and repose.—I have been wondering whether I could in any way match the stoicism of Grace's brief allusion to her own illness by some stern intimation of assent to her recovery. But tho' one may be stoical on one's own behalf, one can't successfully, on that of the friends of one's heart; and I therefore confess to a weak-minded and in fact *maudlin* satisfaction in her great tribulation having slowly melted away—I trust forever. I wrote some time since to Jane, as Grace mentions the receipt of my letter and I regard a bountiful response as one of the bright certainties of the future.—While I am in this lovesome mood I wonder if I may venture to lay my heart at the feet of Miss Theodora? She will at least not trample on it. Silvia Watson is, I believe, still in Florence. Pray recall me in spite of time and space to her cheerful remembrance. I have not said half I wanted to: but there chiefly remains to say I want mostly to hear from you. Heaven speed the day.

Yours
H. James Jr.

1. Bayard Taylor (1825–1878). His translation of *Faust* was published in two volumes during 1870–71.
2. Lowell's volume of essays was entitled *My Study Windows* (1871).

To Elizabeth Boott

Ms Harvard

Cambridge [April 1871] Friday

My dear Miss Lizzie—

A destiny at once cruel and kind forbids my acceptance of your amiable proposition for Monday evening. I am engaged to meet the Bret Hartes[1] at Mrs. Howells's. An opportunity to encounter these marvellous creatures is, I suppose, not lightly to be thrown aside. On the other hand I shall pine for the marvellous creatures assembled in your *atelier* and *salon*. But sich is life!—Such as it is, however, I pray it may last till we meet again.—Primed with your compliment, and your father's, about the P[assionate P[ilgrim],[2] I shall really quite hold up my head to the author of the Heathen Chinee. With cordial regards to your father and many regrets,

Yours most faithfully
H. James jr.

1. Francis Bret Harte (1836–1902) was at the height of his fame when he visited Boston, having just published "The Luck of Roaring Camp."
2. "A Passionate Pilgrim" appeared in the *Atlantic* XXVII (March-April), 352–371, 478–499.

To Grace Norton

Ms Harvard

Cambridge
July 16*th* 1871

Dear Grace—

This response to your last lovely letter and missive from Venice can hardly be called speedy: it is not so speedy by half as I dreamed of its being, in that glowing hour when I received them. But my thoughts have been winged, tho' my hand has not and they have fluttered about you in all gratitude. Your letter was a masterpiece and divinely redolent of Venetian things. I must believe that beside the great pleasure it brought to me, the very writing of it must have brought much to yourself, and your Venetian satisfactions have profited largely by your projecting them so vividly from your mind. At all events, the letter is here—reread, prized, preserved. The photo. was admirably to the point—when I look at it, I feel again that liquid swing of the gondola and that cooling shadow of those melancholy walls. But now these things are, for you, as well as for me, memories and musings and melancholies altogether. And what now are your realities? I have been looking up Innsbruck in various works at the Athenaeum, so that I may at least spend a few summer hours with you in spirit. They all agree upon its great picturesqueness—I hope it's not too picturesque for comfort. You are sure to have had an admirable journey getting there: I hope your mother endured it fairly well, and as far as possible enjoyed it. The Tyrol! I have great notions of the Tyrol. From the standpoint of mid-July in Cambridge they acquire peculiar vividness. Of all this, dear Grace, as well as the thousand and one other reserved places of discussion, we will confabulate, in that teeming future. Have you ever a superstitious sense of having to give some *quid pro quo* for your particular pleasure? If so, know hereby that the penalty is fixed—infinite narration and endless retrospection in the library at Shady Hill, of winter nights, to a fond but inexorable listener! My chronic eastward hankerings and hungerings have been very much quickened of late by the perusal of a little book by our friend Leslie Stephen called *The Playgrounds of Europe*.[1] He has possibly sent it to

Charles and you may have read it. It is much charminger than I should have fancied him likely to make it—and my fond memory and fonder hopes lending a hand—it was altogether charming to me. I want hugely to know how you are lodged and "located." I don't deserve to, I know; but neither Jane nor you have ever treated me according to my deserts, and I take it you're not going to begin at this time of day. A summer of summers to you—with long days too short to hold this peaceful house. From Charles, just before getting your letter, I received a most interesting account of some of his Venetian impressions. Pray tell him with my love, that he shall receive the answer he deserves. His letter came to me as a real benefit and aroused a swarm of the most substantial memories. I hope he continues well enough to observe and reflect to so good purpose as when he writes. But thank him in especial, until I do so directly, for his generous estimate of my *Passionate Pilgrim*. I wrote it, in truth, for him and his more than for anyone, and I'm glad to find it going so straight to its address.—While you are about it, dear Grace, just take yourself by the two hands and shake yourself handsomely, with the ardor of appreciated genius. My writing may be good but your reading is quite a match for it. If you could only be infinitely multiplied into my public!—At all events, I shall write in future for you—as much better and better as I can—and the "public" may take what suits it.—I am dwelling here, in mid-summer solitude, with my brother Wilky; my family being established at Scarboro' Beach, coast of Maine; whence, good folk! they write in gentle raptures of all things. It is evidently a charming place and they are very well off to be there. Later in the season I shall take a look at them. They are hearty and revelling in the sea-breezes and bathing —on which line my brother is especially engaged in working out his salvation. With them are Mr. Boott and his daughter who on Aug. 1st—detestably happy creatures!—return for an indefinite period to Italy.—This is a warm still Sunday morning; as I sit scribbling in this empty house the scratching of my pen seems the only sound in Nature. Wilky, with a friend who is staying with him, has gone round to breakfast with Arthur—with whom, as he too is foresaken of his family, we frequently commingle solitude. It's a clear warm equal summer, as far as we've got, and Cambridge comes in for a fair share of the good and bad. For myself, I make a very pleasant life of it. I linger in a darkened room all the forenoon, reading lightish books in my shirt-sleeves; the afternoon I spend abroad; the evening generally gossiping with Arthur on the piazza. I have of late taken to frequenting these Waltham and Arlington hills and I fancy I like them very nearly as well as Jane—on whom, as I lie deliciously stretched on their bosky slopes, I chiefly meditate. They remind me, tell her, of Italy only in so far as they remind me of her. They are utterly uninfested, full of sylvan seclusion and sweet shady breezey coverts which look down on the great blue plain of Boston and its bluer copes of ocean. I lie there, often, on the grass, with a book in my pockets, thinking hungry eastward thoughts: but thinking too that we have very good things near us home— witness these untrodden hills and woods—so utterly unhaunted that I can people them with what shapes I will with this vast outlook into purple distances and nameless inland horizons fretted by superb undulations—which all simply mean honest Massachusetts.—This is a little private fact of my own. The main public fact just now is not nearly as pretty—being nothing less than the murderous Irish riot in New York about which, I suppose, you'll see in the *Nation* all you'll care to see. For a few hours it was really quite Parisian: the belief seems to be, however, that the thing will have punctured a link in the Irish dispensation there. For the present, very little politics seem to be talked.—You will now gradually be creeping into the Germanic zone of feeling—I shall be curious to hear your impressions of it. You are booked, I take it, for Germany next winter; you'll ere long begin to smoke with German culture and I shall have to "consult" upon your letters as my brother William does on those of his correspondence from Frau Grimm.—I am drifting to a close dear Grace—with a sense, as usual of leaving unsaid what I most want to say. Much of what I have in mind belongs perhaps to the unutterable; but I should like to get you to do it some sort of justice.—I wish very much to get fairly into relation with you in your new medium and atmosphere. Bear this in mind and whenever you are afflicted with an excess of impressions remember whither- ward to work them off.—Not hearing otherwise, I assume your mother's condition to be for the present, comfortable. I know, of course, how at best, it must color your days and thoughts. Pray let her know, with my most affectionate sympathy, how distinctly present it is to mind.—I hope the children are well again and their poor little coughing throats at rest. How they must be growing while I write. Don't let them grow out of all memory of me; for when they grow older (Lily especially) I propose to claim privileges dating from infancy. To ensure this, commend me most devotedly to my friend, their mother. Tell Susan I would give a deal to know what *she* has to say in *these days;* but of course she has plenty of people to say it to, without minding me. But I love her still the same. Tell Miss Theodora that I lament my sister's absence chiefly because of a haunting fear that she is about now getting a letter from her which I shan't hear.—I have on my pen's end a special message to Jane—but it's too long for this sheet and this hour—I shall give it very soon a letter to itself. Farewell. I send you herewith a little story—not meant for folks as fresh from Italy as you—the fruit of a vague desire to reproduce a remembered impression and mood of mine.[2] The lady herself is a gross fit. At the time, I wanted something to happen; I have improved on vulgar experience by supposing that something *did*. It is not much you'll see, and such as it is, not perhaps an improvement.

Yours ever dear G.—

HJ jr

1. An account of Stephen's Alpine adventures.
2. "At Isella," HJ's tale embodying his first impressions of Italy, had appeared in the *Galaxy* XII (August), 241–255.

To Charles Eliot Norton

Ms Harvard

Cambridge Aug. 9*th* '71

Dear Charles—

Your delightful Carpaccios came to me a couple of days since—just in time to catch the letter I was meditating. Hearty thanks for them. They bring back all my surprised enjoyment of the painter, two years ago. He is certainly one of the best of the best—and I would quite prefer (with you, I fancy) to have painted those admirable postulants before the king than all the Andrea del Sartos and *hoc genus omne* in Florence—well as I love it—. So real and yet so graceful—so simple and yet so deep—it does one good to look at him. It is I think, from the painters of his stamp—the early fellows, who wrought into their work their own hard authentic experience and not that of others, transmitted and diluted—that one learns most. These photographs give the hand to your excellent letter of now two months since. It was no small pleasure to me, I assure you, to catch the afterglow of your impression of our friend Tintoret. It's a portentous thought that you should have a couple of his things and that Shady Hill—and I—shall yet behold them. To all you said of him I breathe a fervent Amen. My own memory of him remains singularly distinct and vivid and I feel as if the emotions wrought by his pictures had worked themselves into the permanent substance of *my* mind, more than I can feel it of any other painter—or of any works of art perhaps, save those good people at San Lorenzo.—May you know this good fact in later years! The only trouble is to express at all adequately the breadth and depth of the sensation he provokes. Even Ruskin, I think, has failed to do it. He appeals to such nameless feelings and faculties and seems as it were, to reveal to one one's own imagination.—Your letter had a melancholy note which afflicted me—tho' I wouldn't have a letter from Venice too cheerful. I know what you mean by it all—the change, the lapse, the decay, the hard fare measured out to the beautiful. It does indeed seem as if a certain sense that once flourished and was mighty had now passed out of the world and that, herein, what civilization had grasped with one hand she had let drop with the other. But oh, for some such high view of facts as would suggest that tho' eclipsed this sense, this need, were not lost; that they are masquerading awhile in strange garments, but that some day we shall see them stand forth with unforgotten faces. Narrow optimism, however, is as bad as narrow pessimism, and if the love of beauty as the Renaissance possessed it, is dead, let us sing a splendid requiem. Let us build for it a mighty tomb—as grand as those in Verona. Let us take ages to carve it and adorn it and finish it and inscribe it and then let us perform a daily service around it for ever more. By that time perhaps, we shall all have become so good, that beauty as such, will be altogether *de trop* and we shall be wrapped about in virtue as in so much Titianesque brocade. Then we shall have the satisfaction of at least having kept up the tradition. But I'm scribbling this sweet prattle as if you were still where the shadow of St. Mark's lies blue on the white piazza. You are now, I take it, worshipping beauty, as the Germans understand it, in goodly Innsbrück, whither I have got news of your at least partial removal. With this too I hear of your mother's amended condition—in which I feel with you warmly. This must be an interesting moment for you—the passage into a new society and atmosphere. I should like vastly to know how it all strikes you. Some day perhaps you will drop me a hint. Remember there is but one Italy and don't be too hard on poor Germany. I suppose there is a Germanic charm as well as—say an American! When you have found it—you see I don't hurry you—let me hear. You're sure at all events to have been seeing brave things *en route*—my notion of all that journey is of a perfect revel of picturesqueness. Am I not right? But when I remember how pitiless in spirit I was to poor old France (with the shadow of coming misery even then upon her) when I passed out of Italy, I can't exact much mercy for Germany.—I talk of these things (as if you hadn't settled them all among yourselves) because Cambridge at midsummer is not prolific in themes. Did you ever try it? I am summering here alone in this empty house, and in a quiet way quite enjoying it. Even now and then I vaguely scheme to take up my valises and walk; but the days one by one are melting away, the crickets are filling the nights and the rare yellow leaves beginning to syllable the autumn: yet here I am still, taking it all out in reading the time-tables in the *Advertiser* and wondering which were the deeper joy—Cape Cod or Mount Mansfield. I have taken a good many near-home rambles however and made great discoveries in prettiness roundabout Cambridge. Everyone apparently is away but Arthur, F. J. Child and Miss G[race] Ashburner. We sit a good deal evenings on the Kirkland Street piazzas and await the cool midnight with warm weather talk. Howells too is here (tho' soon to go for a month to Canada with his wife and young ones) and

261

him I generally see on Sunday afternoons. I don't know that there is anything "rich and strange" to tell about anyone. Howells is now monarch absolute of the *Atlantic*, to the increase of his profit and comfort. His talent grows constantly in fineness, but hardly, I think, in range of application. I remember your saying some time ago that in a couple of years when he had read Sainte-Beuve etc. he would come to his best. But the trouble is he never will read Sainte-Beuve, nor care to. He has little intellectual curiosity; so here he stands with his admirable organ of style, like a poor man holding a diamond and wondering how he can use it. It's rather sad, I think, to see Americans of the younger sort so unconscious and unambitious of the commission to do the *best*. Our friend Dennett[1] *e.g.*, who began with such excellent promise a few years ago seems to come to little. For myself, the love of art and letters grows steadily with my growth and I hugely wish, my dear Charles, that you were in the neighborhood, to gossip withal; as, save my brother William, you are the only man I know who loves as I love. I find myself tending more and more to become interested in the things for which you have said so much—art and the history of art and multifarious Italian matters. My passion is ludicrously *a priori*, however, and my gossip would be rather poor fun for you until I had mastered a handful of facts. But the sentiment is there and whatever becomes of it, I trust it will at least last me out as a pretext for going again to Italy. *À propos:* I have omitted to thank you for your very kindly estimate of my *Passionate Pilgrim*. I know no one whom I should have cared more to have like it so well. I have begun to print in the *Atlantic* a short serial story[2] which you will see. The subject is something slight; but I have tried to make a work of art, and if you are good enough to read it I trust you will detect my intention. A certain form will be its chief merit.—I should like much to know what you are occupied with, all these months. One of these days I shall learn. Meanwhile all peace and happy purpose to your hours. Will your stay in Germany interrupt your Italian studies—or complete them? Or shall you dabble in something new?—I believe I never close a letter without saying I have left the heart of the matter untold. So it must be this time. I seem to see a great vague surplus—chiefly sentimental, perhaps—lying unhonored and unsung—but quite "unwept," doubtless by you. I must compress it roughly into a message of universal affection to all of you, from your mother down to that young daughter of Florence to whom I lack an introduction but love none the less.—

Yours ever dear Charles—

H. James jr.

1. John Richard Dennett (1836–1874), member of the *Nation* editorial staff.
2. This was the short novel *Watch and Ward*.

To Grace Norton

Ms Harvard

Cambridge, Nov. 27th '70. [71][1]

My dear Grace,

Your excellent photograph has come—accompanied by your still more excellent note. Blessings innumerable upon your head for your ingenious kindness in sending the picture. Yes, my well-remembered Frati are all there and my little *compagnon de voyage*—and *almost* the Prior. It's a leap out of my own unwritten journal. I won't interpolate here any vain apologies for my long delayed notice of your magnificent letter of August from Innsbruck—deep in the tangled web of my existence some palpable excuse might be discovered; but I thank you now as freshly and heartily as if the letter had come yesterday. I have just been reading it over. It is charmingly graphic about poor old Innsbruck and charmingly amiable about poor old me,—poor Roger, Nora,[2] the signora *e tutti quanti*. It is hardly worth while now, attempting to enlighten you upon any point of the master-piece in which the former creations figure; by the time you get this you will have perused it to the bitter end—and you will have been confirmed or confuted as fate and occasion decree. But if it has beguiled a few of your dolorous Germanic half-hours, and given you a theme for a moment's thought or talk—"the author will not have labored in vain." Really, I'm not writing a preface; I merely wish to thank you beforehand for any sort of final sentiment you may entertain on the subject. Have you or Charles or any of you, by the way, been reading in the recent *Revue des Deux Mondes* V. Cherbuliez's new novel?[3] If not, do it at your earliest convenience. It is tremendously fine—with all sorts of finesse and is quite the author's *magnum opus* as yet. But this *en parenthèse.* In looking over your letter, there is everything to re-read; but nothing definitely to answer—save indeed, those confidential remarks about Howells and his wedding-journeyers.[4] But touching them, too, you will by this time have been confirmed or confuted. I suppose I'm not far wrong in guessing the former. Poor Howells is certainly difficult to defend, if one takes a stand-point the least bit exalted; make any serious demands and it's all up with him. He presents, I confess, to my mind, a somewhat melancholy spectacle—in that his charming style and refined intentions are so poorly and meagerly served by our American atmosphere. There is no more inspiration in an American journey than *that*! Thro' thick and thin I continue however to enjoy him—or rather thro' thinner and thinner. There is a little divine spark of fancy which never quite goes out. He has passed into the stage which I suppose is the eventual fate of all secondary and tertiary talents—worked off his less slender Primitive, found a place and a routine and an income, and now is destined to fade slowly and softly away in self-repetition and reconcilement to the common-place. But he will always be a *writer*—small but genuine. There are not so many after all now going in English—to say nothing of American.—These are Cambridge topics—what have I to add to them? really nothing—save that I count off the days like a good Catholic a rosary, praying for your return.

Nov. *30th.* I was interrupted the other day and now that I begin afresh, it's a terrifically cold, windy dusty Thanksgiving. I'm glad I didn't finish my letter, for scribbling thus to you is a service very appropriate to the day. Alice and Sara S. have gone down to spend it at Newport and you may believe that your health will be drunk in the two places in this hemisphere which know you best. I believe I was on the point, just above, of attempting a sketch of the *vie intime* of Cambridge, at the present moment; But it's well I came to a stop; it would have been a sketch without a model. Shady Hill still exists, I believe, I take it on trust—I shan't fairly know it till you are back again. There are no new social features. Mrs. Doctor Freund *née* Washburn, and husband have come to dwell here—the latter a graceful winning *distingué* German—a German Jew, yet apparently a Christian Gentleman! Mrs. Wm Washburn, née Sedgwick-Valerio, is also expected, I believe, on a visit. This will interest Susan. Also Mr. J. T. Fields lectured here on *Cheerfulness* lately (as who should say: I know I'm a humbug and a fountain of depression, but grin and bear it) and Mr. Longfellow feasted him afterwards at supper. Apropos of which Mr. Longfellow is just issuing a new poem *The Divine Tragedy*,[5] on the Passion and Crucifixion. I don't suppose it will be quite as strong a picture as the San Cassano Tintoretto; but it will have its points. Lowell seems to write nothing. I believe he is given over to the study of Low French —I use the term in a historic and not a moral sense. I'm told furthermore that he is going abroad in the Spring; this of course you know. —You lead quiet lives; but you can match this base gossip, I imagine. —Your tremendous sally on the beauties of the German tongue did me good. I have an apprehension that I shall never know it decently and I am ravished to believe it's not worth my while. But don't come and tell me now that you like it better for knowing it better; for I count upon you for backing me in my scorn.—I try and figure Dresden and your walks and haunts (if the word is not too flattering) as I have always tried to do, with your successive *eménagements,* and with tolerable success, perhaps this time, as I have my brother William to prompt and suggest. But he, poor creature, speaks kindly of Dresden, knowing it only in Summer, and especially—miserable mortal!—never having been to Italy.—You allude, with a kind of mitigated enthusiasm, of the Gallery. Has Deutschland rubbed off on Titian and P. Veronese?—Do they—have they learned to—speak Italian with a German accent?—I think I can say as something more than a figure of speech that I envy you your musical opportunities; for I find as I grow older that I listen a little less stupidly than of yore, and as I zealously cultivate my opportunities,[6] I don't despair of being able someday to recognize an air and the five hundred repetitions. Tell Sally, with an embrace, that I hope in a couple of years, to be wise enough to know how well she fiddles.—I should like vastly to get a hint of Charles's impressions and opinions of Germany. I hope they are not all as unfriendly as I am sorry to hear Germany threatens to be to him. I wish he would write a couple of letters or so to the *Nation* which doesn't seem to grow rich as it grows old. But really I am very generous, wishing him to write to the *Nation;* if he has any spare inclinations in that line, do tell him with my love, that I wish he would direct his letter to me. (I suppose, by the way—I believe I never mentioned it—that he got safely a letter of mine some three months since.)—I must leave myself space to assure you of the interest I take in your various recent mysterious hints about the "nearness" of your return. I don't know whether I care exactly to have this "nearness" translated into literal months—whether I don't prefer to leave it vague and shadowy and shrouded in the hundred potentialities born of my mingled wish to see you and my desire that you continue to see what you may in Europe. I wish you at once to stay as long as you can and to come as soon as you can. Does that mean next autumn—does *that* mean next summer in England? I think the ideal thing for a long stay in Europe is to spend the first and the last few months in England. But these are doubtless very premature and importunate inquiries and reflections. I have only the distinct request—do come, for heaven's sake, so that we can have a good stretch together before I realize that fantastic dream of mine of another visitation of England and Italy. I want to talk things threadbare with you before I see them. But you'll think I've made a pretty good beginning now! I begin to sniff the sacred turkey, and to hear the rattling evolutions of the parlor-maid. You have I suppose a little corner of patriotic piety in your mind—sufficient to feel the pleasant pang I would fain evoke at this image of the classic Yankee feast. Farewell. Commend me most affectionately to one and all—especially to your brother—

Yours always dear Grace—

H. James jr.

1. This letter is of 1871 in view of the references to Innsbruck and HJ's allusions to *Watch and Ward,* then appearing in the *Atlantic.*
2. The principal characters in *Watch and Ward.*
3. *L'aventure de Ladislas Bolski* was published during Oct.–Dec. in the *Revue.*
4. Howells's first novel, *Their Wedding Journey* (1871), was being serialized at this time.
5. Published in 1871 and later included in *Christus* (1872)
6. In spite of this cultivation, HJ was never much interested in music and knew it only in its most conventional forms. He was made aware later, however, of the vogue of Richard Wagner through various Parisian friends.

To Elizabeth Boott

Ms Harvard

Cambridge Jan. 24*th* [1872]

My dear Miss Lizzie—

There came to us this morning from you a letter not, alas, addressed to me! But as I had the pleasure of hearing the greater part of it, I cannot refuse myself the license of answering, and thanking you for that which I appropriated, whether lawfully or not. Your letter was so redolent of Italy and delicious old memories that I must work off in some fashion the ecstasy into which it has plunged me; and who knows but that by doing it thus, I may not incur the favor of your despatching me directly some fine day half-a-dozen pages worth of the same divine aroma?—My brother, too would like to express without delay his great pleasure in hearing from you and as his eyes still remain unserviceable, conveying you his thanks gives me a further pretext. I relish vastly hearing that you still enjoy Italy so much and that the good old land comes up to time. If it is still fresh and eloquent to you after your twenty years of it, what will it be to me, with my appetite whetted by my five months?—We have been most sympathetically interested in your visit to Rome, of which we had already heard; I think I may claim to have outdone the rest of the family, knowing, as I do, just what a visit to Rome means. Your happy touch about the "afternoon light" of the Campagna and Italian scenery generally was worthy of Shelley and brought tears to my eyes. To your raptures about Perugia I say

267

Amen with all my soul. It is a place to make a painter of the dullest Yankee clod and to give a real painter brain-fever. I long since registered a vow to spend some month of May there. Can't we agree to rendez-vous there for that of next year? But aren't all the old towns on the road from Florence to Rome—perched on their mountainsides and boxed and belted in their black walls—the most enchanting old visions in the world?—My ideal of perfect earthly happiness is a slow spring pilgrimage through the whole chain of them, from Arezzo to Narni.[1]—But a truce to this desperate drivel! let me turn to sterner facts! The winter here is working itself away without the help of the Beato Angelico, the Bargello or the Pitti, but with that of a good deal of splendid Yankee sunshine and a certain amount of Yankee sociability. I am leading a rather quiet stay-at-home life, but my brother goes out for two, or nearly so and is becoming an accomplished diner-out. He has just been describing to me a dinner yesterday at Mrs. Craft's (*née* Haggerty) in honor of Miss Nina Greenough's (your cousin's?) engagement to Mr. Atherton Blyth of Philadelphia. Mr. A. B. has a name as in a novel, but Miss G. is certainly a good solid reality. Willy met there Miss Nina Mason whose name and charms this winter almost crowd those of Miss Amy Shaw off the lips of mankind. I met the latter magnificent being by the way, a month ago at a dinner at Mrs. Barr's—who is at her old tricks—and our talk was much of you. You were a Godsend under the circumstances and I assure you, were turned and re-turned and thoroughly discussed. So you see that in your absence, you still play an important part in society. Miss A. S. is hugely handsome. Miss Tappan says that Boston is agog about her simply because she has a straight line from the part of her hair to the end of her nose. So she has—and various other charms; chiefly the "grand air." My only other festivity save the above was to go the other night with Mrs. Bell to a concert of the "Dolby Troupe"—i.e. Southy Cummings, Edith Wynne etc., which was pretty well for an unmusical man. Do you read the new musical *critiques* in the *Atlantic*? They are (if you don't know it) by your friend Apthorp junior. How sound they are, I don't know, of course; but they seem to me mighty "smart"—or rather, very well written, as literature. I hardly dare in the same breath, to mention that the little art-notices, if you look at 'em, are by your humble servant. The thing is hard to do, for want of matter and occasion. If I only had Beato Angelico to start me up! But he, poor man, has been done to death! That is the worst of all Italy—to me who must someday scribble my way through it!—But I must not veer about to Italy again, until I have finished my home gossip. There is not much left however, but to say that Alice has gone for a week, with Mrs. Walsh, to New York—chiefly, I believe, to buy a "party-dress"—though her parties are rare. My brother Bob lately spent a week with us—and Wilky pursues the even tenor of his Western work. It is rather odd getting as we do these opposite blasts from East and West—I mean from you and from my brothers. Sometimes, when, impatient of Cambridge, I hanker furiously after Rome, I remind myself that I *might* be lodged in one of the innermost circles of the Inferno—in Wisconsin.—I have seen little of any of your own especial friends—by whom I mean the Gurney and Harper race. Miss C. H. is holding a German Club, to which my brother and I belong, nominally, but as yet not practically. John Gray came home from Europe in the autumn the same old John and I believe hankers vaguely to return.—From the rest of your great circle of course you receive direct news—a form, to me, a vague outlying swarm of "swells".—I congratulate you on Mr. Gryzanowski[2] and his metaphysical lessons. My brother has just helped to found a metaphysical club, in Cambridge, (consisting of Chauncey Wright, C. Pierce[3] etc.) to which you may expect to be appointed corresponding member.—I congratulate Mr. G moreover on not having come to Cambridge. I have a subtle conviction that he would have detested it. We are just now witnessing the forlorn and homesick state of poor Dr. Freund—husband of Miss Washburn that was, who is striving vainly and pitifully to acclimatize and domesticate himself—. I remember M. Hillebrand[4] very well in the *Revue des Deux Mondes*. He writes French so well that I always fancied him a native—I'm afraid that I can give you no native literary news of an at all high flavour. If you have seen the last two *Atlantics* you will have probably read the beginning of the very charming and promising papers by Dr. Holmes. So at least they seem to me. How does your father like them? I heard read in

MS. the other evening a new story by Bret Harte (for the next *Atlantic*) better than anything in his "second manner"—though not quite so good as his first. Every one here is reading Taine's *English Literature*, provoked by the late translation, and fancying it something new under the sun. You and your father have read and relished it, I suppose, of old. What of the remaining literary group in Florence? Is Miss Blagden[5] productive—do you see the Trollopes[6]— does the shadow of Browinng hover through the city? By the time you get this, you will be sniffing great mild perfumes of Spring. What must it be to see it deepening and planning over the hills from the terrace at San Miniato! Even with the faint far-off foretaste and whisper that we shall soon be getting of it here, it seems a thing so divine, that I can imagine the sense of it at Florence only as a kind of treacherous dream or ecstasy. You say nothing of your plans for the later months and the summer. Is is impertinent to wonder what they may be? I take a kind of artistic pleasure in thinking what people in Europe *may* do. A month hence I suppose, my father will be writing to poor old Scarboro to retain rooms. I went there, you know, shortly after that parting of ours over your open trunks—and found it a charming sort of raw Paradise.— *Àpropos* of my own doings, I feel like first writing PRIVATE in huge letters, and then, in a "burst of confidence," as Dickens says, uttering a certain absurdly vague hope I have of getting to Europe by hook or by crook, in the late summer or early autumn next. If I should, I don't see how, for the winter, I could stop short of Rome and Florence. Then we might see a thing or two together! "Porphyro grew faint."[7] This plan is so pitifully embryonic, that it's really cruel to expose it to the rude blasts of the World. Take it up tenderly —lift it with care!—I am glad to hear my letter reached your father safely—it was not good enough to get lost.—Give him my tender regards. He is kept in my mind by the commiseration I feel for him when, in my frequent walks over the bridge, I think he has lost this pleasure!—Farewell. Write to me with an amiable absence of delay and believe me ever my dear Miss Lizzie,

yours most truly
Henry James jr.

1. The pilgrimage was carried out in 1873 and is recorded in "A Chain of Cities" in *Italian Hours.*
2. Dr. Gryzanowski, a former diplomat of Polish extraction and German education, was a neighbor of the Boott's in Florence.
3. Chauncey Wright (1830–1875) mathematician and philosopher, instructor at Harvard and intimate of WJ; Charles Saunders Peirce (1839–1914), physicist, logician and primary founder of the philosophy of pragmatism popularized and developed by WJ.
4. Karl Hillebrand (1829–1884), German writer living in Florence.
5. Isa Blagden, Browning's friend, lived on Bellosguardo near the Bootts. She is described in HJ's life of Story.
6. T. Adolphus Trollope, brother of Anthony Trollope lived in Florence.
7. A quotation from Browning often used by HJ.

To Charles Eliot Norton

Ms Harvard

Cambridge Feb. 4th '72.

My dear Charles—

I hear of you from time to time but I have an unsatisfied desire to hear from you—or at any rate, to talk *at* you directly, myself. Alice received a couple of days since a charming note from Susan, which was an approach to immediate news of you and has done much to put my pen into my hand. Let me use it first to thank Susan most tenderly for her altogether amiable mention of myself—both as man and author!—I am in constant expectation of a letter from Jane or from Grace and I come down to breakfast every morning and stride to my plate with a spiritual hunger for this possible letter hugely in excess of that which coffee and rolls can satisfy. But as yet I have to content myself grimly with the coffee and rolls. Jane and Grace may be affected by the knowledge that this state of things is not conducive to that breakfast-table cheerfulness and smilingness which I presume figures in their programme for a Christian life.— It is not that I have anything very new and strange to relate. In fact, when one sits down to sum up Cambridge life *plume en main,* the strange thing seems its aridity. A big hustling drifting snow-storm is the latest episode—and we try to believe that, owing to the remarkable "open weather" that has preceded it, it has a certain

271

charm. I have been spending a quiet stay-at-home winter, reading a good deal and writing a little. Of people or things in which, for whom, you are interested especially I have seen little. But who and what are the particular objects of your interest? You must write and tell me—for I hardly know what tastes and sympathies you may be forming in these many months of silence and absence. To the formation of what tastes does a winter in Dresden conduce? A few *dis*tastes, possibly come into shape. Tell me of these too, for I want to be assured that in the interest of "general culture" a winter in Germany is not *de rigueur*.—I have vague impressions of your being disappointed in the gallery. But happy man, to have a gallery even to be disappointed in!—But it will be made up to you in New York, when you come back, by the rare collection of old masters who are to form the germ of what it seems so odd to have the *Revue des Deux Mondes* calling the *Musée* de New York. You will of course adjourn thither from shipboard!—But I'll not talk of your coming back yet awhile, but try rather to forward you some native odds and ends.—The public mind seems to be rather vacant just now, save as to a vague contemplation of the close of the English Treaty. I fancy there is something irrational and premature in the present English irritation on the subject. I doubt whether our directing demands, in so far as the country supports them, are not such as can be fairly satisfied. The English seem exasperated by the very copious setting forth of our injuries. I suppose we have stated our case strongly, to gain moderately. At all events the matter is not, thank heaven, in the hands of the two big foolish nations, but, I trust, in that of men of the last discretion, who feel that the vexing ghost *must* be laid.—Among those who ask about you when we meet is Gurney—though we meet but rarely. I don't know whether it's fancy, but he has to me the air of a man almost oppressed and silenced and saddened by perfect comfort and happiness.—Lowell, to my regret, I never see. With Longfellow I lately spent a pleasant evening and found him bland and mildly anecdotical. Have you seen his new book—the *Divine Tragedy*? I believe it's noted but a partial success. He is not quite a Tintoretto of verse. Howells is making a very careful and business-like editor of the *Atlantic*. As a proof of his energy—he has induced me to write a monthly report of the Fine Arts in Boston!! It's pitiful work and I shall of course soon collapse for want of material.—You, like all the world here I suppose, have been reading Forster's *Dickens*.[1] It interested, but disappointed me—through having too many opinions and "remarks" and not enough facts and documents. You have always I think, rated Dickens higher than I; so far as the book *is* documentary, it does, not, to my sense, add to his intellectual stature. But this we shall discourse in coming days over the succeeding volumes. —Have I come to the end of our common acquaintance? You know, I suppose, the Charles Perkinses—with whom I lately spent an evening. Mrs. P. is spicy and Mr. P.—sugary, shall I say?—No, full of sweetness and light—especially sweetness. He is repeating before the Lowell Institute a course of lectures on Ancient Art, which he gave last winter to the University. Careful and sound, but without the divine afflatus.—There is more or less good lecturing going on. John Fiske is giving a long course in town on Positivism—quite a large performance, in bulk and mass, at any rate;[2] and Wendell Holmes is about to discourse out here on Jurisprudence. The latter, some day, I think, will *percer,* as the French say, and become eminent—in a speciality but to a high degree. He, my brother, and various other long-headed youths have combined to form a metaphysical club, where they wrangle grimly and stick to the question. It gives me a headache merely to know of it—I belong to no club myself and have not great choice of company either to wrangle or to agree with. If it didn't sound weak-mindedly plaintive and fastidious, I would say I lacked society. I know no "nice men"—that is, passing few, to converse withal. The only one we often see is Arthur Sedgwick—who by the way, has gone to New York to comfort and assist Godkin in his present illness.—I suppose of course you always see the *Nation.* I don't know whether it strikes you as it does us; but I fancy its tone has been a good deal vitiated—and in a miserable, fatal sort of way. Godkin seems to me to come less rather than more into sympathy with our "institutions." Journalism has brutalized him a good deal, and he has too little tact, pliancy and "perception."—I confess that my best company now-a-days is that of various vague moonshiny dreams of getting to your side of the world with what speed I may.—I carry the desire (this confession is mainly for Jane) to a morbid pitch, and I exaggerate the merits of Europe. It's the same world there after all and Italy isn't the absolute any more than Massachusetts. It's a complex fate, being an American, and one of the responsibilities it entails is fighting against a superstitious valuation of Europe.—It will be rather a sell, getting over there and finding the problems of the universe rather multiplied than diminished. Still, I incline to risk the discomfiture!

Feb. 5th A.M. I was obliged to interrupt myself yesterday and must now bring my letter to a close—if not to a point! the twenty-four hours have brought forth nothing momentous—save a little party last night at Mrs. Dorr's (*arida nutrix leonum!* as someone called her) where I communed with a certain Miss Bessy Minturn of N.Y., whom Mrs. D. tenders you as *"probably* the most learned woman now living!" Imagine the grimace with which you accept her! But if she's blue—it's a heavenly blue. She's a lovely girl.—I was going on to say above that no small part of this scandalous spiritual absenteeism of mine consists of fantastic encounters with you and yours in various choice spots of the shining Orient—so that I shall listen with infinite zeal to any hint of your future movements and tendencies.—It seems to me I have now been about as egotistical as the most friendly heart can desire. Be thus assured of the value I set on the practise! Tell me how you are and where you are,—morally and intellectually. I suppose you can bring yourself once in a while to read something not German. If so, I recommend: *Taine's Notes sur l'Angleterre* and Renan's *Reforme Morale:* the latter curiously fallacious in many ways, but a most interesting picture of a deeply conservative soul. And in the way of a novel, Cherbuliez's last. I don't see how *talent* can go further. I have heard of Grace, Theodora and Eliot's journey to Berlin. If I might have the story from Grace! Your mother, I trust, continues well. Give her my filial regards— and commend me fraternally to Susan, Jane and the rest. Your children, I suppose, are turning into so many busy little heroes and heroines for Otto Pletsch. Farewell, dear Charles. Respond only at your perfect convenience and believe me ever yours

H. James Jr.

1. John Forster's life of his friend appeared during 1872–1874.
2. John Fiske (1842–1901), chief popularizer of Victorian philosophy and science in the United States.
3. HJ reviewed Taine's English notes in the *Nation*, XIV (25 January 1872), 58–60; he would be a close reader of Renan (1823–1892) whom he later met.

To Charles Eliot Norton

Ms Harvard

Cambridge
May 6*th* [1872]

My dear Charles—

It was very kind in you to answer my note and very brave in you to answer it just as you did. But as the weeks have passed away you have more and more I suppose, sounded the depths of your loss[1]— only of course to find deep within deep—and if we were sitting together would speak to me now with even more intelligent calmness. You have always appeared to me to have so profound and sincere a religious sentiment that I have found great satisfaction in thinking of what it must lately have been to you. To have had this tested by a cruel sorrow and found not wanting is something that an observer (feeling at once all the force and all the vanity, of sympathy) is almost tempted to speak of as a gain.—And yet indeed when I think of how the daily lapse of life must at every step deepen to anguish your sense of the *difference*—as Wordsworth calls it—I wonder I can do anything but lay down my pen, overwhelmed by the fatal, absolute fact. One thing however by this time you know a good deal about—the mysteries of sorrow and what the soul finds in it for support as well as for oppression. The human soul is mighty, and it seems to me we hardly know what it may achieve (as well as suffer) until it has been plunged deep into trouble. Then indeed, there seems something infinite in pain and it opens out before us, door within door, and we seem doomed to tread its whole infinitude; but there seems also something infinite in effort and something supremely strong by its own right in the grim residuum of con-

275

scious manhood with which we stand face to face to the hard reality of things. I venture to talk to you thus, dear Charles, out of my own unshaken security, and because I have in my own fashion learned the lesson that life is effort, unremittingly repeated, and because I feel somehow as if real pity were for those who had been beguiled into the perilous delusion that it isn't. Their hard day when it comes, is hard indeed. The voluntary life seems to me the only intelligent one, and if there be such a thing as heaven, I take it to mean the state in which *involuntary* life is secure.—A woman like Susan can have only one fault; that of making this life seem better and safer than it is. The effacement of a personality so pure, so charming, so instinct with nature's deepest sweetness as hers, seems the very essence and symbol of death. But against such effacement your heart of course protests with every wave of her influence that it transmits to your coming life and that of your children.—I felt many more of these things than I can write or you would care to hear, at the funeral at Shady Hill. You will understand what I mean when I say that the saddest part was there, rather than at the grave. Dr. Newell's short service was perfectly simple touching and irreproachable. You would have been satisfied. The day was extremely sombre—a momentary relapse into winter. While we stood at the grave the snow flakes began to fall heavily. We had been having a horribly *garish* winter—dry, monotonous blue sky for months together; and I remember feeling as we drove to Mount Auburn, a supreme relief in the first rolling grey clouds I had seen in an age—and a sense of the superior seriousness of cloud-scenery. I received yesterday Grace's inestimable letter from Cologne—as I had of course done the note she enclosed with yours. Thank her warmly, pray, for both. She shall soon hear from me. It is proper even to talk about *seeing*, I trust, as well as hearing, for my departure for England with my aunt and sister is now but five days off (May 11th.) I am very anxious to hear what the date of your own arrival in England is likely to be, and your movements when you get there, so that I may narrow down my confidence in our meeting to a certainty. My own plans are vague. Alice wishes to leave London and its fatigues to the last; I think we shall try and find rural diversion on the North Devon Coast (Ilfracombe etc.) for the first three or four weeks. Then to Switzerland and thence, in the late summer, I trust, to Italy, for a month.—Very welcome was Grace's mention of your having found on your way from Dresden, some incidental diversions at Halle and Brunswick. I can imagine your mind turning not unkindly to the chance of talking Dante with your German friend. I trust Paris will have something to interest you; though Paris has remained to me now for a long time an obstinately sombre fact—Alice has just come in to announce—from Annie Ashburner— the arrival of Theodora S., safe and well. I shall see her early tomorrow and have late news of you. You will have heard of Greeley's nomination at Cincinnati. He will carry but a small fraction of the country (I suppose) as against Grant, and the Cincinnati convention is therein a failure.[2] It is not a pure misfortune however that it should be forced to await stronger maturity. With all deeply affectionate message to everyone, dear Charles, and the hope of a speedy meeting,

yours ever—

H. James Jr.

1. The death of Norton's wife.
2. Horace Greeley was the presidential candidate of the Liberal Republicans and Democratic parties but he was defeated by General Grant.

5
Travel and Opportunity

1872-1874

To Mrs. Henry James Sr.

Ms Harvard

Queen Hotel, Chester, May 23 [1872]

Dearest mother

The above is a feeble sketch of the position and circumstances of your exiled daughter. She sits before a great bow-window, looking out into an elegant and verdurous garden. The ivy crawls and clambers in along the edges of the casement; the birds make deafening music in the shrubbery and the high-walled garden is filled with dark, rich greenery and mild, moist cloud-broken sunshine. Behind her sit Aunt Kate and I, driving our respective pens, not far from a gentle fire which harmonizes with this English May. The fruit of Alice's present exertions you will doubtless receive with this, but you will not object to a letter from each of us. You will have received the hasty scrawls Aunt Kate and I despatched from Queenstown and learned that our voyage was prosperous and reasonably comfortable. After Queenstown it became as pleasant as anything can be at sea, and as we steamed up the Irish channel between a blue sea and a blue heaven and sat watching the pale chiaroscuro of the Welsh coast through the mild haze, we almost forgot that we had been spending ten days in muttering curses not loud but deep. The voyage then was very fair, as voyages go, and if I could strike a bargain never to fare worse at sea, I shouldn't feel that I was being cheated. Alice bore it really well, with the inevitable abatements; but these were not such as to be fatal to tolerable comfort (from a strictly sea-sick point of view) and she is now not only revived but ravished and transported by the little (very little as yet) she has already seen. We landed at Liverpool just at the end of our tenth day and a half, in exact season to turn at last into Christain beds at the Adelphi. We lay long and late on the morrow, but we had time to drive about Liverpool and do various things before proceeding hither. Chief among them was securing a state-room on the Algeria for Oct. 15. We weighed the matter duly and decided that taking one thing with another we couldn't do better. Aunt Kate and Alice know the ship and its people, its best and its worst and feel perfectly satisfied to try her again. In most points (in all really essential ones) she is capital. I find England just as I left it, —still, to American eyes, full of the old world. Our little journey from Liverpool here was full of the native English charm and Alice could not have had a better introduction to English verdure than the blooming garden-scenery which borders the railway. We are here at a singularly agreeable hotel, where we have invested for perfect rests, and easy chairs' sake in this little sitting room with its huge clear window giving directly into the quiet and elegant garden whose dark complexity of verdure colors the very light and stillness in which we sit. The ladies devoted their remnant of afternoon, yesterday, to repose; but I snatched a quiet stroll through the town, into which I shall soon lead them forth—feeling already qualified to be a *valet de place*. It is a mighty fine old thing of its kind and there is a certain winding and rambling and turning and bending two miles of old wall, along which three may walk abreast between a rare old city-view and a great screen of shrubbery, which is about as handsome as need be. I am impatient to close my letter and put Aunt K. and Alice into a cab and dump them in the midst of it all.—I shall write again, a couple of days hence, with further accounts of everything.—I find here no news of these twelve days' making, save that the Alabama treaty[1] seems haggling on. Oh for an end of it.—I hope that your prosperity in Cambridge has been as obstinate. That you fondly miss us, we suspect, but if you could take a look at us, as we sit here, your regrets would be tempered by the fierce pangs of jealousy.—We think of you with affection unadulterated by envy. I do hope that I am not inconveniently missed around the house—especially by Willy. I have at any rate the sense of being of great use to my two fair *protegées*. Believe in my affection and receive the blessing of your faithful son and brother

H. James Jr.

1. An allusion to the U.S. claims against England for destruction of shipping by the Confederate battleship *Alabama,* constructed by England during the Civil War for the South. England in the following year paid the U.S. $15,-000,000 as compensation for breach of neutrality.

To Henry James Sr.

Ms Harvard

Chester, Queen Hotel,
Wednesday May 29th [1872]

Dear Father.

We are still at Chester you see; and you will hardly be surprised, as by this time you will almost have received our letters of a week ago and learned our brilliant first impressions.[1] These have been most delightfully confirmed and we have spent a series of charming and comfortable days. There has been no flaw to our prosperity. The country has no disappointments and Alice no *défaillances*. She passes from delight to delight with daily growing strength and has enjoyed a week of those rare first impressions which remain forever memorable. No place could have supplied these more richly than this one, and we feel as if we have been seeing the cream of common England. I have seen nothing as good, myself, as this Chester region. The town itself is full of ancient charm and color, and the country is if possible better. We have strolled on the walls and loitered in the Rows, and lingered in the old churches and driven twice through Eaton Park and along lanes and villages unutterable. On Sunday Alice and I had an excellent morning. We sat out the service in the Cathedral—nestling, so to speak, in the old brown stalls of the choir—and heard Canon Kingsley preach.[2] The service and the *mise en scène* were most agreeable but poor Kingsley is in the pulpit a decidedly weak brother. His discourse (on the Athanasian Creed) was, intellectually, flat and, sentimentally, boyish. Two days we have devoted to delightful excursions by rail, both of which Alice has vastly relished. One was to Buston Castle, a noble rugged ruin on a dark blue hill top, which first won our hearts as we saw it planted across the end of the great vista you view from the terrace at Eaton Hall. Twenty minutes in the train; then a short walk across meadows, stiles and lanes; then a request for the key at certain ivy-smothered gates, then a climb up the long grassy slopes and a couple of delicious hours on the turf in the crumbling old heart of the ruin—with an immense and charming view of all the fair Cheshire country beneath us. It was a truly English day. Yesterday we had a Welsh one. We took the train down to Llangollen and spent half a dozen lovely hours there. It's a romantic vale, squeezed between great hills, with everything picturesque in the way of town and bridge and stream, and a first-class ruined abbey (with the sweet name of *Valle Crucis*) accessible by a short drive. This too was a great success. Alice thrives visibly, and is able to do everything she wishes. We of course interpose large opportunities for rest. Your two letters have been heartily welcomed. Home seems very innocent and primeval. We are daily eager for more—more letters. Dear house-cleaning Mother would rejoice in these quarters of her children. It is luxury, on which we daily exchange remarks, and reminders of the parental bounty. We have fixed on *Rawseley* near Haddon Hall, Derbyshire, as the next of the three of four stations we are likely to make and shall go thither *via* Lichfield tomorrow. Farewell, with much love. Address to Brown Shipley and Co. in London. I will continue to report regularly—

Ever, dear father—

H. James jr.

1. HJ's impression of Chester was recorded in an unsigned travel paper in the *Nation*, XV (4 July 1872), 7–9, reprinted in *Transatlantic Sketches* (1875). Thirty years later he would set the opening scenes of *The Ambassadors* in this ancient town near Liverpool.
2. Charles Kingsley (1819–1875), the clerical social reformer and novelist.

To Charles Eliot Norton

Ms Harvard

Peacock Inn. Rawseley
Derbyshire.
June 1*st* [1872]

Dear Charles—

Your note came to me a day or two before leaving Chester and the interval has been consumed in rather active travel. I am extremely sorry that our meeting has been deferred by your not coming to England; but I cannot altogether deplore the fact as a consequence of your resolve to spend another year abroad. I hope your doing so is not such a disappointment as to make it sound unkind in me to be glad that your inability to get your house gives you a pretext, a motive, a cause, or whatever it may be.—I trust, seriously, that you are comfortably resigned to your non-departure. I think of course especially of your mother—to whom pray give my most affectionate wishes for a prosperous summer. You are not likely to remain in Paris, I suppose, after the warm weather begins and I shall be interested in hearing what summer quarters you select. Whereever they may be, I still hope to see you. We shall pass through Paris on our way to Switzerland about a month hence, as I suppose, and be there again for two or three weeks on our way home again. I can imagine the impression the place makes upon you and hardly expect to enjoy it as once I might. Indeed, can one enjoy anything as one once might? I find I am taking England in the calmest, most prosaic manner—without heart-beats or raptures or literary inspiration of any kind. After a certain hour, one can't live on the picturesque and extract essential nutriment from it. Here we are in a show region—rather too utterly one—yet I think if it wasn't for my sister, I should take the train straight for London, mankind and the newspapers.—This morning we have been "doing" Haddon Hall and Chatsworth, at one swoop—two fine things, certainly, especially Haddon. But they leave me cold and dull.—My sister happily is more generous and enjoys things immensely. We put a day on our way hither at Litchfield, where I confess the cathedral was a sensation.[1]—You are as weary of the *Treaty* as we, I suppose, and as sick of the whole business. Our government, I think, is not doing things handsomely. Shall we be certain of so doing them if we have Horace Greeley to preside at our destinies? *Qui vivra, verra.*—I am very sorry to have to defer the much talk of many things, to which I have been looking forward. Of your further plans I hope soon to hear. Much love to Jane and Grace;—from your letter I infer that Grace had got mine. Alice thanks you for your message, which quite hits the case with her, and joins with my Aunt in cordial regards.

Yours ever
H. James jr.

1. HJ's unsigned "Lichfield and Warwick" appeared in the *Nation,* XV (25 July 1872), 57–58 and was reprinted in *Transatlantic Sketches* (1875)

To His Parents

Ms Harvard

Randolph Hotel, Oxford. *June 4th* [1872]

Beloved parents.—

I resume my report of the young lady you have committed to my care.—Lo! Just as I take my pen, arrive two blessed letters of May 21 and 24th—Father's and Mother's and the *Atlantic*—sent apparently from the shop.—We have been breakfasting on them, as well as upon the daily ration of chops; we have ordered a carriage for Blenheim, and meanwhile I devote the half hour to my letter. Your home news was welcome and pleasant and by this time you will have written again to say that you have got our Queenstown despatch—scribbled on the tumbling washstand in the malodorous stateroom, hardly more than a short fortnight ago—which seems like a good three months. Our exploits during the past week have had much to do with thus crowding the calendar. I wrote you just a week ago, on the eve of our departure from Chester. We proceeded thence to Rawsely Derbyshire, thinking this a likely place for the famous "settling down," which has figured so largely in our programme. We broke the journey by an afternoon's and night's stop at Lichfield—where we saw the truly divine Cathedral which Alice vastly enjoyed. This was a most paying investment. Rawseley turned out not so paying. After we had seen Haddon and Chatsworth we had come to the end of it—in spite of a charming ancient inn, seated just at the lovely confluence of the Derwent and the Wye —a spot as lovely as this conjunction of names imports. The Derbyshire scenery was a singular disappointment—being, for England, strangely raw and vacuous. But Haddon Hall covers a multitude of sins and we spent an enchanting morning there. Nevertheless a couple of days satiated us and we determined upon a vigorous and immediate push to Oxford, to nail it before Commemoration and Vacation. Vigorous we were, behold you. Leaving Rawseley at 9 A.M. we reached this at 9 P.M., having done Warwick Castle and Leamington most deliciously during the day. The Castle, and all the gentle Warwickshire Country we rolled through were most

Alice James

lovely, and I think we enjoyed these hours as much as any we have spent in England. Those that have since elapsed here (yesterday) have been prodigiously good, and Oxford is the same old Oxford still. Alice enjoys everything to ravishment, and, what is better, endures everything *à merveille*. We spent a large portion of yesterday strolling from college to college and from garden to garden and the pleasure was great.

5 P.M. We have been to Blenheim and are ready to die—not with fatigue. It is all more lordly and lovely even than when I saw it before. After driving through the park and seeing the pictures, we spent a long delicious hour in the gardens strolling on a turf which we could almost back to match mother's new carpet—among myriads of gnarled and ivy-throttled oaks—and great mountains of rhododendrons—"rosy-dendrums" the gardener called them—and colossal bouquets of azalia—a world of bloom and of verdure which must be seen to be appreciated.—To say Alice is getting through all this very well is almost to understate it. She is really making a capital traveller and when we have done what she is able to do we have all pretty well done what we desire to do. In short, her undertaking has already proved a most distinct and brilliant success. She enjoys, admires, appreciates and observes to the utmost possible extent. Aunt Kate is of course, inestimable, invaluable and invulnerable. She has been a little unwell according to her ancient wont, but thanks to her native buoyancy we have not been interrupted by it. She seems quite well again and you had better make no allusion to it.—We find your scraps of home news of surpassing charm—especially Mother's mention of recent rain. May the baleful spell have been raised! I have been haunted ever since I left by those clouds of dust in which we quitted Cambridge. May they have been laid forever!—We have had blessedly fine weather.—Father at this writing, we suppose, is "doing" Milwaukee, as we Oxford. May he find it half as pleasant. The boys of course will vastly prize his visit and I hope that he may find enough in it to make up for fatigues. He must write us everything about every one.—We envy Willy much his new society. I should like indeed to hear Herbert Pratt's[1] tales and see Chauncey Wright lying in

W's arms! Our further plans are indefinite; but the "settling down" vision has evaporated (as for England). Our present notion is to go hence for 'three or four days to the Wye, thence to London, and start July 1st (after a fortnight in London) for Switzerland. "Settling down" here on an economical basis is too dull and travelling too dear. You shall hear duly from Alice and the Aunt—. You have heard I suppose of the Nortons not returning. Love to you, dear parents—and to our brother. To our friends as well. Mine especially to Sara and Theodora and T. S. Perry.

Ever—H. James jr.

1. Herbert James Pratt (1841–1915) doctor and traveler, friend of WJ and boon companion of HJ in Venice in 1881. See HJ's *Notebooks* (1947), p. 31. Pratt graduated in medicine from Harvard in 1868; after briefly practicing in Denver, he devoted the next forty years to travel, investigating the greater part of the habitable world. HJ embodied some of his characteristics and speeches in Gabriel Nash in *The Tragic Muse*.

To Grace Norton

Ms Harvard

[Thusis, Switzerland]
Aug. 8*th* [1872]
Hotel della Via Mala.

Dear Grace—

I received from you yesterday a letter too charming and too welcome to remain long unanswered. I should have got it and you should have got this, sooner, but that owing to our recent travel our letters have lost some time in meeting and overtaking us. It was more than a month yesterday since I had had any news of you, and it was with great satisfaction that I learned that in all this time the world has gone well with you. With yours came Charles's answer to my note—a fuller and better one than its brevity deserved. These had been sent back to us from the Engadine, where you will probably be glad to hear we are not—to put it broadly—such fools as to be going. We came hither, by a week's slow carriage-journey from Grindelwald, meaning to push forward to Pontresina, but everything has conspired to deter us and we have ended in acquiescing—indeed, in rejoicing in the verdict of chance. We have been a week in this singularly lovely place—a place that almost reconciles us to Switzerland—and shall probably remain a week longer, after which we shall probably move upon Venice. I don't know that I quite agree with you in pronouncing this (with admirable lucidity on your own part) an *odious* country; but somehow I grudge it more than a measured experience and doubt that of my own free will I shall ever come here again. So much the worse for *you*!—Thusis cries out—and I think that if I could give you some faint picture of Thusis you would say yes. Perhaps you remember the spot—on the Splügen road, at the entrance of the poor old hackneyed, but still romantic, Via Mala. This Grisons country is to our mind, almost the most beautiful and all together the most interesting part of Switzerland, as we know it. It has as many castle-tipped crags as the Rhineland—an antique lingo (the Romansch—a strange jumble apparently—you will appreciate the combination of German and Italian) of its own and divers little ruinous towns, with quaint old armorial bearings on their house-fronts. A long day's drive we took hither from Andermatt on the St. Gothard, through the wondrous Vorder. Rheinthal I shall always remember as one of the rare facts in my travels. And today, as I strolled about within sight of the hotel and saw the lovely mixture of lavish foreground bloom and verdure and dell and stream and far blue cliff and crag—a feast of color and a perfect oppression of lovely shapes—it seemed to me that really and deservingly to enjoy such beauty demands all one's senses and powers and that to do so, one ought to gladly withdraw them from visions of a corrupt civilization. At any rate, I shall make the most of Thusis while it lasts and one of these days shall try and describe it to you.—*À propos* of description, dear Grace, you are a mistress of it, and you put before me with lovely vividness the various episodes of your recent days—M. Brill's fireworks—(as to the "taste" of which Sainte-Beuve, I think, would have agreed with Eliot) the *tête à tête* of the Fraulein and the Grischin, with her truly inimitable account of it—and the former's "incompatibility" with Eliot. Thank you heartily for it all, it renews those excellent hours I spent with you.—The only regrettable thing you mentioned was your mother's indisposition, which I hope is quite at an end. Lily too is off the bed again, I trust, and as amusing as she was amused.—I have hardly the heart to reply to your kindly mention of my letter to the *Nation*; it made such a shabby appearance in print. Besides the usual generous allowance of misprints, it had suffered the loss, on the way, of a page of the M. S., which subtracted from the body of the letter, made an absolute jumble of the surrounding context.—Tell Charles with my love that so long as such things happen, I shall not discontinue to agree with him that it is better to read than to write.—Please tell him furthermore that if we reach Venice as we hope to, he shall hear from me there. My kindest love to your mother and Jane and the blessed boys and girls. Yours ever dear Grace most faithfully

H. James jr.

To His Parents

Ms Harvard

Botzen, Austrian Tyrol
Sept. *9th* [1872]
Zum Kaiserkrone

Dear Parents,

My last letter announced our arrival in Venice and mentioned the letters from you we found there. Here we are, having departed thence, on our way *via* Innsbrück, Munich, and Strasburg, to Paris and more letters. Alice wrote to you from Venice, so that you will have learnt that we had determined our stay should be short. Even if we hadn't, however, I think circumstances would have been too many for us. By "circumstances" I mean *mosquitoes,* from which we suffered such nightly martyrdom as even Venice was hardly a good enough cause to make endurable. The curtains pompously affixed to the beds were a mockery and a delusion, and the only way to attain sleep was to burn certain stifling pastilles within the net and to woo oblivion while the ravenous beasts were temporarily stupefied.

This of course was not wholesome in the long run, and the great heat (from which our first week in Italy was entirely free, and which overtook us only at Venice) did not make it more so. We gave ourselves four full days and on the fifth departed for Verona. Most delightful days they were, for it was only the nights that were obnoxious. We left nothing unseen that we wished to see, lived in our gondola, and found abundant coolness on the water and in the darksome churches. We went to Torcello—an ever memorable excursion; to Murano; twice to the Lido, (which has been sadly "improved" since I was there last) but where we dined most breezily on a platform where bathers and diners were strewn in true Italian promiscuity; spent much time in St. Mark's, and had ample leisure to see all the desirable pictures. The weather was perfect, we ate innumerable figs, ices every night at Florian's and bought a few very beautiful photographs (all of pictures, many of which you have not seen) so that our four days were a great success and seemed more like a fortnight. We have been in Italy only a fortnight, but it seems almost like a couple of months—it has been so crowded with sensations surprises and pleasures. I have enjoyed Italy not, perhaps, precisely as much as the first time, but so nearly as much as to leave little difference. As for Alice, I think she has had no disappointments, but has gained a multitude of impressions which she will forever value. Two occasions stand out in our retrospect in a sort of supernatural relief—our little boat-journey on the Lake of Como, which it seems almost absurd that our present vulgar flesh should have partaken of; and my afternoon, just mentioned, at Torcello. We had two mighty gondoliers, and we clove the wandering breezes of the lagoon, like a cargo of deities descending from Olympus. Such a bath of light and air—color and general luxury, physical and intellectual! Verona, too, we greatly enjoyed; and I found it, as I had left it, one of the most interesting of Italian cities. There, too, we managed to see in our single day everything noticeable. We have preferred to break the long journey to Innsbruck, over the Brenner at this place, where we find an excellent inn and a little town sufficiently picturesque; but poor Italy already defunct and Germany in every stick and stone and uglier than ever by contrast. It is a most singular thing—the immediacy with which national differences begin and their universal pervasiveness. There is a sort of cathedral here which is as ugly and graceless and displeasing, as if the lovely churches of Verona were on another planet, instead of just across the Italian frontier. We shall have time, however, I hope, even in our few days in Germany to learn to cease to make invidious comparisons, and to judge things by German principles. Munich we expect much to enjoy, that is as to its collections. Lizzie Boott lately wrote us thence that the gallery of old masters was immensely rich. The Bootts by the way failed to overtake us in Venice as they had planned to do—not with our concurrence. If they carry out their design, they will be arriving there now, having crossed us at Verona. Poor Mr. Boott will enjoy neither the heat nor the mosquitoes, and Lizzie has done a rather inhuman thing to drag him down there so early, in the absence of any pressure of time. They crave society—naturally, and have had plenty all summer, having never been without a large *entourage* of Bostonians; but they seem to prefer ours, to any other, and hurried their journey to Venice for the mere chance of being with us four or five days. It was impossible we should wait for them, and yet I'm afraid they won't forgive us for not having done so. But I hope they may be waiting for us in Munich. Whatever Munich may have in store for us, I am glad at last to find ourselves facing towards Paris again. We have allowed ourselves time for three complete weeks there and for a journey to London inclusive of a stop at Boulogne—of which Willy will be glad to hear, and which was in our minds when we passed it ten weeks since. If Alice enjoys Paris half as much as during our first visit, the great profit and pleasure of these five months will be complete. We shall have been travelling, by that time, pretty steadily from the very first, and there will be a delicious tranquillity in a stretch of three weeks without thought of trunks or trains. —My own desire to remain abroad has by this time taken very definite shape. In fact, I feel as if my salvation, intellectually and literarily, depended upon it. I have had too little time to write, to lay up any great treasure to commence with; but I shall need but little to start with and shall be able to add to it fast enough for comfort. I *have* laid up on the other hand a great treasure of health. On this point my dearest mammy's last made particular inquiries, which I should be sorry to leave unsatisfied. During my first month in Switzerland, I was poorly and had to struggle with adverse atmospheres; but before that and since (more especially) I have done nothing but improve. My improvement is going on now at so very rapid a ratio that I feel an almost unbounded confidence in my power to do and dare. In short, I am really well, and am confident of being able to work quite enough to support myself in affluence.—I have left no space for asking questions or making conjectures; but I shall find all possible ones answered I trust in the letters even now piling up for us at Munroe's in Paris, where we expect to claim them about a week hence. *A propos* of *money* above, has the *Nation* ever sent you any cheques? I suppose not, or you would mention them. I can't as yet suspect you of secreting the gains of your toiling and loving child

H. J. jr.

To William James

Paris, Hotel Rastadt
Rue Neuve. St. Augustin.
Sept. *22d* [1872]

Dear William

I found awaiting me at Munroe's a couple of days since your delightful and excellent letter of Aug. *24th* from Scarboro; and I must let my usual Sunday letter, today, serve as an answer to it. It found us arriving in Paris rather sated with travel and pleased at the prospect of a three weeks' rest. These weeks will slip rapidly by and then I shall find myself turning away from the ship's side, at Liverpool and (if I remain of the same mind that I am of now) leaving my companions to take home such accounts of me as may seem to them veracious. The five months that we were looking forward to such a short time since, now lie behind us, having changed their blank vacuity for the rich complexion of a mingled experience. They have done more for us, I suppose, than we yet can measure, and I have gathered impressions which tho' now wofully scattered and confused by incessant travel, I hope never all together to lose. We have really seen a great deal; and I think Alice, in the tranquil leisures of home will find that her mind is richly stocked with delightful pictures and memories. As regards her health, I don't see how the journey could have been a more distinct success; but it is needless to talk of this now, for you will soon see her and make the same judgment.

Sept. 28th I wrote the above a week ago, was interrupted, and have lacked time since to resume—having devoted my mornings to doing something for the *Nation* about our Italian journey[1]—which there was no chance for at the time and yet is a sort of thing very difficult after the immediate glow of experience is past.—The week has gone pleasantly albeit for Paris, quietly. I already feel so much at home here that I lack the spur of curiosity to drive me into the streets. Alice and Aunt Kate, even with their moderate demands, find plenty of occupation with milliners and dressmakers—and have even now sallied forth on an expedition to the Bon Marché. Aunt Kate's energy and capacity in this as in everything else, shine forth most powerfully. A letter has just come in from father, enclosing a piece from the *Tribune* about my new story. The critic is very polite and makes me curious to see the piece, which I have rather forgotten, so long ago was it written. Father also says that you have not come back with J. Gray from Conway and leaves me wondering how you found it there and what you did. It was just thus, last year, that I was there and somehow wasn't charmed with it. I hope at any rate you have found some impetus to your physique—and may perhaps have sounded the mysteries of J. Gray's *morale*. You, too, will have had a somewhat diversified summer and will have seen more of human nature, at any rate, than we, who have seen none worth mentioning. Lately we have been spectators of the familiar virtues and vices of the Tweedies, who live here below us and dine with us every day. The Nortons too are here, and J. R. Lowell and wife, and Chauncey Wright and Rowse. C. Wright seems in Paris just as he did in

Cambridge—serenely purpurine. He lives at the Grand Hotel, and I frequently see him trundling on tip-toes along the Boulevard, as he did at home along the Main Street. The Nortons are excellent, but I feel less and less at home with them, owing to a high moral *je ne sais quoi* which passes quite above my head. I went with Charles the other day to the Louvre, where he made some excellent criticisms, but he takes art altogether too hard for me to follow him—if not in his likings, at least in his dislikes. I daily pray *not* to grow in discrimination and to be suffered to aim at superficial pleasure. Otherwise I shudder to think of my state of mind ten years hence. Paris continues to seem very pleasant, but doesn't become interesting. You get tired of a place which you can call nothing but *charmant*. Besides, I read the *Figaro* every day, religiously and it leaves a bad taste in my mouth. Hereabouts, moreover, the place is totally Americanized—the Boulevard des Capucines and the Rue de la Paix are a perfect reproduction of Broadway. The want of comprehension of the real moral situation of France leaves one unsatisfied, too. Beneath all this neatness and coquetry, you seem to smell the Commune suppressed, but seething. Alice, Grace Norton and I went the other night to the Comédie Française to see Musset's *Il ne faut pas badiner* etc. Perdican was beautifully played, but the piece is too exquisite not to suffer by acting. The only other noteworthy things I have seen were two pictures of Henri Regnault, yesterday, at the Luxembourg, the *Exécution Mauresque* and the Portrait of General Prim. They are very juvenile works, but they make one feel that their author if he had lived and kept his promise, would have been the first of all modern painters, with much of the easy power which marks the great Italians. He seems to have thought, so to speak, in color. You have learned, by my recent letters, that I mean to try my luck at remaining abroad. I have little doubt that I shall be able to pull through. I want to spend a quiet winter, with a chance to read a good deal and to write enough. I shall be able to write enough and well enough, I think: my only question is how to dispose of my wares. But in this, too, I shall not fail. Your criticism of my *Nation* letters was welcome and just: their tendency is certainly to over-refinement. Howells wrote to me to the same effect and you are both right. But I am not afraid of not being able, on the whole, and in so far as this is deeply desirable, to work it off with practise. Beyond a certain point, this would not be desirable I think—for me at least, who must give up the ambition of ever being a free-going and light-paced enough writer to please the multitude. The multitude, I am more and more convinced, has absolutely no taste—none at least that a thinking man is bound to defer to. To write for the few who have is doubtless to lose money— but I am not afraid of starving. *Au point où nous en sommes* all writing not really leavened with thought—of some sort or other—is terribly unprofitable, and to try and work one's own material closely is the only way to form a manner on which one can keep afloat—without intellectual bankruptcy at least. I have a mortal horror of seeming to write thin—and if I ever feel my pen beginning to scratch, shall consider that my death-knell has rung. I should prefer to spend the winter in Florence or Rome—rather the latter, in spite of its being, I imagine, pretty distracting. But it would pay me best, I think, and the *Nation* would value letters thence. But enough of my own affairs. All we hear of Wilk and Bob and their prospective mates is very interesting—especially father's mention this morning of Bob's possible marriage in November. I hope he knows what he is about. If so 'tis excellent. I read your Taine and admired, though but imperfectly understood it.[2] Charles Norton praised it to me the other day.—Proceed, and all blessings attend you! Howells lately wrote me that there was a chance of T. S. Perry getting, subordinately, the *North American Review*. Good luck to him! From allusions in letters, he seems to be still in Cambridge. Is he then keeping his place? Give him my love and tell him that I have a constant design of writing to him. You sometimes see Wendell Holmes, I suppose, of whose matrimonial fate I should be glad to hear something. Farewell. I have another letter to write and the morning is ebbing. Alice and Aunt Kate are counting the days. —It seemed to me that I had much more to say—and I have: but I must keep it for another day.—

Yours ever—

H. James jr.

301

1. "From Chambéry to Milan," *Nation* (21 Nov. 1872), pp. 332–334.
2. WJ had reviewed Taine's "On Intelligence." According to Ralph Barton Perry, in *The Thought and Character of William James* (1937), this was the first of WJ's publications which gave a hint of his philosophical leanings.

To His Parents

Ms Harvard

Paris, Hotel Rastadt
Sept. *29th* [1872]

Dearest parents—

I have let rather a longer interval than usual pass without sending you a line—but no news, in this case, has meant perfect good news. I wrote yesterday to Willy, who has no authority for not showing you my letter. These agreeable days in Paris are ebbing away very fast and bringing us to the fated 15th October; so that in less than a month you will fold my fair companions in your arms. We hear from you with delightful regularity and nothing is wanting to the even flow of destiny which bears us so caressingly forward. Our little hotel has turned out a real *trouvaille*, and our solitude is agreeably tempered by the vicinity of the Tweedies, with whom we almost daily dine and who relieve the mutual monotony of our by this time extremely familiar selves. Alice and Aunt Kate have been rather immersed in shopping, but are now getting their heads above water, so that we shall be able to occupy ourselves a little more aesthetically. Alice has just shewn me a ravishing bonnet which will certainly next winter, be the wonder and envy of all Cambridge. It belongs to the class of bonnets of which a milliner yesterday said to me on my admiring some on her table—"*Ah Monsieur, sur des jeunes têtes c'est divinement beau!*"—Yesterday came a letter from father enclosing Mrs. Moulton's genial notices of my tale. Many thanks to father for his labor in reading my proof; if he has to consult my M. S. often, it is no light one. But I feel very comfortable that the thing should have passed under his eyes. I have not yet got the *Atlantic,* and the story was written so long ago that Mrs. Moulton's stirring synopsis really excites my curiosity.[1] Father's mention of Bob's possible marriage was interesting. If Mr. Holton gives a house, all will go well, I suppose, so long as the larder is kept at par, which doubtless Mary's economical talents will contrive. I have seen nor done nothing in Paris of exceptional interest. The Nortons are here, whom I see every day or two, with J. R. Lowell and wife and Chauncey Wright, who seems to do nothing but loaf and absorb knowledge apparently from the asphalte of the Boulevards.—It is strange to think of our journey being so nearly over and that what seemed so full of mysteries and wonders beforehand should have passed with such tranquil regularity and punctuality. It has been however, a very fruitful one and I think that when Alice is fairly established at home again you will feel that for her its fruits have been considerable. Now that I look back upon it all, we seem to have seen a vast deal and to have had innumerable delightful days and hours and sensations. I wonder sometimes what can have become of so much experience—in what part of our being it is stored away. We have really I suppose, become considerably older and wiser by it and we shall measure our profits little by little as life goes on. In retrospect it all seems now to have been absurdly easy—and indeed our wheels have been liberally oiled by the paternal bounty. One of your recent letters hopes that we won't venture into Italy—a hope that we greet with amiable derision. For nothing you could offer would I have had Alice miss that fleeting fortnight of delight.—I suppose you are resigned to not seeing me this autumn. I can't say that I am to my prospects of exile, but I try to steel myself. Seriously speaking, I expect this coming year or two, over here, to do a great deal for me. It will not be my own fault if it don't. As to the practical side of it, once I get started I have little fear of not keeping afloat. If I had had a more disengaged summer I should have a larger capital to begin upon; as it is however, I have a decent little sum owing me by the *Nation* and the *Atlantic,* which I have written them to send me forthwith. Beyond this I may have to ask you for a little money and I may not. My plan is to return directly from England to Paris, after having packed off my companions. Once in Paris, simple immediate economy would dictate my remaining here; but after due reflection, I incline to think that a whole winter here would not be profitable, and that a season in Italy would stand me in better stead. The *Nation,* for one thing, has a Paris correspondent, but no Roman one, and would be glad to have letters from me—I may safely conjecture. Various other good reasons cooperate. What I submit therefore is that you kindly permit me to draw enough money to get me a few clothes in London and to help me on my way to Italy; for the clothes and the journey together would rather diminish my private fund. I roughly estimate that by the time I place Alice on shipboard, we shall have spent about £480.[2] (This covers of course her Paris purchases.) How much money I shall need I can't yet say, but I will use our letter discreetly. I think £50 would comfortably start me in life and carry me ahead for a long time, as regards clothes. But I shall of course write you again before the 15th. Continue to address everything care of John Munroe & Co. 7 Rue Scribe. Farewell. Ever, beloved parents, your affectionate

H James jr.

1. Louise Chandler Moulton (1835–1908), poet and novelist. HJ's allusion to his tale and to the *Atlantic* is confusing. He had published no tale in that journal thus far in the year 1872; and his father had just read proofs of "Guest's Confession" which appeared in Oct.–Nov. 1872. The tale noticed by Mrs. Moulton was probably "Master Eustace," *Galaxy* (November 1871), pp. 595–612.
2. About $2,400.

To His Parents

Ms Harvard

Charing Cross Hotel Oct. 10*th* [1872]

Beloved parents—

You mustn't think I have wantonly abandoned my good habits in letter writing—for I think it is more than a week since I last wrote. My last days in Paris were rather preoccupied ones and I finally gave up even trying to write until our arrival here. This took place last night comfortably, in spite of a very *mauvais quart d'heure* on the channel. We came to our old friend the Charing Cross, not as ideally comfortable, but as combining many advantages. Our last days in Paris were busy, but pleasant, and though Alice and Aunt Kate had a fierce fight toward the end to get their outstaying parcels sent home I believe they accomplished it and suffered no irreparable disappointments. I envy you, in Quincy Street, the spectacle of their disinterred treasures and have little doubt that you will feel that they have combined zeal with discretion. I meant to have dropped Willy a line about his overcoat, but I suppose he has taken my silence as assent. Fearing that we should have too little time to have the coat made in London (as it has turned out we perhaps might have effected it) I ordered it in Paris of a well recommended English tailor and it seems to me a satisfactory and excellent garment. It cost 180 francs: very much less than Randidge. I hope it will suit him, for color texture and weight. It must propitiate him in some degree for our not having stopped at Boulogne—once more! On coming to the point I found that Alice and Aunt Kate were both indisposed to do so: Alice on the ground that she had been too young to have any memories of the place—and Aunt Kate on the ground that she was too old to care to refresh hers. But I don't yet despair of stopping there myself. London is the same terrible great murky Babylon as ever. Blood-drenched Paris[1] seemed as a glittering bauble beside it. It is something overwhelming—even more so at this moment than when we saw it in the season: for the autumn fogs magnify all the swarming street vistas and give them a kind of monstrous immensity. Alice and I took a prodigious drive in a hansom this morning, over to the new Bethnal Green Museum[2], where there is a beautiful lot of pictures, ancient and modern, loaned from Paris by Sir Richard Wallace, heir of the famous Lord Hartford. But it's a diamond on a dunghill, if there ever was: for the grimy squalor of the whole vast circumjacent district is inexpressible. Alice will give you her own final impressions of Paris; even if they were wholly unfavorable, an arrival in London might quicken them into some sort of kindliness for by contrast, in everything that makes much of the indispensable charm of life, Paris is ineffably more gifted. Even after all its tragedies Paris has a certain graceful natural wholesome gayety which is a blessing of heaven: but oh, the grimness of London! And oh! the cookery of London! Aunt Kate and Alice will give you anecdotes.—We parted with the Tweedies the day before we left Paris: they starting for Switzerland to pick up Mrs. Temple and take her to Italy. My ladies will also give you a harvest of anecdotes on Aunt Mary [Tweedy], whose idiosyncrasies they consider to have greatly increased. Tweedy is amiable, apathetic and elderly. I don't know that I mentioned that the Masons and Bob James very diligently called on us in Paris.— Nor have I mentioned your various more recent letters which came in frequently during our last ten days in Paris and culminated with one to me from Mother and one to Alice from Father (of dates which I forget) telling of the Holtonian visit etc. We rejoice in the latter having passed off so smoothly, and are most curious to behold the remarkable Holton *père*. Mrs. H. we had glimpses of in Paris, in situations not favorable to conversation.—But it is needless I should keep scribbling on, for my letter will precede the Algeria by but very few days. (Why in the world, by the way didn't Mother *enclose* the letter from Gail Hamilton, about her magazine, she so pregnantly alludes to? It is all a mystery. She says Father will explain, but Father has not explained, and I await the elucidation.) On my return to Paris, I expect to get in some sort regularly at work—of some sort. —Aunt Kate's eyes remain about the same, and I don't understand their condition and cannot help suspecting that it is less serious than she thinks. I haven't combatted her unwillingness to go to a European oculist, because if there is anything to be one, she has not been well placed for it.—At any rate, she will be glad to get home, and will have fairly earned a long rest. She has had no heart evidently in our journey on her own account, and yet her devotion to Alice has been *immeasurable*, and has been everything in seconding the benefit of our travels. Farewell. I will drop another line before the 15th *if there* seems a chance for it to go. We go to Liverpool on Monday. Yours ever

Yours ever
H

1. An allusion to the Commune in Paris of March–May 1871, which had been suppressed with great violence.

To Henry James Sr.

Ms Harvard

Paris [Nov. 1872]

Dear father:

I received promptly your letter of Oct. 14th: and I had a couple of days before received the last *Atlantic.* For both many thanks. The photograph from John La Farge's drawing, and Bob Temple's letter were both welcome, too, in their respective and very different manners. The drawing seems to be a weaker thing than John ought to be doing, now-a-days, (though certainly very pretty;) and Bob's letter is touching in its amiable demoralizations. It's an event worthy of Thackeray that his *spelling* should have degenerated!—I have not yet heard from Aunt Kate and Alice; I must allow them a few days more. By this time, I suppose, you feel as if they had never been away. The dresses are unpacked, and the photographs, and the stories told, and Alice is all ready to take ship again. You must remind her that she is to write me the most *intime* details of her impressions of home. My love to Aunt Kate, who will have written me, I trust, whatever she is able to do. May she, on reaching home, have found this more than it seemed to be here!—I am fast becoming a regular Parisian *badaud;* though, indeed, I led a far madder and merrier life in Cambridge than I seem likely to do here. The waiters at the *restaurants* are as yet my chief society. The weather, since my return, has been wet but soft, and I have had a blissful respite from suffering with the cold. This little room of mine, in the Hotel Rastadt, is a most delightful spot: hardly larger than a state room on the *Algeria,* but with everything needful and all the warmer for its smallness. Today is bright and the sun is pouring in over the opposite house tops in a way that I wish Aunt Kate could see. A gentleman has just come in to try me on a shirt. Imagine Mr. Chaffin calling in Quincy Street for this purpose or entertaining the idea that a shirt could be tried on! Mine is an elegant fit and *très echanchré*

307

in the neck.—I did wrong just now to speak slightingly of my society; for I have struck up a furious intimacy with James Lowell,[1] whom I lived side by side with for so many years in Cambridge without sight or sound of. I called on him the other day, with a message from Charles Norton; he returned my call, the next day and we went out to walk and tramped over half Paris and into some queer places which he had discovered on his own walks. There is a good deal of old Paris left still. Lowell is very pleasant and friendly, and apparently very happy: driving great bargains in old books, some wonderfully handsome and cheap. The cheapness of books here must make Paris a paradise of bibliophilists. A few days later I went over and dined at Lowell's *table d'hôte* in the Rue de Beaune, just off the Quai Voltaire. He lives in a little old genuine French hotel, in a snug little apartment, with fabulous cheapness. The dinner at 3 frs.50 was the cheapest entertainment I ever enjoyed, not only on account of the food which was very *savoureux*, but of the company, which was more succulent still. The scene was indescribable; I only wish Willy could have seen it. It consisted of a political fight between four conservatives (one the Marquis de Grammont, a deputy and legitimist,) and a solitary republican, a Wallachian by birth. All the classic qualities of the French nature were successively unfolded before us, and the *manner* of it beat the best comedy. One of the conservatives, a doctor of the complacent sapient epigrammatic sort, was a perfect specimen of a certain type of Frenchman, and the way he rolled his eyes and chucked his epigrams into the air with his chin (as if he were balancing a pole on the end of it) was something not to miss. He clamored for a despotism stronger than any France has ever had, absolute suppression of the press and that all radicals should be *fusillés*. The Marquis de Grammont thought *suppression* of the press a little severe, but went in for *lois très répressives* and declared that his party hoped to carry such in the next session of the chamber. He then worked himself into a rage, against the Wallachian, more purple, more frantic, more grotesque, than anything you can imagine. The wildest parody couldn't approach it, and it was wondrous to see the rest of them quietly eating their dinner instead of running for a straight-jacket. I shall know in future what to *s'échauffer* means. The state of mind exhibited by the whole thing was incredibly dark and stupid—stupidity expressed in epigrams. If the discussion was really as typical as it seemed to be, the sooner France shuts up shop the better. I mean to return often to the Hotel de Lorraine, and if the other table d'hôtes in that region are as good, I shall take them all in turn. Mr. John Holmes,[2] by the way, is with the Lowells, with his aroma of Cambridge quite undiluted.— Rowse and C. Wright have gone and the latter, I suppose, will have turned up in Cambridge before this reaches you. I know of no one else in Paris whom I am likely to see, except the Masons and Bob James, whom I mean to reserve till every other resource has failed. —For your liberal advice about drawing money, beloved father, many thanks. I shall do very well without ruining you. I mean to act in accordance with what you say about having my cheques sent to you; it is the best plan. Tell Alice and Willy to read the *full correspondence* of Henri Regnault, just published. I have just sent a review of it to the *Nation*.[3] You say nothing about the boys, so that I suppose there is nothing new with them. Tell Willy I mean soon to write to him. Love to my incomparable mammy. Address Hotel Rastadt etc. Farewell. Ever your loving son

H. James jr.

1. James Russell Lowell was fifty-six at this time and HJ twenty-nine.
2. Brother of Oliver Wendell Holmes.
3. Unsigned review of *Correspondence de Henri Regnault* in the *Nation*, XVI (2 January 1873), 13–15.

To Charles Eliot Norton

Ms Harvard

44 Rue Neuve St. Augustin
Tuesday evening. Nov. 19. [1872]

Dear Charles:

I thought your first note excellent when it came, but I think it is even better now, since it has brought your second. Of your criticism or your repentance I don't know which I prefer, and thank you heartily for the affectionate tenor of both. You say the inventor of a work of art is always right. In a certain sense; but the critic is always right too; that is the impression of an intelligent observer has always an element of truth and value. I should be sorry never to write anything which mightn't suggest a question of its being right or wrong, at points. But ah, *probability*! Bugbear of the fictionist! Who will ever hit the happy medium between the too little and the too much—the prosaic matter of course?—All is well with me, as you kindly hope, and I am glad to hear it is with you in spite of rain and mud and early darkness. I am fighting the same enemies, backed up by the cold, and viewing every day that the Paris climate is too detestable for another day's endurance. But I like my life here and shall probably endure it for some weeks more—unless indeed M. Thiers and the Assembly between them treat us to another revolution and make an exodus prudent. We are *en pleine crise* and I suppose you will have got the news of yesterday's session. Is this unhappy people booked for eternal chaos—or eternal puerility? I don't know what the day has brought forth and am curious for tomorrow's news; the Republic may even now be decapitated.— I dwelt in a serener air for a couple of hours this morning, in walking thro' the Louvre with Emerson. I found him at Lowell's hotel, with his daughter when I went over there to dine on Sunday, according to my wont, and he then benevolently suggested our seeing the pictures together. Even when he says nothing especial, his presence has a sovereign amenity, and he was peculiarly himself this morning. His perception of art is not, I think, naturally keen; and Concord can't have done much to quicken it. But he seemed to appreciate freely the splendor of the Louvre, and that of Paris generally. But he's not one of your golden Venetians, whose society I decidedly envy you. Golden indeed they must seem in murky London. Love to everyone—*especially to Grace,* for her delightful answer to my letter of ten days since. N. B. This last message to be conveyed *literatim.* I believe she hath a conscience.—Goodnight.

Yours always, dear Charles,

H. James jr.

To William James

Ms Harvard

Paris 44 Rue Nve. St. Augustin.
Nov. 31*st*. [–Dec. 1] '72.

Dear Brother:—

I have not written home for nearly a fortnight. I suppose the domestic circle has begun to wonder at my silence. But it has not been caused by calamity of any kind. I am well, active and joyous and have been kept from writing only by a series of accidental interruptions and delays—humiliatingly trivial now that I look back on them. Meanwhile I have received an excellent letter both from Aunt Kate and Alice. That of my sister, which was extremely satisfactory, shall be answered within a reasonable period. Aunt Kate's contained such blessed good news about her eye that I am surprised at myself for not having immediately despatched her a note of congratulation. I enclose her a few lines in this.—I have from yourself a letter a month old which I have read over several times since getting it and should be unjust to leave longer unanswered. Aunt Kate and Alice both expatiate gleefully on that threadbare topic, as I believe you consider it, the remarkable salubrity of your appearance and I have ventured to reflect upon it with some complacency. If you are but half as well as they make out that you look I shall be perfectly satisfied. I hope, in spite of your improvement that you did nothing in the way of putting out the great Fire.[1] Aunt Kate's and Alice's letter contained the first details on the subject that had reached me, but as they wrote on the following day, these were still scanty. Anything more of especial interest I suppose some of you will transmit. There are some "views" of the burnt district in the last *Illustrated London News* which give the *débris* a grandly romantic appearance and make them look like the ruins of Palmyra. If they are as good as that I might as well be enjoying the picturesque at home.—The picturesque at any rate, has been with you and departed again, I suppose, in the shape of Bob and his plump little spouse.[2] Mother and Father can hardly fail to write me all about them and the impression they produced singly and unitedly. I hope everything seemed propitious for their happiness and prosperity.—With me the weeks chase each other along at a steady pace, none of them bringing as yet any great amount of grist to the mill. I have been busy the last fortnight writing a little story, which now that it is finished I hardly know what to do with—having other designs on the *Atlantic* I shall probably send it to the magazine (*Wood's Household*—degrading connection!) for which Gail Hamilton lately appealed to me.[3] My life is composed of many elements, but they have seemed hitherto quite sufficient. Mornings and very often evenings in my room; afternoons in the streets, walking, strolling, *flanânt,* prying, staring, lingering at bookstalls and shop-windows; six o'clock dinner at a restaurant (generally Hill's, on the Bvd. des Capucines, where I get a *rosbif saignant* and a *pinte*—a pot of prime English ale.) *De temps en temps* the theatre, which I don't enjoy quite as wildly as I expected; but quite enough to be thankful for. I have enjoyed nothing more than a night of Molière recently at the Odéon: the *Précieuses Ridicules* and the *Malade Imaginaire.* He was certainly the heartiest and most heroic of humorists. The *M.I.* is a broad farce with a vengeance but, acted as they do it at the Odéon, it's the sublime of the comic and a thousand times more wholesome than anything now going in Paris. I walked over to the Odéon in the rain (it hasn't stopped in three weeks) and enjoyed through the flaring dripping darkness from the Pont du Carrousel the great spectacle of the moment, the enormous *crue* of the Seine. The endless rains of the last six weeks have swelled it prodigiously and it stretched out from quay to quay, rushing tremendously and flashing back the myriad lights from its vast black bosom like a sort of civilized Mississippi. Not so very civilized either; if the rain keeps up, it will soon be in the streets. The weather is a great trial and makes of one's walks a rather dreary potter in the mud and wet. But one gets used to everything—even to seeing the sun but once a month. The rain too has kept away the cold and I haven't suffered at all from that bugbear. I cross the river once or twice a week to see Lowell, with whom I haven't exactly sworn an eternal friendship —but we have at any rate struck a truce to the mutual indifference

312

in which we dwelt in Cambridge. He is very friendly, entertaining and full of knowledge; but his weak point will always be his *opinions*. Poor little Mr. John Holmes, the most *unassimilable*, in Europe, of New Englanders, lives with him and they make a little Cambridge together. Of other society I have had that of Chas. H. Dorr, who called on me and chirped away as usual for half an hour; of Mr. and Mrs. Theo. Lyman and Miss G. Russell (with whom I dined the other day) and of the Dixwell family, whom I lately met at Munroes and was invited to call upon. They live a good bit off, near the Parc Monceau and are at housekeeping. Mrs. Dixwell is extremely handsome—her eye bluer and her complexion fresher than ever—and most emancipated and delighted with Europe.— Most of my social intercourse however consists of looking at people in the streets, theatres and restaurants. I find they excite my curiosity far more than at home—often doubtless *à tort* and always vainly. The Americans in Paris (as observed at Munroe's, the Grand Hotel etc.) excite nothing but antipathy.—I enjoy very much in a sort of chronic way which has every now and then a deeper throb, the sense of being in a denser civilization than our own. Life at home has the compensation that there you are a part of the civilization, such as it is, whereas here you are outside of it. It's a choice of advantages. I have the same feeling as you in coming to write, that I have made a note of a hundred things to say, but can't say them because they are a hundred and not two or three. I have made serious reflections about the French; but they are a threadbare topic and I'm tired of them. I've done them justice, mentally and arrived at a sort of ultimate feeling about them. I doubt if they are ever again a first class influence in the world; though they can't fail to be a precious second class one.—Politics are just now very lively and quite interesting and comprehensible even to politically stupid me. There has been a prolonged battle between Thiers[4] and the majority (monarchical) in the chamber, ending or tending to end in the discomfiture, well-deserved, of the latter. Thiers is really a sublime little creature, in his way, and since listening to that row at Lowell's table that I wrote you of, I can believe anything of monarchical blindness and folly. But every crisis, like the present, this republic outweathers and worries through in the regular parliamentary way, the less hope for either Bonapartists or Orléanists.

Monday A.M. *December 1st* It struck midnight as I wrote the above sentence, and I suddenly discovered that I was sleepy and went to bed. The morning brings nothing new but rain—which isn't at all new, and a letter from Lizzie Boott, from Rome. Àpropos of this, I have pretty well decided to repair thither a fortnight hence. A fortnight ago I thought of sticking it out in Paris two or three months more and letting Rome pass for the present. But I have come to the conclusion that this would be a tolerably—in fact an extremely—unremunerative course, and that if I have a chance to nail Rome I ought to do it without delay. I expect therefore to start about the 15th and beg you to address your letters till I give you a permanent address Care of *Spada, Flamini & Co. Bankers.* If anything comes to me here after I leave I can trust Mme Thuillier to forward it. Lizzie B. is enchanted with Rome and seems to be in the midst of a host of Americans—who, I can't say form an unmitigated attraction. Still, I shall brave them. Aunt Mary Tweedy has just written me a second time at great length, reviling the place as a "nest of abominations," and I am afraid from what Lizzie B. says, that in spite of her coupe with a "snowy stud" she is unhappy there. She offers me a room in their apartment, which I shall discreetly, and I hope, unoffendingly, decline. It would make one feel that the world was terribly small.—There were several things in your letters which I had at heart to reply to, categorically; but I must leave them till another time. For the present, farewell. Yours ever

H. James jr.

Was your overcoat satisfactory—and the Wordsworth?

1. The fire of 9–10 November 1872 in Boston's business section ruined the richest quarter of the city. An area of 65 acres was devastated; 776 buildings valued at $75,000,000 were destroyed.

2. Robertson James had recently married Mary Holton.

3. The magazine seems not to have materialized and the tale, probably "The Sweetheart of M. Briseux," appeared in *Galaxy*, XV (June 1873), 760–779.

4. Thiers had been president since the previous August.

314

To Henry James Sr.

Ms Harvard

Rome

33 Via Gregorian

Christmas morn [1872]

Dearest father.

"I was writ in a Roman Chamber," as Clough's poem says.[1] It is not mine however, but a little crimson drawing room, adjoining poor Mr. Tweedy's. I say poor Mr. Tweedy's, because he is lying ill with gastric fever, with which he was taken down some ten days ago. The worst is over, however, the doctor says, and Aunt Mary begins to breathe more freely. I found a letter from her in Florence denoting a good deal of anxiety on his account, and so came directly on day before yesterday. His fever has very much subsided, but he seems exhausted and despondent and talks about never getting up again. This of course is mere depression, for the doctor considers him satisfactorily convalescent and is waiting for him to pick up his strength with a returning appetite. Aunt Mary, for two or three days was alarmed and considers that he had had a close shave from typhoid; but Mr. Boott says he seemed very poorly for three weeks before he broke down and thinks he will be the better for it, when he gets up. He is there in his bed, staring through his window at St. Peter's dome, with his poor old melancholy eyes more dumbly appealing than ever; but I have no doubt that when I next write I shall have better news to give you.—Otherwise our friends are very well off; in a beautiful little apartment with the cream of the Pincian view, and a neat blue-lined *coupé*, and a venerable English *Cox*, for a "butler." The "pantry" is at last justified. But I am beginning at this wrong end of my story. You will have got my last letters from Paris, and have followed me sympathetically on my journey. It was very comfortable and much less cold than I expected. I came through in twenty-four hours to Turin, rested there a day; proceeded in another to Florence; spent a lovely day in that lovely place and came hither by day on the *24th.* [23rd] I have therefore been here but one complete day; long enough, however, to rec-

315

ognize Rome—and its changes. These are numerous—almost painful; and consist not so much in special alterations as in a kind of
modernized air in the streets, a multiplication of shops, carts,
newspaper-stalls etc., and an obscuration of cardinals' carriages and
general picturesqueness. It all promises me great pleasure, however,
and I shan't prejudge. The vast sunshine is divine, and I walked
about yesterday thinking my summer coat would be better on my
back than in my trunk. The Bootts are natural and friendly, and gave
me a Christmas-eve dinner of turkey and applesauce; and today I am
to feast with Aunt Mary—and Cox!—The above address doesn't
imply that I am staying here. I'm at the Hotel de Rome, till I find a
lodging, which I can't look for till after the festa is over. I will give
you my address as soon as I am fixed. I'm to drive with Aunt Mary
to St. Peter's at 2 o'clock; which is the only attempt we are making
toward the Christmas ceremonies. I must therefore return to my
hotel and get ready; and let this hasty scrawl suffice, with the addition of a great deal of love, for today. Address always till further
notice Spada, Flamini & Cie: from whom tomorrow I expect
forwarded letters. The Pope's Christmas blessing on you all!—I feel
the kindlier to him, since seeing Rome profaned at such a rate under
his apostolic nose.

Ever dear father—
your loving H.

1. HJ is quoting from Clough's *Amours de Voyage*, first printed in the
Atlantic Monthly and later included in Charles Eliot Norton's edition of *The
Poems of Arthur Hugh Clough* (with a memoir by Norton), Boston 1862.

To Mrs. Henry James Sr.

Ms Harvard

Rome, Hotel de Rome
Dec. 29th [1872]

Dearest Mother—
    You will have received before this my letter of three or four days
since, giving you an account of my arrival here and my first im-

pressions. My first week is almost over; it is a Sunday morning and by nature a time for letter writing, and I dispatch you these rapid lines in the interval of two visits. You will want first to know about Mr. Tweedy. He is better—is in fact doing very well. I see him every day, generally more than once. His fever has quite gone, and his strength and appetite are beginning to return. His convalescence I am afraid, will be rather slow and wearisome, and perhaps may end in their leaving Rome for change of air. He is enthusiastic about his doctor, an allopathic German, strongly resembling Willy, who has cured him with big doses of quinine (Aunt Kate's friend, Camillo Liberali he first tried, but without good results.)—My week seems to have been a very busy one, though much of it has passed away in the small doings that one forgets or dislikes to remember. I have resolutely sacrificed it to accident and chance but hope tomorrow to get to work. Some of it I spent with Mr. Boott, tramping up dark staircases in quest of lodgings. These are so scarce and dear that I combine more convenience and economics by remaining at my hotel, which is very "reasonable". I have a luxurious little room on the fourth floor with sun all day, for 4 frs. per diem. The best lodging I saw was 200 frs. a month (first price—the woman would have come down: but the situation was inconvenient.) Please therefore next address me here, where I shall remain, unless something better turns up.—I write this at my wide open window through which the sun is pouring and bathing me with warmth and light. This is our coldest day: the others have been of midsummer. I have gone slinking about in the shade, and last night killed a mosquito in my room. Aunt Mary has been very friendly and kind and has taken me every afternoon to drive in her little open carriage. This is a keen pleasure and one of the ways one most enjoys Rome. Today she asked me to dine with her and in the evening I go—where do you think? To the Cambridge Greenoughs confound 'em. I have not come to Rome for Cambridge tea fights, and shall content myself with this tribute to our ancient enemies. The chapter of "society" here—that is American society—opens up before me; but it remains to be seen if it is deeply interesting. I doubt it—having read the first pages. I went a couple of nights since to a little party at

317

Mrs. Cleveland's which its being in Rome didn't seem to make [it] very different from one of Miss Ashburner's least vivacious. There I met the famous Mrs. (Kemble) Wister[1] who is very handsome, and who nailed me for last evening, when I met everyone, including the terrific Kemble[2] herself, whose splendid handsomeness of eye, nostril and mouth were the best things in the room. Me *voilà* already intimate with Mrs. Wister to the point of having promised to go with her to the Villa Medici, the Academy of France; where she wishes to "shew me something she is very fond of." On this mysterious object I shall report; also as to whether I am growing very fond of her. This I don't foresee. I vaguely mistrust her. She is almost beautiful and has the handsomest hair in the world; but she is "intensely conscious," and diffident and lacks a certain repose comfortable to herself and others. She greatly resembles her mother; but beside her, Mrs. W. looks like the echo of Mrs. K. the voice.— I have just been interrupted by a visit from two Englishmen, one of whom I left in Florence whither I had travelled with him from Paris. He arrives this morning ushering a friend—a gorgeous London swell with a Jewish nose and name—Lucas. A converse with genial British simplicity and soon depart. So you see what with visiting and being visited I am making up for my Paris solitude. I must wash my hands and change my coat for Mrs. Wister, and will finish on my return. *5.15 o'clock.* It is over and I suppose I've had a mighty privilege—. We didn't go to the Villa Medici; but to the Colonna Gardens, where we wandered for nearly a couple of hours among mossy sarcophagi, mouldering along heaven-high vistas of ilex and orange and laurel, and lingered at the base of damp green statues and communed with the ghosts of departed Colonnas. After this criticism would be graceless. A beautiful woman who takes you to such a place and talks to you uninterruptedly, learnedly, and even cleverly for two whole hours is not to be disposed of in three lines. But I can't finish my letter even now. I must dress to dine with Aunt Mary and proceed thence to the Greenoughs', but will close off before going to bed . . .[3]

. . . Paris, a bottle of medicine from him in a sad state. The bottle seemed to have smashed on an early stage of the journey and the

medicine had evaporated. I shall try and get the same here, should
I need it. There is an excellent pharmacy.

Ever dearest mother your H.

1. Mrs. Sarah Butler Wister (1835–1908), daughter of Fanny Kemble the
actress and the southern plantation owner Pierce Butler. She was the mother
of the novelist, Owen Wister.
2. Frances Anne Kemble (1809–1893), celebrated actress and writer was
sixty-two when HJ met her in Rome. They remained close friends to the end
of her life.
3. This letter consists of two sheets, apparently a further sheet is missing
and only the last few words of the letter remain written on the margin of the
first sheet.

To Thomas Sergeant Perry

Ms Colby

Rome, Jan. 1*st* [1873]

Mine ancient Tom—

I rec'd yesterday your little editorial note,[1] relative to Théo.
Gautier; and meditated all day on your proposal. Forgive me when
I say I don't think I can undertake the task on exactly the scale you
would prefer. To write a really exhaustive article, I should have to
re-read him all carefully, with an eye to extracts, and distribute these
through a tissue of finely-wrought eulogy. The task is formidable
and almost impracticable. First: I am much preoccupied with some
other work. Second I have none of his books, and am pretty sure
I can't get more than one or two here. I should have to send for
them at much expense and considerable delay.—I should like very
much however to say a good word for our rare old Théophile,
whom the world doesn't seem to me to hold in a decent esteem. If
you like therefore, I will write a short notice, *à propos* of his last
volume, and try and say as many things in it as I can. If it should
expand in the writing, you can print it as a body article; but this I
doubt, and for want of references, at any rate, it would be inevitably
incomplete.—*Dunque,* I shall assume that you would rather have
this than nothing; shall begin it forthwith, and let you have it *au
plus tôt.*[2]—I would indeed you were with me, *Tommaso mio,* in this

319

wondrous old Rome which that ripe culture which has made you an editor would fit you so well to enjoy. I wish your note had been a little less confined to business. The next time you write treat yourself less exclusively as an editor and me less as a contributor. For these last eight months you have appeared to me fitfully illumined by flashing allusions in letters from home, as hovering on the dim confines of the Cambridge horizon: but of explicit statement as to your whereabouts and tendencies I have had little. I am very glad you are so honorably occupied—not that I'm surprised. Infuse your youthful life-blood into the *North American Revue* and be successful and happy. My people, and William, especially, must tell you about me: in this way I have written you many unanswered letters. I was introduced last night to an ingenuous young cousin of your's: Mr. Crown?—or Cram? He rides greatly on the Campagna: happy youth.—I will do what I can then, for T. Gautier. Don't be disappointed if it's very little.

Ever yours, dear Tom,

H. James Jr.

1. Perry had become an assistant editor on the *North American Review*.
2. "*Théâtre de Théophile Gautier: Mystères, Comédies et Ballets*" appeared as an essay-review in the *North American Review*, CXVI (April 1873), 310–329 and was later reprinted in *French Poets and Novelists* (1878).

To William James

Ms Harvard

Rome, Hotel de Rome

January 8*th.* [1873]

Dearest William.

I am so heavily in your debt for letters that I despair of discharging my obligations at a single sitting. Nevertheless, I must make a beginning. Shortly before I left Paris came to me your large and delightful communication of Nov. 24th, and since my arrival here I have been overtaken by your note of Dec. 8, enclosing T. S. Perry's petition to write on Théophile Gautier. I have had the beginning of a letter on my pen's end many times these last ten days, when Rome has been peculiarly suggestive and it has seemed a pity to swallow my impressions like a greedy feeder without offering some one a taste of it. You will know through my letter to mother of my having been here a fortnight, how I got here etc. I am taking Rome much more quietly and prosaically than before (—to this complexion do we come at last!)—but a certain restlessness was inevitable during the first days. This I have well worked off and now really feel at home. But I ought to tell you without delay of Mr. Tweedy, whom I found tolerably ill. He has been mending steadily ever since my arrival and it seems to me that his smooth recovery proves more in favor of the Roman climate than against it. His trouble was in no degree "Roman fever"—he is confident he would have had it anywhere as he had been for many weeks gastrically deranged. For the past day or two he has been a little less well; but the interruption is transient and I think he expects very soon to drive out. Aunt Mary, somewhat mellowed by tribulation, has been very hospitable and gracious to me; indeed I feel, dining and driving with her, as if during poor Tweedy's eclipse I were enacting a sort of *caro sposo*. Her dinners are of course good—and her drives (when she doesn't use up too much sunshine in a preliminary round at the butcher's and baker's) must be taken to be appreciated. She has a most affable coachman who talks, not Italian, but Roman—delicious stately full-lipped *Latin,* which adds greatly to the local color of a drive on the Appian Way.—I received a couple of days since a blessed letter from Mother, full of all goodness and especially of tender injunctions as to the care of my health. They are not superfluous, but I am incapable of being imprudent. I have made an excellent *début* in Rome in this respect. In Paris, I may say, I was not especially well for some five or six weeks before leaving; but since my arrival here all is changed and I am better than ever, almost. I don't know whether it is Paris's fault or Rome's virtue; but so it is and so may it remain! It is hard to think any ill of a climate in which on the 8th of January, you sit as I am doing now, fireless and coatless at your open window, with your room more than warmed—heated, by the strong sunshine. It is a blessed change from drenched and draggled Paris. The flies are irritating my nose, I have just killed a mosquito on my window-curtain, and in half an hour I am going (by invitation) to drive with Miss Cleveland and Lizzie Boott in the Villa Wolkonski.—Mother's letter spoke cheerfully of most things at home save of father's health. I am very sorry to hear of his having again those strange visitations (as I infer the case to be) of last winter. Give him my love and my wishes for their leaving him as suddenly as, if I remember right, they did before. I have had lately a good batch of home news in the shape of a letter from Aunt Kate. and one from Mother (as well as my own) to Aunt Mary Tweedy, which the latter gave me. Aunt Kate mentions Uncle James's death, of which I hadn't heard; a relief of course to every one. Yesterday came an *Atlantic* with my *Bethnal Green* notice and its other rare treasures. The B.G.N. doesn't figure very solidly as a "Lady-article"; it was meant as a notice. But it is as good as the rest, which, save Howells' two pieces, which his genius saves, read rather queerly in Rome. As I ought to be decently punctual for Miss Cleveland, I postpone further utterance to this evening which I shall devote to you.—Calling last evening, by the way, on Miss C. to tell her in answer to a note that I would drive with her, I found her mother in *tête à tête* with Mrs. Kemble, of whom I had thus half an hour's contemplation. She is very magnificent, and was very gracious, and being draped (for an evening call) in lavender satin lavishly *décolleté*, reminded me strangely, in her talk and manner, of the time when as infants, in St. John's Wood, we heard her read the *Midsummer Night's Dream*. It was very singular how the smallest details of her physiognomy come back to me.[1]

Evening. The Wolkonski is of course charming, but the visit was one of those party affairs which are (to me, at least) so deadly unprofitable. Miss Cleveland had invited the two Miss Greenoughs and Lizzie Boott and I stood round holding their shawls and listening to their prattle and grinning and wishing them at the deuce—and resolving I would go there before I got entrapped again.—I dined at the Tweedys' (an occasional privilege which bad Roman *tratterias* makes most valuable) and sat for an hour conversing by Tweedy's bedside.—I have been reading over your fine long letter to me in Paris, and find it contains a bewildering amount of answerable matter. Often in Paris I felt as if I had a hundred things to say to you, but I came away before the best of them got written, and now such of them as will keep must wait for future days.— It was a very pleasant and profitable couple of months I had there, and though to be at one's ease in Paris probably seemed to you in Quincy Street a more rich and wonderful fortune than it did as a regular thing to me, yet at certain hours I enjoyed it all keenly and gathered a host of impressions. Every thing Italian and especially every thing Roman, that is not a ruin, a landscape or a Museum, has such a deadly provinciality and more than American dreariness, that in coming here with a mindful of Parisian memories, one seems to have turned one's back on modern civilization. I regretted much in Paris, however, never having the chance to exchange a word with a typical Frenchman, and there grew to be something irritating at last in this perpetual humiliating sense of ungratified curiosity. There came enclosed yesterday in mother's letter a note from T. S. Perry offering me (if I would write back and ask for it!) an introduction from J. La Farge to Paul de Saint Victor. If it had come while I was there, I should have been very glad to use it; but if I had had to wait till John had heard from me and brought himself to send it out, I should, short of a miracle, have waited six months. But the mere daily and hourly spectacle of human life in Paris is greatly suggestive and remunerative.—*À propos* of all this, I thank you for the trouble of writing to sustain T. S. Perry's request to do something for the *North American Review* about Gautier. I immediately wrote to him that I wouldn't undertake anything on the large scale you recommend, having just now neither the inclination nor the opportunity (lacking his volumes) to re-read him all, *plume en main:* but I shall do something shorter which I hope he may make serve.—I am far from surprised at the admiration you express in your last for *Middlemarch.* I read it all in Paris and sent a review of it to the dilatory *Nation.*[2] (The *N.* has now *five* unprinted things of mine: of course I shan't add to the number till they begin to disgorge.) I admired and relished *Middlemarch* hugely, and yet I am afraid you will think I have spoken of it stingily. I necessarily judged it I suppose, more critically than you. Nevertheless I didn't make perhaps, a sufficiently succinct statement of its rare intellectual power. This is amazing.—You ask me to tell you what I am reading and thinking. I have been thinking (if thinking it may be called) almost too many things and reading too few. No new books—cropping simply on the few old volumes I brought with me. (About sending you *Middlemarch* by post—I left my set of it in Paris, to be kept at the Rastadt with a small pile of other books. It would have cost more than you seem to think—certainly more than *Harper's* cheap reprint.)—What I find Rome and am likely to find it, it is hard to say in few words. Much less simply and sensuously and satisfyingly picturesque than before, but on the whole immensely interesting. It is a strange jumble now of its old inalterable self and its new Italian assumptions—a most disturbing one for sentimentalists, such as generally all educated strangers are, here. It is an impossible modern city and will be a lugubrious modern capital, such as Victor Emmanuel is trying to make it. It has for this purpose both too many virtues and too many vices. It is too picturesque to spoil and too inconvenient to remedy. Of course in living here one isn't perpetually wound up to the seventh heaven of "appreciation" and sensation, but every now and then there come to you great gusts of largely-mingled delight such as no other place can give. Generally, what one feels and inhales, naturally and easily, with every breath, is the importunate presence of tradition of *every* kind—the influence of an atmosphere electrically charged with historic intimation and whisperings. Practical profit from so huge an influence as this must disengage itself shortly, but I hope eventually to get much. I shall stay on here as late as possible into the lovely spring and give myself a chance to react.—American "Society" here as far as I can judge of it, is a rather meagre affair, and the Bootts and Tweedies stand up in familiar shape like dusky terminal stones along the social horizon. However I am invited to dine on Sunday by Mrs. Terry (née Crawford,)[3]—or rather made Crawford, and née a sister of Mrs. Howe. She lives in great state in the Odescalchi palace and has a very agreeable and clever daughter. I am also bidden on Saturday evening by Mrs. Wister whom I have before mentioned and whom every one greatly admires. She is at moments, in certain lights and with her hat on, a startling likeness to Minny Temple; but the likeness is all in the face.—The "artist" society in Rome I have as yet seen nothing of. As far as it is American, I doubt that it amounts to much. I hear of no interesting men. I see the Bootts occasionally and find them of course unchanged. Lizzie is as sweet and good as ever, and is greatly enjoying Rome. She has a little studio, where she paints little tatterdemalion Checcos and Ninas— with decidedly increasing ability. She also rides three or four times a week with Miss Cleveland and a groom—and that would be enough to make misery smile. Lizzie has still the attribute of making you fancy from her deadly languid passivity at times, that she is acutely miserable. But she is evidently very happy and has plenty of society. Boott also greatly relishes Rome—that is his daily half-dozen walks with his overcoat on his arm. But they are fixed, I believe, to return in July.—I am writing such a letter as will ruin me in postage, and yet I haven't said any of the things which I have had it in my mind to say.—You suppose me of course to be growing all the while in wisdom and skill from association with those objects which you keenly feel the absence of. I grow more slowly than it must seem in Cambridge, than I ought to; but that I do grow, I hope continually to prove. I find I can work quite enough: but that I have everything to learn in the way of *how* to work.—I would write a short notice of Morley's Rousseau if I could have the book: but I can't get it here in Rome without great expense. I am now doing something for the *Atlantic*.—By this time I suppose you have begun to lecture or teach or preach, or whatever it is. Amen! This letter is for Alice as well as you: so that I send her no vain message but my love. This also to my parents. Farewell.—What a poor business is writing after all! Answer my letter nevertheless. Ever yours

H.

1. HJ's recollections of Mrs. Kemble's readings were incorporated in his memorial of her in *Essays in London* (1893).

2. HJ's review appeared in *Galaxy*, XV (March 1873), 424–428, the *Nation* having assigned the work to another reviewer.

3. Louisa Ward (1823–1897), wife of Luther Terry, American painter, and widow of the sculptor Thomas Crawford. She was the mother of F. Marion Crawford, the novelist.

To Henry James Sr.

Ms Harvard

[Rome Hotel de Rome]
[Jan. 8, 1873]

Dear father:[1]

Wishing to be thoroughly business-like I hereby notify you that I have just drawn on my letter of credit, the complement of the 250£ you have been holding for me. I draw the full sum in gold; but the difference will be more than made up by a cheque for my Bethnal Green Museum which must come to you from the *Atlantic*. If I should draw when you are actually without instalments of my revenue in your possession, you may generally count on some such soon overtaking the draft. I hope never to leave you out of pocket uncomfortably long.—I am very sorry to hear that you have not been well. May it be a transient trouble. I wish you were as comfortable as I! I am fixed still at this good hotel de Rome, where I find it healthiest, comfortablest and, all things considered, cheapest, to live. A hotel gives one a disagreeable *tourist* feeling, but this one is so large and grave and tranquil, that I feel as if I were a pensioner by the year in some soundless old convent. My little room has sun and stillness and perfect salubrity. I more than heed your and mother's injunctions about care. I am here in what has come to be considered (the middle of the Corso) the healthiest part of Rome. The *high* places are quite exploded. It is for me to say take care of *yourself*. Tweedy is getting well, smoothly but slowly. It has been a great experience for the poor old fellow and I think a consolatory letter from you would be very welcome. Addio.

Your loving H.

1. This letter was enclosed in the preceding.

To Henry James Sr.

Ms Harvard

Rome Jan. 19*th* '73.

Dearest father—

Your excellent letter of Christmas eve came to me safely a few days since and would have received my immediate reply but that I had despatched the day before a long letter to Willy and thought you would relish further tidings of me more after a longer interval. Your affectionate wishes and loving benedictions admit of no reply save that I should deserve them more in the future than I have ever done yet and that the tender and grateful thoughts they aroused should really fructify in my life.—It seems half strange indeed to be receiving such ungrudging good wishes from home—my lot being one to excite your hatred rather than your kindness!—plunged as I am in elegant leisure over here in this rich old Europe while you are bowed beneath the heat and burden of existence in your dreary America! I don't like to think of it and your attitude proves a rare magnanimity in one and all of you. My blessings on you;—but I shall bless you somehow or other with the fruits of my absence. These, as yet, are rather green however, and Rome is a wonderful place for stealing away your time, and giving you it may be much and it may be little in return. Just as I was shaking myself down with something of a productive mood again, I was visited by an interminable cold—about the worst I have ever had—which saddled me with a ten days' seediness. I treated myself mainly with going every day from one to three and sitting on the parapet of the Pincio to *cook* myself through—to bake it out of me. This was efficacious and I an now myself again.—Poor Mr. Tweedy is not getting well so expeditiously. His relapse is slow to pass away and he is condemned day after day to keep his bed. His patience is great; but his situation rather dreary. He has a very clever German doctor; but I believe both he and Aunt Mary consider the course of his malady a condemnation of allopathy—I don't know with what justice. He has no fever and a good appetite, but the derangement of the bladder continues. I have no doubt however the end is drawing nigh. Aunt

Mary expends a great deal of sharpness on people and things in general (and Cox the butler in particular;) but I come in for all her sweetness. Since my cold I have given up driving with her, but I often dine there and find it very wholesome. She is thankful for society—though she says that all her time is devoured by closing the doors and picking up the little chunks of wood as they tumble off the queer Roman hearths. Having been shut up much I have seen and heard little. I dined yesterday with the Bootts and Miss Connie Hall of Florence, a charming English girl and beautiful musician who is staying with them. Near ten o'clock I went to Mrs. Wister's weekly reception and conversed with Mrs. Sumner, Miss Bartlett,[1] Mrs. and Miss Story, Mrs. George Ward and Mrs. Kemble—in purple velvet and Venetian lace. Mrs. Wister seems to have marked me for her own—having again bidden me come to her this P.M. and be walked somewhither by her. She has a fierce energy in a slender frame and has always some social iron on the fire. She rides, walks, entertains, has musical rehearsals, writes largely (I believe) and is very handsome in the bargain. But as I believe I said before she isn't "easy." Aunt Mary has a great story of Mrs. Kemble—who was lately lamenting to her (A.M.) the decay of her accomplishments for beguiling solitude. She had lost her voice and couldn't sing, and her fingers were grown so stiff she couldn't play, etc. Whereupon A. M. in dulcet and insinuating tones: "Ah, but Mrs. Kemble, you can always READ!" To which Mrs. K., staring: "Yes, thank God, I can *read*,"—choosing, characteristically, to treat A.M. as if she had meant the newspaper.—I have now (proud privilege) the *entrée* of three weekly receptions—the Terrys, Storys and Mrs. Wister's. So you see I lack not society.—But enough about myself.—I have been reading sympathetically about your great Christmas snowstorm and your terrific cold—in which I hope poor Wilky was not buried nor frozen in his homeward journey. I am looking tomorrow for another letter telling me how much you must have enjoyed him and he you. Poor dear boy—how I should like to see him and hear from him the tale of his love and his strivings. May they be crowned with prosperity not too late. What a fierce affair your snow and your ice must have made for you. From over here, you look, at home, as if you were suffering a deluge of tribulations.—A recent letter of Aunt Kate's to Aunt Mary mentioned the failure of Mr. Sherman in Albany as affecting the Van Burens. Has it reached you? I suppose not—and I hope not the poor Gourlays. The Van Burens are indeed heavily afflicted.—All this time the winter here is no winter at all—the weather sublime, the days and nights wondrous with sun and moon. While I was unwell I treated myself to a dose of homesickness and fell to loathing Rome. But a better taste is coming back to me. Rome is indeed a strange compound; you can pick it to pieces and leave it not a stone to stand on—and yet it stands! But I will talk of this some other time.—I hope you are feeling better than when Mother wrote. Love to her, to Alice and to William. Write soon and often dearest father and believe that I treasure your words—

Ever your loving son
H. J.

1. Mrs. Charles Sumner (1838–1913). In 1873 she was awaiting her divorce, after which she resumed her maiden name of Mason. Alice Bartlett, a friend of Lizzie Boott and Mrs. Mason, later married a man named Warren. It was probably she who told HJ the anecdote which became "Daisy Miller."

To Thomas Sergeant Perry

Ms Colby

Rome, January 24*th*, '73

Dear Tom—

I enclose you today in another cover the paper on *T. Gautier,* which I trust will reach you safely. I have made more than a "notice" —but I am afraid you will think not quite an article. I suppose it will make some *fifteen* pages of large print. You will see that it is but slightly bibliographical, as I lacked time and material to make it so; but you will probably find it a prettily enough turned compliment—a sort of monody on his death. I gave it my best care and it is—I may say it—well written. May it serve your turn—and my hieroglyphics not bother you too much.—A word on its sure arrival will relieve my anxieties—the Roman P. O. being very eccentric.—

I suppose you have got my note of three weeks since and I hope are healthy and happy. Won't you walk with me this afternoon to the arch of Caius Quadrifrons. Do write me a brotherly note with a few *intimes* facts. A propos of *intimes* facts I have just heard of J. Gray's engagement. Passing strange!

Yours ever
H. James jr.

Direct your answer
Hotel de Rome

To Mrs. Henry James Sr.

Ms Harvard

Rome Jan. 26th, 1873
(Sunday)

Dearest mother—

I am in happy possession of your letter of January 6th with its delightfully copious news of all sorts—such a letter as you alone can write—as Alice and I used so often to say last summer. Ask her! —I came in an hour or more ago from a long walk upon which I had projected myself this morning with an energy increased by excessive confinement during the week's bad weather which has just been reminding us of our mortality. Rain in Rome brings out the dirt as darkness does a photographer's negative, and makes the streets impassible to the fastidious. I am not fastidious, but I hankered for exercise and walked down the Corso to the Forum and thence to the mouldy Temple of Vesta by the Tiber and thence along to the Gate of St. Paul, the Pyramid of Caius Cestius and the Protestant Cemetery which holds Shelly and Keats so picturesquely. I don't recite these fine names to aggravate you, for I regard the places far less gushingly than when I was here before and they often seem to me so shabby and rubbishy, too stale and *exploités* to deserve another thought. Today, however, under a beautiful cool light, (in which the sun made warm enough shadows however), it was all picturesque enough and satisfactorily Roman.—The days are passing terribly fast, the daisies and wild flowers are already starring the colorless grass, and though in places you are cool without your overcoat you are everywhere over-warm with it. Nothing has happened to me—and I want nothing to happen but that the weeks should smooth themselves before me and allow me to do an even stretch of work. The cold I mentioned in my last has wholly evaporated, and I feel much better than before I had it. Rome evidently agrees with me, and you may be assured that as far as I am concerned your fears as to its insalubrity are altogether vain. I hear of no illness and I apprehend none. Mr. Tweedy is almost well and has begun to walk and drive out very freely. His brother John Tweedy, with his wife and daughter, have just arrived, so that he will end his winter more jovially than he began it. The Bootts I see rather less than I have it on my conscience to and than Boott, I infer by signs which Alice will describe to you, thinks honorable of me. But I dined there a few days since and assisted afterwards at a tea party—rather heavy and dusky but relieved by fine music from the handsome Miss Hall they have staying with them from Florence. Rome is a place in which time disintegrates so strangely that in self preservation I cut down my "social" performances to the limits of courtesy. Society (American) here seems a very poor affair indeed. Limited and isolated, without relations with the place, or much serious appreciation of it, it tumbles back upon itself and finds itself of meagre substance. I am going tonight to a reception at the Storys, which apparently I shan't enjoy, as people don't pretend to. But fortunately they don't go before half-past *ten*! Don't father wish he was going? Mrs. Wister I see from time to time;—she is a "superior" woman but a beautiful Bore. Tell it not in Philadelphia—where I don't believe they know it. Going with her the other day to the Villa Medici, we beheld Edmond About walking in the garden— stout, and conspicuously clever-looking.—In all your home facts I was deeply interested, beginning with poor Wilky's visit. I'm sorry indeed that his work is so repulsive and uncongenial and promises so little change for the better. Poor boy! he has been much tried—it would seem it ought to have been for some better use than his present one. I trust Bob's cheerful hopes for him may come to something. Bob's own situation and state of mind seems to leave nothing to be desired. His religious convictions seem to me very admirable and it is a fine thing to see them so real and ever-present and capable of playing such a substantial part in his life. I hope his Prairie du Chien move is in effect an era in his destiny. With such a spirit and such a wife he certainly ought to conquer fortune?—I heard of Willy's first lecture without a desire to throw pence at him, and feel sure that his pupils by this time have been charmed by his accents like the forest-brutes by Orpheus. May he profit both himself and them!—John Gray's marriage is interesting, and one can't think ill of a girl whom he thinks good enough to be his wife. I suppose he will "educate her up" to him; and I hope that whether she stays up or down, she will make him happy.—*Monday morning.* I was obliged to suspend my letter yesterday and must finish now. Today dawns superbly—as clear as your finest winter and as mild as April. I sit, as usual, at my open window alongisde of the flooding sun.—The sequel of yesterday brought forth the Storys' reception which was very pleasant:—Mrs. Story fair, fat, and fifty, her daughter "chatty and an agreeable partner" and very handsome withal and Mr. Story friendly, humorous and clever. An apartment in a Roman palace is a very fine affair, and it certainly adds a picturesqueness to life to be led through a chain of dimly lighted chambers, besprinkled with waiting servants, before you emerge sonorously announced, into the light and elegance of a reception-room with a *roof,* not a ceiling.[1]—I lately called by the way on Miss Sara Clarke, who sent me an invitation through the Tweedys. She has a jolly apartment (if you reach it with an unbroken neck, through the midnight of her staircase) and seems a most worthy woman. She showed me a lot of drawings she has been making of spots in Italy reputed to have known the tread of *Dante's* wandering foot. The drawings are mild, but it has been a delightful errand for her, these several years past, to look up the localities.[2] She sent many messages to father, you and Aunt Kate. I have just heard a rumor that the Ashburners are here, and shall look them up and report to Alice on Annie. But it may be false. I recd. this A.M. (from the office—a great compliment!) a copy of the *Nation* with my Paris

Stage letter, with "blood-stained *pavements*" printed blood-stained *garments* (!)—*amuseur* "amateur"—and other similar delights.[3] Has the *Atlantic* by the way sent father a cheque for my *Bethnal Green*? Please tell Howells that I wrote him a fortnight ago. And to T. S. Perry when you see him that I lately sent him a thing on Gautier which will have fallen due—I trust indeed Stokes will be hanged.[4] I have just been reading in the Roman papers an account of the queer scene on the rendering of the verdict. It sounds queer enough in Italian,—but it must have been disreputable even in American. Poor Smith Van Buren! And amazing Mrs. Lombard! I shall expect to hear from her.—Send my letters to Aunt Kate when they seem worth it. Farewell dearest mother. Love to father sister and brother from your

H.

1. Story occupied for many years a large apartment of some fifty rooms in the Palazzo Barberini.
2. Sarah Freeman Clarke, sister of the Unitarian James Freeman Clarke, friend of HJ Sr. and of Emerson. She studied with Washington Allston.
3. "The Parisian Stage," unsigned, in the *Nation*, XVI (9 Jan. 1873), 23–24, reprinted in *Transatlantic Sketches* (1875).
4. Edward S. Stokes had shot and killed the financier James Fisk, the previous year, and was now on trial in New York. HJ, always interested in murder trials, had apparently been following the lurid case which involved Josie Mansfield, Fisk's mistress, who became the mistress of Stokes.

To Henry James Sr.

Ms Harvard

Rome February 1st. [1873]

Dearest father—

I have just received your long and most satisfactory letter about the proof of my story and Howells's restrictions, invitations etc. The former I regret, and as far as I can remember the "immoral" episodes don't artistically affront. With such a standard of propriety, it makes it a bad look out ahead for imaginative writing. For what class of minds is it that such very timorous scruples are thought necessary?[1]—But of course you were quite right to make all convenient concessions, and I am much obliged to you for your trouble. Evidently, too, Howells has a better notion of the allowances of the common public than I have, and I am much obliged to him for performing the excision personally, for of course he will have done it neatly. About his offer to have me write monthly for the *Atlantic Monthly* I shall directly write to him. I am charmed and ask nothing better.—I shall have to ask you a further service: Viz:—I sent six weeks since a short MS. Story to Miss Dodge, according to her invitation (which I thought seemed to promise remuneration) for *Wood's Magazine*. I yesterday hear from her that she has had bilious fever, *Wood's Magazine* is exploded, and what shall she do with the precious packet? I have written her to send it you; and would like you to forward it (marked visibly outside with my initials—or even name) to F. P. Church, Editor *Galaxy,* whose address you will find in the corner of the magazine and to whom I enclose a note for you to post.[2] I don't offer the story to Howells, because, like the *Madonna of the Future,* it hinges on a picture, and because I am on the point of sending him something else.[3]—This doesn't pretend or propose to be a letter. I shall write sentimentally in a day or two—being now about to start to lunch with the Baroness von Hoffmann (Lily Ward —none other!) at her ravishing villa, which I saw on calling there the other day, though I didn't see her. She politely immediately invited to me lunch. I will report of it when I write next. But the day will all but spoil it, for the rain is unceasing and I must expend on a cab.—

3.30 P.M. Back from the Hoffmann's—a long drive in a torrent of rain and the villa with its lively *entourage* of the Coliseum, the Baths of Caracalla, the Arch of Constantine etc. perhaps a trifle lugubrious. Our party, beside the hosts, Dr. Wister (a very good fellow) Baron Ostensaaken (something in the way of a Danish envoy I believe) and Mr. Parker a musty and famous old antiquarian. Von Hoffmann a friendly and polite little German, and Lily amiable and loquacious as ever. She sent affectionate messages to you all, and hoped some day to see you all in Rome! We lunched in a dining room with a roof like the Dome of St. Peter's, with three lackeys behind our chairs. Altogether it was pleasant enough. Nothing else of great importance has lately happened to me. Aunt Mary last night gave a little party to feast Mr. Tweedy's recovery (which is now complete)—though indeed its numbers were scanty for the purpose; the Bootts, their friend Miss Hall and little Miss Crane a rather pretty but rustic niece of the Marshes. On these last, by the way, I'm assured it's my duty and interest to call; but I haven't yet acquired a realizing sense of it. Perhaps it will come to me. I went yesterday to the studio of that worthiest of men Mr. Terry, husband of Mrs. Crawford and step-father (dreadful trade!) of Miss Annie C.[4] I didn't know how worthy he is, till I saw his pictures—the Artist's Dream, the Vision of St. John etc—the queerest old survivals of the American art of thirty years ago. It is an agreeable curiosity to see their author sit and look at them seriously and expound his intentions and yet be on the whole a sensible man of the world. His studio is one of those delightfully odd nooks which constitute the superiority of Europe to America. A squalid house in a squalid street, promising gross darkness within. You ring and the door is opened by an invisible agency; you ascend a long stone staircase and find yourself in a delightful little second story court or hanging garden, open to the sky and bedecked with verdant bower and trellis. Straight out of this opens the large still studio.—The main episode of the last week for me was my at last making a beginning with a scheme that I had much at heart in coming to Rome. The thought of it indeed was the thing which really uprooted me in Paris. I took a delicious two hour's ride on the Campagna and can now believe all the ravings of the people who ride here. I took a couple of turns first at the _manège_ to remind myself how it felt to brave the slippery saddle—forgotten since the days of Moses—and then got hold of a docile beast recommended by Julian Story.[5] It was an immense pleasure and has brightened my outlook on existence. I can stick on a horse better than I supposed and have a very tolerable seat, and at the end of my two hours I came bounding back through the Porta del Popolo as if I had never done anything else. It has been my dream that a couple of months riding may supply me with a valuable sort of exercise—to say nothing of its intrinsic delights (and its extrinsic—such as gallops with Miss Alice Bartlett)—prove in short a physical, intellectual and moral education. If this degenerate weather doesn't spoil everything and I can fix on a good horse I shall try it again and let you hear more of it—loathe me as you will! If it is really the peculiar pleasure I imagine it to be, it ought to do great things for me—and one ought to do great things in consequence, to prove one's right to it.—Father mentions little news save that Alice is having headaches—beloved and cruelly afflicted child. She must try and stick it out till she can come to Rome, where I will await her and then on the best horse that can be found, she will have a winter of gallops on the Campagna. That will fix her for a lifetime. I will soon write to her.—I should like to hear one of Willie's lectures. Does he hear anything as to how the students like them?—I suppose you are pulling heroically through your winter of snow-drifts, duly toned up to the scratch by unremitting icy blasts. I wish the 1st February marked your way downhill as it does here. The violets and anemones have been out for a fortnight. This is my first complete experience of a mild winter—for up to the time I left Paris there had been no cold to complain of. I must say I kind o' like it—and like above all this early nearness to spring.—I have thought much of poor Wilky since you last wrote about him—but can only hope for him. —After all, I have written a letter, but must end it now.—I don't think there is anything to add to my remarks in the beginning. Carnival is to begin in a few days; but I believe it has fallen into great shabbiness.—Love to my beloved mammy, and thanks dear father, for all your services. Love to William to whom I lately sent a long letter.—

Your affectionate H.

I have just heard from and written to Aunt Kate. Mention it in writing to her.

1. HJ alludes to "The Madonna of the Future," *Atlantic*, XXXI (March 1873), 276–297. Howells took exception to the speeches by the cynical artist friend of the protagonist who constantly compared the human race to "cats and monkeys."
2. "The Sweetheart of M. Briseux" appeared in *Galaxy*, XV (June 1873), 760–779.
3. Probably "The Last of the Valerii," *Atlantic*, XXXIII (January 1874), 69–85.

4. Luther Terry, the painter, was step-father of Annie Crawford, later Countess von Rabe, and of F. Marion Crawford.

5. Son of William Wetmore Story

To Alice James

Ms Harvard

Rome February 10*th* 73—

Dearest sister:

I think it is not much more than a week since I last wrote home and you can not quite yet have begun to conjecture that the hand of death has been laid upon me. I am very much alive—especially when I stamp and swear at the non-arrival of letters from home—which I have lately been left to do for a little longer time than usual. Something must come today or tomorrow, or I shan't know what to think of it.—I continue remarkably well and prosperous and the days chase each other along with amazing speed. The faster the better, till celestial spring arrives and the crowd thins out and we can see Rome, as my intimate friend M. Hébert[1] (the French painter says) *renaître à elle-même*. Sight-seeing barbarians are oppressively numerous—and among them, by the way, the familiar *Andrews*. I yesterday espied Miss Edith flitting through the corridor and hailed her and was taken by her to her mamma in the dining room. They are just arrived from Naples and are to be here the rest of the winter. Mrs. A. seems about the same at the Hotel de Rome as at the Hotel de Scarboro! Bessie I haven't yet seen, but will look them up today and give you further news of them. I don't know that I have anything amazing to relate. Rome doesn't amaze—it quietly, profoundly, intensely delights and satisfies. As the weeks pass by I find myself settling down to it, morally, with less and less reluctance and more and more devotion. It is partly the inevitable attachment one forms for any place one tries to *live* in (I think I might even—such is the force of this tendency—have grown fond of Münich!)—but chiefly of course the fact that taking bad and good together Rome abounds in interest and ever-varying charm. The first month I was here I was acutely homesick for the high civilization of Paris

337

—especially in the evening, at the hour the theatres go in—when I groped homeward from my dinner through a narrow black alley lighted by a single lamp, in which, here and there, in a dusky caffé a lot of frugal Romans were huddled round a lot of empty tables. But there are compensations—and one by one I am learning them. I mingle enough in society to give a flavor of magnificence to my life—am moreover getting fond—which is the only footing on which you can acquire any sense of permanence here—of the very barbarisms and miseries and uncleanesses of Rome. I might as well let my hair grow at once like a German religious painter, or begin and prattle about the Holy Father, like the Baroness Von Hoffmann. —I had an errand this morning at the Piazza Barberini—(the Bootts') and found Lizzie in her studio, *en tête à tête* with one of the very swell models—a wondrous youth in a sheepskin jacket and bandaged legs and flowing curls and the most pictorial complexion. The color of all the tribe of models here is far superior to their "shapes," which must have degenerated of late years, for they are generally very meagre and common. Lizzie is very busy, happy and good. (She recently received a letter from you.) I am trying to arrange to ride with her, but innumerable obstructions (including a good deal of woeful rain) have hitherto prevented it. It was in my last I think I mentioned that I had made my *début* in the saddle. Since then I have twice repeated the experiment and now feel capable of going anywhere my horse will take me. I have this morning ordered this amiable brute to the Porta Salara for three o'clock and as the day is brilliant, it will go hard but I get my money's worth. My first ride struck me as a revelation of bliss; the two second were rather spoiled by dark weather and bad roads, but today I expect again to find myself wishing that you might be hounding at my side. If this strain displeases you I will stop—but would that you might nevertheless!—I have enjoyed besides this week, my usual modicum of parties—beginning with a grand musical flare-out given by Mrs. Terry. She has a beautiful concert-room attached—thrown in—to her apartment and she has good music and all the world to listen to it. Miss Reed (sister of Mrs. Paran Stevens) sang luxuriantly, and the chorus performed a composition of Mr. Boott's, which was very well received. On Saturday I went to Mrs. Wister's reception and conversed with Miss Trench, daughter of the Archbishop of Dublin (the gentleman who writes on *Words* etc.) chiefly on *Middlemarch* from which like a well-drilled English maiden, she recited many passages from memory. Also with M. Hébert the French painter and director of the Villa Medici—an easy mannered, friendly little personage, who invited me to his Sunday evenings at the Academy. With him, Regnault was the theme. He knew him well and praised him warmly—even to his *sourcils bien acquis* and *barbe bien plantée.* He said that the volume of R.'s letters is very incomplete. He had been asked for none of his own and he had many better than those printed. Yesterday I dined at the Storys, in company with the Wisters, the Marchese somebody, a mellifluous Italian master of ceremonies to the King and the extraordinary little person known as Hattie Hosmer.[2] The latter looks like a remarkably ugly little grey-haired boy, adorned with a diamond necklace, but she seems both "vivacious" and discreet and is better, I imagine, than her statues. The Storys, if you take them easily, are very good. Story himself is evidently a rare organization and he does you a service by shewing you his singularly handsome, expressive and vivacious physiognomy. It's a very remarkable face and reminds me a little of Dickens's. Miss Story is a girl of whom her friends say that she is much less "spoiled" than she might be. She doesn't strike me as offensively so, and is, moreover very pretty and sings deliciously. "*Ce frémissement dans votre voix, mademoiselle,*" said Hébert to her after a song the night before at Mrs. Wister's— "*est-ce la peur ou est-ce l'art?*" "*C'est la peur.*" "*Elle vaut bien de l'or, cette petite peur là!*" said Hébert. And meanwhile I was standing gawkily by, wondering what the deuce to say to Miss Story on her singing.—After the dinner—at 11 o'clock, while you were all virtuously snoozing, I repaired with Mrs. Wister to the Villa Medici. Here, in a great saloon, hung all round with antique Gobelins—a most delicious apartment,—were congregated the twenty students of the Academy, a knot of effete young *attachés,* and three or four formidably fine French ladies. A great deal of solemnity, a little music, and no introductions. I should have sate twirling my hat but that an amiable young fellow whom I had met at Mrs. Wister's introduced me to an intimate friend of Regnault's, a certain Blanchard, who talked agreeably about him—beginning characteristically with the statement that he was a *nature bien seduisante, aimant beaucoup les femmes et très aimable avec elles.* Toward one o'clock we departed, through a tremendous tapestried library and wondrous portico, looking out on the gardens of the Villa, flooded with magical moonlight.—In the way of prosier pleasures I daily see the Tweedies and frequently dine with them. Tweedy is altogether restored and seems more jocund and youthful than in a long time. He is extremely well pleased to be living here and resists Aunt Mary's proposals to go home and try Virginia—or Canada! To such eccentricities is she pushed by the irritation of her Roman housekeeping. She takes the small things of life too hard for her own comfort or that of other people. They think, I believe, of going to Albano, for a week's change of air. The John Tweedies have gone to Naples. My alarm, by the way, about the Ashburners was false, for I neither see them nor hear of them.—The wretched sky is darkening up and I'm afraid I shall miss the great thing—the *effets de soleil* on the mountains. But this is a calamity over which I can hardly expect you to shed tears.—I've heard no *news,* from home, now in sometime. My last letter was from father about my *Atlantic* matters and my appetite for domestic tidings is getting sharp. I was truly grieved to hear, dearest sister, that your head has become feeble again and that you can use it but little. I hope you find enough to do in a frivolous way, to help you to let learning alone. I have dilated at such length on my worldly pleasures that I have earned the right to hear of yours. Have you been to any parties and worn the Montreux dress? I suppose you see much of the Sedgwicks—and I wish you would give a very affectionate message to them from me— especially to Sara. Have you formed any new ties or had any new sensations? I suppose you still sometimes muse in the watches of the night or the sleepy hours of the day, as I do, upon last summer's doings. They have become to me as the shadow of a shadow. But may we try something like them again and find that they are real!— I got lately a long good and apparently cheerful letter from Aunt

Kate from whom I suppose you often hear. I hope you sometimes, as always, send her my letters. Tell me when you write everything about every one. Do you ever see Fanny Holmes? Is John Gray's engagement yet explained? Does T. S. Perry live in Cambridge etc? You will also have heard from Bob, on his arrival at Prairie du Chien. I desire news of that, and of poor Wilk's estate and fortunes. Has he got B's place? I must scribble to a close and go forth to mount my steed. Farewell, sweet sister. Love to each. I trust father is being let off easily with his queer trouble. Write me promptly—believe me your adoring bro.—

H

1. Ernest Hébert (1817–1908), artist-director of the French Academy in Rome, the Villa Medici.
2. Harriet Goodhue Hosmer (1830–1905), American sculptress, whose work was admired by Hawthorne. She is described by HJ in his life of Story.

To Mrs. Henry James Sr.

Ms Harvard

[Rome] Feb. 17th [1873]

My own dear mother—

A week ago came to me your letter of Jan. 21st and last night arrived father's of the 31st. All thanks for both. Yours contained some quotations from a letter of Bob's about poor Wilky, which gave one rather a dismal feeling about him—dismal and yet hopeful; and father last night hints that Miss C. under the circumstances is not an especially tonic influence. He says this is a mere guess however, and I hope it may have been a wrong one. I can't but believe that Wilky will pull through—and at any rate, I feel so ill fitted here in Rome to conceive or appreciate his circumstances and his difficulties, that I can hardly bear to think of him. I have been meaning any time for a month to write to him. Give him my especial love when you write and tell him he shall very soon hear from me. Bob seems to be going ahead and fame and fortune already dawning on him. May they swell to a noonday blaze of prosperity! He certainly deserves it! Prairie du Chien! Think of it—and if you could think of it, as I do, with the Corso and the Roman Carnival hub-hubbing outside of your window. But Prarie du Chien contains, I warrant, nothing so drivelling:—so foolish as this same hubbub. It takes the capital of "Latin" Christendom to produce that sort of thing.—Both your and father's letter contain urgent inquiries as to "what I am living on?" I am surprised that Messrs. Brown Bros. should lately have given you a hint. In Paris I lived on certain moneys which I had. Just before leaving I drew from Munroe £30 to pay off bills for clothes, hotel etc. and journey hither. On Jan. 7th I drew twenty pounds which has lasted me to this morning. These two draughts, fifty pounds (£50) represented to my imagination the 250£ which father wrote me the *Nation* had sometime since sent him for my five summer letters. (for two later ones—one not yet published—it had subsequently paid me.) As I drew in gold, I of course overdrew the 250£, but other things to come to father will cover the difference. From the *Nation* he ought to receive another cheque for my two last things at least; and from the *Atlantic* there should have come a *cheque* for my *Bethnal Green*. Nothing was sent to me and I had fully meant to make a point of asking Howells to have it addressed to him. I have written to ask H. whether it was really sent. If I omitted my request it was strange forgetfulness. As the thing has not come they ought to give another. The *Nation* has treated me very shabbily about *Middlemarch:* I didn't expect it of them. I wrote to Garrison last summer when the book was half out that I would review it and he replied that he would be charmed. I sent the review promptly and he answered me that it had come and was in the printer's hands. A week ago arrives the *Nation* (they have sent me the last few numbers from the office) with this foreign article instead of my own—and nothing since in the way of apology or explanation, till father tells me that Dennett had told Willy that they had sent my thing to the *Galaxy*. It's all unrighteous: the throwing me overboard at the last minute for a stranger, after an agreement and after my long service—the sending me no notification of it, and the disposing of my M.S. in that irresponsible way. Dicey's[1] article was very good, but as a general acct. of the book mine (I make bold) was better. But I see there is to be 2d part in which Dicey will perhaps overtake me. I should have preferred to have them offer my thing to Howells. But I trust you may duly hear from the *Galaxy* about it.—You will have received by this time a note from me, asking you to forward to Church (*Galaxy*) a package (M.S. tale) which Gail Hamilton will have sent you. I send today to Howells a similar package, and if you see him mention it, so that he may know it ought to have arrived. With what I have sent, am sending, and shall continue to send, (the cheques always to be sent to you) I think I shall not fail to keep you funded up to the point I draw on you. But I am surprised you haven't had news of my two last drafts. I this morning drew £20 more from Spada & Flamini; which cheques for the three things lately printed ought to cover.—Life in Rome is but moderately expensive and I ought to live here comfortably for about *half* of what I could live at home alone and comfortably for. My weekly bill for instance at this hotel for everything except dinner (room, service, breakfast—beefsteak potatoes etc— fire and lights) is about 70 francs—Italian paper. For this I live *luxuriously*, I may say, and I certainly couldn't get the same at a poor Boston boarding-house for $14. The restaurants are poor—very poor—but they are cheap. The cabs are 16 sous a course—anywhere within the vast *enceinte* of Rome. Most other things (except the rent of apartments which is abnormal) are proportionate. It must be added that much that is cheap—shops etc—is decidedly bad. My riding is my only serious expense—11 frs. for as long a ride as you please or 300 frs. for a horse by the month. But this is so substantial a pleasure and profit that I can manage it. In fine, I shall be able, I think I may claim, (especially as time goes on and I learn to produce with less waste of labor) to make comfortably and very comfortable subsistence here.—This long economical statement has been provoked by your tender questionings. Your blessings on it!—What terrible tricks your thermometer is playing you!—tricks which even father's rhapsodies about the effulgent light and the crystal skies and the unsullied snows don't persuade me to prefer—in thought, to my present privilege—my open window, my unlit fire and the muslin curtains drawn to temper the sunshine. We have been having however a week of frost and crisp *tramontana* weather—and behold the effect—the debauching effect—of luxury, in climate as in other things. This mild severity of the air seemed to me hideous and I prayed (wholesome as it was) that it should end. It *has* ended, and I suspect that we are going to slide warmly into spring.—The days pass and resemble each other—not too monotonously. Carnival began two days since; but it seems to me strangely shabby and charmless. Its chief merit is that it concentrates the accursed *forestieri* in the Corso and leaves the rest of Rome freer to wander in. —I took a long walk with Lizzie Boott throught the heart of the city and to several churches, yesterday afternoon (Sunday) and observed duly the keen holiday-keeping passion of this Southern race. In the evening I went to the Terry's reception and talked for an hour and a half with a Mlle. Giliucci, a daughter of Clara Novello, the once celebrated singer, who sometime since married an Italian count who lives on his patrimonial estate in the Marshes of Ancona and brings his family to Rome for a couple of months in the winter. She was a nice, simple Italian maid, speaking very pretty English.— Today I dine at the Von Hoffmanns—a large party, I believe. A couple of days since I rode with Lizzie Boott and shall soon do it again. These facts belong to the superficial sort of information which father says Willy wishes me to replace by statements as to what I read, think and feel. As to this, I lack, not the will but the means. I think and feel a good deal, but the less said about my reading the better. I have read nothing but a little Italian and a volume of Montaigne since I have been in Rome. What with my slow and laborious writing, my going out evenings, my making calls, my afternoon walking riding and sight-seeing, my daily inquiries after Mr. Tweedy's health—I have had little time for reading. And yet Rome and Italy make one long to handle books. I have surrendered myself to seeing "life" here, in so far as it offers itself; I shall work through it however, and then read as far as I can. But yet while I can't read very actively during the days I'm writing. —With practise I shall learn to write more briskly and naturally. Practice tells slowly with me and it seems, as yet, the successive difficulties that chiefly dawn upon me. But eventually I shall write none the worse for having learned slowly. Meanwhile I keep up a devil of an observing, and would write much more easily if I heeded things a trifle less.—I read Italian regularly for a short time daily and find it very easy. I had it at heart when I came here to try and hire some pleasant fellow to come and talk with me; but I must wait till the season tapers off and especially till I give up riding.—The Tweedies are gone to Albano for a few days and I believe are enchanted with it. The Temples (Capt. and Mrs.) are daily expected. The Andrews are living here luxuriously, without apparent loss of fortune or serenity, and are showing a laudable energy in sightseeing. Mrs. A. is very appreciative. Continue to address H. de Rome. I expect to stay here till May 1st. I wrote last week to Alice. Blessings on you all. Love to William who must write when he *can*, but not before.

H.

1. Albert Dicey (1835–1922), fellow of All Soul's, essayist and literary journalist.

To Henry James Sr.

Ms Harvard

Rome, March 4*th* [1873]

Dearest father—

I haven't written for a longer time than usual, because I have been waiting for a letter from home—which doesn't come. The last, now more than a fortnight since, was from you. Since then I have written to mother, and I hope my letter will not be lost, as possibly one of yours has in this interval. But I hope not. I had rather you had not written at all. I am well and happy and still rejoicing in Rome. The spring has begun in earnest and the sun is getting decidedly fierce. I foresee that my generous south-window will become a nuisance before long and that I shall incline to change my room. I am sick of hotel-life to which I have now been restricted for nearly ten months and long for perfect privacy.—*Vedrèmo!*—Since I last wrote the Carnival has died and been buried—greatly to the relief of everyone lodged on the Corso, which for ten days was transformed into a squeaky pandemonium. But I am on the point of enclosing some remarks on it to Howells, to which I refer you for details. Lent has now begun and I am hoping that the unprofitable little invitations to which I have been sacrificing myself for the last two months in the hope of some latent profit, will die a natural death. What do you think—what does Alice think—of my having to go tonight to the Greenoughs—having declined them before? There I shall bury my dress coat. Last night I was bidden again to the Archbishop of Dublin's (who seems fairly *hungry* for my society) and to Miss Sarah Clarke's to meet the Emersons, back from Egypt. I let them both alone; but in the morning I had called on the E's and had had the pleasure of serving them by giving them my passes to the Vatican. They are very serene and appreciative and Emerson was as lovely as ever. Of course you will see them and learn everything about their travels.—The Tweedies and Boots rub along and I rub against them as usual. Tweedy is quite himself again—but poor Aunt Mary is passably erratic and uncomfortable. She is in a state of chronic dissatisfaction with everything. Mrs. William Temple has just come to them for a month. The Boots I see pretty often, especially now that I have begun to ride pretty regularly with Lizzie. I have taken a very nice little horse for a month, as that was the only way to get him—he being engaged twice a week to follow the hounds and to be had neither on those days nor the morrow's. I didn't judge myself *de force* to go round trying horses promiscuously: so now for a month I am master of a great privilege. He has a charming little character and yet is sufficiently lively to assist me somewhat; to learn to ride. For some ten days past, I have been incapacitated by—to speak plainly—a *boil;* but before that I had one day a famous ride with Mrs. Sumner and Miss Bartlett: both admirable horsewomen, especially Miss. B., and both very handsome in the saddle. We went far away in to the rolling meadows, where the shaggy-vested shepherds feed their flocks and had a series of magnificent gallops, of which I acquitted myself *à mon honneur*. But for me and my infirmities, they ride at rather a tiring rate, and as Lizzie depends upon me, I shall be chiefly her companion.—The rival houses of Story and Terry have each been having theatricals—each indifferently good—in spite of the two clever heads presiding at each—Story himself and Miss Annie Crawford. The latter (Miss C.) is quite the most remarkable person I have seen in Rome. She has every gift (including a face so mobile and expressive that it amounts almost to beauty) but she is as hard as flint and I am pretty sure will never have an adorer. He will have to be a real Lion-tamer.[1] She is supposed to lead her step-father (poor Mr. Terry) a terrible life. She told me a few evenings since right under his nose, that she *hated* people who had no "modelling" in their faces; and I have no doubt that poor Terry who has as roughly-finished a plebian a countenance as you often see, keenly realizes the fact.—A much sweeter girl, as well as a very clever one, on whom I occasionaly call in the dusky half hour before dinner, is Miss Lowe[2] (of Venice) of whom Alice will have heard Lizzie Boott speak. She is very handsome, very lovely, very reserved and very mysterious, and ought to have many adorers. But I am not yet regularly enlisted as one of them. I have seen no one else in society here (the very small society I have been in) who has caused a pulse of curiosity in the least to beat. Mrs. Wister has beautiful hair; but on the whole I don't at all regret that I'm not Dr. Wister.—Your little admirer, Eugene Benson, has called on me twice; in consequence of which I went lately to his studio and saw several careful and conscientious but very uninspired little pictures.[3] I don't know whether I have mentioned going also to the Storys'. *His* inspiration is very unequal: though his cleverness is always great. His things, on the whole though, are fatally un-simple.—Everyone seems to be in Rome and I constantly pass in the street carriage-loads of people I know. But I fix a stony stare on some merciful column or statue: for life is too short to go to see them all.—The Andrews have left this hotel and gone to a smaller, where I dutifully called on them and found them happy. But I *almost* notified them it must serve for evermore.—These shoals of American fellow-residents with their endless requisitions and unremunerative contact, are the dark side of life in Rome. They really abridge very much the sense of all that one comes for, and make one ask very often whether under such circumstances Rome pays. If I come here again next winter, I shall break with them altogether. The trouble here is that there is apparently no interesting or "cultivated" native society, as in Paris and London. On the side of "culture" Rome seems pitifully barren and provincial.—Here is enough gossip, in conscience: it may beguile the family fireside—the fireside near which, I suppose, you are still unhappily huddling.—Not a word about my moral life or my intellectual!—I have enough of each left to think Cherbuliez's last novel in the *Revue des Deux Mondes* very inferior to anything he has done.[4] It seems to me *almost* poor. I suppose you have been reading it.—My moral life all goes to wondering how you are and what you are doing, and why I don't hear from you. I hope much that William will soon be able to send me a line or so. I am very well *indeed,* and ought to be able to work along prosperously enough. I shall do so better, when all this stale party-going subsides. I gave myself up to it thinking it wouldn't be stale, and that new and various forms of life would be revealed to me: but it is in Rome as in Cambridge. Peace be with it!—How is society with you?—with Alice especially? I should like much to hear from her, what she is doing and whom seeing. Has she been going into Boston at all?—I swore just above at the Greenoughs. But I advise Alice on their return (this summer, I believe) to make their acquaintance: for they are both very nice girls, and I should think she might take very kindly to the elder one (Fanny.)—Mr. Emerson sent you (father) very friendly messages, and asked me what you are now writing. But I couldn't tell him—and the fault is yours. I hope you are better of your late discomforts and able to do your work. Enlighten me about it and don't abate your recent frequency in writing to me. I am always homesick, but in the midst of this lavish loveliness of the Roman spring—the thought—even of certain March-moods of our Yankee heavens, causes me to groan with filial tenderness.—Farewell, dearest father. It is not the moods of the skies only, but those of the paternal and maternal souls conjoined, that make me hanker for home.—I suppose Aunt Kate is still in New York and I hope well and prosperous.—Mention always the last news from the boys. I would give my hand for a talk with William. But farewell, again. Furious kisses to mother and sister.—

Your everlasting H.

1. HJ was prophetic: Annie Crawford married a Prussian and became the Countess von Rabe.

2. Elena Lowe of Boston. See *The Conquest of London*, the chapter "Six Women," for Miss Lowe's possible relation to HJ's heroine Christina Light, Princess Casamassima.

3. Eugene Benson (1839–1908) American artist, devotee of the Venetian School of Painting; later stepfather of the author Constance Fletcher (George Fleming). He may have been the "original" for Singleton in *Roderick Hudson*.

4. Cherbuliez's latest novel, then serialized, was *Meta Holdenis*.

To Grace Norton

Ms Harvard

Rome March 5*th* 73.

Dear Grace—

Your letter was a letter to have been answered the day it came. It was not answered, because there were several sterner duties to perform on that day (and the following ones)—and by keeping it constantly before me, as one does an unanswered letter, I have learned its great merits, as one does, with time, those of all supremely best things. I've carried about with me, meanwhile a heart full of sympathy for poor Charles. What a miserable season! Your letter gives me a painful sense of far-away unhelpfulness to your troubles. But they are melting away I trust, and Charles's cold being thawed out of him and his patience rewarded by even such lukewarm whiffs of spring as a London March affords. How all your trouble, in so far as it's a physical matter, would dissolve in the influence of this vernal sun of Rome! But a little endurance more and you will have an English April—a thing I know well, for I drank deep of it for two successive years.—Already here, in the sunny places, there is a certain scorchingness: but such a loveliness everywhere—such a solid blue in the sky and such a carpeting of anemones and violets in the untrodden places in the Villas.—It would all have been worth waiting for, even if the winter had been half as goodly as it has.— Your picture of your London fog-world was really Turneresque, and Charles lying in the midst of it ill—and with Smollett (has it one *l* or two?) for his healer a truly pathetic image. Has Smollett done his share of the work? If so, I will treat him tenderly when I come to write my great projected work—*A History of Prose Fiction since Cervantes*.[1] Seriously dear Grace, give Charles my tenderest love and my heartiest congratulations, if he is as much better as I hope he is. Your mother, I would fain believe, is out of her room and her serenely vigorous self again—and the children enlivening the high respectability of Cleveland Square by the vocal music of their sports.—Thank you for envying me all these Roman opportunities so much: your good opinion of them reminds me how precious they are. Of regular sightseeing, *Murray* in hand, I have done little this winter—owing partly to want of time, partly to the cold damp atmosphere of most places of resort and partly to a strange feeling of familiarity with most of the lions, begotten I suppose, by intensely zealous scrutiny of them on my former visits. But I have had lovely random walks and rambles and droppings into places, and have perhaps been taking the best course really to know Rome—I have surrendered myself freely to the current of "society" here—but it has landed me on rather sandy shores, enriched chiefly by the stern experience of its unprofitableness. One's inevitable (or almost so) entanglements with the American colony here are a dark side to a brilliant picture, and make one think twice about deciding on a second winter here. It contains nothing novel, individual or picturesque enough to repay one for any great expenditure of time. I doubt that any society here does. There must be some very good scattered individuals: but I haven't met them. On the other hand, (not to be misanthropic) I have met lots of amiable people.—Your own hints about your London world excited my curiosity more than they satisfied it. Some day, perhaps, I shall have a glimpse of it, and shall walk safely by the light of your impressions. In the way of scattered individuals, Mr. Emerson is here with his daughter, back from the Nile, serene and urbane and rejuvenated by his adventures. He is on his way to London, and will relate them of course to you, as quaintly as he did—a little—to me.—Of people you know, I doubt that I see anyone but the Storys, who give pleasant enough parties, at which their handsome daughter sings with a delightful voice, with the strangest most tremulous sort of vibration in it. (Privately) I imagine the touching effect is a matter of voice rather than of *âme.*—I went lately to Story's studio and found him in the midst of an army of marble heroines, which were not altogether unsuggestive of Mrs. Jarley's waxworks.[2] They are extremely (though unequally) clever, but I think almost fatally unsimple.—However criticism in the case is really ungrateful: for they offer a perfect feast of ingenuity, inventiveness and fancy.—*Àpropos* of criticism, the Nation *Middlemarch* is not at all mine—*mais pas du tout.!* It is by Mr. Albert Dicey (I am told) whom I think you know. I had sent them a notice, but at the eleventh hour they displaced it for this one, which is doubtless better as going more into details. But if mine is printed elsewhere you shall see it. What you write me about Lewes's anecdotes was most interesting and welcome. I wondered whether you were hearing anything about George Eliot. Her book, with all its faults, is, it seems to me, a truly immense performance. My brother William lately wrote me that he was "aghast at its intellectual power." This is strong—and what one says of Shakespeare. But certainly a marvellous *mind* throbs in every page of *Middlemarch.* It raises the standard of what is to be expected of women—(by your leave!) We know all about the female heart; but apparently there is a female brain, too. In fact, dear Grace, there are two of them!—I have read very little else this winter and written little, though something. Thank you for liking the Bethnal Green notice. *Criticism* of pictures is less and less to my taste and less and less useful—to my perception.[3] An easy-going profession of amusement in them is more philosophic, I think. In fact criticism of all kinds seems to me overdone, and I seriously believe that if nothing could be "reviewed" for fifty years, civilization would take a great stride. To produce some little exemplary works of art is my narrow and lowly dream. They are to have less "brain" than *Middlemarch;* but (I boldly proclaim it) they are to have more *form.*—I don't know whether I mentioned in my last that I had lately taken to the saddle and been exploring the wondrous Campagna. I see indescribable things, many of which you can doubtless close your eyes and see glowing in faint violet through the mists of years. Yes, it's all solemnly beautiful, and strange and still as you remember it. I ride often with Lizzie Boott, who is a very nice girl, and who, when you go back to Cambridge, will rejoice to know you.—Do you know Mrs. Charles Sumner? I went the other day with her and like her much. With her great beauty (which on horseback is enormous) she has great honesty, frankness and naturalness.—I gave your message to the Tweedies who received it gratefully. They are enlivened (though perhaps that is hardly the word just now) by having Mrs. Captain Temple (Mrs. T's sister in law) with them. Not that she is not a particularly nice woman, I only meant she is a little drooping. Mr. T. is altogether salubrious and happy. The Storys profess to believe that *Lowell* is still to turn up: but I doubt it, from what he told me in Paris.—Farewell, dear Grace. I wrote lately to Jane; my letter must have crossed yours. My universal love. I should like extremely a single line, saying that Charles is better—and your mother. I shall soon write to Charles. I think of Jane and you, as always, as of two things in heaven.

Your perpetual worshipper
H. J. jr.

1. HJ is apparently being facetious. He seems never to have planned a work of historico-criticism of this nature. It was the sort of book that might have been written by his friend Perry.

2. In Dickens's *Old Curiosity Shop*

3. He would hold to this view for the rest of his life and write a comedy, *The Outcry,* mocking expertise and connoisseurship.

To Charles Eliot Norton

Ms Harvard

Rome, March 13th 73

Dear Charles—

Some days since I heard from Grace the sad story of your last illness and this morning comes a letter from Jane with further mention of it, of a kind that makes me feel how trying it must have been. Ten days ago—a week ago—you were still in your room, with the single compensation, apparently, that though that was dismal, the outside world was more dismal still, and you had not the torment—as you would have had here—of seeing squares of deep blue sky in your window and long streams of sunshine over your walls and carpet.—But whatever your skies and winds, I hope by this time you have made their acquaintance again and have even had another walk or so with Carlyle. You have had all my sympathy in your illness and you would have a good deal of my envy (perhaps not quite *all*) in those walks. I have been seeing a great *mess* of people this winter and they have none of them diminished my sense of the value of the company of a man of genius. For instance: I a few nights since heard W.W. Story read (at Mrs. Wister's, to an audience composed simply of herself, her husband, Mrs. Kemble and myself, whose presence was accidental)—a five-act tragedy on the history of *Nero!*[1] He got through three acts in three hours, and the last two were resumed on another evening when I was unavoidably absent. The performance was the result much less of an inward necessity, I surmise, than of a most restless ambition, not untinged with—what an impertinent little word stands for, beginning with *v* and ending with *y*[2]—as I say, I should have enjoyed particularly just afterwards, half an hour of Carlyle's English and Carlyle's imagination.—I gather from Jane and Grace as I did from your letter received several weeks since and which I now tardily acknowledge, that you have been having a rather interesting winter but not an especially cheerful one. You must have had a dreary dose of climate—and I think of all that with a shudder; but I inevitably think of the moral climate of London as a murky, dusky, oppressive medium too;—only to be comfortably outweathered if you have laid up a private store of intellectual sunshine. Yet I also confess that I am fond of English *chiaroscuro,* in the material landscape and relish it somewhat in the social as well. And you have some opportunities that are foreign enough to us—such as the show of old masters at the Royal Academy which Jane speaks of in her today's letter. You remember how quickly one can number the first-rate pictures in Rome.—Fortunately Rome is itself a picture—now in these mild March days more than ever. Of the charm that is stealing over the place with every deepening breath of spring, I can hardly soberly speak; and you have your memory and Jane's and Grace's to consult.—I know how your memory has been charged of late with another burden. Your illness has at any rate done you the service of helping you to be alone with your thoughts.—Jane tells me that you are to sail on May 15*th*—sooner even than I supposed—not too soon, I hope for a peaceful voyage and a—what shall I call it?—philosophical arrival. I suppose you'll hardly see much of Cambridge before the summer is over, but I shall nevertheless feel tempted to beg you to interpret my absence to our fellow-citizens as eloquently as you may feel moved to.—I ought myself to justify it by doing much more than I have done this winter. But how can I write good tragedies when I am liable to find myself in for a three hours' audition—a poor one?—Your children I hope are better of their colds and are able to watch the hawthorne springing as I suppose it does or soon will, in Cleveland Square. Your mother, I trust, has had no cold nor any other small misfortune, to get rid of and will be able to await serenely the day of your departure. My affectionate remembrances to her—please thank Jane profusely for her letter, and mention (the Roman postoffice is rather lax) to Grace that I despatched her one, in answer to her own, about a week since. Farewell dear Charles, with vigorous wishes for a return of strength and of all good influences.

> Yours most truly
> H. James jr.

1. For an account of this evening, remembered many years later, see HJ's life of Story, II, 254.
2. The word, fairly obviously, is "vanity."

To Mrs. Henry James Sr.

Ms Harvard

Rome March 24*th* '73

Dearest Mammy.

Since writing last, almost a fortnight since, I have been blessed with three letters: one from Willy, one from you, and one, yesterday, from father. All were supremely welcome and all excellent in their diverse manners. I am well and undisturbed, in spite of my long silence, and have not written chiefly because of much other occupation. I have rejoiced in your home news when it was good—and deplored it when it was not, as for example when you touch upon your furious snows and frosts—you, dearest mammy, upon your grievous domestic fatigues and woes, and Willy upon Alice's spoiled dinner parties.—But I hope by this time the tender grass is peeping up along the border of the Brattle street fences, where I used to watch it so lovingly last year,—that Maria and Lizzie[1] have recovered their health, and Alice has ornamented all the feasts to which she has been bidden.—Here, midspring is already upon us and I walk abroad in my summerest clothes and am warm therewith. Yesterday I spent the whole afternoon rambling in the Borghese Villa, drinking in the vernal influences with a satisfaction tempered only by the regret that you, sweet mother, might not be trampling the anemones, in the shadow of the grim old walls of Rome and plucking the violets from the roots of the high-stemmed pines. The days follow each other in gentle variety, each one leaving me a little more *Roman* than before. Lent is well on and party giving, though I continue to get pitifully entangled in stupid little engagements which deprive me of the pleasure of spending my evenings in meditative solitude. But every day now brings a little more liberty. The Boots leave in a week, the Wisters the same (also for America) and various other people are more or less shutting up shop. The Tweedies thrive, somewhat ponderously, and Mrs. Temple who is staying with them, stands forth in scintillating relief. I continue to dine there quite often, in spite of the sufferings engendered by Tweedy's passion for converting his rooms into an oven. I have had no fire in five weeks but he still revels in a temperature which is positively fabulous, and Aunt Mary, Mrs. Temple and I fan violently by the hour. The Butler was recently threatened with expulsion, but has been kept and the pantry still flourishes. I see a good deal of the Boots and can't help thinking that Lizzie will miss her Roman resources in Cambridge more than she apprehends, and that their stay there will be short. Going up early the other morning to make a riding appointment with her, I found her in her studio with a certain little Peppina—the most enchanting little nut-brown child model you can imagine: in structure, color, costume, everything, the handsomest little miniature woman. There sat Lizzie happily painting this delicious object. Where will she get a Peppina in Cambridge? The Park doesn't grow them alas. Lizzie, by the way, has painted much this winter and has enormously, or at least, strikingly improved. I was present the other evening at an exhibition she gave of all her things (including a lot of sepia and watercolor sketches) to a couple of young artists, Boit and Crowninshield,[2] and they, like myself, were much surprised at her fertility, inventiveness and general skill. She ought now to paint, or more especially, to draw well enough, to sell her things and make herself if she wishes, a career.—I have been riding with her a good deal, and also with Mrs. Wister. I have now had for some three weeks the luxurious, the *princely,* sensation—of keeping a saddle-horse. I am a little disappointed in the immediate profitableness of riding, which I thought would be a very good muscular exercise. It is a fair one, but I find it doesn't take the place of walking. In a general way, however, and morally and intellectually, it is magnificent. The only drawback is that at present and for sometime back, the mild weather gives too little *tone* to the air for really exhilarating movement. If to the boundless Campagna, Rome added a climate with a little snap and lift to it, riding here would be Paradise. I went out the other day with Mrs. Wister and her husband. They led me rather a dance, but I took four ditches with great serenity and was complimented for my close seat. But the merit was less mine than that of my delightful little horse, who is a brave jumper, and would just suit Alice if she would come out and try him. To cease this heartless jesting. I am now in the position of a creature with *five* women *offering* to ride with him: Mrs. Sumner, Mrs. Wister, Mrs. Boit, Miss Bartlett and Lizzie Boott. I shall fight shy of Mrs. Boit who, I believe, is an equestrian terror. Pray don't repeat these fatuous speeches.—Everyone, more or less, is here—several in whom Alice will be interested. I called the other night on the Dixwells, and found them fresh and hearty and wholesome. Tell Alice our *Whitwells* of Berne are here, Miss W. handsomer than ever, and with a wondrous pretty but less

satisfying sister, who fell into my arms and asked about her (Alice.)
Àpropos of our last summer's friends, she will be interested in
hearing that I met Mr. *Duggin* of the Algeria etc. Imagine my horror
on learning from him that our lovely friend Miss Bailey had *died*
in Paris, in October last, of congestion of the brain brought on by
the excitement and fatigue of shopping for her *trousseau*. She was
to be married on her return. Alice will tell you all about her: she
was an enchanting creature. (Send this on to Aunt Kate)—Your
three letters contained a good deal of home talk, which was all
devoutly relished. Thank Willy, to whom I will soon write a
specific answer. I owe father one too, which he shall soon have.
Thank him meanwhile greatly for his story of Mr. *Webster*. It is
admirable material, and excellently presented: I have transcribed it
in my notebook with religious care, and think that some day something will come of it.[3] It would require much thinking out. But it is
a first class theme. Thank him also for his trouble in discussing with
Osgood[4] the matter of my bringing out a volume. He mentioned
it sometime since and it has been on my mind to respond. Briefly,
I don't care to do it, just now. I value none of my early tales enough
to bring them forth again, and if I did, should absolutely need to
give them an amount of verbal retouching which it would be very
difficult out here to effect. What I desire is this: to make a volume,
a short time hence, of tales on the theme of American adventurers
in Europe, leading off with the *Passionate Pilgrim*.[5] I have three or
four more to write: one I have lately sent to Howells and have half
finished another. They will all have been the work of the last three
years and be much better and maturer than their predecessors. Of
these there is only one—*A Light Man*[6] (published in the *Galaxy*) I
should not rather object to reissue. That showed most distinct
ability. The money I should get would not (probably) be enough
to make a sacrifice for—so long as (as I properly) I can keep making
enough to get on with comfortably.—I should loathe, too, to have
you spending money on my plates—though it's noble to offer it.—
If I should think better of this a few days hence I will let you know.
But there is the impossibility of the thing's being printed as they
stand, uncorrected. They are full of thin spots in the writing which

I should deplore to have stereotyped, besides absolute errors, to which I was always very subject.—A blessing on all that concerns you. The letter enclosed by mother from Bob, was lovely. Happy boy! Mention to Wilky I lately wrote him.—My especial love to Sara Sedgwick, and my friendliest sympathy in her disturbed health. Happy Arthur with his *work* and his 2500$!!—Is Aunt Kate back? My love to her always, and send her my letters.—Where is Mrs. Lombard and does anyone hear from her? I thought she might write me. Farewell, farewell, dearest Mother. A smoother kitchen and many happy months ahead. Love to sister and to her poor head, and to Father and William

Your fondest H

1. Apparently domestics in Quincy Street.
2. Edward D. Boit (1840–1915) and Frederic Crowninshield (1845–1918) were among the painters HJ came to know in Rome and used in his novel of American artists, *Roderick Hudson.*
3. HJ used this subject several years later in "Crawford's Consistency," *Scribner's Monthly,* XII (August 1876), 569–584
4. James R. Osgood (1836–1892), Boston publisher.
5. *A Passionate Pilgrim and Other Tales,* HJ's first volume of fiction, was published by Osgood in 1875.
6. "A Light Man," *Galaxy,* VIII (July 1869), 49–68, revised and reprinted in *Stories by American Authors,* vol. V (Scribner, 1884).

To Henry James Sr.

Ms Harvard

Rome, *101 Corso* Feb. [March] 28*th* [1873][1]

Dear Father—

I shall not write a letter: I wrote a long one last week. I only want to drop a line to tell you (what I might have done a fortnight since) to cease directing to the Hotel de Rome and send to Spada & Flamini.—I have just changed my quarters. My hotel, with the increase of the mild weather, had become insufferably warm and suffocating; and living in one small room, especially at night, on the terms one has to be on with one's windows in Rome, an uncomfortable affair. There has lately been a great emptying of

Alice Mason (Mrs. Charles Sumner)

lodgings and I have taken this excellent one for a month. Two fine rooms—one upholstered in cobalt and the other in yellow—with magenta *portières* in the doorways—on a *4° piano*, with a spacious view and a goodly balcony, and the most devoted of little *donne* to wait on me. She would even satisfy mother, I think,—in spite of her having nailed my card, which I gave her to affix to the front door, *upside down!*—No news—save that Rome grows every day more divine. These last have been perfect days—pure as crystal and cool as the sea. My month with my horse is soon up and I am taking my last rides. You should see the beds of asphodel shaking in the wandering wind on the Campagna. People are leaving somewhat— and I bade farewell two days since to my friend Mrs. Wister. I used some brutal phrase about her in one of my early letters, which I hope you never repeated. I immediately retracted it and have regretted it ever since. She is a fine person—not "easy", but perfectly natural. I took her last ride with her away and away under the shadow of the acqueducts. She is most broken-heartedly to exchange Rome for Germantown! The Bootts leave on Wednesday next—(today being Sunday.) Lizzie is having regrets, I think, and measuring her losses. I *imagine* they will at last come back and stay. I rode with her yesterday among the cork woods on Monte Mario. Forgive me!—I have seen a good deal of late of Mrs. Sumner and adore her.—I'm going tonight to the Storys with hopes of meeting Matthew Arnold whom I saw a day or two since, lunching with his wife and little girl at Spillman's. Tomorrow I dine at the Terry and Crawford's. Every week I hope "society" is over—but it spurts up again. I have deliberately taken all that has come of it and been the gainer: but now I hope for a month—two months—of quiet work. This has lately suffered various impediments. But every *lapsus* leaves me hankering after it more. My plan is to remain here till May 15th: then go for three or four weeks out to Tivoli. Beyond that I have no plans.— The Clover Adamses[2] have been here for a week, the better for Egypt, but the worse for Naples, which has made them ail a little. I saw them last P.M., and they are better and laden with material treasures, *à la* Harper.—The Tweedys are well—or rather, not: poor Edmund being rheumatic, and Aunt Mary fertile in restless schemes for his going hither and thither, which infuriate him. But he is mending.—I enclose a note from Charles Eliot Norton which will please you as much as it did me.[3] *Keep* it privately and jealously. Forgive this bundle of egotism. Kiss everyone for me and believe me dearest dad your loving child—

H. James jr.

If you see Howells, tell him I have just heard from him.—Tell T. S. Perry I *haven't*.

1. The February date was a slip of the pen: the letter was obviously written 28 March 1873.

2. Henry Adams and his wife.

3. Norton, in England, had written HJ on 23 March 1873 (ms Harvard) of a day spent with Ruskin who praised HJ's letter to the *Nation*, XVI (6 March 1873), XVI 163–165, "From Venice to Strasbourg," and especially the passages on Tintoretto. "It would have been pleasant for you to see the cordial admiration he felt for your work, and to hear his warm expression of the good it did him to find such sympathies and such appreciations, and to know that you were to be added to the little list of those who intelligently and earnestly care for the same things that have touched him most deeply and influenced his life most powerfully. You may be pleased from your heart to have given not merely pleasure, but stimulus to a man of genius very solitary and with very few friends who care for what he cares for." Ruskin, said Norton, had been "eager" that HJ might have been appointed Slade Professor of Fine Arts at Cambridge instead of Sidney Colvin, lately named.

To Charles Eliot Norton

Ms Harvard

Rome, 101 Corso 4°p. March 31*st* [1873]

Dear Charles—

Nothing could have given me more substantial pleasure than your note about Ruskin—the indivious comparison as to Mr. Colvin included.[1] If there is any stimulus in the case it is certainly I who have felt it. I can well understand that it should be a gratification to Ruskin to encounter late in life a cordial assent to a cherished opinion never very popular and to which years have not, I suppose, brought many adherents. Tintoret I have never seen (save by Ruskin) spoken of with the large allowance that he demands.—Your letter has been the great news with me—I don't know that I have any other. I am growing daily fonder of Rome, and Rome at this season is growing daily more loveable. My only complaint is of the climate, which takes a good deal more strength from you than it gives. But Rome with a *snap* in the air would not be Rome, and the languor that one continually feels has something harmonious and (intellectually) profitable in it. "Society" continues, in spite of the departure of two or three of its ornaments. Last night at the Story's I met Matthew Arnold and had a few words with him. He is not as handsome as his photographs—or as his poetry. But no one looks handsome in Rome—beside the Romans.—So you're acquainted with Story's Muse—that brazen hussy—to put it plainly. I have rarely seen such a case of *prosperous* pretention as Story. His cleverness is great, the world's good nature to him is greater.—I am very sorry your harsh weather continues, for an English spring is too good a thing to be spoiled. I wish I could take you out on my balcony and let you look at the Roman house-tops and loggias and sky and feel the mild bright air. But this is questionably kind.—Your note of ten days since came safely and was most welcome. There were several things in it to reply to which your story of Ruskin has chased out of my head.—I do, for instance, believe in criticism, more than that hyperbolical speech of mine would seem to suggest. What I meant to express was my sense of its being, latterly, vastly over-done. There is such a flood of precepts and so few examples—so much preaching, advising, rebuking and reviling, and so little *doing:* so many gentlemen sitting down to dispose in half an hour of what a few have spent months and years in producing. A single positive attempt, even with great faults, is worth generally most of the comments and amendments on it. You'll agree to that.—Again, I wished to repudiate the charge of my patriotism being "serene". It has come to that pass, you see, that I'm half ashamed of it. I wish it *were* serene. I don't pretend in the least to understand our national destinies—or those of any portion of the world. My philosophy is no match for them, and I regard the march of history very much as a man placed astride of a locomotive, without knowledge or help, would regard the progress of that vehicle. To stick on, somehow, and even to enjoy the scenery as we pass, is the sum of my aspirations.—As to Christianity in its old applications being exhausted, civilization, good and bad alike, seems to be certainly leaving it pretty well out of account. But the religious passion has always struck me as the strongest of man's heart, and when one thinks of the scanty fare judged by our usual standards, in which it has always fed, and of the nevertheless powerful current continually setting towards all religious hypotheses, it is hard not to believe that *some* application of the supernatural idea, should not be an essential part of our life.— I don't know how common the feeling is, but I am conscious of making a great allowance to the questions agitated by religion, in feeling that conclusions and decisions about them are tolerably idle. —But I meant to write you no letter—only to thank you: and this is more than a note and less than what it should be otherwise. Farewell dear Charles. Love to each and all—I sent you a criticism of *Middlemarch* in the *Galaxy* lately. Did it come? If you positively don't at all like *M.* you will probably say that such criticism as that ought to be silenced.

Yours always
H. James jr.

1. See the preceding letter.

To William James

Ms Harvard

Rome 101 Corso
April 9th 73

Dear William:—

I have had in hand from you for some time a letter of Feb. 13th. which gave me great pleasure on its arrival and of which I have just been refreshing my memory. Three days since too came a letter from father of March 18, which I shall answer at my next writing. Many thanks to him meanwhile. As always, when I write, I feel that in some mood a week or two before, I would have had a good deal more to say and that the full stream of utterance is not turned on at this particular hour. But we must say what we can—and *read* it. From all my letters as they come, you get, I suppose, a certain impression of my life, if not of my soul. In fact, my soul has not been quite as active as a well regulated soul should be. (By soul, here, I mean especially brain.) The winter is at last fairly over, and I can look at it as a whole and decide that though under the circumstances I am fairly satisfied with it, I shouldn't care to spend another just like it. All of it that has been of pure Rome (with the exception of one point) has been delightful: but there is little left here now of which that can be said and the mark of the fiend—the American fiend—is on everything. I surrendered myself with malice prepense when I came, to whatever social entanglements should come up. They multiplied actively and took up my evenings pretty well for three months; but on retrospect they don't seem to have been very remunerative. I have seen few new people and no new types, and met not a single man, old or young, of any interest. There have been several interesting women "round"—Mrs. Wister being the one I saw most of—but none of the men have *fait époque* in my existence. Mrs. Wister has gone, to bury her regrets in Germantown, Penn., and I have of late been seeing a good deal of Mrs. Sumner and Miss Bartlett, who live together, are now my neighbors, and since I have given up my horse have amiably invited me several times to ride one of theirs—having three. They are both superior and very natural women, and Mrs. Sumner a very charming one (to Miss B. I feel very much as if she were a boy—an excellent fellow)—but they are limited by a kind of characteristic American want of culture. (Mrs. Wister has much more of this—a good deal in fact, and a very literary mind, if not a powerful one.) For the rest society (for Americans) is very thin and such at home as we would dream of coming somewhere else to get something superior to. Storys and Terrys soon pall, and such is our fatal capacity for getting *blasé* that it soon ceased to be for me, what it was at first, a kind of pretty spectacle to go to their houses. At the Story's however, the other night I met and conversed for a few minutes with Matthew Arnold, whom, if I had more ingenuity, I suppose I might have managed to see more of. He is handsome but not as handsome as his fame or his poetry and (to me) he said nothing momentous. But I think I mentioned all this in my last. This in parenthesis. I suppose there are interesting individuals to know in Rome, but I doubt that there is any very edifying society. And I doubt that one meets interesting—generally interesting—individuals anywhere by going round and hungering for them. If you have some active prosperous speciality, it introduces you to fellow-workers, and the interest of such is the one, I suppose that wears best.—My own speciality has suffered a good deal, for the immediate hour, by my still unformed and childish habits of application having been much at the mercy of the distractions and preoccupations of my daily goings and comings, innocent as they have been. I have written less than I have supposed I should and read not at all. But in the long run I have gained for it has all after all been "quite an experience" and I have gathered more impressions I am sure than I suppose—impressions I shall find a value in when I come to use them. And for the actual writing now that life is growing quieter, I shall sufficiently overtake myself. The point at which, above, I took exception to Rome in itself is one I have only gradually made up my mind about—namely, the influence of the climate. (This has had much to do with my intellectual idleness.) When I first came and the winter gave it a certain freshness, I felt nothing but its lovely mildness; but for the past eight or ten weeks I have been in a state of ineffable languefaction. The want of "tone" in the air is altogether indescribable: it makes it mortally flat and dead and relaxing. The great point is that it is all excessively pleasant and you succumb to languor with a perfectly demoralized conscience. But it is languor (for me at least) languor perpetual and irresistible. My struggles with sleep have been heroic, but utterly vain, and to sit down with a book after eight P.M. (and after a rousing cup of *caffé nero*) and not snore the evening ignobly away has been a dream never realized. It seems to me that I have slept in these three months more than in my whole life beside. The soft divine, enchanting days of spring have of course made matters worse and I feel as if, for six weeks past, I have been looking at the world from under half-meeting eyelids. But I am going to fight it out to the end, for I don't know when I shall ever be here again. Nothing of all this means that

I find the air unwholesome: on the contrary. It makes me thick-headed and a little head-achy; but the languor and the "fever" are two very different matters, and I have been steadily living and still live, in the most salubrious conditions.—Of Rome itself, otherwise, I have grown very fond, in spite of the inevitable fits of distaste that one has here. You feel altogether out of the current of modern civilization and in so far, very provincial, but (as I believe I have more than once said) I often hanker for the high culture and high finish of Paris—the theatres and newspapers and booksellers and restaurants and boulevards. But the atmosphere is nevertheless weighted—to infinitude—with a something that forever stirs and feeds and fills the mind and makes the sentient being feel that on the whole he can lead as complete a life here as elsewhere.—Then there is the something—the myriad somethings—that one grows irresistably and tenderly fond of—the unanalysable *loveableness* of Italy. This fills my spirit mightily on occasions and seems a sort of intimation of my learning how to be and do something, here. These last—or first—weeks of spring have been strangely delicious, and it has seemed a sort of crime to be keeping them to myself. The weather has been perfect; as it has been constantly since my arrival, and perfect Roman weather seems somehow, beyond all others, the weather for the *mind*. My riding has put me in the way of supremely enjoying it and of course has doubled the horizon of Rome. Physically, I doubt that it will ever do wonders for me; but morally and intellectually it is wondrous good. Life here (after one has known it) would be very tame without it and to try it is to make it an essential. Like everything that is worth doing, riding well is difficult; but I have learned to sit a well-disposed horse decently enough—the Campagna, with its great stretches of turf, its slopes and holes and ditches, being a capital place to acquire vigilance and firmness. I wish *fratello mio*, that you might come and take a turn at it.—But you'll soon be thinking that my only mission in life is to preach amusement.—Of Italian, *per se*, I have learned much less than I had dreamed of doing—not having (with so many other things to do) hired the intelligent young Roman of my vision to come daily and converse with me. But I read it fairly well and to speak it after the fashion of a rank foreigner is not hard. I lately formed a contract with Miss Bartlett to come twice a week and read *Tasso* with her (delicious stuff!) and this I hope will progress as finely as my inevitably falling into a three hours' dead sleep over my dictionary will allow. I have been now for a fortnight in these rooms on the Corso (extremely good ones) where I have more observation of *moeurs Italiennes* than at my hotel. The *padrone* keeps a little shop of Catholic images in the basement and lives with all his family (wife, three children, sister-in-law, maid servant and various female hangers-on) behind a curtain, in an alcove off the vestibule to my two rooms, which being on the front, with a balcony, are the main source of his subsistence. It's a pathetic old-world situation and I feel as if (if I were not a brute) I would invite them in to air themselves in my apartment.—Your letter was full of points of great interest. Your criticism on *Middlemarch* was excellent and I have duly transcribed it into that *note-book*[1] which it will be a relief to your mind to know I have at last set up. Better still was your expression of interest in your lectures and of their good effect on you.—Without flattery, I don't see how you could fail to please and stimulate your students, and hope the thing will develop and bring you larger opportunities. That your health too, should keep pace with them is my cordial wish. Your praise of my articles was of great value. I feel myself that I constantly improve, and I have only now to strive and to let myself go to prosper and improve indefinitely. So I think! I mean to spend a not idle summer. Our friends here are in eclipse. The Tweedies, with Mrs. Temple have gone to Albano, for a change of air, poor Mr. Tweedy having lately been suffering acutely from rheumatism. Rome doesn't agree with him and I should think he would be glad to get away. His brother (John T.) has had his daughter ill at Albano for many weeks with typhus fever (brought from Naples,); so that the whole family has been roughly used. Aunt Mary is on the whole rather tragical (not to call it comical) and I pity their want of a central influence or guiding principle. (Such as their children would have been.) They don't know where to go, what to do, or why to do it. They have been full of hospitality to me.—The Bootts after a few days at Albano, are gone to Naples, prior to a month at Bellosguardo again. I have seen a good deal of them all winter; and miss them now. Lizzie wears better than her father, whose dryness and coldness and tendency to spring back to calling you Mr. again like a bent twig, is ineffable. But still, if you get him laughing (as you so easily can) you forgive him everything. Lizzie still makes one pity her—though I don't know why. Her painting has developed into a resource that most girls would feel very thankful to possess, and she has had a very entertaining winter. Her work will always lack the last delicacy, but if she would only paint a little less *helplessly*, she would still go far—as women go. But with her want of *initiation*, it is remarkable that she does as well. I should think she might make very successful little drawings for books. She has made a lot of excellent sketches.—In the way of old friends we have been having Henry Adams and his wife, back from Egypt and (last) from Naples, each with what the doctor pronounced the germs of typhus fever. But he dosed them and they mended and asked me to dinner, with Miss Lowe, (beautiful and sad) and came to Mrs. Sumner's, where I dined with them again, and shewed me specimens of their (of course) crop of bric-à-brac and Adams's Egyptian photos (by himself—very pretty)—and were very pleasant, friendly and (as to A.) improved. Mrs. Clover has had her wit clipped a little I think—but I suppose has expanded in the "affections."—I have been meeting lately at dinner for ten days young *Ireland* (Miss I's brother) who used to dine with us on Sundays. He is travelling hereabouts and spending a month in Rome and seems rather helpless and listless and lonely and thankful for chance company. He has a more amiable air than in former days.—There have been hordes of other people here, before-seen, most of whom I have contrived to elude. The Andrews have gone to Florence, having much enjoyed Rome. I surrendered lately an evening to the Dixwells—who were very wholesome and lively, especially Mrs. D., whom Europe animates and beautifies. I have first or last seen in a cab in the Corso every one I ever saw anywhere before—including (tell Alice) Ella Eustis and mamma—the latter, apparently, with the same ink stain on her nose she had at Oxford! Also the Dr. Kings and in fine, every one!—But my letter is eternal. Continue to say all you can about the boys. Bob evidently will thrive, and our blessings and hopes must go with Wilky. I'm glad Alice was to have been in New York, and hope it will have tuned her up to writing me a line. My blessings on her. Did Aunt Kate come back with her? If so, a line from her again when she can, will be welcome.—Love to every one else. There were some things in father's letter I wanted to answer but I must wait. Kisses in profusion to my inestimable mammy. I am wearing all my old under garments, though in rags, because they have her needle work.—Farewell, dear Bill. I haven't said twenty things I meant but it must serve.

Ever yours
H. J. jr.

1. This notebook did not survive among those published in 1947, but portions of it were used in "From a Roman Notebook," *Galaxy*, XVI (November 1873), 679–686.

To Alice James

Ms Harvard

Albano, Friday April 25*th* [1873]
Albergo di Parigi.

Dearest sister:

I have received during the past two weeks a letter from father and mother each, to which properly I ought to reply, I suppose, before writing to you, from whom I have not heard for so long. But knowing that your silence has been caused by your infirmities, I don't propose to stand on ceremony with you: indeed I am moved by a strong desire to console you for your ills. If you show this letter to my parents (I suppose you generally intercommunicate my missives, more or less) they may be placated till the next arrives, which shall be addressed punctually to one or other of them or to both. Mother's letter was of April 1st; father's of about a week before, and they were both welcomed as usual. Reassure Mother as to her fears that I sometimes miss your letters. As well as I can make out, nothing that has been sent has failed to come sooner or later. I trust as much can be said for my own things. I have not written now for more than a week—a delay which my *déménagement* will help to account for. I came hither three days since and behold me established at the top of this wondrous old ex-palazzo, now an inn, with two great windows sweeping the whole expanse of the mist-bathed Campagna. Mist-bathed is a flattering epithet; rain-washed would be true; for I have fallen upon evil weather and today promises ill. But I don't despair of getting a walk this afternoon. This rural seclusion is a great change from life in Rome, which I see distinctly with all the domes and spires from the edge of the town. I felt that I should be the better for change of air, for I had grown rather unstarched with the lovely relaxation of the Roman Spring. Besides I wanted to see Albano—and should have wanted much more if I had known what a paradise of picturesqueness I was to find here. It is in truth an enchanting spot: I have talked of the picturesque all my life: now at last, by way of a change, I see it. Charming air I find here too—air, within an hour of Rome, almost as bracing as—Andermatt. This is a merit you will appreciate. The scenery is superior even to that of Andermatt and is something ineffably fair. The walks are innumerable, the views divine. Half an hour away is the Alban lake—hidden in the woody cup of the most exquisite rotundity; and half an hour thence the lake of Nemi, deep down in a smaller and boskier oval, and flanked with its little high-perched black-walled towns, Genzano and Nemi. All the roads hereabouts, plunge down on one side, into the Campagna which lies out as blue and vast and iridescent as the sea, or on the other into one of these little high-rimmed lakes; and they are all so grassy to the feet and bordered with such great arching greenery of twisted oak and stunted elm, and ilex and olive, and so haunted with throbbing nightingales and so adorned all along, at an hour's interval, with these dark little mouldy villages, (each with a church as big as the Music Hall)—that, in short, it's no great bore to have nothing to do here but to walk. It's very jolly, too, having quiet evenings to read after I have paid my respects for half an hour, to poor Mr. and Mrs. John Tweedy, who are still detained here by their daughter's illness. She is now convalescent and sitting up, but she has had a hard time. Her parents are plain folk, though of course excellent. But from the aesthetic point of view, John is to Edmund as a Satyr to Hyperion. I left Edmund and Mary in their usual yearning and wondering Roman mood. Aunt Mary's last proposal was *Athens* for next winter, and Mr. Tweedy's reply, as usual, a groan. For the summer at any rate they will probably go to Kissingen, recommended to Mr. Tweedy (Aunt Mary had just got mother's letter.) Rome was still lively and I went to a couple of dinner parties just before leaving. One at the perpetual Terrys, small and select at the request of its heroine, Lady Ashburton, who is a great swell and, I believe, makes the terms on which she is entertained.[1] In this case they were, to begin with, that she should keep us waiting exactly an hour. But I sat next to her and found her very amiable and humble-minded in her talk. Anyone seems humble-minded however within five miles of Miss Crawford who has a prodigious measure both of cleverness and conceit. As she talks of nothing but herself and her own most *intime* physical and mental idiosyncrasies, I feel very well acquainted with her. She is free-spoken to a degree, and proposes to become a great "decorative" painter. She will probably succeed, for her touch is wonderful, and her taste very handsome; but her things will always lack a certain interest.— 'Tother dinner was a vast and ponderous banquet at the Von Hoffmann's for Matthew Arnold and lady—all flowers and footmen and dreariness. Von Hoffmann is a very good little fellow, but a pitiful underfit to his big house and rather swelling position; the Baroness is still as "chatty" as ever and I only hope that for a whole dinner Matthew Arnold found her an agreeable partner. I have met the latter several times and had a little talk with him. He is not delicately beautiful, but he has a powerful face and an easy, mundane, somewhat gushing manner. Up to a certain point, it is very good: but the rest belongs too much to the little glass he screws into one eye. This little glass is rather a *mécompte* to me in the poet of Obermann.[2] But I fancy he is a fine man.—I doubt, however, that his wife is a fine woman—in the American sense. She is of that thin-lipped English type we used to notice last summer, and I think, on occasion, might behave like your jealous lady of Lausanne. Apropos of your *table d'hôte* neighbors, I have those of the [Hotel] Byron (the good-looking, white haired *dame de compagnie* with the morbid mistress) in the rooms next mine: and I still observe that the former's toilet seems to consist simply in blowing her nose.—Rome, in all ways, has been growing more and more charming with the advance of the spring, which brings out its individuality with tenfold distinctness. Everything interesting, suggestive, picturesque seems to become a hundred times more intensely itself, in the atmosphere of April. The place is born again and your old resorts and walks put on a new fascination. The Villas (Doria, Borghese and Ludovisi) become most strangely fair, and you can hardly keep out of them. I had (from the atrocious Tilton,[3] the transcendental painter) a second permit for the Ludovisi, where I conducted young Ireland, whom I believe I had mentioned as being around—his unfriended and apparently unelastic condition having much appealed to me. He is a very good boy, and not a fool, and I spent there a memorable morning.—*Tilton*, whom I have just mentioned, is the only painter (save the irrepressible Eugene Benson) that I've seen; and is a very queer genius. He is great on sunsets and does them (and all sorts of aerial luminosities etc.) very well: but he is the most blatant humbug in his talk you ever heard—assuring you, every twenty minutes, that Emerson is the "lens of the Almighty." *À propos* of Emerson, Miss Bartlett told me a good story lately about Ellen. She travelled with them on the steamer last autumn, from Nice to Genoa, and was compelled by some imposition of one of the functionaries, to remonstrate vigorously,—in the presence of the Emersons when it was over—"The thing itself is small," she said to Ellen, "but I do hate injustice." ELLEN. "I don't know that I have ever known injustice. Father, have we ever known injustice?"[4]

Welcome was everything savoring of home in father's and mother's letters. I was especially glad to hear of Wilky's change back to Milwaukee and his inammorata. *À propos* of her, mother tells me she encloses a new photograph—and as usual, the enclosed treasure is not enclosed. Do have it sent in the next letter. But the great matter was your visit to New York—about which, if it has cleared up your head a little, I should so like to have you write me. I devoutly trust it may. I have greatly deplored your having lost anything in the way of strength that you took home; but patience and it will come again. —In Willy's continued prosperity with his class I have constantly rejoiced; may it lead to something great.—Mother gave me sad news of Fanny Lombard—the first I had got of them since hearing they sailed. I meant to have written Miss Lombard on her arrival, but had no address and have none now. Please send if, as is probable, you have it. What a situation! And Ned marrying in the midst of it. Strange Miss Butts!—I met your friend Miss Ella Eustis the other night at the Story's. She had the same quiet *distinction* as ever, and was very inquisitive as to you. They have been everywhere apparently, and are going everywhere else. I met also Miss *Addie Hare,* back from Syria: but I believe she was one of my intimates, rather than yours.—I'm sorry Sara Sedgwick is in such indifferent health. Poor sweet girl! I hope the Nortons' return will help her along. Mother lately gave a brave account of Arthur—and of the *Atlantic Middlemarch* being his—which I had vaguely conjectured it might be. He is having a brilliant destiny, certainly. The *Middlemarch* was superficially very good; but it had his characteristic laxity. I have been enjoying very much Howells's *April* number of his tale.[5] But what a pity, that with such pretty art, he can't embrace a larger piece of the world.—*Saturday April 26th.* I broke off my letter yesterday to profit by a momentary cessation of the rain and get a walk; and when I came in I was too late to overtake the mail, so that I have kept over my letter.—I got my walk under my umbrella, after all: but it was not so very much less charming; along the road— the gallery, as they call it here—to Castel Gandolfo and the cope of the Alban lake. Afterwards, after dinner, my affable waiter, for entertainment, took me about the house and showed me its faded splendors. It was once a goodly old palace and though pitifully inconvenient as a hotel, is charminger to stay in than if it had a steam elevator. Such halls, such ceilings, such cold cavernous staircases, such a fine fantastic grand saloon, such a queer little chapel and such a wealth of dim old landscape frescoes on all the walls representing the various properties of the Prince Corsini who owned the place in the last century.—Today is cold and grey but not actually raining, and I shall go somewhere or perish. For an hour after breakfast I went down to the little Villa Doria, and strolled among the damp ilixes and listened to the thick-singing birds.—Tomorrow, if the weather is at all decent, I shall walk up Monte Cano, past Palazzuola, the Franciscan monastery—through Rocca di Papa, black little high-clinging city, into the chestnut woods. Envy me—and forgive!—Monday or Tuesday I shall go back to Rome.[6] I hardly expect to be in Rome later than May 12, when the lease of my lodging is up. My plans, after that, are undetermined—further than that I shall go to Florence and (I hope) spend the month of June. Please therefore begin to address me to *Emile Flazi and Co. Bankers,* Florence, where my letters had better come for the next two months or so. I want to cling to Italy as late as possible and not be driven over into Switzerland at all if I can help it. I dream vaguely of going to Siena, for July and making for the Lakes (or Monte Genneroso above them) for August. But this is wholly uncertain, and will depend on my physique and the climate. If necessary I can be very happy in Switzerland, and could pass cheerfully six weeks at *Berne*—even at the Faucon. And you, sweet family, what is to become of you, while I thus heartlessly prattle and scandalously roam? Tell me all your plans and hopes and fears. —I shall send Mother's message to the crazy Bootts, whom I shall probably see in Florence.—Thank father and mother for their information about my two cheques ($160.) They have lately felt me pulling at the purse-strings, but there is money owing them at home. Howells has three unpaid mss.[7] (one I at least sent a few days since) in his hands. I have now money in hand to last me some time. *À propos* of which I sent to Bob's wife through Lizzie Boott a little wedding-jewel (a mosaic cross) which I should like you to transmit. —Love to every one and everything, and especially, sweet child to yourself. I hope you have been able to drop me a line. But let it alone unless it's perfectly easy. May it soon be easier to!—My love always, particularly, to Sara Sedgwick.—Farewell!

Your devoted brother
H. James jr.

P.S. I am glad to hear from mother my *Gautier* is liked. I suppose it has been sent me.

1. A prominent member of the foreign colony in Rome. See HJ's life of Story, I, 195.

2. An allusion to Matthew Arnold's verses and his essay on Étienne Pivert de Sénancour, a precursor of romanticism who wrote several introspective novels, notably *Obermann* (1804). Arnold's *Obermann* (1852), *Obermann Once More* (1867), and his essay in *Academy* 9 October 1869 introduced Sénancour to English readers.

3. J. Rollin Tilton (1828–1888), New Hampshire landscape water colorist, had an apartment in the Barberini.

4. The Jameses, led by HJ Sr, invariably alluded to Emerson's "innocence" and his unawareness of evil.

5. Howells was serializing his novel, *A Chance Acquaintance*, published later that year.

6. HJ recorded his stay in Albano in "Roman Neighborhoods," *Atlantic*, XXXII (December 1873), 671–680.

7. These were "A Roman Holiday," Roman Neighborhoods," and "Roman Rides," all published in due course.

To His Parents

Ms Harvard

Rome, May 4*th*. 73. 101 Corso 4° piano.

Beloved parents.

Feeling this morning rather more in the affections than in the intellect, I can't forebear to write you a few lines; although since I wrote copiously to Alice at Albano a week ago (heaven speed the letter) nothing of moment has transpired. The chief events are 1° my return to my charming little apartment here after just a week of somewhat rainy and extremely cold, but altogether exhilarating weather at Albano; and 2° the arrival of a thrice welcome letter from Willy, of April 6th. Let me immediately repeat in answer to his questions as to the receipt of *all* your things that I have consciously missed nothing. The *North American Review* has not come, tho' there is time; but I suppose it will yet turn up. They ought in

375

politeness, have sent it to me from the office. *Enfin!*—I have been back in Rome a week and have returned to it as to an old friend or an old love. It's a monstrously amiable place. The weather has been abnormally cold—in Florence and the north I believe most cruelly so—killing vines and fruits and flowers: but it has tuned me up comfortably and I feel primed for another fortnight in Rome. It's impossible to make up one's mind to leave it. The Tweedies are so-so; poor Mr. Tweedy rheumatic and seedy. He lives like a salamander, and is reduced to that point after which the sooner one leaves Rome the better: that of driving, in a closed carriage. I heard this A.M. from the Bootts, who have been shivering in Florence and regretting Rome. But Mr. B. writes (in answer to mother's message) that he would much rather summer in Pomfret or in Scarboro than in Switzerland. Alice will tell you how hard he took Switzerland last summer; and this will help to explain their movements. I see no one new, and among the old no one often but the Tweedies and Mrs. Sumner and Miss Bartlett—who lead that life and are of that turn that they rather tend to appropriate and absorb a likely young man: but they have had no more of me than I find it convenient to give, for though they are very nice women, I am meant for better things—especially since the other day, I became THIRTY![1]—solemn fact—which I have been taking to heart. The Barbarians are thinning out here very blessedly: I shall devote a portion of this last fortnight to going to various places where I have been waiting all winter for them to clear out. They still muster thick in Florence I believe and I am not sorry to be lingering here and giving them a chance to depart.—In Willie's letter I rejoiced greatly and it shall soon be copiously answered. I think I have mentioned that I wrote him at length some three weeks ago. Meanwhile thank him for his remarks on my *Gautier* and for his advice: none of it shall be lost. Alice I suppose is back from New York: full of vigor and anecdote, I trust. The latter perhaps may spill over in a few lines to me. Has Aunt come with her? My gracious love to her, if she is present. I suppose you are beginning to discuss the respective merits of boarding-houses, beaches etc.: to a happy end, I pray. You are not unlikely, I suppose to have the Bootts again for company. Don't shrink from

376

them. Enriched with a fund of European reminiscence they will be very pleasant comrades. Lizzie ought to be able to spend a month in talking about Rome—and (if it's a recomendation) giving sketches of my career there.—Willie's letter mentioned the happy fact of Wilky's promotion and return to Milwaukee, on which I have reflected with fraternal sympathy. May it open the gate to prosperity. You, dear mother, in your last, of March 21st offer to send a new photograph of Miss Cobb—*ma non c'è!* Do send it still: for I suppose Wilky's improved prospects make his marriage more probable and my curiosity therefore greater. Do mention please, on your first chance to Wilky and Bob each that I wrote them long since each an unheeded letter: to Bob in December from Paris: to Wilky a couple of months (or more,) ago.—Thank father for sending me the proof of his letter to the Advertiser on *Hanging:* it seemed to bring with it to this musty old Rome the aroma of the New Jerusalem. I believe I never spoke of getting Willy's *Insane* letter;[2] but it too came and was read with profit.—I picture Cambridge in these young tenderly-blooming spring days (here the verdure is already stale and an old story—something of a penalty) and I find that, as poor Mrs. Lombard would say, I "care for it" still. I remember so many spring walks and sensations there: so many hopes and fears and emotions of the far away past, before my last birthday. Even now, just after the Lake of Nemi, methinks I could enjoy the blessed Yankee ether, as it hangs about Fresh Pond.—To touch for a moment on money matters; I have made two drafts within the past six weeks (£60 in all) necessitated by late expenses and of which father may have felt the strain. The 160$ you mention the receipt of (*Bethnal Green*, *Nation* and *Middlemarch*:) the Gautier and the story sent the *Galaxy* ought to almost refund him for this: or rather as they were partly absorbed by drafts made before which in some degree exceeded the $250 from the *Nation* to start with (nay, *much* exceeded it as they amounted to 70£) he must count upon the price of a story sent Howells some time since and which he said he would immediately publish. I'm afraid it's not in the *May* Atlantic: but I hope it's in the *June*. In other words here is a table which I hope won't sicken you.

Drawn by me since Dec. 18th		Paid and to be paid father on my account	
	£		$
		From *Nation*	250
Paris	30	" "	75
Rome	20	" Atlantic	60
"	20	" Galaxy	30
"	40	" N.A.R.	75 (?)
"	20	" Galaxy (for story I think I asked)	$150
	£130	" Atlantic (for story forthcoming)	100 *at least*
= $650 *in gold* = (I suppose not more than) $575 at most in paper.			
	$575	$640	$640

By this rough computation I shall by the time this reaches you (I trust) have made about $575 and drawn $640.[3] I owe father therefore $65, about: which he will have to wait for, from forthcoming things. Howells has two sketches of travel and I have just finished a third: and I have other designs. My last draft will last me some time. I hope all this doesn't bore you overmuch: of course we must keep things regular. You'll say it's hardly for me to say so with my heavy anticipatory drafts. But it will take me some time yet to get ahead of my expenses (I mean throw things out whereof the payment shall come in like a revenue.) It will take six months—or more. Meanwhile I trust to your being able conveniently to meet my drafts. Forgive all this sordid stuff, and believe me,

Ever your loving child,
H. James jr.

P.S. Excuse my stupidity: I find that by my hasty addition I have made $640 (sum earned) of what should be $740. So that I am about abreast with my drafts.

If Alice or (any of you) wants a good tonic beverage for warm weather I recommend: vermouth quinine and seltzer! It's delightful and I drink it regularly. Much vermouth and little quinine, of course.

1. HJ's thirtieth birthday fell on 15 April 1873.
2. On WJ's interest in mental health.
3. HJ's addition is faulty: the total should be $740; see his postscript.

To Sarah Butler Wister

Ms Congress

Rome, May 9*th* 101 Corso [1873]

My dear Mrs. Wister:

Your excellent letter came to me a couple of days since after a little longer delay than was necessary at my Banker's and put a very welcome end to certain melancholy musings. The memories of that blessed last winter of ours are fast turning into sad-faced phantoms and I had become capable of wondering whether your promise to write was simply to haunt my mind like a spirit a little more disembodied than the rest of them. But praised be fortune and your admirable charity, it is a good stout reality, such as I hope to know more of.—Your letter gave me a singular feeling, which you will doubtless partly understand. Lingering on here in these lovely languid days of deepening spring, I felt as if I were standing on some enchanted shore, sacred to idleness and irresponsiblity of all kinds and watching you tossing amid the waves of life and subject to all kinds of strange chances. Some of your chances, though, sound very pleasant and I envy you. I could alternate willingly a morning at the Lanari with one at the Vatican and (willingly indeed!) an evening at the Français with the entertainments of Ernesto Rossi (*Amleto, Otello* etc.) at the Apollo.—Still, I grant you that Rome is all you so tenderly describe its being and heaven knows I have for the last six weeks been feeling its daily deepening charm. You feel and express this charm so well that I needn't to attempt to tell you what it is we have been living on here since you departed and left life meagre.—About the winter I feel indeed very much as you; it seems a hundred years ago, and that last ride of ours by the Acqueducts savors strongly of a former state of being—or a future one! I have been taking a kind of satisfaction in the fact that the spring in a certain way rather vulgarizes the Campagna and scatters wheat and oats and other useful products over the fine bare stretches we galloped over. I came in the other day from Albano and looked out of the train and remembered my rides, but somehow but half believed in them.—The crowd has thinned out in the happiest way: the Corso is empty, the Pincio dull and the galleries silent and delightful. I try to believe that I'm coming back next winter, but I'm behaving as if I were not and going about spoonily and taking looks at things which will serve, if need be, as good-byes. The weather is deliciously cool and brilliant and I have been pitying the good people who left religiously a month ago because it was the tenth of April. For the most part, though, I don't want to recall them.—The frantic dissipations of winter are over and I see very few people—chiefly the Tweedies and the household in the Via della Croce.[1]—I took several rides with these latter ladies in the first days of April, but that is all over and we do so little that if it wasn't Rome, life might seem dull.—I went with them as I say, last night to see Rossi in *Otello*. Rossi was bad, though he roared rather handsomely at the end; but I found a kind of picturesque account in the thing; and then, the ingenuous Wurts came in and told us who all the ladies in the opposite boxes were; and I really felt a trifle the wiser to know that they were the Lavaggi and the Calabrini. (The *fine fleur* of the female nobility were there in a row: but on one side were a couple of boxes full of American women who I think were really finer flowers.)—Some time since I began to read *Tasso* with Miss Bartlett and though he is very delicious I have let it become rather desultory. May 11th. I have let it become rather desultory for the same reason that I broke off this letter the other day—that I have been feeling of late rather heavy-headed and seedy and absurdly incapable of dealing with book or pen. It is simply the delicious and atrocious Roman Spring weather, which doesn't at all suit me, but which it has been very well worth while staying on to get a good "square" impression of. I have got mine, and I shall soon be going. I don't know that there is anything momentous to add to that record of my daily doings but that I *didn't* drive one lovely day to Ostia with Mrs. Sumner and Miss Bartlett and the Tilton family; but went instead out to Albano and spent an expensive but most delightful week at the Parigi. It was fabulously cold and uncomfortably wet: but I got a good many long walks and was prodigiously pleased with everything. The whole region seemed to me a perfect Paradise of picturesqueness and I was moved to scribble some of my impressions, which in the good time of the Editor of the *Atlantic,* you may peruse. I had a short time before attempted to turn a few phrases on Roman rides and these too I bespeak your indulgence for. They will need it, for the thing is rather a humbug and about the rides properly there is very little said.[2]—I thank you cordially for your kind reassurance of the pleasure you extract from my literature. It shall be none the worse for feeling that you care about it.—*À propos* of literature (and indeed in answer to your own question) I did meet M. Arnold at the Story's—two or three times, besides dining with him rather drearily at the Von Hoffmann's. I had first and last a little small-talk with him. It remained small-talk and he did nothing to make it *big,* as my youthful dreams would have promised me. He's a good fellow I should say, but he is decidedly a disappointment, in a superficial sense, Besides, I never had pictured the author of the *Obermann* verses with a little glass screwed into one eye. But that was simply *my* want of imagination.—I went again to one of Hébert's receptions—*deceptions,* it would be better to call them. I was served, in a corner, with an insufficient quantity of ice-cream and I listened to some playing *à quatre mains* and that was the extent of my entertainment. I remembered that I was a free born American and departed abruptly. Mme. de Catalquinto was of course there, in all her—what shall I call it?—her immoral beauty. I think I have literally seen no one else to speak of—Miss Lowe once or twice only, though I have tried oftener. The Story's Sundays have become quite desolate and the last time I felt really like a lion—the only other guest being an insignificant little Englishman.—I have been out twice for the day to Frascati and spent the most ineffable hours on the grass at the foot of the ilexes, in the Villas Aldobrandini and Mondragone. The latter (if you know it) is the loveliest place in the world and I would give a round sum, if I possessed it, to be able to spend the summer there. It's an Italy, within Italy.—You meanwhile are dealing with nothing more Italian than the pavement of Bond Street: unless indeed you are just now in the country and treading the Warwickshire meadow-paths. There are places there *all but* just as good as Mondragone. It's just this "all but" that makes everything less loveable than Italy. Nevertheless I imagine the happiest things for you and I hope you find your sister stronger than you last mentioned her being. I confess I rather envy you your London pleasures—and even pains, the high civilization of Bond Street and the general spectacle of London. Just a little later than this a year ago I got a great impression of it all. As a spectacle it is certainly the biggest thing conceivable. If in the midst of your turmoil you find a spare half hour I should be very thankful for a hint of what and whom you've been seeing. I have seen some newspaper mention of Desclée's being about to appear with the French company in London. If this is true, I hope you may see her, for she is really unsurpassable.[3] There's a chance for disappointment! But I'll risk it—for both of you.—This sprawling letter, however, is threatening to bid defiance to envelopes; so I must close.—Doctor Wister, I sincerely hope, has found his better self again and is as well as his best friends can wish. Please give him my kindest regards. I should like also to offer whatever caress is appropriate to his years to your fine young Roman of a son. Farewell, and believe me, dear Mrs. Wister most faithfully yours

H. James Jr.

P.S. I should have liked to hear more of the lady *née* Musset. Some day I shall. And Lefèbvre *père* and his [word illegible] fibs French enough.

1. Where Mrs. Sumner and Miss Bartlett shared an apartment.
2. "Roman Rides," *Atlantic*, XXXII (August 1873), 190–198.
3. Aimée Olympe Désclée (1836–1874) established a large reputation at the Gymnase Theatre in Paris by her roles in the plays of Alexandre Dumas *fils*.

To William James

Ms Harvard

Perugia. May 19*th* [1873]

Dearest William:

I haven't written home for two long weeks, and my conscience gnaws me accordingly. I hasten (now) to put it to rest and beg you all to forgive my silence which will not have again the same efficient cause. The cause was simply that my last week in Rome was extremely occupied with doing twenty things (chiefly sight-seeing) which I had been purposely leaving all winter till the foreigners had cleared out and left a free field; and then that the *scirocco* was blowing vigorously and producing a lassitude not favorable to an even very light use of one's brain. The atmosphere didn't at all suit me; but I staid on from day to day, to get certain impressions which I should have been sorry to miss. Then, (yesterday,) I clutched my traps together and departed. I reached this lovely Perugia in the afternoon, after a six hour's journey through a landscape of surpassing fascinations and rejoice greatly in the delightful change of air I find here. I mean to pause two or three days and enjoy it.—I forget whether it was before I last wrote (to father and mother) that your letter of April 6th had come. I think so, and that I acknowledged it. Many thanks for everything in it. Alice's letter of the 13th is still unacknowledged, which I hereby do, embracing her in the lovingest manner, *en attendant* that I answer it. The enclosed scrap from the *Advertiser* about my *Gautier* was very agreeable. *À propos* of which, do you know the authorship of the *Nation* notice? The general style of the article didn't read like Dennett, though the phrases about my thing were obscure enough for him. Whoever he is, he is very silly.—I hardly know what to tell about my last days in Rome. It had become very empty and very fascinating and I would gladly have staid there till July 1st. The weather was beautiful and the heat not intense: but with the peculiar quality of the air I grew visibly on worse and worse terms and I continued to breathe it only for the sake of everything else and of my growing doubt that (on this very account) I should soon behold Rome again.

All the last weeks I was there I found it almost impossible to read or write; but the enchanting experience of Rome in April and May was too valuable to be sacrificed: so I said to myself: "Get your impressions now; you may never have another chance; and *use* them afterward." Indeed, now that I look back at my five months there (almost) from an external standpoint, I see that they were languid months and that I enjoyed but the half of my moderate capacity for work. I had always an incipient headache. But for all that the episode has been immensely profitable. My impressions will abide, and in this breezy Perugia the headache has already past away. As for the work, that I shall easily overtake. I go into all this because I must have seemed to you for a long time very unproductive. But I am a great deal wiser.—The Tweedies had left Rome a day or two before me, and poor Mr. T. certainly needed it. You will think I have found out Aunt Mary's soft spot when I tell you that *a couple* of hours after her arrival in Florence, after twelve spent in the railway train, on a hot day, she wrote me a copious and affectionate note. They are still in Florence, where I may possibly overtake them. They go thence to the lakes where they hope to meet Lady Rose,[1] and thence to Kissingen. I saw no one else in the last days of Rome, save the ladies of the Via della Croce (Mrs. Sumner and Miss Bartlett) who were both rather wilted, and preparing to depart for the chateau at Dinant in Brittany which Mrs. Sumner has taken for the summer. The Terrys and Storys were thriving and I spent my last evening in the most affectionate manner with the latter, for whom I don't care an inordinate number of straws. Story is too much occupied with himself, and Madam with the Duchess of Northumberland. Mlle, is on the whole the most satisfactory as well and the handsomest. I dined a day or two before at the Terrys *en famille*, and had a better time there than ever before. The two Miss Crawfords had just come back from a wonderful ten days' tour through a dozen old Sabine and Etruscan cities with Hare, the author of the *Walks*,[2] and Miss Annie was *intarissable* with characteristic cleverness—although she did intimate at table that poor Terry was a *beast*.—You may despise these trivial personalities, but they will interest mother and Alice: the latter too will be glad to hear that the poor pallid von Hoffmanns are to spend the summer at a pension at *Berne:* a change from the Villa Mattei. But a personality in which you will be interested is one (or rather two) I encountered this morning, in the breakfast room of this inn. A German and his wife were drinking their tea with a great reverberation, but with an amiable air which led me to make overtures (in French) to conversation. The husband replied with alacrity and we conversed long and agreeably, chiefly about the contrasted characteristics of Rome and Florence, where (at F.) he had been spending three months, *"dans un but scientifique."* His wife seemed to speak no French, but took a kind of tacit part, by play of feature, in the talk. After we had parted, it was borne in upon me that they were the H. Grimms;[3] and so in truth they were. I hope they will be round at dinnertime, and I will introduce myself over you.—An individual I shall certainly see in Florence is Hillebrand who lives there and whom Boott has introduced me to. He and Gryzanowski are two very good social elements in Florence—and such as I have greatly missed the like of during the past winter. An intelligent male brain to communicate with occasionally would be a practical blessing. I have encountered none for so long that I don't even know how to address yours and find it impossible to express a hundred ideas which at various times I have laid aside, to be propounded to you.—Looking over your letter, I perceive your adjuration to prepare articles etc. on the French, G. Sand, Balzac etc. I may come to it, some day, but there are various things I want to do first. Just at present I shall write a few more notes of travel: for two reasons: 1° that a few more joined with those already published and written will make a decent little volume; and 2° that now or never (I think) is my time. The *keen* love and observation of the picturesque is ebbing away from me as I grow older, and I doubt whether a year or two hence, I shall have it in me to describe houses and mountains, or even cathedrals and pictures. I don't know whether I shall do anything better, but I shall have spoiled for this. The real, natural time,—if I *could*—would have been when I was abroad before. Mysterious and incontrollable (even to one's self) is the growth of one's mind. Little by little, I trust, my abilities will catch up with my ambitions.—I am glad to hear you have decided on the Physiology and Anatomy place for next year. Father mentioned it in a letter received about the same time with Alice's, whether before or after I can't remember, and can't verify, as it is in a trunk downstairs. I hope you will go on from success to success. But I shall be interested to hear how you have compromised with the desire to give time and strength to other things.—Your account of Child and his tribulations was very touching. The poor little man looms up to me like a perfect Colossus of domestic heroism. In Theodora Sedgwick too I am interested; but short of marrying her, I can't give her a social start. (Not that I could by this.) Is anything more heard from Wilky and does this man ahead show any signs of making room?—

Later. Evening. They *are* the Grimms and I have just had a most effusive meeting with them in the dining room. They weren't at dinner but I caught them over their beefsteak-tea a moment before they went to the little theatre at which for three francs they had taken a box holding four persons. They asked me to go with them, but I preferred finishing my letter to you. I reintroduced myself and they exclaimed greatly and delightedly, asked much about you and said *sie liebten Sie sehr* etc. I shall probably see them again tomorrow. Why is Mrs. G. the only German woman of condition who don't speak French? There is something extremely taking about her—a wondrous frankness and sweetness. She of course asked me if I too loved *die Künst Peruginos*. I met little Richard Staigg (whom I had seen several times in Rome) with his nice wife; and she gave me news of C. Atkinson, to whom through her I sent a message. I should like to see that good creature.—But I musn't write forever. You shall have more about Perugia in print. I hope to make excursions to Assisi and Cortona and combine the three.—There are by this time, I trust, letters forwarded to Florence for me—letters full of home and all I long to hear. I wrote last that you were to address *Fenzi* (*Emile*) Florence. Love, love, love.

Yours ever
H. James Jr.

1. Lady Rose, wife of Sir John Rose, was the former Charlotte Temple (d. 1883), sister of Mrs. Edmund Tweedy.

2. Augustus Hare (1834–1903) compiled numerous guide and travel books, notably his *Walks in Rome*.

3. Whom WJ had known in Germany.

To Mrs. Henry James Sr.

Ms Harvard

Florence, H. de l'Europe [May 1873]

Dearest mother—

I reached Florence last night, and the first thing this A.M. went in quest of letters. I was rewarded by the bestowal of two—yours of April 27th, and one from Aunt Kate from New York. Your letter was ten times blessed, beloved mother, and I lose not time in answering it. I wrote to Willy eight days ago from Perugia, after an unduly long interval: but by the time this reaches you, you will have been reassured and comforted. I transacted the little scheme with which I left Rome and "examined" minutely after leaving Perugia, Assisi, Cortona and Arezzo, gathering materials for one of my charming articles.[1] They are all very curious old places and I ought to be able to say something worthwhile about them: but I won't expatiate now, because you will enjoy my impressions more when I put them into better form. I find the Tweedies departed; for the lakes, I suppose. They have left no tidings behind and I must communicate with them. My own designs are rather "mixed," and difficult to arrange. I am divided between an impression (not however amounting to a certainty) that I ought before long to leave Italy: and an inability to decide where to go. I have already mentioned that I left Rome rather "seedy," and though my week at Perugia was beneficial, the barbarous food there and at the other lovely spots I touched at rather took off the edge of the benefit. I find just now a rather heated and heavy atmosphere in Florence which if it continues, will not be just the thing to tone me up. But I shall try a few days of it and then decide. Three months of Switzerland, before the 1st September, are rather formidable: but any place where I am well and can do a little daily work I shan't complain of. My "daily work" for some time past has been a struggling with

387

adverse influences; but I console myself with thinking that I have a mine of *impressions*. Be patient all of you; and you shall see them assume the most enchanting forms. Don't be scared sweet mammy, at my talking thus freely of being a little under the weather. It's an evanescent ill and I shall soon come to the surface again. I mention it only, because, as considerations of salubrity *do* affect my movements I always fancy these must seem erratic, unless the former are touched upon. What I had rather built upon was staying here till July 1st, and then trying the Baths of Lucca. This would have a greater charm then a mere renewal of acquaintance with poor old Switzerland. Be assured of this, however, that I shall act with perfect discretion; and implore you not to let my situation ever cost you anything but a benevolent smile.—Your letter was full of welcome odds and ends about home affairs; and your mention of oysters tomatoes and apple-pie most harrowing. Fried artichokes (toasted shavings they might be called) are the only delicacy that has crossed my path these ten days. I am glad to hear Alice and William are at the lifting business again: they ought by this time between them to have lifted the world into a higher plane. I am glad, too, that you dine and are dined: my blessings on every mouthful you swallow.—I am not at all glad, though, over your news about Howells' putting off my "article." I don't know which one it is he means. I have sent him three in the last two or three months and have heard of the arrival of but one—a story.[2] I suppose it's that. It's a pity, and it's hard, to have to write such very short things. A story in five or six Atlantic pages is impossible, and I shall have to give up that. But of course if it's a condition positive, I must sing small. I have all written, in my bag, an article (about Albano, Frascati etc.) which I was on the point of posting to him: but as its predecessors are of nine or ten pages (I conjecture) it would not see the light for many months, and I must try and dispose of it elsewhere. The *Galaxy*, as you say nothing, I suppose gives no sign about my story: which it seems to me it ought to do before I send it anything else. My piece is really very *nice* writing and I am rather averse to sending it to Scribner or Lippincott. This, however, I must of course do: though they too will probably find it too long.

I therefore take the liberty of enclosing it to father and of asking him first: if by the time it comes, he has an answer from the *Galaxy* about the story, to send them this: second if not, to send it to Lippincott's or Scribner's as he thinks best. If it were a *newer* subject, I am pretty sure I could get Leslie Stephen to put it into the *Cornhill:* but I had rather make a better beginning with the C. This I mean to do. I presume to be able to do *Cornhill* writing. The M.S. will not reach father for two or three days after this; and if he transfers it into another envelope, I beg him to mark it externally with my initials and send with it a *separate* letter, calling attention to it. Bless him for his trouble. It seems to me that his name and MINE!! conjoined ought to make their attention tolerably immediate. I suppose I ought to name a price for it, and not be modest either. £75 ought to be the minimum. I would rather it were the *Galaxy* than the others. A word more on a cognate theme. I recently sent the *Nation* another letter.[3] The *Nation* isn't polite: but where is one to turn? They were so long in printing my last that I told Garrison that rather than keep it *indefinitely,* I would have him transfer it to father. I hope he will print it within a reasonable time, but if he shouldn't, I must ask the latter to do something with it. Say the *Evening Post.* A word from father to Godkin would probably get a place for it: though in strictness it is too *précieux* for the place, and (I fear) overlong. Excuse all this personal stuff: you will appreciate the needfulness of it.—I am not surprised at the Bootts requisitions; I thought I saw them *hatching* them in Rome. I placed as many words, here and there, as I could, to avert them: but in vain! I don't think you need fear any fatalities however. You will get on very well with Boott: the only thing is that Lizzie will oppress her victim of Grindlewald and Berne.[4] But she has been a good deal tuned up by Rome and her subsequent experiences, and will not be so dead a weight. Take 'em easy!—By this time the Nortons will have reached Cambridge I suppose: but for the present, you will not see much of them. Take *them* easy when you do. I shall be much interested in your summer designs as they develop. Let me hear everything, and may everything be agreeable. You say nothing about the boys; so I suppose they prosper in their own measure. Tell William I saw more of H. Grimm at Perugia. He staid over the next day and I had much talk with him. Mme. G. was very communicative, but all in German, of which I lost the greater part. I took greatly to G. who sent W. his love; and his wife an unintelligible outburst in German. As my movements are so uncertain address *E. Fenzi Florence.* You shall hear again as soon as possible.—Meanwhile, dearest mammy, I fold you in a passionate embrace—you and all the blessed family.

Your loving
H

1. "A Chain of Italian Cities," *Atlantic*, XXXIII (February 1974), 158–164.
2. "A Roman Holiday," "Roman Rides," and "Roman Neighborhoods." The story was "The Last of the Valerii."
3. "The After-Season at Rome," *Nation*, XVI (12 June 1873), 399–400.
4. A reference to their travels the previous year when Alice James was abroad.

To William James

Ms Harvard

Florence May 31*st* [1873]

Dear William.

I got this morning with pleasure your note of May 11*th*, enclosing Bob's. The latter I greatly thank you for. It is most wonderful and beautiful. What a marvellous child he is. One may certainly hear with pleasure that, with such feelings and views, he's going to become a father. Your note was otherwise equally welcome—and a voice (unheard by me for many months in the profitless society which is the dark feature of one's expatriation here) from the world of serious things.—There seems something half-tragic in the tone with which you speak of having averted yourself from psychology. But I hope you have settled down calmly to it, and will have no irritating regrets. You know best, and one must do not what one plans, but what one can. For the chance I miss to review books by being absent, I suppose there is something in it: but not over much, for I am struggling through long delay to get at something better

390

than book reviewing. Mind is a slow progression, but a progression, I believe, it is. I saw Pater's *Studies*[1] just after getting your letter, in the English bookseller's window: and was inflamed to think of buying it and trying a notice. But I see it treats of several things I know nothing about.—I wrote less than a week ago to mother, just after my arrival in Florence and as well as I can remember, my letter must have been rather plaintive. There is no need to *piangere*, even tho' I probably *shall* shuffle off from Florence tomorrow. I am confirmed in my impression that I had better be moving out of Italy. Though as yet we have had no heat to speak of, I find the Italian spring atmosphere curiously and obstinately relaxing. [*Private*.[2] You will be interested to know just how; and probably guess that I mean in its effect on my well known idiosyncrasy. Even so. Ten weeks ago (after an excellent winter) I began to break down and ever since have suffered from perfect torpor and inaction of the bowels; I suppose too of the liver as I am as yellow as an orange. I see every reason to believe it's the climate. Places in which I am very sleepy immediately tell on this point (I verified this distinctly twice last summer in Switzerland) and here I am always soporific and heavy headed. It makes me sick and seedy and unable to work and it's too great a loss of time to see it out further. I hope, reasonably enough, that as my improvement becomes confirmed by time I can stand Italian springs. But it's better to knock under now and depart. Besides, of the whole spring I have drunk deep: and this is the summer, which makes many exiles, and I am not a lonely victim. This for your interested ear: but don't let it trouble you. I'm a vastly better man than a year ago.] I shall make straight from here to Lago Maggiore and station myself on the Simplon road—at Bavino or Pallanza. I shall try a few days there—if I find them propitious a few more; so as to eat as much off as possible from the cope of THREE MONTHS twice in Switzerland. Alice will envy me! But I am very content and look forward to a healthy, tranquil, somewhat productive summer. I had my jocund summering all winter in Rome. I shall go straight either to Lausanne or Glion (Montreux), according to the moment at which I arrive. Please therefore begin and address Poste Restante, Montreux, as I shall probably be there at the right

391

moment to get your letters and will advise you of new addresses proportionately. Two or three will probably suffice for the whole summer.—I have been strolling about gently and looking at Florence, but finding in her I blush to say how little of her old magic. Rome has murdered her—Rome a hundred times more wondrous in retrospect. Her great smiting hands have snapt the tender chords of perception to which Florence appeals. I should vainly try to tell you how one looks back on Rome and hungers for her again. How I envy the people—lethargic Terry and tough Story—who thrive there till July 1st!—I have seen no one here but Gryzanowski whom I shall probably see again. I have been shy of calling on Hillebrand as I meant, *on* my short stay. Gryzanowski isn't, in talk, quite as "masterly," as in writing, but he is very superior every way, and delightfully bland as a companion.—You say nothing of the family summer. Is it fixed? Let me hear, oh beloved ones all.—I send to father by this mail, in another package, the M.S. I wrote last about: I wish it a safe journey. Please mention also to T. S. Perry that I sent him yesterday a review of Cherbuliez's novel.[3] It, also, heaven speed.—My blessings, dear brother, on all your renunciations and undertakings. Love to all.

Yours ever,
H. James jr.

1 Pater's *Studies in the History of the Renaissance* had just been published.
2. Presumably the word "private" was a signal to WJ not to read the subsequent portion of the letter aloud to the family.
3. Unsigned review of "Meta Holdenis" in the *North American Review*, CXVII (October 1873), 461–468.

To William James

Ms Harvard

Glion—June 18*th* 73.

Dear William:

I received last evening your letter of May 25th and mother's of the same date, (for which please thank her.) I wrote a week ago to Alice, so that you will already know of my having migrated to these parts. Your letters were forwarded from Florence, which involved some delay: but now that I have got yours I lose no time.— I am very sorry to hear that your strength has increased less during the past winter than I supposed and that your work is so much of an effort to you. If this is the case, I well understand why you should be indisposed to deal with your augmented class, and that some such plan as you ask my advice about, should have its attractions. I'm strongly inclined to think that you might subsist very comfortably *in Rome* on the footings you set forth. The place has more resources in one way and another than any in Europe and is peculiarly adapted to help one get through time. I found for myself that it stole away many hours—quite too many—in which I would have preferred being shut up to myself. Of course I was more active than you could be: but even the difference would, I should think, leave enough in your favor to make your idle hours tolerable. You would find a good many people to drop in upon: sitting round in the villas and churches is in itself a great resource, and hack hire is extremely cheap. This without counting the galleries. Wishing a sedative climate you might not (probably would not) find that of Rome too relaxing; and if the winter were reasonably fine, you would be able to spend much of it in the open air. Altogether counting up all the various chances of Roman life I can hardly doubt that they would serve your need. Of course my society would fill up a great many crevices.—These things I can undertake to say of Rome alone. Florence would be less favorable for though there are a good many people there, there are vastly fewer resorts and lounging places and a much harsher climate. In Naples you would get a warm but exciting atmosphere and a *belle nature*, but very little society. Rome in short is quite apart. My own plans for next winter have been vague, and I have been divided about Rome: partly because of the (for me) too sedative climate, and partly because of the importunate demands of the American village (which is a proof that you could kill time.) But if you were to come to Rome, I would willingly and joyfully decide to go back, because I enormously want to. I could avoid over-relaxation by leaving early in the spring. My plan otherwise had been to spend the autumn and spring in Florence and the midwinter in Naples. But Rome has such a hold on my affections that I only want a pretext for going back. Another winter I should know how to play my cards (both physically and socially) more profitably.—This is the whole story, I think, as far as it may be told. I hope you will find the *data* sufficient to help you to a tolerably easy decision. It can't be very easy I know; and for me to *advise* is impossible. But this I can say: that with my high opinion of Rome, I don't see how to an observant and reflective man even a loafing winter there could fail to be profitable. You will have Lizzie Boott to interrogate: I imagine she would confirm my impression. It is a pity they are gone, as their house would help you to loaf.—If you come I will do all in my power to help you through. We should certainly have much profitable talk.

I received several days ago father's letter, telling me of T. S. Perry's engagement. Thank him (father) and tell him I shall very soon answer it. The engagement surprised me somewhat, but not altogether. I always fancied T. S. Perry would never marry: but if he does it seems to me in character that he should marry a Miss Lilla Cabot.[1] I suppose they will have to wait. Meanwhile I shall write him a note. I'm very glad Silvia Watson is provided for. She will be a providence to her provider. I was interested in A. Sedgwick's $4000 a year. I wish you would tell me by what papers he makes it and how much they pay him. Does it all come from the *Nation* and the *Atlantic*? For what else does he write?—I'm sorry you didn't like my *Galaxy* tale,[2] which I haven't seen. Has it been sent? I hoped it was sufficiently pleasing. But one can't know. I wrote you what I remember as a rather plaintive letter from Florence a fortnight ago which I hope you'll not let afflict you. I did well to come to Switzerland, though I haven't chosen just here a very happy resting place. I had a curious experience last summer on the influence of this immediate region. I hoped it was confined to Villeneuve, but it has removed itself here—as is but natural as the places are hardly more than three-quarters of an hour apart. I shall leave this as soon as the present rainy spell is over and go *via* Berne (where I shall stop awhile) to Thusis which took my fancy greatly last summer and suited me apparently though it didn't suit Alice.

It will be rather a dull *séjour* for two months, so I shall try and break the back of the summer at Berne which I also greatly liked last year. Your letters for a while will have concentrated at Montreux: but direct them henceforth: *Poste Restante—Thusis, Grisons, Switzld.* It would have been wiser to give you this address from the first. But I was uncertain.—Don't bother a jot about my ailment. I am wondrous well and content and shall be much better for this Swiss summer. I was at first indisposed to come here: but it was the thing to do. My winter in Rome was a poor working winter and I have done less than I hoped: but it was very educative and will tell before long. Mother tells me you are going to see the boys. All prosperity to your journey. Write me something about it, if only a few words. —I have said nothing about the Boston fire! What can one say? I hope the suffering isn't great. Love to W. Holmes: I don't expect him to write to me but hope (that is mean) some day to write to him. I think there is nothing more to say about the subject of your letter. I can only give you the *data* on this side. Let me hear in due time of your conclusions.

Yours ever
H. James jr.

Excuse misfolding of letter

1. Perry married the daughter of the Boston surgeon Dr. Samuel Cabot. Her mother was Hannah Jackson, a cousin of James Russell Lowell. "You will have a wife at once very clever and very devoted," HJ wrote to his friend.
2. "The Sweetheart of M. Briseux."

To William Dean Howells

Ms Harvard

Berne, Switz. June 22d [1873]

My veritably dear Howells,

Your letter of May 12th came to me a week ago (after a journey to Florence and back) and gave me exquisite pleasure. I found it in the Montreux post-office and wandered further till I found the edge of an open vineyard by the lake, and there I sat down with my legs hanging over the azure flood and broke the seal. Thank you for everything; for liking my writing and for being glad I like yours. Your letter made me homesick, and when you told of the orchards by Fresh Pond I hung my head for melancholy. What is the meaning of this destiny of desolate exile—this dreary necessity of having month after month to do without our friends for the sake of this arrogant old Europe which so little befriends us? This is a hot Sunday afternoon: from my window I look out across the rushing Aar at some beautiful undivided meadows backed by black pine woods and blue mountains: but I would rather be taking up my hat and stick and going to invite myself to tea with you. I left Italy a couple of weeks since, and since then have been taking gloomy views of things. I feel as if I had left my "genius" behind in Rome. But I suppose I am well away from Rome just now; the Roman (and even the Florentine) lotus had become, with the warm weather, an indigestible diet. I heard from my mother a day or two since that your book is having a sale—bless it! I haven't yet seen the last part and should like to get the volume as a whole. Would it trouble you to have it sent by post to Brown, Shipley & Co., London? Your fifth part I extremely relished; it was admirably touched. I wished the talk in which the offer was made had been given (instead of the mere résumé), but I suppose you had good and sufficient reasons for doing as you did. But your work is a success and Kitty a creation. I have envied you greatly, as I read, the delight of feeling her grow so real and complete, so true and charming. I think, in bringing her through with such unerring felicity, your imagination has *fait ses preuves*. I wish I could talk over her successor with you, sitting on the pine-needles, by Fresh Pond. This is odiously impossible: but at least let me hear what you can, as the thing goes on. I suppose it's to begin with January.—Are you in the new house yet? Let me know how it's arranged—that is where your library and the *dining room* are, that I may sometimes drop in in a vision. I've just seen Aldrich's *Marjory Daw* in the *Revue*[1] looking as natural as if begotten in the Gallic brain. It's a pretty compliment to have translated it and well-deserved. Perhaps they'll try you next.[2]—I can fancy that Keeler[3] should be more divine than ever. I suppose the recent letter in the *Nation* about Sir A. Cockburn was his. It was very well said and he has learned to write at least like a mortal. I should like to tell you a vast deal about myself, and I believe you would like to hear it. But as far as *vastness* goes I should have to invent it, and it's too hot for such work. I send you another (and for the present last) travelling piece—about Perugia etc.[4] It goes with this, in another cover: a safe journey to it. I hope you may squeeze it in this year. It numbers (in pages) more than you desire; but I think it is within bounds, as you will see there is an elision of several. I have done in all these months since I've been abroad less writing than I hoped. Rome, for direct working, was not good—too many distractions and a languefying atmosphere. But for "impressions" it was priceless, and I've got a lot duskily garnered away somewhere under my waning (that's an *n,* not a *v*) *chevelure* which some day may make some figure. I shall make the coming year more productive or retire from business altogether. Believe in me yet awhile longer and I shall reward your faith by dribblings somewhat less meagre.—I'm very glad to hear of Fiske's coming out and of his friends' generosity. His long labors richly deserve it.[5]—I say nothing about the Fire. I can't trouble you with vain ejaculations and inquiries which my letters from home will probably already have answered. At this rate, apparently, the Lord loveth Boston immeasurably. But what a grim old Jehovah it is!—Are you to be in Cambridge for the summer? May it be happy and kindly for your wife and children, wherever spent. Commend me tenderly to your wife and recall me to the expanding nurseries of Winny and Bann.

My blessing, dear Howells, on all your affections, labors and desires. Write me a word when you can (Brown & Shipley, London) and believe me always faithfully yours,

H. James jr.

1. Thomas Bailey Aldrich's short story appeared in 1873.
2. HJ himself would shortly be translated in the *Revue des Deux Mondes*.
3. Ralph Keeler (1840–1873), friend of Howells, a former cabin boy on Great Lakes steamers and a Californian vagabond; he wrote fiction and travel articles for the *Atlantic*.
4. "A Chain of Italian Cities."
5. His *Outlines of Cosmic Philosophy* was about to be published.

To Sarah Butler Wister

Ms Congress

Homburg, Germany.
Aug 10*th* [1873]

Dear Mrs. Wister—

It seems long ago now that I answered the excellent letter you were so good as to send me at Rome. It's not really so very long, but it seems long because everything connected with that blessed place has melted away into a kind of misty, fabulous past. If I may say this, I suppose you can with even better reason, and yet I should be sorry to think that my poor letter had become so utterly a thing of the past as to have lost all chance of resuscitation in one of your leisure hours and your kindliest moods. I think you expected America to bring you a great many of the former—and I defy it altogether, at its unimaginable worst—to rob you of the latter. I really haven't in the least expected you to write to me; I am very sure you have had more urgent duties—and I hope keener pleasures. But I only want momentarily to assume that you *might* have written, as a pretext for sending you a few lines—which I beg you will think of answering only at your perfect convenience. I remember by the way that I don't at all know your American address; but I suppose I shall be safe in trying *Germantown*. This little fact proves that I have heard very little about you since your letter came to me. Nothing at all in fact: I left Rome very soon after, saw no one who could give me news of you and was left to imagine you in London, imagine you at sea, and at last imagine you looking your native land—a trifle grimly—in the face and settling down to your *tête à tête* with it. But now I confess that though my imagination demands no more congenial topic than you and your fortunes, I long for a little plain certainty. You *have* crossed the sea, you *are* at home, I suppose, and you have taken the measure of the situation. Give me a sketch of it, I beg you, and send me a hint of your impressions of everything. If I thought it would be anything of a bribe to you, I would relate my own *histoire intime* since we parted—or since I left Rome at least; for I didn't feel as if I had really parted with you till I had done that, too. But the topic has little intrinsic interest and

I have had very few adventures. The summer is melting away (melting, alas, literally), very fast and I feel rather blue when I I think of the meagre sum of its contributions to my experience. I lingered on in Italy till about the tenth of June and then came doggedly over the Simplon and spent three or four weeks in Switzerland. I have been at Homburg a month, having come here, out of sorts, to attempt a "cure" with the waters. I have ceased to drink them—the "cure" not responding to my appeal; but I am staying because I like the place and have a constitutional shrinking from fleeing to ills I know not of. Do you know Homburg at all? It's very pretty—German pretty—and is cool and shady and comfortable generally, and still amusing enough, in spite of the death and burial of the gaming. The Kursaal stands there like a great cavernous tomb—a tomb however in which they have concerts, a reading room and a café. I have seen no old friends all summer and made no new ones who have caused me any particular emotion. I have heard nothing of any of our Roman associates—save the Tweedies, who are here—not a word about Mrs. Summer and Miss Bartlett, to whom, however, I have lately written.—I feel as if I might sentimentalize inordinately about Rome, if I gave myself leave, but you probably do your own sentimentalizing, and better than I can.—Some of my published attempts in this line you may lately have seen—a couple of things in the *Atlantic* and a thing in the *Galaxy*—which latter however is probably not yet out. There are to be a couple more Italian scribbles in the *Atlantic,* which I know I can trust your friendship for both theme and scribbler to read kindly. You will recognize an allusion or so in the rather highfalutin *Atlantic* Rides and in the *Galaxy* piece.[1] Enjoy them and forgive them according to need. You will see—I had to make up for small riding by big writing. But what's the use of writing at all, unless imaginatively? Unless one's vision can lend something to a thing, there's small reason in proceeding to proclaim one has seen it. Mere *looking* every one can do for himself.—I actually have been seeing something in Germany—a thing I never expected—and let my imagination dance a little jig on it the other day for the *Nation.*[2] I take a voluptuous pleasure in putting you thus *au courant* of my literature.—not having had speech these three months, of any one to whom it—or anyone else's—the least bit mattered.—I don't quite venture to say to myself that I shall go to Rome for the winter, but I venture still less to say I shan't. It would be an immense help to know that you were to have a fireside there by which I might sometimes sit in that before dinner dusk. Has Miss Lowe, by the way, gone home? I met her at Assisi, uncertain, and attended by the painter Bellay. I heard afterwards that it was a case for a more suggestive word than that I have just used: but isn't this vile gossip to send across the sea? Have you had further news of ce bon Lefèbvre?[3] This is a small specimen question of a hundred I should like to ask you. But they mustn't crowd into the particular inquiry I wish to make about Dr. Wister and the friendly message I wish to send him. I hope he is a quite well man and not too much bothered as a new settler. Pray give him my kindest regards. For yourself, I have more good wishes than I have left room for. Do show me that you have guessed some of them by finding a leisure half-hour some day to write to me—Care Brown Shipley, London. Yours always, dear Mrs Wister, most faithfully

Henry James, jr.

1. "Roman Rides" in the August 1873 *Atlantic* and "From a Roman Notebook" in the November 1873 *Galaxy* contained several allusions to HJ's outings in Rome the previous winter with Mrs. Wister.

2. "Homburg Reformed," unsigned, *Nation*, XVII (28 August 1873), 142–144.

3. Bellay and Lefèbvre were painters Mrs. Wister and HJ had met at the Villa Medici.

To William Dean Howells

Ms Harvard

Homburg Sept. 9th [1873]
5 Kisseleff. Strasse

Dear Howells—

I have been meaning for many days to write and tell you that your book came safely and very speedily to hand; but have put it off for reasons doubtless not good enough to bear telling. The work is at any rate by this time the better digested. I had great pleasure in reading it over, and I have great pleasure now in recurring to it.[1] It gains largely on being read all at once and certain places which at first I thought amenable to restriction (or rather certain features—as *zum beispiel* a want of interfusion between the "scenery" element in the book and the dramatic) cease, quite, to seem so in the volume. But your people are better than their background; you have done your best for the latter but your story is intrinsically more interesting. This of course, however. Vivid figures will always kill the finest background in the world.— Kitty is certainly extremely happy—more so even than I feel perfectly easy in telling you; for she belongs to that class of eminent felicities which an artist doesn't indefinitely repeat. Don't be disappointed, then, if people don't like her later-born sisters just as relishingly. If they do, however, you will have taken out an unassailable patent as story-teller and shown—what is the great thing—-that you conceive the particular as part of the general. The successful thing in Kitty is her *completeness:* she is singularly palpable and rounded and you couldn't, to this end, have imagined anything better than the particular antecedents you have given her. So! In the House of Fable she stands firm on her little pedestal. I congratulate you!—Arbuton I think, now that I know the end, decidedly a shade too scurvy. The charm of Kitty, as one thinks of her, is that she suggests a type—a blessed one, and the interest of the tale as one gets into it is the foreshadowing of a conflict between her type and another. But at the last, the man's peculiar shabbiness underlines this interest by making you think that she had simply happened to get hold of a particularly mean individual— one, indeed, that she would't have even temporarily felt any serious emotion about. I know that a great part of the idea of the story is that she shall be impressed by his unessential qualities; but as it stands, you rather resent her drama—her own part in it being so very perfectly analysed—having a hero who was coming to *that!* I was hoping that it was she who was to affront him. She does, indeed, come up by her shabby clothes; but this is an accident that she should have done something, I mean, which even had she been dressed to perfection, would have left him puzzled, at loss, feeling that she wasn't for him. This wouldn't, indeed, have necessarily implied his being snubbed, but was that inherent in your plan? Your drama, as you saw it, I suppose was the irreconcileability of the two results of such opposed antecedents and not a verdict on one or the other.— But you'll be amused at my "something", and ask me to dream it up for you. Heaven deliver me. Your own at least is very neatly executed.—But I didn't mean to dig so deep. How are the Venetian Priest and his fair one coming on?[2] I suppose that they're to begin in January and that you're giving them touch upon touch and line upon line. I wish you quiet days and propitious moods. The wish for the former sounds sarcastic: for I suppose Cambridge is still Cambridge, in your new house as well as your old; that your new roof covers you is almost all I've heard about you in a long time. The Arctic explorations of my own family have made their letters rare and slow to arrive. I wrote you from Berne, in June and you get the letter, because you sent me the book: but don't let that be the only answer. I sent you also a paper ("A Chain of [Italian] Cities") which I trust you received and can sooner or later use. I've not had a very productive summer—directly at least; but indirectly, yes; as I came here unwell and shall be leaving permanently better as I trust, and apt for turning production, ever more. There isn't much to say about my summer. It has been ten quiet weeks of Germany.— Even while I wrote, half an hour ago, came your letter of Aug. 26th. Your forty letters about your story make me blush over all the foregoing stuff. But with them and Miss Lane's reports, you needn't heed late-coming praise or blame. I'm sorry your Venetian Priest is still so far off. So my Chain of Cities did arrive. I'm sorry it seems "meagre"—an idea that makes me weep salt tears. This, however, I fondly hope, was less owing to my own poverty than to a constant fear to amplify and make it too long.—I'm very glad to get news of you, but your letter was cruelly brief. But I suppose such things must be with editors and householders. I'm glad your house is so good, and should like vastly this horrible afternoon (a foretaste of November) to spend an hour before that wonderful fire-place. Farewell. I shall send you more things in these coming months, and I shall heed your advice about unlaboriousness.[3] I know I'm too ponderous. But the art of making *substance* light is hard. Love to your wife and kids.

Yours always,

H. James Jr

1. *A Chance Acquaintance* had just been published.
2. Howells was writing *A Foregone Conclusion*.
3. Howells had written to HJ (26 August 1873) accepting "A Chain of Italian Cities" and "Roman Neighborhoods" for the *Atlantic,* adding "They are both good enough, but I wish you would write for the *Atlantic* as unlaboriously as you seem to write your *Nation* letters, putting all the minor observation and comment that you can into them." It is possible that the *Nation* articles were written more spontaneously because they were published unsigned, whereas in the *Atlantic* all of James's writings bore his name.

To William Dean Howells

Ms Harvard

Florence October 18 [1873]

Dear Howells—

I send you another bundle of hieroglyphics (apart from this, in a second cover) with hopes that matters are not immutably disposed against its coming to the front early rather than late. If it suits you to have me figure in your January number, if my two last sketches are printed and my story is too long for the purpose—*if* all this is blessed fact—here's your chance. Siena, you'll see is my theme and I have tried to remain brief.[1] My only fear is you'll find me too brief. Bald, however, I've tried not to be, nor yet too artfully curled and anointed. In short, consider me discreetly light and agreeably grave and print me when you can!—I am distinctly in Italy again, as you see, and am spending three or four weeks in Florence previous to settling in Rome for the winter. If I could have my wish I think I should remain quietly by the Arno and write enchanting stories; but my brother is at present crossing the ocean to join me (as of course you know) and Rome is his goal. I had last winter there a bad time for work; but I must, can and shall do better now.—I wrote you some five weeks ago from Homburg, just at the moment your last letter reached me. Mine I suppose you duly received.—I know nothing about you now save that you are watching the autumn days drop like bright colored leaves. My memory is full of uneffaced Cambridge Octobers, and every now and then I drop a tear on them and I seem to hear a little leafy rustle deep down in my spiritual parts and to see a dim haze before my eyes. Here yet, it is frank summer, but I don't complain, for I don't like cold weather any better as I grow older. If I only overtake the warmth yet in Rome I shall have had almost two months of it at a stretch. Envy me, *ma non troppo;* for there are uncountable drearinesses in exile. In some future remission of it I'll tell you them. —What are you to be doing this winter, before that picturesque fire-place? Is your novel coming on in a manner to make life tolerable? And your wife, without the consolations of authorship, does she find the days pass lightly? Of course they do when they march with the patter of one's children's feet. What I meant was,— is she well and a happy housewife? My love and compliments. Whom shall you see this winter whom you've not seen before?— When you wrote you were going to Ohio; was it done and done prosperously? Ohio! I make this vague purposeless exclamation, simply as a Florentine.—I hope you will extend some social charity to my people this winter, who, with my brother William now also absent, will be very lonely.—Do you often see the Nortons—and what of Charles? I hope this winter to find Lowell in Rome. Oh for a man to talk a bit with!—Farewell. With every good wish and tender invocation upon your wife, your children and your genius—

Yours,

H. J. jr.

1. HJ had just returned to Italy from Germany via the St. Gothard, and finding Florence still very hot had spent a few days in Siena. This yielded the article "Siena," *Atlantic,* XXXIII (June 1874), 664–669.

To Henry James Sr.

Ms Harvard

Florence Oct. 26*th* [1873]

Dear Father—

I have been waiting to write again until I had heard from Willy and could let you know that I was in communication with him. This morning his letter from Liverpool arrived, and I delay no longer.[1] He speaks with pleasure of his voyage and says seasickness was *nil;* but this he will have written you. When he will reach Florence he is yet unable to say: not, I suppose, within ten days. I wrote last upward of a fortnight since, to Alice, who, I hope received my letter. It was from Siena, to which on arriving at Florence I repaired to escape the mosquitoes. I have now been back here some twelve days and have found the weather charming and the mosquitoes departed. Meanwhile have come three letters—mother's of Sept. 22d, and her note and yours of Oct. 3d and 4th. Many thanks for all. I am sorry you should have had any worry of mind about sending me back the Turgenieff M.S. and most glad you decided to do so. I shall not fail to do everything I can to amend it. I am not a little disappointed to know it leaves so much to be desired, for I wrote it with great care, zeal and pleasure and said to myself when it was finished that it was the best thing I had done and would help me to some reputation. In my elation I offered to do a series of other articles for T. S. Perry. It shows how poorly we judge our own performances. But I have no doubt that I can improve this, and I am a hundred times thankful to you for giving me a chance. I will send it back as promptly as possible.[2] Apropos of such matters, I am sorry to hear such accounts from you of the dishonesty of Sheldon and Church.[3] They have two M.S. of mine—one a piece on Rome and one a story in three parts of which I can obtain no tidings whatever. I will write to them immediately either to let me hear something about them or of their intentions concerning them or else to enclose them to you. You in that case will please send them to Lippincott. I lately sent a M.S. to Scribner and am on the point of sending them another—a story in two parts: so that they are for the moment choked with my wares. Poor Howells is chronically; besides, he would not publish the *Galaxy* story on account of the subject, I'm afraid. (It's needless to say that *I* think the subject all right—in fact very fine!) But please mention to H., when you see him, for safety's sake, that I sent him ten days since a short article on *Siena*.—I have it at heart to say more about this matter of my writings and their getting published and paid for.— I am better and better in health (as you will be glad to hear on other grounds than its' helping simply to write)—better, indeed, I may say, as I never have been before. I feel more and more apt for writing, more active and ambitious. At the same rate of improvement for the next year I shall be able to do really a great deal. Meanwhile I am able to do amply enough to secure a comfortable—an easy—monthly income. I have been working smoothly and prosperously for the last six weeks and have taken the measure of what health allows me to do. But I had got so much behind during the preceding six months that I had been degenerating in health—that I'm afraid I have been rather heavily testing your power of letting me draw on you while waiting for my own efforts to produce something. Their doing so—I can answer for it—their producing enough to completely cover all my expenses—is only a question of time. The point is—is not the temporary inconvenience to you very great? I bear it in mind and draw no more money than I absolutely need. I don't spend a sou idly; what I spend goes simply to my living— which must of course be fairly comfortable. My recent travels have made me draw more rapidly than I could have wished—as well as the need of winter clothes etc. But as I say, I can count upon soon overtaking all these drafts, and more, with my *envois* of M.S. It is a matter of these coming to light, and of my getting thoroughly started. This start has been delayed pitifully long by my being in poor working order; but I really feel now as if I had passed through my last tight place. I shall never be able, I believe, to work *largely;* but I shall—I already am—to work in the modest manner that will bring me, say $3000 a year—a sum on which I can in Europe, live handsomely. I can assure you, I think, that at the end of six months I shall be even with my drafts, without at all hurting myself.

I wish, with all the uses that you have for your money, that it might not take so long; but I shall try and manage it. Meanwhile, short of real inconvenience, bear with me.—If all this bores you, give it to mother to read. I had to say it; I can't go on using my letter of credit without giving you some sign that I am conscious of the situation. I have sent home since last June the worth of at a moderate estimate (or at least not an exaggerated one) $600 (in gold.) It must all come into you, sooner or later; and in the coming winter I shall be able, with my better health, to at least double the sum. I have drawn in that period (since June 1st) 100£. I am by no means living, as you see, at the rate of $3000 a year—in spite of my expensive summer travelling. But enough of this.—I have been enjoying Florence extremely; it has never seemed pleasanter.—I have seen a few people. Mrs. Lombard, I wrote you, I see every day or so, oftener than in Cambridge! She is ill much of the time but keeps wonderfully cheerful and says she is better at least than at home. She has many friends—and seems to have made many since coming abroad, and both she and Fanny delight in Florence—especially the drives. The Andrews are here for the winter. I called and kept awake—or at least woke up in time to hear them send much love to you. Bessie is no thinner, but very sweet, and Edith charming. The Henry Greenoughs are here for the winter—after a summer in Innspruck.—But this is all my news. I am hankering fearfully to see Willy and have all my curiosities and questions answered. You must have already begun to feel lonely, but keep up your spirits. Wilky's nuptials are at hand and will give you something to think about.— Please tell Lizzie Boott that I received her charming letter and will answer it at my earliest leisure. Farewell dear father, with all thanks and blessings on your head. Much love to mother, Alice and Aunt Kate. Don't let William's having joined me keep you from writing. —I suppose you recognized the letter from Darmstatt in the *Nation* as mine.[5] How much has the *Nation* paid for that and the *Homburg?* Address Rome: Spada and Flamini. Your affectionate

H. James jr.

1. As foreshadowed in their correspondence, WJ had taken leave of absence from Harvard and was joining his brother in Italy. For details of the continuing

rivalry between HJ and WJ see the relevant chapters in Edel, *The Life of Henry James,* and especially the chapter "Angel and Brother" in "The Conquest of London."

2. HJ Sr, an ardent reader of Turgenev's novels, had read his son's article critically and made a number of suggestions for revision. James based his essay on three Turgenev tales published in German, including "The Torrents of Spring" and "A King Lear of the Steppes." The review-article appeared in the *North American Review,* CXVIII (April 1874), 326–356.

3. The editors of the *Galaxy;* that journal published HJ's Roman essay in November 1873 and "Madame de Mauves" during the following February and March.

4. Howells had apparently shied away from the delicate sexuality of "Madame de Mauves" and felt it unsuitable for the *Atlantic.*

5. "An Ex-Grand Ducal Capital," unsigned, *Nation,* XVII (9 October 1873), 239–241.

To Henry James Sr.

Ms Harvard

Florence Nov. 2*d* [1873]

Dear Father:

I wrote to you a week ago, telling you of Willy's being on his way to me—and I had hardly sent my letter when he arrived. He had travelled very fast, stopping only a day in Paris, in his impatience to reach me. A compliment to me! I have delayed writing, as I wished to be able to tell you how he seemed, after a few days' observation. He felt, he said, the fatigue of his long journey from London very little and is at least as well as he expected to be. In appearance he is even more *sohnst* than your accounts have led me to suppose. He looks indeed in exuberant health, and I am immensely struck with his change in this respect since I last saw him. He is very much charmed with Florence and spends a great deal of time in going about the streets and to the Galleries. He takes it all as easily as possible, of course, but he already manages to do a good deal and has made a beginning which augurs well for the future. He has fallen upon indifferent weather, but the air is happily still very mild. I find great pleasure in seeing him and have plied him with all imaginable questions about you all. I feel almost as if I had been

spending a week in Quincy Street. Would to heaven I could!—
Your letter of Oct. 17th has just come in, to our great satisfaction.
I'm glad to hear of your breakfasts and dinners and of your meeting
foreigners of distinction. May such alleviations of your solitude not
be wanting.—We shall remain in Florence a week or two longer—
as long as the weather remains at all mild and then shall proceed to
Rome. How or where we shall arrange ourselves I don't know. We
shall have to decide, taking all things into account, when we get
there. Considering our experimental (especially as regards William)
relation to the Roman climate, we shall do nothing that will bind
us for more than from week to week. William finds the Italian
climate very soft and "flat", but not disagreeably so. I have very
good hopes of the profit of his undertaking, now that I have seen
the apparently strong basis of muscular health that he enjoys.—
His arrival is my only news. I live quietly devoting my mornings to
work.—I was very sorry to see that the *Atlantic* had again played me
false.[1] This long initiatory waiting is quite *accablant* and in sombre
moods, I feel as if I had no business to be over here, compromising
you in the delay. This very moment, I would give—I don't know
what—for an hour's talk with mother and you. But I wrote you
last week on this matter, and will add no more now. My only
course, for the present, is to keep as well as possible and do my daily
work. Give me your blessing!—Willy tells me that he is going to
write, so that I will let these lines suffice. Florence, apparently, is
filling up for the winter with Americans. A day or two since I met
Mr. Bradford. The same old Mr. B. He is going to Rome. Florence
still is charming, but as the autumn advances, I, too, feel the attraction! Love—love to all. Ever dear father

Your affectionate H.

From your not mentioning it, I suppose the *Galaxy* too is void
of my work.

1. HJ refers here simply to the delays of publication, there being sometimes
almost a year between the time of his dispatch of his manuscript and its appearance in the American magazines. Only in the *Nation,* since it was published weekly, did his work appear with some promptness. But by unremitting
toil HJ managed to build up a back-log so that ultimately his work appeared
consistently and regular payments were sent to his father.

To His Parents

Ms Harvard

Florence Nov. 16*th* [1873]

Dearest parents—

Willy wrote you less than a week ago, so that I have allowed a longer time than usual to pass in silence. He acknowledged in last writing mother's good letter to me, of Oct. 21st. When I wrote he had been with me but a few days; but now his presence is quite an old story, and we have got pretty well used to one another.—You are of course anxious to hear how he seems now that I have had prolonged observation.—He varies a good deal at different times but he seems on the whole in a very promising condition. There have been times when he has had the appearance, the manner and almost the activity of perfect health. His activity is very considerable and much greater than I expected to see it. Not having seen him for a year and a half I am greatly struck with his improvement in almost all ways. He is evidently in a much better vein of feeling about himself—more optimistic and taking things easier, and it seems impossible that with his immense gainings (as they strike me) he should not, at no distant time, be in good working order. He enjoys Florence very heartily and explores the galleries and churches, day after day, like a regular vigorous tourist. He is of course often tired, but as the strongest people are tired with the same work—. He admires the Florentine painters greatly and his talk on all that he sees is most suggestive and edifying to me. He strongly inclines to think that the Italian climate is what he wants; and in short his adventure seems to me up to this point quite as successful and as promising for the future as was to be hoped. He has been moreover, for the greater part of his stay here, at the disadvantage of bad weather which has prevented his sitting and loafing much out of doors.—We are lingering on in Florence, as you see, and shall probably do so till the 1st December. There has been some sharp weather which makes me long for the Roman softness, but we shall probably have it soft here again, as it is too early for winter.

I have a very pleasant large room in which Willy chiefly dwells and our life is very harmonious and comfortable. He is now sitting by the fire writing to Wilky; it is a beautiful bright Sunday; we are just going to have some lunch and then are going up to San Miniato. I wish we could make a family party of it.

Monday A.M.—I had to break off my letter yesterday to get my lunch. Our walk was beautiful but cold. I have no especial news for you. I'm getting on myself very fairly and the great improvement in my health continues. My liver is somewhat out of tune with it and I don't *feel* quite as well as I ought: but this is, I am sure, but a transitory phase of the long row I have had to hoe and will gradually pass away. Cold weather causes me especial discomfort and I expect to be in a better way in Rome.—We have been with you in spirit, these last days, over your expectations of Wilky's advent with his wife. I suppose they are with you at this present moment and that you are feasting your curiosity on Carrie. A blessing on all your impressions—and a full account of them to us. I hope Wilky's marriage will be to him even a fraction of what Bob's is.—I received the last *Atlantic* and *Galaxy*, with great bitterness of spirit at the non-appearance of my *Albano*. The notes in the G. were badly printed and I regretted their being stuck into that obscure corner. But I am thankful to be printed on any terms. They are to send you $75.00 for the piece.—The *Nation* as you say is appreciative and I shall cling to it devoutly. I have just sent it a letter from Florence. I could easily review a book a week for it, if I could only get the books. (I suppose you recognized the *Dumas* and *Goethe* as mine.)[1] If you see a couple of short notices (*Sandeau* and *Merimée*) they are also mine.[2] You might mention (for safety's sake) to T. S. Perry if you see him that I lately sent him two reviews—Howells's *Poems* and Pater's *Studies*.[3] I am now at work on the Turgeniew which I bless you for sending back—We dined two days since with the H. Greenoughs, who are most loving. I see Mrs. Lombard every few days—always invalidical but serene, and with plenty of kind friends here. She is socially much appreciated and moves in a higher circle than at home. Her caps are the prettiest in Europe. Fanny seems

411

very hearty.—Farewell, dearest parents, sister and aunt, if she is still in C. This is a thin letter, I know, but you shall have a better next time.

Ever your loving H

Begin and address *Rome: Spada and Flamini.*

1. "Dumas and Goethe," unsigned review of *Faust* in a new translation by H. Bacharach with a preface by Alexandre Dumas *fils, Nation* XVII (30 Oct. 1873), 292–294.
2. Jules Sandeau's *Jean de Thommeray; Le Colonel Everard,* unsigned review, *Nation,* XVIII (5 Feb. 1874), 95; Prosper Merimée's *Derniéres Nouvelles,* unsigned, *Nation,* XVIII (12 Feb. 1874), 111.
3. "Howells' Poems," reviewed in the *Independent* (8 Jan. 1874), p. 9; there is no record of any publication of James's review of Pater's studies, and no manuscript has been found.

To Henry James Sr.

Ms Harvard

Rome 101 Corso Dec. 3d [1873]

Dearest father:

We found yesterday at the bankers your blessedly welcome letter of Nov. 14th, which was soothing balm to our spirits in the midst of the inevitable puzzlements and small drearinesses of a first installation in Rome. Willy wrote to you a couple of days since—a letter teaming, I imagine, with his first impressions of the place; but you'll not be sorry to have a sketch of the situation from me as well—and for my own satisfaction, I must write a word. We have been here now some four days and are "settled"—at any rate for a month or two. We left Florence with regret, for we had both grown very fond of it. If I had been alone, I should have subsided for the whole winter there, I think. It had begun to be very cold, however, and it was time for Willy to address himself to the superior resources of Rome. We had a lovely day for our journey and a lovely first day here—a great felicity for W. He appreciated it fully—especially a moonlight walk to the Forum and Colisseum, of which he gave you an account.[1] I value greatly *his* impressions; they are always so lively and original and sagacious that it is a real profit to me to *receuillir* them. His society in this way, as well as lighter ways, is altogether

412

advantageous to me. We spent a couple of mornings looking about for rooms—discouragingly as regards finding anything at a reasonable price that would do for both of us, and that would be obtained for a month at a time. People are all bent on letting their rooms for the season—till the first of May, at least. We collapsed as the only solution, on a common basis, into a couple of sun-bathed chambers at the Hotel de Russie. But yesterday the landlord of my old quarters of last winter came out with a reasonable offer for a single month and we decided to separate. W. remains at the hotel which is his wisest and most comfortable course and I have just unpacked my things here, where I sit writing this in my warm and pleasant little parlor. It will amount to the same as our really dwelling together by day, as he will have the perpetual resource of my fireside and my balcony, and we shall always lunch and dine together.—He has just gone off to the Capitol, and I am to rejoin him shortly over our two o'clock *colazione*. You want of course to know promptly how he seems and progresses. I don't know what report he has given of himself; but it seems to me that I am justified in giving a very encouraging one. He does more and more, all the while, with little serious fatigue, and in power of general locomotion and exertion I see little difference between him and a usually well person. His last days in Florence, his journey, and his first days here have been a constant call for activity which he is apparently quite able to supply. His walking power has most materially increased, and this, it seems to me, cannot possibly fail to bring total improvement with it. His spirits, on the whole, are very good, and his appearance excellent. He longs acutely and constantly, I think, to be at work; and is doing all this *à contre coeur* but is nevertheless well satisfied with the sensible effects of it, and the promise that two or three months more of the same sort of thing, even at the same rate, will leave him with a really solid gain. I fully underttand his impatience of his idleness and the spirit in which he often exclaims—"Oh, if this were only a real vacation after a long stretch of work—not a simple prolongation of the effort to get well—how much more I should enjoy it!" Nevertheless I think that mentally as well as physically, he is laying up substance which he will feel himself much the stronger for. To walk much and sleep well this is the result for him to arrive at—the result which will mean real health again; and I weigh my words when I say that it seems to me to be steadily arriving. He has slept well, with insignificant interruptions, and it was only this morning that he expressed a sense of the large and incontestable increase of his power of locomotion. He *did* Florence, at any rate as unstintedly as any traveller need.—Rome is still the same old Rome, *minus* Tweedies, Bootts, Wisters etc. I wish for William's sake the Tweedies were here, with their fireside, their carriage and their dinners. But we shall do well enough. We have already lunched at the Von Hoffmanns!—owing to Sam Ward's inexplicable alacrity in calling on us. He met us in the train coming from Florence told us that his wife and Miss Bessie were lying ill with measles at the hotel, that he was staying at the Villa, and that he would come and see us etc. He did the next day and invited us to lunch, of which yesterday we partook.—I have seen no one else. Rome is as yet very empty and apartments abundant. The weather for two or three days has been very dusky, but we hope for better things.—Your letter was redolent of Wilky's hymeneal atmosphere —which I hope seemed thoroughly salubrious on a near acquaintance. We count the days till your report of Carrie arrives. Wilky's letter, which you enclose, was strange and characteristic, but I trust of purely good omen. All your mention of household things (and persons) was pleasing to us. May they long remain as pleasant! I shall be glad to get at last the poor old *Villegiature*. The letter from Albany was from a silly man wanting me to write him a *letter* to put in his collection of autographs! Such is fame—and such is idiocy. But I must join W. at lunch, and have only time to add my kisses for all and my thanks, dear dad, for all your repeated benefits. Think of us most contentedly, and often of your affectionate

H. J. jr.

Of course we wonder about *Spain* etc: and think that bloody as was the deed it would be most shabby in us to fight with that distracted land.

1. HJ continued to spell Colosseum erratically. WJ's account shows that he did not appreciate the Colosseum or Rome as his brother believed. If Henry

had not been with him he would have fled "howling" from the place, WJ wrote home. He also intensely disliked the "churchiness" of Rome and the Italian hill towns HJ had admired and described so glowingly in his travel articles.

To Elizabeth Boott

Ms Harvard

Rome 101 Corso 4° po. 10 Dec. [1873]

Dear Lizzie—

Your lovely letter reached me some six weeks ago and was prized as it deserved: but I have delayed answering it because—first, William's almost simultaneous arrival gave me for some time a good deal of out of door occupation and abbreviated my writing hours; and second because I wanted to address you rather from this old Rome and secure for my letter at least such value (in default of a greater) as the Roman postmark would give it in your affections. Not that you are especially fond of the Roman post-office: it is probably the thing in Rome that you like least: but nevertheless you may feel kindly to even a poor letter of Roman origin. We came hither about a fortnight since, and owing to a good deal of troublesome delay in getting domiciled it is only lately that I am beginning to feel shaken down and settled. This has been helped along by the usual vicious cold with which I inaugurate the winter: which keeping me indoors for several days has enabled me to become desperately at home with my carpet and wall-paper. These indeed, however, are an old story as I am back in the room I occupied last spring. They are excellent quarters and I am very comfortable. I had been some two months in Florence when I left and William about a month and we had both grown so very fond of it that it was not at all easy to depart. If I had been alone, I am sure I should have staid, for there is something about the whole constitution and nature of Florence that suits me wonderfully well. I had drunk deep of Rome last winter, and was quite willing to let it serve for the present. We shall probably go back early to the Arno-side. My winter here however promises to be of a much tamer

415

pattern than the last, and indeed I feel already very low in mind and haunted with the ghost of all our old revelry. Rome itself is unchanged of course, and has been putting forth her characteristic charms through the lovely weather of the past fortnight. But I feel here always the importunate *muchness* of the place—all the memories and materials and elements which one can't assimilate and do justice to. But it has an indefinable loveliness surely. William, rather to my surprise, doesn't as yet take to it as kindly as he did to Florence (for which he quite emulated my own *gusto*)—but one is safe in the long run, to let Rome take care of itself, and I expect him to come in some day and tell me that, after all, he rather likes it. He wrote you I think, from Florence, and probably told you, how, as we wandered about, your name and your papa's were forever on our lips. You were the genius loci. We peregrinated most tenderly twice, out to Bellosguardo, which, I found more adorable even than I remembered it. The view (from your back windows) has a most extraordinarily poetic and solemn sort of loveliness. It seems strange that you should have been "raised" upon it, as it were: or rather, it seems not at all strange in the sense of being surprising; but most awfully enviable. We had in Florence a rather social time—seeing a good deal of the Greenoughs, (who were most kind and friendly,) the Huntingtons, who were blooming in their ruddy beauty (Miss Laura handsomer than ever;)[1] the Whitwells, the Lombards and Andrews,—and somewhat, Dr. Gryzanowski and Karl Hillebrand. The Doctor endeared himself to both of us; he is a wonderfully likeable man, certainly, and a clever withal. He says nothing about anything that isn't worth hearing. We also became intimate with Mrs. G., who showed us her apartment, minutely and separately, lamp in hand and "pride in her past." It is very handsome, certainly, but terrifically cold.[2] The drawing-room is as big as Papanti's hall, and marble-paved; cosy on the December nights! To Hillebrand we took very kindly and have seen him since here. William saw more of him than I, however; as I was *vocalizing* all the evening to Mme. Laussal and her mother. What a queer household: it reminds me of Doctor Johnson's.—I have seen no one here as yet, and am disappointed in not being able

Elizabeth Boott (later Mrs. Frank Duveneck)

Francis Boott

to report from the Palazzo Odescalchi[3]—I was going there last Sunday, but my cold prevented me. But I shall see Miss Annie in good time and you shall have my impressions. Rome is as yet very empty, and I hear of no one coming to chase away last winter's ghosts. So be it: I prefer the ghosts: I'm afraid even my rides will be ghostly. We have eaten the inevitable dinner at the V. Hoffmann's; but I haven't seen Miss Bessie Ward, who is laid up with the measles. Farewell. I'm glad to hear that Cambridge serves your turn and that you can get up a fond illusion in your studio. But I don't despair of some more Italian days with you, sometime. Affectionate regards to your father to whom I intend to write. Ever dear Lizzie most faithfully yours

H. James jr.

1. The Greenoughs and Huntingtons were old American-Florentine families. Miss Laura Huntington would become Madame Wagniere and remain a friend of HJ in later years. The Huntingtons owned the Villa Castellani on Bellosguardo in which the Bootts had an apartment for many years.

2. The visit to the Gryzanowski apartment is mentioned in James's "Florentine Notes" in *Italian Hours*, where he speaks of the apartment as having the spaciousness "of a Russian steppe."

3. For details of the Palazzo Odescalchi, its personalities and sociabilities, see Edel, *The Conquest of London*, the chapter entitled "The Two Palaces."

To Henry James Sr.

Ms Harvard

Rome Dec 22*d* 73

Dear Father—

I received a few days since your letter enclosing *Scribner's* note and was going to answer it immediately, but I found that Willy was just writing to Alice, and I waited, to let my letter gain more relief. I am sorry Scribner could not print my notes; but I suppose they have, in fact, a great deal of that sort of thing on hand.[1] I am much obliged to you for having the thing sent you. Since it is written, it seems a pity that it shouldn't be used and something or other got for it. As the *Galaxy* printed the other, I suppose it would print this, and I beg you therefore to forward it with the note that

I enclosed. I don't like the *Galaxy's* manners and customs, but one can't afford to be too fastidious, and the best thing is to hang on and make the G. do what it will. Scribner in spite of its refusal, seems agreeably hospitable. I lately sent it a tale in two parts and am just sending it another of the same dimensions. I hope the January *Atlantic* has managed to squeeze in something of mine. The December number came duly to hand. So much for such matters, for the present.—Willy will have written you about himself and given you, I hope, as good accounts of his progress as he daily gives me, and as his whole appearance and daily exploits testify to so eloquently. He seems greatly contented with his condition and is sensible of its growing constantly better. He has just been into my room, flushed with health and strength, to see whether I had found any letters at the bankers this morinng and to ask where he should go today. Seeing me writing he says—"Give them my love and tell them I am doing splendidly." He does in fact, a great deal, and walks, climbs Roman staircases, and sees sights in a way most satisfactory to behold. It has been a measureless blessing that the weather ever since our arrival in Rome has been the finest on the whole I ever saw;—as brilliant and clear and still as our finest Octobers and yet even milder than our mildest autumns. The last day or two has come grey skies and soft sirocco; but it is still winter with all the edge melted off—still delicious out of door weather. I am sorry to say that I found nothing at the Bankers this A.M.—nothing save a very pleasant letter from Lizzie Boott to Willy, with an enclosure to me, for which when you see her, please thank her. Tell her also, if you remember, that I wrote to her ten days since. (Three or four days since Willy wrote to Alice.) A propos of messages, here is one from Mrs. Ward. (We dined there a week ago and are to dine again on Christmas day, besides dining today at the oft-recurring Hoffmanns.) "Give my love to your father and thank him for his lovely note. But tell him I can't answer it, because my heart is so full of *tendresse* for him that if I were to dictate to my *donne de compagnie* such a letter as alone I would write, she would be so shocked that she would leave me. She thinks me very

religious and my letter would cast discredit on my professions."
Mrs. Ward and Bessie are up, smiling, from measles, and Sam is
unwontedly genial and friendly.—I am having socially (thank the
Lord!) a much quieter time than last winter. I have paid my respects
to the Storys and Terrys but don't expect to see them, as formerly, to
satiety. The S's moreover are to be "quiet" on account of Mrs.
Story's health: *i.e.* receive not on fixed days twice a week, but
every evening, regular! I have seen (Mother and Alice will be glad
to know) Miss Crawford's young man, who is youthful and
ordinary, but a gentleman, and backed by a very vigorous old
dowager of a mother, with a big jaw, a high forehead and enormous
hands. Also by a very charming sister; the most attractive German
she I ever met. Miss Crawford told me *everything,* among others
that she was to be none too rich. She has received a certain unwonted
grace of softness from her engagement.—At this moment, in comes
Willy, with Alice's blessed letter of Nov. 30th, describing the party
for Wilky and Carrie. I thank her for it much and will answer it
soon. It is pleasant to get such accounts of the success of the fete;
but we are sorry that Alice didn't touch upon Carrie personally.
The most fearful thing in letters from home is to be told that some
one else has told us all about such and such a matter. Father and
mother had indeed sketched Carrie quite vividly but what we hoped
was that Alice might have added a few lights to the picture—not
shades. I am sorry Wilky's wife is not more interesting to those who
are fond of him: but that matters little, so long as practically she
proves a help and not a hinderance. I devoutly trust she may, in
spite of her diamonds. I had dreamed of offering her the tribute of
some modest Roman toy; but the diamonds put me out of countenance, and I think I shall let it slide.—Your news of Bob and his
Baby is most exhilarating and father's extracts from B's letters
extremely beautiful. I long to see the wondrous child and pull its
cheeks and pinch its legs. (I mean Baby's—not Bob's.) I await
with anxiety its baptism. If it should be a Henry no. 3., I shall feel
queer, so sandwiched between infancy and maturity. You and
mother must be in a terrible state to behold it. It's a pity it can't
be sent on by express, to spend alternate weeks at Cambridge and

at home.—Very sad certainly is poor Emily Atkinson's death—and sadder her poor husband's state of mind.—Alice's letter contained an adjuration to me, from Howells, to print a volume of stories. Good advice, doubtless, but I must wait, to apply it, till I get home, when I shall attempt also to put forth a volume of articles and letters about Europe.[2] I have written enough to make a very good one. I have an increasing feeling that I ought to go home to start myself on a remunerative and perfectly practical literary basis. I wrote you a couple of months ago (I hope you got the letter,) about my re-maining abroad for the present—*i.e.* for six months more. This would bring me home towards the close of next summer, and I should get a better market for my wares and more definite work to do (especially in the way of reviewing books) than in this far-away region. My view of the case is to make a short winter here, go back to Florence soon (in a sanitary way it suits me much better) and remain there till I'm ready to go home. I could spend four or five months in Florence at a cost moderate enough not to force me to draw unendurably on you, while waiting, always, for the realization of my investments; and it would, moreover, break the back of the summer. I don't feel as if I have by any means sucked the European orange dry: but I am content to defer the completion of the process.—*Àpropos* of Howells, *tantôt,* do you remember hearing him mention receiving from me long since an article on *Siena*? He may not be able to use it in some time; but it is as well to know that it reached him. I don't know that I have any more news for you—or any to add to what I said about Willy—which on reading it over doesn't seem to me at all too *couleur de rose.*—Cer-tainly, a man couldn't look better—and what he distinctly says of himself quite justifies his looks. He got some days since a charming letter from John Fiske, whom we may meet later in Florence. Lowell is still there, now I believe, but unlikely to come to Rome. Story, last evening, was in despair at not being able to produce him, in the world.—Willy, who at first hung fire, over Rome, has now quite ignited and confesses to its sovereign influence. But he enjoys all the melancholy of antiquity under a constant protest, which pleases me as a symptom of growing optimism and elasticity in his own disposition. His talk as you may imagine, on all things, is most rich and vivacious. My own more sluggish perceptions can hardly keep pace with it. Ever dear father, with love to all, your loving

H J jr

W. encloses a scrap to Alice. Happy Christmas!—

1. *Scribner's Monthly* had been founded in 1870 and shortly after this letter proved distinctly hospitable to HJ's work.
2. HJ had already planned a volume of tales, but acutally published first his book of travel articles—both volumes appearing in 1875.

To William Dean Howells

Ms Harvard

Florence Jan. *9th.* 74.

Dear Howells—

Your good letter of a month ago reached me some ten days since, just as I was leaving Rome, and I have just been reading it over, under these less balmy skies. My brother had a mild stroke of malaria, in consequence of which the doctor ordered him away, under penalty of being probably worse; so he retreated upon Florence as the next best thing, and I have followed him to keep him company. From the Cambridge point of view I suppose Florence ought to be a very tolerable *pis aller,* even from Rome: but I confess to utter corruption from that terrible Roman charm, Florence seems to me a vulgar little village and life not worth the living away from the Corso and the Pincio. With time however I don't despair of settling down, doggedly, to my hard fate. Meanwhile, to beguile the heavy hours, I turn to communication with you. Many thanks for your letter, which was most agreeable. The news of the sale of the *Atlantic*[1] set me wondering about you and I needed your own word for it that you are contented to soothe my startled sympathies. All prosperity to the new dispensation and fame and fortune to both of us. I'm sorry you have to go and watch your flock across the sands of Dee, as it were, but I suppose there is a daily excitement in it. I have just received the new *Atlantic*, which makes a very handsome appearance. I don't like the new type as well as the old, which was remarkably pretty; but the cover and the paper make me feel as if one were ministering to the highest culture of the Age. Give Aldrich[2] my compliments on his novel, which opens out most agreeably. There is something in all the regular New England scenes and subjects, in fiction, which strikes in a chill upon any soul; but with Aldrich, I imagine, we shall get a great deal of prettiness. But for heaven's sake, do hurry up with your Venetian priest; he can't help, at the worst, being prettier than Parson Wibird. Thank you for speaking well of my own tale; it reads agreeably enough though I suppose that to many readers, it will seem rather idle.[3] Let me explain without further delay the nature of the package which will go with this, in another cover. It is the first one half of a tale in two parts, for use at your convenience. I have been reading it to my brother who pronounces it "quite brilliant." I was on the point of sending it to Scribner, but your words in deprecation of this course made me face about. I am much obliged for the esteem implied in them; but it remains true, in a general way, that I *can't* really get on without extracting tribute from that source. It's a mere money question. The *Atlantic* can't publish as many stories as I ought and expect to be writing. At home, it could, for then I needed scantier revenues. But now, with all the francs it takes to live in these lovely climes, I need more strings to my bow and more irons always on the fire. But I heartily promise you that the *Atlantic* shall have the best things I do; and it is because this *Eugene Pickering* (being perhaps unusually happy in subject) is probably better than its next follower will be, that I now make it over to you.[4] The second half will follow by the next mail: heaven's blessings attend it.—I should like to gossip to you about Rome, which in this last month I have been spending there, laid hold on me again with a really cruel fascination. But talking is vain, for the thing can't be described; it must be *felt*, as a daily, daily blessing. I believe that if I could live there for two or three years I should finally, by my doing so—my thinkings and feelings and scribblings—quaruple the circulation of the *Atlantic*. Don't you want to pension me for the purpose?—But you remember it all, more or less, of course. Nay, I thought I did from last spring; but it all came rushing back in a wonderous wave, and melted me into daily stupefaction. It's either very good for you, or very bad: I don't know which. My sternly scientific brother thinks the latter: and there is indeed much in that view. Thank your stars at all events, that you are not living in a place whereof the delight demoralizes; and when you are buffetting the breezes in that Campagna which leads to Riverside, reflect with complacency that you are not a cringing parasite of the Beautiful. Florence, after Rome, seems tame and flat and infernally cold. It's cruel after basking for a month on the Pincio to wake up in the region of chapped lips and chilblains. But happily, even the Florentine winter is short and before long I hope to be sniffing the vernal breath of the Tuscan poderes.—I am very sorry the *North American Review* couldn't give a corner to my notice of your poems. It was written quite from my tenderer parts, and I think would have found assenting readers. But I trust it may still find them somewhere.—I think I have no news for you. In Rome I saw few people, and here I bid fair to see no one. No one, that is save Lowell, who is lingering here on his way to Rome and with whom I lately passed an evening. He was very jolly, tho' homesick, and taking Europe with the sobriety of maturity. He says he positively can't work here— and like Bryant and May's matches won't go off unless struck on his own box. He goes home in July, and if that will start him up, let him hurry.—I'm not surprised at your finding Charles Norton an impracticable comrade. He seemed to me to be ripening for home discomfort, when I last saw him. But I suppose your are tired of the theme. Whom *do* you see, then?—You'll see me, I apprehend, before very long: that is I hope to manage to stay abroad another six months and to turn up in Cambridge toward the close of next summer. I don't know that I shall undertake the winter in Cambridge; but I shall spend the autumn there. We shall have plenty to talk about—the more that in that case I shall remain in Italy till almost the last.—Farewell! My affectionate regards to your wife and blessings on all your house. Yours, dear H., always,

H. James Jr.

1. The *Atlantic Monthly* was bought by the publishing house of Houghton Mifflin Company. Howells continued as editor until his resignation in 1881.

2. Aldrich had begun serialization of his novel *Prudence Palfrey*.

3. "The Last of the Valerii" had just appeared in the January *Atlantic*.

4. Howells accepted "Eugene Pickering" as a two-installment tale, *Atlantic*, XXXIV (Oct.–Nov. 1874), 397–410, 513–526.

To Grace Norton

Ms Harvard

Florence Jan. 14*th* 74.

Dear Grace—

Your are almost cruelly kind and you understand to perfection the art of making a man hang his head and scourge himself with spiritual stripes. I have in hand both your letters—the long ago Ashfield one and the one of the other day. I certainly exercised no ingenuity to not answer the first, but circumstances were somehow ingenious in my despite and I have had these many weeks the daily grievance of seeing myself prevented from doing the thing I most wanted to do. But here I am stranded on a kind of sand bank in the surging sea of life and labor and I am almost selfishly glad that, not having written to you sooner, I have it as a consolation now. By a sand bank I don't so much mean Florence as my present humor with it. I have been jerked away from Rome, where I had been expecting to spend the winter, just as I was warming to the feast, and Florence, tho' very well in itself, doesn't go so far as it might as a substitute for Rome. It's like having a great plum-pudding set down on the table before you, and then seeing it whisked away and finding yourself served with wholesome tapioca. My brother, after a month of great enjoyment and prosperity at Rome, had a stroke of malaria (happily quite light) which made it necessary for him to depart, and I am here charitably to keep him company. I oughtn't to speak light words of Florence to you, who know it so well and with reason love it so well: and they are really words from my pen's end simply and not from my heart. I have an inextinguishable relish for Florence and now that I have been back here for a fortnight this early love is beginning to shake off timidly the ponderous shadow of Rome. But the truth is that when one has come to know Rome well and feel its vast and various charm, and depend upon it for one's daily impression, it is impossible for any other human habitation not to seem pale and tame and meagre. I have never felt its charm more than during this past December. It was empty, the weather was divine and I was getting from my brother's enjoyment an echo of all my own first impressions. One's wanderings in Rome, during the mild sunny afternoons of midwinter are a most prodigious intellectual dissipation. The whole place keeps playing such everlasting tunes on one's imagination, that it seems, at first, when such a music stops, that one's whole intellectual life has stopped. But Florence is as good as need be, and I am getting reconciled to it so fast that I already think as well of it again as a quarter of an hour since, when I began my letter. I shall probably be here for several months to come, after which, if present prospects hold, I shall be making you my bow at Shady Hill.—We are having here a very keen but most brilliant and beautiful winter. The sun is pouring into my little southward facing room as it has done for a fortnight and promises to do for a fortnight more. In this little room much of my life goes on. We see very few people and I hear of no one who especially inflames my curiosity. In fact I have seen no one but the Lowells who as I suppose you know are lingering here on their way to Rome—but lingering at a rate which makes me doubt of their ever arriving. Lowell is jovial, but as Charles says, most lustily homesick, and profoundly convinced, I think, that the Charles is *par excellence* the beautiful river of the world. If you haven't drawn this moral from your own European experiences, I imagine you will have several bones to pick with him.—But all this while I am not telling you how much I valued and how much I thanked you for it, as I read it under the trees at Homburg, your truly interesting letter of last July. But I confess that immediately I was not disposed to answer it for the humor of it was rather sad than joyous and yet I couldn't bear to assume in writing that you were not elastic and serene. In fact I'm not answering it now. But do we, in talk or in writing, ever really answer each other? Each of us says his limited

427

personal say out of the midst of his own circumstances, and the other one clips what satisfaction he can from it.—Just as I was leaving Rome came to me Charles's letter of Dec. fifth for which pray thank him warmly. I gather from it that he is, in vulgar parlance, taking America rather hard, and I suppose your feelings and Jane's on the matter resemble his own. But it's not for me to blame him, for I take it hard enough even here in Florence and though I have a vague theory that there is a way of being contented there, I am afraid that when I go back I shall need all my ingenuity to put it into practice. What Charles says about our civilization seems to me perfectly true, but practically I don't feel as if the facts were so melancholy. The great fact for us all there is that, relish Europe as we may, we belong much more to that than to this and stand in a much less factitious and artificial relation to it. I feel forever how Europe keeps holding one at arm's length, and condemning one to a meagre scraping of the surface. I have been nearly a year in Italy and have hardly spoken to an Italian creature save washerwomen and waiters. This you'll say, is my own stupidity; but granting this gladly, it proves that even a creature addicted as much to sentimentalizing as I am over the whole *mise en scène* of Italian life, doesn't find an easy initiation into what lies behind it. Sometimes I am overwhelmed with the pitifulness of this absurd want of reciprocity between Italy itself and all my rhapsodies about it. There is certainly, however, terribly little doubt that, practically, for those who have been happy in Europe even Cambridge, the Brilliant, is not an easy place to live in. When I saw you in London, plunged up to your necks in that full, rich abundant various London life, I knew that a day of reckoning was coming and I heaved a secret prophetic sigh. I can well understand Charles's saying that the memory of these and kindred things is a perpetual private joy. But pity our poor bare country and don't revile. England and Italy, with their countless helps to life and pleasure, are the lands for happiness and self-oblivion. It would seem that in our great unendowed, unfurnished, unentertained and unentertaining continent, where we all sit sniffing, as it were, the very earth of our foundations, we ought to have leisure to turn out something handsome from the very heart of simple human nature.—But after I have been at home a couple of months I will tell you what I think.—Meanwhile I aspire to linger on here in Italy and make the most of it—even in poor little overshadowed Florence and in a society limited to waiters and washerwomen. In your letter of last summer you amiably reproach me with not giving you personal tidings, and warn me in my letters mistaking you for the *Nation*. Heaven forbid! But I have no *nouvelles intimes* and in this solitary way of life I don't ever feel especially like a person. I write more or less in the mornings, walk about in the afternoons, and doze over a book in the evenings. You can do as well as that in Cambridge.—I was extremely glad to hear from Lowell that Charles is to occupy his college chair—glad, I hardly know which most, for the chair and for Charles. Certainly the main condition of a contented life with us, is having some absorbing definite work. I hope Charles will find all kinds of satisfaction in his. Apropos of messages pray tell my dear tho' of late so distant Jane that I *did* write her in England, last May (about the first) But I shan't count her the letter. Farewell dear Grace. My most affectionate regards to your mother, my love to Charles and Jane, my blessings on the children, and my thanks to you for all your benefits and forbearances.

Yours ever
H. James jr.

To His Parents

Ms Harvard

Florence Feb. 5*th* [1874]
Corona d'Italia

Dearest parents:

I can't write much of a letter; but I must scrawl a line or two, to tell you that I am better of the stupid malady from which Willy will have let you know that I have been suffering. Not only better but quite myself again and beginning to eat and sleep and move about like sane mortals. Willy will have told you, in so far as it was tellable, what was the matter with me, but in truth it was a strange and mysterious visitation and it would be hard to say just what it was. It was an affair chiefly of the *head* which caused me much pain for many days and nights and would not be comforted. Ultimately, however, it was, and since then I have been steadily mending. I was ten days in bed; on the eleventh I rose, and after some graceful convalescene in my rooms, went out to drive. Yesterday I walked and did wonders, and today feel as good as new. In a few days more I shall be leading the normal life again. I have had every blessing from the first. Willy has simply been a ministering angel, and nursed and tended me throughout with inexpressible devotion. For three nights I had a good Italian matron who hovered about me with the softness —and the size—of mother, Aunt Kate and Alice rolled into one. I had also a very capable and sagacious little doctor (Parisianized German) the sensible efficacity of many of whose remedies was most gratifying. Lastly, this house has been a paradise to be ill in— from the quiet, the good servants and the ease of getting things done to suit one.—These little details will interest your sympathetic hearts which I hope have been agitated by no superfluous anxiety. As I say, my illness was strange and unnatural and I can't tell you the whence or the whereof of it. It arose in great manner from my chronic indisposition, and was complicated by local and temporary influences. But now that I am better, I flatter myself that it has been a sort of crisis which I shall emerge from into more brilliant health than ever. Let me interpose, lest dear mother should crazily murmur something, that it had absolutely nothing to do with any use, over-use or abuse of my head. My use of my head has never been such as would make a baby wink.—But I must not expatiate: I will write again in three or four days. Two blessed letters have come from you these last days: mother's of Jan. 13th and father's yesterday, inclosing *Independant* etc. of 18th.—Willy is most vigorous and brilliant. He seems *entirely* the Willy of our younger years again—in looks, spirits, humor and general capacity.—I can't help adding that I have been revising my plans in the watches of the night, lately, and have pretty well made up my mind to return home during the coming spring. I merely touch on this: I must keep reasons (which you will guess at, however, and appreciate) and a decisive statement till I next write, a few days hence. Whether with William or not would depend on the date of his voyage. Much love dear parents, and regret that you should have been troubled in thinking of all this. It is over now, for good I trust. Much love to Alice. Pray enclose this letter to Aunt Kate. Ever yours

H. James jr

To His Parents

Ms Harvard

Florence Feb. 27th [1874]

Dear Parents:

I have been waiting for several days for another letter from you, and tho' none comes, I won't revenge myself by keeping you waiting longer than this. Some days since it is true, arrived a long and charming one from mother which I immediately despatched off to Willy, but I have had a sort of feeling that another was due. In a day or two, I suppose it will come. Meanwhile I trust you have not been without news of us, for Willy must have sent you more than one characteristic commentary on his late adventures. You know that he left me nearly three weeks since to join the Tweedies in Dresden whither he journeyed by way of Venice, Verona, the Brenner and Munich. The enterprise has evidently been a great success, and feeling rather languid when he left Italy he wrote me that on touching German soil he began to feel "hunky." Dresden, the Tweedies and Mme. Spangenberg have quite wound him up. Just now, however, I am without news of him and am anxiously expecting it. He *probably* sails for New York by the Bremen Steamer (the finest of the line he wrote) on March 4th: but I am yet to learn the certainty. He left here so intensely impatient to get home and return to work that I shall not be surprised at his decision, and I hope you won't be made uncomfortable by it. He had had a surfeit of holiday and was uncomfortable at idling and spending money longer. That he should decide on Bremen is also natural enough when the alternative was the expensive journey to England. If he *does* sail, I wish him every blessing and comfort. I think you'll find he's a much better man. I can't imgine all that he has done here *not* having infused a great deal of permanent strength.—For myself, Florence still holds me, and if I can do as I dream, will hold me for some little time yet. Now that Willy is on the point of sailing and I am not hurried to meet him or overtake him, it seems the best thing I can do to stay on here till the really mild weather. I desire on no grounds to make for the present a long and money-using journey to England, and by lingering awhile here I think I shall feel strongly disposed to sail by the line of steamers (extremely good ones) from Leghorn. A south Atlantic passage in the fine season ought to have no horrors at all and would have the advantage of costing at most half of the other enterprise. I feel within the last three weeks so well and so competent to work that I desire greatly to make the most of my being here under these improved circumstances, as heaven only knows when I shall be here again. I'm really quite my better self again and proving the truth of what I suggested—that I thought my illness was really a contribution to my health. I am active, cheerful, sound and altogether on the right track. I have in mind half a dozen things to write about which will complete the series of my Italian sketches and make a very pretty book. I don't know whether my two or three recent letters have led you to expect that I would turn up hand in hand with Willy, but you will appreciate the merits of the above exposition and defer for awhile with a good grace the realisation of your caresses—and mine. I don't think that for the time I remain I shall drain you inconveniently. My things seem to be getting better started at home in publication and I shall be now regularly sending more. I am just posting three chapters of *Florentine Notes* to the *Independent*: they are too pretty for it, but the note father enclosed me makes me think it a profitable organ. So here they go, to be followed by a fourth.—I have no news, save that with the deepening breath of spring, Florence grows daily more lovely. I have quite forgotten Rome. I see few people, but enough. There are some tolerable ones in the house here, and I make the most of others. Mrs. Lombard goes soon to Leghorn, to complete her convalescence which is slow. I have lately been taking Fanny about to galleries etc: a great charity and no bore, from her amiability and good taste in the picturesque. I went (tell Alice) to some theatricals arranged by Miss Whitwell. They were poor save for Edith Andrew, who was brilliant and might make an actress. Greenoughs, Huntingtons, etc are hospitable. Hillebrand offers me the *entrée* of *any* Italian society *au choix*.—I trust you are all well and happy and sniffing the spring, too, in your measure and that I shall soon get a letter to tell me so. Farewell to all—love to all. Endure my absence yet a while longer and I will return to you primed for immortality! Your all-loving

H

To The Editor, *Independent*

Ms Yale

Florence, March 1*st* 1874.

Dear Sir:

I enclose you herewith (in another cover) three chapters of "Florentine Notes," which I hope the *Independent* will find available. I trust also that the *quantity* will not seem excessive and the quality entertaining enough to carry it off. Indeed, a few weeks hence, if these are found useful, I should like to add another chapter or two. I have divided the MS. into what I hope you will find suitable lengths for three numbers, but you will see that, if necessary, the subdivisions will permit of a different arrangement. You will probably agree with me in preferring the notes to be signed. With the best wishes for the prosperity of my package—[1]

Yours very truly
Henry James jr.

P.S. Please address any word you should need to send me: Care H. James esq. 20 Quincy St. Cambridge, Mass. A cheque also should be made out to my father's name.

1. "Florentine Notes" were published in the *Independent* with several other Florentine pieces: "Florentine Notes." (13 April), pp. 2–3; "Florentine Notes" (30 April), pp. 2–3; "A Florentine Garden" (14 May), pp. 3–4; "Florentine Notes" (21 May), pp. 1–2; "Old Italian Art" (11 June), pp. 2–3; "Florentine Architecture" (18 June), pp. 3–4; "An Italian Convent" (2 July), pp. 3–4; "The Churches of Florence" (9 July), p. 4. Considerably revised, these various papers were used by James in *Italian Hours* (1910) under the general title "Florentine Notes" and "The Autumn in Florence."

To His Parents

Ms Harvard

Florence March 9*th* '74.

Dearest parents—

I received three or four days since your two letters of February 17th, enclosing one from Dr. Holland. Of this anon. Long since, now, you will have been set at rest about my illness and forgotten the solicitude which you so tenderly express. I wrote to you about ten days ago—since when, nothing of moment—save the news of William's departure—has stirred the tranquil current of my days. I'm afraid *his* current has not been very tranquil: but by this time it is near floating him ashore. Tell him when he arrives that I rejoiced in his letter from Southampton and am truly happy that his last impressions of this decaying continent were so pleasant. I live on here safely, soundly and contentedly, liking Florence, Italy and Europe better every day, though I suppose it is disagreeable to you to hear it. I see few people, but I distribute my small social resources as economically as possible, over the days and weeks and manage generally to have a chance for company at hand when I need it. Principally, I am extremely well, and *contentissimo* with my bodily state. I'm much better since my fever than before, and think—if Willy will excuse my saying so—that it was quite worth having. The spring is coming on bravely and the lights and shadows on the mountains and the river, the sunsets and the moonlights, the walks in the dim palace-bordered streets whose shadow is now losing its winter chill—are all quite worth enjoying. These are my principal dissipations and distractions. I have also, since a few days, the diversion of attempting colloquial Italian evenings, with a very nice young fellow whom Hillebrand procured, a Roman, a gentleman, though needy, and a very pretty talker. I expect in a few weeks to rattle the divine tongue like an angel, if we don't exhaust our list of topics *en attendant*. This is the danger.—Tell Willy his beloved Corona d'Italia is odiously full of new-comers, and that I am sandwiched between Miss Heidekoper and Mrs. Mallet—*la bella e la brutta*. Miss H. is charming, on closer acquaintance and her mother is forever talking of *him*. I called lately on the Whitwells and Miss W. was lovely as usual. I went 'tother night to an entertainment at the Lorimer Grahams the American consulate—and saw some gorgeous but uninteresting tableaux. This is all the gossip I can think of (—except that I enclose a card which will amuse Alice.)—I was of course much gratified by Dr. Holland's letter, and have been revolving it these last days.[1] I am well disposed to accept his offer, but there is an obstacle. I feel myself under a tacit pledge to offer first to the *Atlantic* any serial novel I should now write—and should consider myself unfriendly to Howells if I made a bargain with *Scribner* without speaking first to him. I am pretty sure the *Atlantic* would like equally well with *Scribner* to have my story and I should prefer to appearing there. It must depend upon the money question, however, entirely and whichever will pay best shall have the story, and if the *Atlantic* will pay as much as the other, I ought, properly, to take up with *it*. I have a vague notion that *Scribner* would be more liberal and perhaps pay down the money or a good part of it on receipt of the M.S. As for the "honorarium," I don't know what to ask at all and wish I had someone to consult. I don't know, either, what to write immediately to Dr. Holland. I will enclose herewith a note to him, however, to be forwarded by you or not, according to the answer you receive to a note I mean also to write to Howells, and in which I shall request him to communicate with you.—I have decided to ask $1,200 for my story. I thought at first of asking but a thousand; but Dr. Holland evidently wants it and why not profit by such reputation as one has laboriously acquired? 1200$ makes a hundred for each part, which is what I could earn by writing 12 short stores.—One thing I must say, though, that if I begin it within a month, I shall, of course, while occupied upon it, not be sending home many short things, and you may have to wait, for partial reimbursement, at least, till the autumn. But I shall certainly turn out several sketches of places and things here which my heart is set upon noticing before I go away, to complete my little bundle of Italian articles, and make a good volume. Please look out at the *Independent*. I have sent them a review of Mérimée's *Letters*[2]—besides the three Florentine chapters

I mentioned in my last, part of a series of five. Let me say finally that father when he gets answers from *Scribner* and the *Atlantic* had better accept 1000$ rather than let the thing fall. The writing and publishing a novel is almost as desirable a thing for me as the getting a large sum for it. The money-making can come afterwards. As I say, if the *Atlantic* wants the thing and will give an equal sum for it, it must properly have it. I leave my letter unsealed.—No news since yesterday, save a letter this A.M. from Aunt Mary, speaking of Willy's getting off. She wants to come to Italy for the spring but the exasperating Tweedy don't see it. She also quotes from a letter from Bessie Ward which I inclose for Alice.—Farewell, dearest parents, sister, brother and aunt, if she is in Cambridge. Think of me as very prosperous. Tell William I saw Gryzanowski last night, who sent him his love and said he was delighted with his book. I am to dine today at Hillebrand's between two ladies, one stone-deaf and the other warden-deaf. Tell Mr. Boott I wrote to him three days since.

Your devoted

H. James jr

I send *2* notes to Dr. Holland, to be sent, one or the other after father has seen Howells. The letter from Aunt Mary is not detachable. Please send a copy of *Scribner*.

1. Dr. Josiah Holland (1819–1881), editor of *Scribner's Monthly*.
2. "The Letters of Prosper Mérimée," review of *Lettres à Une Inconnue*, *Independent* (9 April 1874), pp. 9–10.

To William Dean Howells

Ms Harvard

Florence March 10*th*. [1874]

Dear Howells—

This is grim business, and yet I must be brief. Your dear friend Dr. Holland has just proposed to me to write a novel for *Scribner*, beginning in November next. To write a novel I incline and have been long inclining: but I feel as if there were a definite understanding between us that if I do so, the *Atlantic* should have the offer of it. I have therefore sent through my father a refusal to Dr. H. to be retained or forwarded according to your response. Will the *Atlantic* have my novel, when written? Dr. H's offer is a comfortable one—the novel accepted at rate (that is if terms agree,) and to begin, as I say, in November and last till the November following. He asks me to name terms, and I should name $1200. If the *Atlantic* desires a story for the year and will give as much, I of course embrace in preference the *Atlantic*. Sentimentally I should prefer the *A.*; but as things stand with me, I have no right to let it be anything but a pure money question. Will you, when you have weighed the matter, send me a line through my father or better, perhaps, communicate with him *viva voce*—This is not a love-letter and I won't gossip. I expect to be in Europe and, I hope, in Italy, till midsummer. I sent you lately, at three or four weeks interval, the two parts of a tale.[1] You have them, I hope? Farewell, with all tender wishes to your person and household. Yours ever

H. James jr.

1. The two-part tale of "Eugene Pickering."

To Alice James

Florence, April 18*th* [1874]
10 Piazza Sta. Maria Novella
1° po.

Dearest sister:

It's a long time since I have addressed one of my punctual missives to you, and I long to renew our sweet intercourse. But in order to be punctual this time, my missive must not be long, as I have but a brief interval before post-time. I wrote about a week ago from Leghorn to mother, in answer to her letter of March 24th. Since then (yesterday) has come father's of the 31st enclosing Howells's acceptance of my story for the *Atlantic*.[1] With this I am very content: especially as it gives me a longer time to write. I shall immortalize myself: *vous allez voir*. I have been back in Florence about a week—having prolonged my tour, briefly, to Pisa and Lucca. It was very pleasant though marred by bad weather—Pisa in especial being delicious. But I won't dilate, as I have just sent off some rather indifferent gossip about it to the *Nation*.[2] On my return, I fixed myself in my present quarters—a little apartment all to myself on the Piazza of all Florence in which it always seemed to me I should choose to live. I am established *à merveille*: and indeed have a "guest chamber," to which you would be welcome, were you here. I have a vast and luxurious sitting room and balcony, two bedrooms, a scullery and a china closet: which at 100 frs. a month is moderate. Blessed Florence! I couldn't face the idea of returning to live in one small room at an inn; and my literary labors will certainly show the good effect of my having space to pace about and do a little fine frenzy. Tell William I find the French restaurant in Via Rondinelli, with the lobsters and truffles in the window, an excellent place to dine, so that I am altogether most comfortable. I am also most well, and better in health, without exaggeration than for many a day. Peco!—What shall I tell you of Florence? The weather lately has been grey and rainy: but I have rather relished it and find the Florentine spring generally less deleterious to my nervous organism than the Roman last year. The Lombards are back in town: Mrs. L. very poorly again. She has come to the nice decision that she ought to leave Italy and I shall draw a long breath when I see her starting northward and facing homeward. I have been taking poor Fanny about to see a few more sights—having been much moved by the pathetic fact, which she casually mentioned, that in the six months she had been in Florence, she had been but twice to the Uffizi Gallery. It is gallantry very well bestowed; for the poor girl is very appreciative. Mrs. L. is able to go nowhere.—I was going this P.M. up to Bellosguardo to Mrs. Stephen Perkins's Saturday reception: but the skies are so black that I have stopped at home: and hence this letter.—I have seen no one new,—unless perhaps Mr. Bradford, *retour de* Rome. He lives across the way, and though his poor little frame seems more ashen grey, and his conversation more desultory than ever, his nose is as big and his virtue as unbounded. I have effected the conquest of Mme. von Limburg, the wife of an old Dutch diplomatist, living here (she was a Miss Cass, daughter of the General.) She is considered a very fine lady, and followed me up, on my being introduced to her, with an immediate invitation to a large dinner party. Unfortunately I was at Pisa, and I am informed that she made no secret of the fact that she was *inconsolable*! I am waiting till Monday, her day, to call upon her again; and if she bids me to another banquet I shall certainly go and report you everything of interest.

Sunday. I was interrupted yesterday, but don't regret it as I have this morning mother's sweet letter of April 3d (describing her dinner at Boott's with the C. Perkinses) to acknowledge. *Apropos* of which I can't imagine how I failed yesterday to mention the receipt of Willy's a week since, containing the portraits. They caused me a sweet emotion—especially yours, which is the best and wonderfully good. It is indeed most lovely and a capital likeness. I tremble for future days when I learn from Willy that even he finds (or at first found) Cambridge mean and flimsy—he who used to hanker so for it here. I should think that his three months in Italy would seem wonderfully charming to him now. To me too they have faded into a sort of half-reality, and I have to look at some visible proof too fast—as for instance—a pair of old stockings he gave me—to believe that he was veritably here. I have long ere this relapsed into my solitary single life, and save that I should like to know an agreeable man or two, I bear it very contentedly. Tell Willy I am delighted to hear that he regrets having "badgered" me about my fondness for these parts, and gives me license to go on liking Italy, irresponsibly. After he had left me, I rebounded, in this direction and haven't had an hour of *défaillance* since. Mother speaks of Wilky's prospects, which I am glad to hear are fair, of getting Mr. Tweedy's photo. and of Bessie Ward. I heard a couple of days since from Aunt Mary who doesn't disguise her extreme resentment at being kept in Dresden for many weeks after she has had enough of it. But the poor Tweedys drift with a kind of melancholy aimlessness when they are set in motion, and I shall pity her rather more when she has to begin to decide again where to go and what to do.—The Wards I am told passed through Florence rapidly a few days since *en route* for Paris, where Bessie is to be married—her lover being still in Rome, too unwell to travel. Last summer at Homburg apropos of the conjugal suffering of the German lady with whom she was staying, she used to rail sharply at German husbands; now she has got one. I hope her railings don't have reason to multiply.—I don't think of anyone or anything here more that may interest you. Mrs. Effie Lowell, I am told, is in Florence, and I will call on Mr. Dorr. Loulie Shaw's property all go to the Hoopers, Tappans etc. Tell Willy I called at Gryzanowski's one warm morning, the other day, and that he can't fancy how charming that dusky old apartment looks by daylight with the back windows all open to the garden and the view of the Cathedral. —Farewell, sweet sister. Prove to me, as I contemplate your photograph, that handsome is that handsome does by writing me a long and sprightly letter. I hope father's indisposition is over. Much love to both my *genitori* and to William and a tender folding in the arms to yourself. Ever your brother

H. James jr.

1. "Eugene Pickering." This cleared the way for the writing of the Roman novel, *Roderick Hudson*.
2. "Tuscan Cities," unsigned, *Nation*, XVIII (21 May 1874), 329–330.

To William James

Florence, May 3d [1874]

Dear William

I wrote some ten days ago to Alice, and I am not sure whether I then had received your letter of April 5th. Since then, at all events, has come to me father's note containing my notice of Mérimée and also the *North American Review* (2d number,) for which I am greatly obliged. I have sent the Review to Turgeneff through Hetzel the Paris publisher, as I could find no other address.—I was glad to get from you any new expression of impressions of home and was much entertained by your thermometrical record. But I could send you one almost as entertaining. After ten days a short time since, of very hot—of really July and August—weather, something very like winter has set in again and cold and rain are the order of the day. Today is a raw, rainy Sunday of anything but an exhilarating kind. The Piazza di Sta. Maria Novella, before my windows is a wide glittering flood, with here and there two legs picking their steps beneath an umbrella. I have already written you of my being established at housekeeping—or something very like it. It wears very well and my rooms are delightful; if I came back to Florence again, I should certainly take them for the winter. The way of life is rather solitudinous—especially the lonely feeding: but I have found a very good dining-place, where I can at least converse with the flower-girl who comes every day to distribute rosebuds for the button-hole. (The place is Victor's, Via Rondinelli, whose window, like those in the palais Royal you must remember.) The days go on with me monotonously enough and I make no new friends. I spend my time very much as when you were here, save that when the warm weather fairly set in, I took to going out in the morning and working during the hot hours from lunch to dinner. There is nothing especial to tell you of your acquaintances here, tho' I continue to see most of them occasionally. I pay frequent short visits to the Lombards, and though long since mortally tired of their nature and conversation am reduced to accepting their parlor gratefully for half an hour as the nearest approach to a domestic *foyer*. In fact I shall miss them, uncomfortably, when they go. Mrs. L. is better and worse, and lately much pleased to hear that Essie was coming out to join her. But E. will not find her anywhere in Italy, as she is constantly on the point of leaving. But she can't imagine where to go.—I have had great pleasure lately in seeing Mrs. Effie Lowell, who is a most lovely being surely. I have seen her only in the evening, however, and haven't undertaken to "go round" with her. She says she doesn't care for "art," and the other day was going to visit the poorhouse in company with a colored doctoress established here! Gryzanowski came in just as I was reading your last letter and told me to tell you that he had received the books you lately sent him and prized them greatly,

441

but that your generosity made him uncomfortable. He is "simpatico" as ever. Hillebrand becomes to me less and less so; he is an unmistakeable snob. I went the other evening to a large and very wearisome party given by Mrs. Taylor (Mme Lannsot's mother,) filled with very ordinary folk, Italian, German and English.—James Lowell and his wife spent a few days here on their return from Rome and have left for Paris—without revealing any new traits of mind or character. I feel as if I know Lowell now very well; but don't feel as I should ever get anything very valuable out of him.[1] They (the Lowells) were very frankly critical of the Storys with whom they staid a while in Rome and seemed to have been chiefly busy after the first day in inventing subterfuges for getting away. The Andrews are here, back from Rome, Edith ill (slightly I believe) with fever, as you were.—Let me say, without more loss of time, that my letter of credit expires (the date not the sum) on May 27th, and that I should like father to please ask Uncle R. to have it renewed for June, July and August. The last was for £500; this had better be (nominally) for £250. I shall draw no such sum, probably; but I had better be able to draw all that I need for my expenses in getting home and making any purchases for you. If this can be done without delay, it will be a convenience to me; as I have left too long speaking of it. I keep your various lists of commissions; though they imply as a *certainty* my sailing *via* England. I have given up all idea of taking an Italian steamer: but if I leave Italy in the early part of June, I may be reduced to going to Homburg as the best place to spend the interval of the seven weeks of July and August. In that case I shall hesitate to think it worth while to go to England, expensively, when I can make the journey from Bremen; and I suppose you won't want me to go there on purpose to buy your things. But there is time to decide on this. Father sent me a rather puzzling request in his last: *i.e.* to buy $75 worth of vertu for the tops of the bookcases. I can't very well buy it here, as to send it would be (I am told) very expensive—costing as much, almost, as the thing itself. Then to carry it about with me would be equally so, and not very convenient. I think therefore I had better let my getting it depend on my being in Paris; where the choice of things is probably better also. I see no reason here to suppose it remarkable. Thank father àpropos of his last, for his care of the proofs of my last story. I suppose it has been sent me, though it has not yet arrived.—I have fairly settled down to work upon my long story for the *Atlantic* and hope to bring it home finished or nearly so. Except therefore for two or three more Italian sketches (if opportunity offers) I shall send home no short things before I leave, and shall have to draw more money than, for the present, I cause to flow in. But if I am paid down, even in part, for my M.S. I shall be able to offer full reimbursement. I lately sent a tale to the *Galaxy*[2] and a couple more reviews to the *Nation*:[3] but I want henceforth to give all my time and attention to my novel. I am determined it shall be a very good piece of work. Farewell, dear brother. Would that you were here for an hour, this dreary day, at my solitary side. I'm sorry Waterman doesn't give you your place since you are disposed to resume it. But such is life. Farewell. My being aches with unsatisfied domestic affection, and just now I could howl with homesickness. Ever yours

H. J. jr.

1. HJ was wrong, and his friendship with Lowell would be a deeply affectionate one in later years.

2. Probably "Professor Fargo," XVIII (August 1874), 233–253.

3. Probably HJ's review of Flaubert's *Temptation of St. Anthony*, unsigned, *Nation*, XVIII (4 June 1874), 365–366 and Montégut's *Souvenirs de Bourgogne*, unsigned, *Nation*, XIX (23 July 1874), p. 62.

To William Dean Howells

Ms Harvard

Florence, Piazza Sta. Maria Novella
May 3d [1874]

Dear Howells—

I received some days ago from my father the little note you had sent him signifying your acceptance of my story for next year's *Atlantic,* and have had it at heart ever since to drop you a line in consequence.—I'm extremely glad that my thing is destined to see the light in the *Atlantic* rather than in t'other place and am very well satisfied with the terms. My story is to be on a theme I have had in my head a long time and once attempted to write something

443

about. The theme is interesting, and if I do as I intend and hope, I think the tale must please. It shall, at any rate have all my pains. The opening chapters take place in America and the people are of our glorious race; but they are soon transplanted to Rome, where things are to go on famously. *Ecco.* Particulars, including name, (which however I'm inclined to have simply that of the hero), on a future occasion. Suffice it that I promise you some tall writing. My only fear is that it may turn out taller than broad. That is, I thank you especially for the clause in the contract as to the numbers being less than twelve. As I desire above all things to write close, and avoid padding and prolixity, it may be that I shall have told my tale by the 8th or 9th number. But there is time enough to take its measure scientifically. I don't see how, in parts of the length of Aldrich's *Prudence Palfrey* (my protagonist is *not* named Publicius Parsons,) it can help stretching out a good piece.—Of Aldrich's tale, I'm sorry to say I've lost the thread, through missing a number of the magazine, and shall have, like Dennett, to wait till it's finished.— Only do you continue to treat me as if I didnt' care to hear from you? I have a vague sense of unnumbered notes, despatched to you as an editor, but in which your human side was sufficiently recognized to have won from you some faint response. If you know how dismally and solitudinously I sit here just now before my window, ignorant of a friendly voice, and waiting for the rain-swept piazza to look at last as if it would allow me to go forth to my lonely *pranzo* at a mercenary *trattoria*—you would repent of your coldness. I suppose I ought to write you a letter flamboyant with local color; but the local color just now, as I say, is the blackest shade of the pluvious, and my soul reflects its hue. My brother will have talked to you about Florence and about me, sufficiently too, I suppose, for the present. Florence has become by this time to me an old story— though like all real masterpieces one reads and re-reads it with pleasure. I am here now but for a few weeks longer, and then I shall leave Italy—for a many a year, I imagine. With ineffable regret for many reasons; contentedly enough for others. But we shall have a chance before long to talk of all this. I return home at the end of the summer (and hope to bring my tale with me substantially completed). To many of the things of home I shall return with pleasure—especially to the less isolated, more freely working—and talking—life.—Don't wait for this, however, to let me hear from you; but write me meanwhile, if it's only to tell me you're glad I'm coming. I have had no personal news of you in an age, but I trust you are nestling in prosperity. It's a hundred years since I heard of your wife's health: but I trust it is good, even at the advanced age which this makes her. What are you doing, planning, hoping? I suppose your Venetian tale is almost off your hands—I long to have it on mine. (I'm delighted by the way to hear you like "Eugene Pickering": *do*, oh do, if possible put him through in a single number.) Lowell has just passed through on his way to Paris. I got great pleasure from his poem, which he read me in bits. I'm impatient to see it all together. Farewell, dear Howells; the rivulets on the piazza run thin, and I must trudge across and quaff the straw-covered *fiaschetto*: I shall do it, be sure, to your health, your *gentilissima sposa's* and your children's. Yours always

H.J. jr

To Sarah Butler Wister

Ms Congress

Florence May 10*th* [1874]
Piazza Sta. M. Novella 10.

Dear Mrs Wister:

This is not a letter—that must be for another day when I've not just been writing one of sixteen pages: (to my mother.)—This is simply a thank you (or rather twenty) for your own letter, which illuminated my existence day before yesterday. It was very good to hear from you; and I shall always value doing so, incalculably, for I feel as if we had had a glimpse of *la beauté parfaite* (or something very like it), together. I shall answer your letter as it deserves on the first possible day:—meanwhile I want simply to enclose this newspaper scrap: which you would never otherwise see. Read the book, decidedly: it's thoroughly interesting.—Here I am at the end of a Florentine winter, which tho' socially most tame and arid has

Sarah Butler Wister

been much more remunerative than I expected when I wrenched myself about from Rome to face the prospect. Florence has worked pretty thoroughly into my consciousness and I have grown foolishly fond of it: but there are no especial details to enumerate. It has been a very *unpersonal* winter—save as regards that very tiresome person myself of whose society I've had a surfeit. Doesn't some one else want to try him?—I can imagine your having deserved to have Boston made amusing to you, but (quite apart from deserts) your story doesn't make it even easy to go thither—which nevertheless I rather distinctly intend in the autumn.—I saw a couple of nights since (or rather mornings and it was at a ball, the only one I've been to all winter) Miss Edith Story, who inquired about you, very prettily. Also Mme de Rabe, née Crawford, with whom nowadays one has to converse in French, as her husband knows no English. I never wanted to marry her, surely, but I don't care for her so much now that another man has done so.—So Porter[1] is painting you? I congratulate him on his opportunities. He will do your dress very well, but I am dissatisfied in advance with the face.—Mrs. Lawrence, on Cherbuliez, was excellent; but not having reviews to write, she has no business to take such good things out of the critic's mouths.—I enjoy greatly your having enjoyed my Turgenief,[2] but think you are wise, morally, not to read his works.—But I am writing the letter I didn't mean to. I hope that that *malappris* of an Adams will make reparation by printing your article in letters of gold.—Yes: the flowers do stand in *shame* against the dark base of the Strozzi, your word makes the picture: but somehow, I don't see or feel and smell and *know* the Spring here, even in May, as I did in Rome last March. With kind regards to Dr Wister: yours most faithfully and gratefully.

Henry James jr.

Excuse the shabbiness of the scrap. I lent it to a friend who returned it so.

1. Benjamin Curtis Porter (1845–1908), American portrait painter.

2. HJ constantly varied his spelling of Turgenev. In the article-review in the *North American Review*, CXVIII (April), 326–356 he spelled the name Turgénieff; later he accepted the French form Tourguénieff.

To Mrs. Henry James Sr.

Ms Harvard

Florence, May 17*th* 74.

Dearest mother—

I have before me two unanswered letters from home: one from Willy of April 16th, received some ten days since: the other yours of May 1st, which arrived yesterday. Many thanks for each; they have helped to console me for the want of your personal society. Your principal news was the snow and sleet of your dreary spring; and unless things have greatly improved since I still excite your animosity by telling you how much better they have been with us here in Florence. A little rain, but nothing to complain of and day after day of lovely, healthy coolness. To those who above all things dread being "relaxed," this postponement of the warm weather is very agreeable. Even yet, though the sky is brilliant, it fails to arrive and today is a radiant blue-heavened Sunday with such a crispness in the air as you might have in early October. But evidently there must be a change and it will be sudden and intense; though Gryzanowski, who is as ingenious an observer of the weather as of everything else, prophesies that this is to be, in Italy, a cool summer.—The days pass here evenly and rapidly in my comfortable little dwelling on this lively (and alas dusty) old Piazza Sta. Maria Novella. (The centre of the square is not paved and the dust hovers over it in clouds which compel one to live with closed windows. But I remove to my bedroom which is on a side-street and very cool and clean.) Nothing particular happens to me and my time is passed between sleeping and scribbling (both of which I do very well) lunching and dining, walking and conversing with my small circle of acquaintance. Florence is supposed to be in a very festal state just now, owing to a great flower show which has brought a crowd; but it is to me personally neither better nor worse than usual. I haven't yet been to the flower show, which I believe is handsome—for Italy, where the flowers don't match our northern ones. I have seen no new person nor new thing—or rather I have; for I went a couple of nights since to a very brilliant ball given by the jockey-club at their

Casino in the Cascine. The omnipotent Hillebrand sent me an invitation and though it required much cold-blooded energy to go trundling off alone at midnight to an entertainment where I should know no one, I went for information's sake. It was very brilliant and elegant and I saw a concentration of the élite of Florentine society, and more tiaras of diamonds and ropes of pearls and acres of *point de Venise* than I had ever beheld before. There were also a few people I know—Miss Story among others, with her hostess the Princess Corsini, with whom I also had a little talk. I left at 3 A.M. when the cotillion was still an hour off!—I came the other day at my restaurant across Mme de Rabe (née Crawford) and her husband who are here "*incogniti*" to escape visiting and visits. She seems very happy and I think has quite tamed her Prussian. Lizzie Boott, I suppose, will have heard of the last engagement of Miss Mimoli Crawford to one Fraser, namely attaché of the English embassy at Rome, a very respectable and worthy youth who is to take her to live in Pekin, whither he has been appointed. They are to be married immediately. The good Terry is going for the summer to America and Mrs. T. is to spend it at Dantzig (or thereabouts) near Mme de Rabe. (This will interest Lizzie.) It will also divert her to hear that Mrs. Carson is reported to be engaged to the blind Duke of Sermoneta and that Edith Story has just refused Peruzzi, aid de camp of the King and nephew of the Sindaco here; but nearly fifty and penniless.—[1] Tell Willy I thank him greatly for setting before me so vividly the question of my going home or staying. I feel equally with him the importance of the decision. I have been meaning, as you know, for some time past to return in the autumn, and I see as yet no sufficient reason for changing my plan. I shall go with the full prevision that I shall not find life at home *simpatico*, but rather painfully, and, as regards literary work, obstructively the reverse, and not even with the expectation that time will make it easier; but simply on sternly practical grounds; *i.e.* because I can find more abundant literary occupation by being on the premises and relieve you and father of your burdensome financial interposition. But I shrink from Willy's apparent assumption that going now is to pledge myself to stay forever. I feel as if my three years in Europe (with much of them so *maladif*) were a very moderate allowance for one who gets so much out of it as I do; and I don't think I could really hold up my head if I didn't hope to eat a bigger slice of the pudding (with a few more social plums in it, especially) at some future time. If at the end of a period at home, I don't feel an overwhelming desire to come back, it will be so much gained; but I should prepare myself for great deceptions if I didn't take the possibility of such desire into account. One oughtn't, I suppose, to bother too much about the future, but arrange as best one can with the present, and the present bids me go home and try and get more things published. What makes the question particularly difficult to decide is that though I should make more money at home, American prices would devour it twice as fast; but even allowing for this, I should keep ahead of my expenses better than here. I know that when the time comes it will be unutterably hard to leave and I shall be wondering whether, if I were to stay another year, I shouldn't propitiate the Minotaur and return more resignedly. But to this I shall answer that a year wouldn't be a tenth part enough and that besides, as things stand, I should be perplexed where to spend it. Florence, fond as I have grown of it, is worth far too little to me, socially, for me to think complacently of another winter here. Here have I been living (in these rooms) for five weeks and not a creature, save once Gryzanowski, has crossed my threshold—counting out my little Italian, who comes twice a week, and whom I have to *pay* for his conversation! If I knew any one in England I should be tempted to go there for a year, for there I could work to advantage —i.e. get hold of new books to review. But I can't face, as it is, a year of British solitude. What I desire now more than anything else, and what would do me more good, is a *régal* of intelligent and suggestive society, especially male. But I don't know how or where to find it. It exists, I suppose, in Paris and London, but I can't get at it. I chiefly desire it because it would, I am sure, increase my powers of work. These are going very well, however, as it is, and I have for the present an absorbing task in my novel.—Consider then that if nothing extremely unexpected turns up, I shall depart in the autumn. I have no present plans for the summer beyond end-

ing my month in my rooms—on the 11th of June.—I hope, beloved
mammy, that you will be able to devise some agreeable plan for
your own summer and will spend it in repose and comfort. I took
great satisfaction in what you say of Wilky's prospects and your
quotation from his letter about his wife. His state of mind is certainly a blessed "providence." Your mention of Howard's situation
and requisitions was sufficiently sickening.—T. S. Perry then is
married! Is it true that his wife is to be constrained to "give lessons"
—as Mrs. Lowell told me she has heard? What a grey prospect!—
Àpropos, I believe I wrote that I have been seeing Mrs. Effie Lowell
—less than I would, now that she is gone. She is a ravishing woman
and I came within an ace of falling wholesomely in love with her.—
Mrs. Lombard (with whom I am not in love) is still lingering on
here, amid ups and downs of health. She is living so comfortably
and cheaply (a charming parlor, two bed-rooms and all her meals
which are very succulent, for 7 frs. a day—and in the Palazzo
Machiavelli, once the home of the great Niccolo, too,) that she fears
to break the charm, though having old designs upon Venice. I have
by this time put Fanny thro' all the sights and conducted the two
the other night to the opera to hear Cimarosa's *Matrimonio Segreto.*
This was poor Mrs. L's one revelry, since she has been in Italy, and
even this outwearied her. I also drove with them the other day to
Fiesole and Vincigliata, and tell Willy I thought most achingly of
him. If that was pretty in January he may fancy what it is in May.
But I have missed nevertheless that entrancing sense of the Italian
spring that I had so fully last winter in Rome. Here there are so
many fewer places to catch it—no Villa Borghese, no Coliseum, no
long walls, overtumbled with cataracts of white roses. But here,
nevertheless, you should see against the rugged brown walls of the
Strozzi Palace the flowers standing in sheathes for sale and climbing
and breaking in verdurous spray away up in the neighborhood of
the second story windows. The Cascine too, now, are enchanting:
but you haven't that delicious invasion of spring that arrives with
March, in Rome. I'm glad to hear Charles Norton has found some
active work to divert him from his dusky opinions. I hope you
enjoyed his Turner drawings: as I remember them there were some

lovely ones.—I received the other day, a *Scribner* with my story:[2] the nature of which (I had never seen a copy before) made me cross myself with gratitude that nothing had come of Dr. Holland's invitation. You speak of some *notes* of mine having appeared in the *Independent*. If they were sent me, they have not arrived; and would father kindly send another copy?—Has the trunk reached Quincy St? Pray guard jealously my few clothes—a summer suit and a coat and two white waistcoats that I would give much for here, now. But don't let father and Willy wear them out as they will serve me still. Farewell, sweet mother, I must close. I wrote last asking you to have my credit renewed. I suppose it has been done. Love abounding to all. I will write soon to William. I wrote lately to Alice.

Yours ever

H.

1. Edith Story married Count Peruzzi, who was a descendant of the Medici.
2. "Adina," *Scribner's Monthly*, VIII (May-June 1874), 33–43, 181–191.

To Mrs. Henry James Sr.
Ms Harvard

Florence June 3*d*. 10 P. Sta. N.N. [1874]

Dearest mother—

I must write today, though I have nothing whatever to relate. Nothing at least beyond the fact that I have just recd. your letter of May 19th; and that a few days since came Alice's of the 10th: both most cheering to my soul athirst for domestic affection. To you I wrote some ten days since. (This morning also came an *Atlantic* and a *Scribner*.) You see I am still lingering on here in Florence—one of the few survivors of the winter colony. The summer has begun in great earnest—you would think so if you could peep with me through the closed lattice of my sitting-room out into the wide, glaring Piazza. It shines so as to scorch the eyes: in the shade on one side is huddled a cab-stand with the drivers all asleep on their boxes, and a collection of loungers of low degree and no costume to speak of lying flat on their faces on the stones and courting the siesta. I am staying on because it is convenient and not uncomfortable. In fact I have so much comfort in being able to

452

expand and perambulate in my three darkened rooms that I dread to begin to travel and live in hotels and one small chamber. My life is profoundly tranquil. I go out in the morning, walk about a bit and court the dusky coolness of a church. The Cathedral just now is divinely cool and picturesque, with its portals flung wide to let the white sunshine of the streets pour in and lose itself vainly in the gorgeous dusk. I lunch early in a beer-garden, in the green shade of a trellis and then come home and dwell through the long hot hours of the afternoon till about 7:30 at which fashionable hour I dine. The evenings I spend abroad in one way or another. On this basis I shall remain here (if nothing expels me sooner) till about the 20th and then probably make straight for Homburg. I suppose it is not at all enterprising to revert thus mechanically to a place I know so well: but I have no time nor money to waste in exploration and I know Homburg to be cool, salubrious, cheerful and propitious to six weeks scribbling. My present design therefore is to arrive there about July 5th. Absolutely nothing has befallen me since I last wrote and I hardly speak to more than three or four persons a week. The Lombards (the consolers of my solitude—for to that had I come!) went off to Venice about a week ago, with Mrs. Dana— (Willy will tell you who she is.) They were in a very feeble way, but I imagine the change of air and the Venice breezes have helped them. The Gryzanowskis rose in their might the other day and invited me to dinner—a great event for both of us: for since Christmas I have dined out but twice, by the charity of Mme. Laussol. Tell William I continue from time to time to see that household, but with effort. I have tried to make a friend of Hillebrand, but I like him too little, and the ladies are really too deaf. Gryzanowski spoke of enjoying much his correspondence with father. I lately got a letter from Wendell Holmes, telling me he was coming abroad, and proposing we should "travel together." This of course is impossible and I am afraid we shall not even meet as with his short allowance of time he probably won't care to touch at Homburg. I regard it as fixed, however, that I shall return home either August 20th or about October 5th. In the first case from Bremen; in the second case from Liverpool. Each has its advantages but I won't decide till I get North of the Alps. Both your letter and Alice's are a mine of advice: Alice's that I must not turn up my nose at home things, and yours that I take a wife. I will bore a hole in my nose and keep it down with a string, and if you will provide the wife, the fortune, and the "inclination" I will take them all.—I am sorry the summer question pesters you so and devoutly hope it will find some happy solution. I am almost shamed to have a German watering place to turn to so easily.—I hear once in a while from Aunt Mary Tweedy, who does not, as you say, write a letter of genius. I wrote about a month ago, asking you to please ask Uncle R. to have my letter of credit renewed for a convenient sum. I hope the letter duly reached you and the thing was done, as my present credit is exhausted (that is, the time the letter was to run) and I shall be left high and dry unless the other arrives. I await it from week to week.—I have said before that I would send home but one or two things more to print this summer as I am occupying myself exclusively with my novel. It is proceeding to my satisfaction—not very rapidly, but very regularly, which is the best way. The produce of it will make up all my arrears.—I ought to have told you in my last that you will have to begin addressing me for the summer care of Brown Shipley and Co. It is the only possible course, in view of the uncertainty of my movements. I had bother last summer in trying to give you local addresses.—I ought to tell you that I am in health continually better and this in spite of the heavy Italian air. But I must close, with multitudinous blessings on all. Won't you send me those *Notes* from the *Independent*?[1]—But I have less and less desire to see my printed things over here, the errors are so distressing, and always, by some cruel fate, such bad ones. Two very bad ones in the *Siena*, and the *Adina* also much spotted. I lately sent an excellent review of Feydau's Gautier to the *Nation*, but I see Laugel has anticipated me. I will write to have it sent to the *North American Review*.[2] Farewell, sweet mammy and all the rest of you. Alice shall have a due response to her brilliant letter.

Ever your
H. J. jr.

1. The series of "Notes" on Florence.
2. This article appeared in the review in October 1874 (CXIX, 415–423).

To William James

Ms Harvard

Monte Generoso
Near Como. June 13*th* [1874]

Dear William

I am sitting under a sort of little shed, on a sort of terrace, over-looking a sort of view—writing this at a rustic table, the rusty nails of which lacerate my wrists as I drive the pen. Opposite are established Mrs. Lombard and Fanny!! But of them anon.—I wrote home last from Florence—speaking then, if I remember, as if I expected to remain there till the 20th. I absconded at a day's notice, just a week ago, under pressure of the terrific heat which suddenly descended upon Italy a few days before and sent all travellers spinning northward. I was greatly *contrarié* to leave, but the atmos-phere was intolerable and work had become impossible. I came on to Milan, grasping on the way a most scorching but most delightful day at Ravenna. Of this I shall write to the *Nation*.[1] At Milan I met the Lombards flung from Venice and much distracted to know where to go. I being minded to come up here to await, if possible July 1st. they decided to come as well: so we ascended together last evening, in a thunder storm which caused them much discomfiture. But this morning we are rested and dried; and though I confess to a certain sinking of the heart at finding myself fixed on a mountain top, with the old too, too familiar Swiss pension life going on about me, and a dozen English clergymen in "puggaries"[2] kicking their enormous heels on the front steps—yet I am inclined to take a cheerful view of things. A small closet five feet square isn't favorable to literary labor, but I shall give myself a chance to get used to it, and doubtless succeed. The air is delicious—Alpine freshness tem-pered by Italian softness—the views enchanting, the food eatable and the company apparently estimable. There are agreeable strolls and shady hillsides and I shall perch till I can perch no longer. (Your letters, meanwhile, must come to Brown and Shipley.) The heat in Italy for the past fortnight has been extraordinary and for a week in especial, intolerable. The journey from Florence and the

455

couple of days at Milan were spent in a mere demoralized *soak* of perspiration. The Lombards say Venice was fatally uncomfortable and seem to have come away with an indifferent opinion of it. I am more than satiated with their society, but they are too feeble for criticisms; and they make no exactions. They will probably depart in a few days for Geneva to join Essie.—I have not heard from home in some time, and am expecting letters to be sent from Florence. Just before starting I got a *Nation* with my letter from Pisa etc. What do you think of this for a misprint:—"idle vistas and melancholy nooks"—"*idle sisters and melancholy monks*!!" In the article on *Siena* the sense of two or three good sentences was also ruined.—But this is not a letter—but only a notification of my whereabouts and I must not embark on details. I am rather stiff and sore with my climb yesterday and must lie off, horizontally. I'm afraid you are all struggling painfully with the summer question, and I wish I had a bosky-flanked Monte Generoso to offer you. The opal-tinted view, the drowsy breeze, the stillness and the tinkling cow-bells are gradually sinking into my soul.—I had been wondrous well in Florence, until the great heat began, and that rather undid me: but on this higher plane I shall doubtless mend. Much love to all: I shall write again speedily. In spite of the temperature, I have been lacerated at leaving Italy. Ravenna is remarkable: I wish I had given a second day to it. I trust you are prospering and that the summer will pass well with you. I have not yet answered directly your letter about my coming home; but I answered it through mother. I shall certainly come.

Yours ever
H. James jr.

1. "Ravenna," unsigned, *Nation*, XIX (9 July 1874), 23–25.
2. A turban-like form of head-covering cultivated at Swiss altitudes.

To His Father

Ms Harvard

Hotel Royal, Baden-Baden
June 23*d* '74.

Dearest father:

I wrote home about ten days ago from Monte Generoso, giving an account of my departure from Florence and subsequent adventures; but I am sorry to say that I have not yet had time to receive the letters which I fondly hope have been accumulating for me at Florence. I am expecting them speedily, but I am unwilling to delay writing until they come lest you should fancy that I had fallen into a precipice of the Generous Mountain or that Mrs. Lombard had poisoned me in a fit of jealousy of my attention to Fanny.—You behold me now in fresh fields and pastures new—among which however, for rest and comfort's sake, I hope to remain long enough to permit them to grow stale and old.—A week of Monte Generoso convinced me that the conditions of life on an even divinely beautiful mountain top were not favorable to my prosperity, mental or physical, so that without losing more time I repaired immediately to this place. By immediately I mean *via* the Splügen pass, Chur and Basel—at which of each latter places I spent a night. I came down from Generoso on Saturday A.M. last (this being Wednesday,) crossed the mountain that night on the summit of the diligence and arrived here yesterday (Tuesday) afternoon. My stopping here, experimentally, was a happy thought, for twenty four hours observation of this enchanted valley have determined me to abide here for the present. I was deadly sick at the idea of going back to that too too familiar Homburg, and yet I didn't know what else to do. This cuts the knot, as far as I can foresee, effectually. Baden, judged by one walk and one seance last evening on the terrace of the Conversation House, listening to the Band is an absurdly pretty and coquettish little *ville d'eaux* embosomed in a labyrinth of beautiful hills and forest walks. In all this it leaves Homburg quite behind— as also in the facilities for frugal living. (I have just concluded an arrangement to dwell awhile at this extremely comfortable little hotel to the tune of 10 frs. a day). It is inferior to Homburg, I believe, in climate; but after Italy I don't believe I shall find the air oppresive. Besides Turgeniew lives here, and I mean to call on him. Many of his tales were probably written here—which proves that the place is favorable to literary labor. Thus encouraged I shall settle down to my own and hope to achieve a quiet summers attention to it. I shall not lack quiet, I imagine, as the racketing days of Baden are said to be well over. I have no further news. Monte Generoso was lovely—but no place to lie all day on the grass, rather than to work indoors or to walk. The Lombards came down with me to Como, and started for Geneva, *via* Mont Cenis—there to await Essie. I can't write more till I have heard from you again. Heaven bless you all, poor Beloved Badenless creatures! I will write again promptly when I have got my letters. Meanwhile I bless you all and remain dear dad your loving son

H.

To Mrs. Henry James Sr.
Ms Harvard

Baden Baden July 28*th* 74.

Dearest mother—

This cannot possibly be a letter, for I have absolutely nothing to write about. I only wish, in the first place to thank you for your letter of July 9th which, with a note from Willy, came to me some days since, and in the second to let you know that I sail from Liverpool, in the *Java*, August 25th. I hope therefore to arrive about the 3d or 4th September, by which time you will have had leisure to return comfortably from the country and settle yourselves in Quincy St. The interval, I trust, will pass speedily for both of us and nothing will mar the felicity of our reunion.—Beyond this, I have nothing to relate, nor even to mention. The days as they follow each other, look so much alike that I can hardly tell them apart. The extreme heat has within a week, somewhat subsided, and existence has consequently more charms. But this is the only thing that has happened. Nothing not only befalls me, but I hear of nothing that befalls anyone else. For a moment there was a possibility of my seeing Wendell Holmes and wife; but that has evaporated, and we shall probably not meet, tho' we sail from England within two days of each other. He is to spent August (I suppose visiting) in England. The Tweedies too are not to turn up, as Aunt Mary writes me they have taken for two months a cottage near her sister's place. She invites me to visit them and I shall probably look at them before sailing. I am here for upwards of another week and then to England, probably *via* the Rhine and Rotterdam. Now that I am booked for home I am intolerably impatient to start and to arrive. I was happy to have you give a cool account of your summer up to the time you wrote. May you have kept cool and be now about to repair as you designed, to Alice and Aunt Kate's resort. I hope this has turned out satisfactory to them and that Willy is lodged somewhere where the breezes play about his brow. His last note contained a request to buy some surgical instruments in Dresden for him, which I shall now not be able to do. I asked father in my last to let me know of anything he wished me to do in London for him. Farewell sweet mammy. I hope this will find you reposing on that "elevated plateau" which Aunt K. describes in a letter to me just received, for which I beg you to thank her. I hear Alice has taken to riding and rejoice in the noble circumstance. I wish I were humping by her side.—Farewell. In one little month—hardly more—I shall press you in my arms. Be sure about Sept. 4th to have on hand a goodly store of tomatoes, ice-cream, corn, melons, cranberries and other indigenous victuals. Love to all—

your H

To Sarah Butler Wister

Ms Congress

Baden-Baden July 29th [1874]

Dear Mrs. Wister—

I wrote you some weeks since from Florence a few lines simply as an advance on a letter more worthy of your own gracious liberality. I hope you safely received it and have not been supposing that I have remained irresponsive and dumb until this hour. The days meanwhile have gone by and I have torn myself away from Florence and am making the best of existence in this degenerate and melancholy spot. In truth, I had better have written my letters out and out in Florence, for my spirits have been chilled and my imagination blighted by the dullest weeks of my life, which I am now bringing to their lugubrious term. Were you ever at Baden Baden, in the good old time of the gaming? With the suppression of this its light has quite gone out and you, even if you are visiting those Quaker relations again about whom you wrote me last summer so charmingly, are not spending days of a greyer hue than those which have been passing over my devoted head, in the shadow of the despoiled Conversation House. Fortunately Baden is enchantingly pretty and I have taken to the woods, like the hunted negro of romance and amused myself with long solitary strolls in the Black Forest. This is really quite fabulously picturesque and has helped to console me for the universal flatness of mankind as represented at Baden. Fortunately, too, I have had a rather absorbing piece of scribbling to do, and the weeks have taken themselves off with a better grace than at one time seemed likely. I scribble in the morning, and walk, as aforesaid, in the verdurous gloom of the Schwarzwald in the afternoon and I sit and listen to the band on the terrace and consume *farce glaces* in the evening. I converse with the waiter and the chambermaid, the trees and the streams, a Russian or two, and a compatriot or two, but with no one who has suggested any ideas worthy of your attention. My literary labor, however, has interested me and I hope, before long, will interest you. I am writing a novel for the *Atlantic* next year (beginning January) and, as I go, have had frequent occasion to think of you. It all goes on in Rome (or most of it) and I have been hugging my Roman memories with extraordinary gusto. The fault of the story, I am pretty sure, will be in its being too analytical and psychological, and not sufficiently dramatic and eventful: but I trust it will have some illusion for you, for all that. *Vedremo.* This is the only fact with color in it that I can offer you, save and except one other which just now rather takes the lead. I sail for America on the 25th of

August (from England)—a rather sudden decision. I had had thoughts otherwise of going back to Rome, but various practical considerations have turned the scale and now that the thing is settled, (though the settlement cost me a grievous pang) I am extremely impatient to have it over, to start and to arrive. It has at least the merit that it will make it possible for me to see you within some calculable period. I have no plans of liking or disliking, of being happy or the reverse; I shall take what comes, make the best of it and dream inveterately, I foresee, of going back for a term of years, as the lawyers say, to Italy. I shall spend two or three months at Cambridge, but I expect to dispose of the winter in New York. Either there or in Boston or in Philadelphia—wherever it can be most gracefully contrived—I count upon seeing you.—All this is a copiousness of egotism which it will take a friendly soul to excuse. Meanwhile, where are you and what manner of life do you lead? Whom do you see—what do you do, or think, or feel? I imagine that your house in the country is by this time "done up" as they say in England, and I hope your days there are *files d'or et de soi.* Is Porter's picture finished and does it please those whom it should please? Particularly, have you seen that brave Miss Bartlett, who, I hear, with her woe-worn friend, is coming back to Rome for the winter. A winter's riding on the Campagna I think, may do much to mitigate even such infelicities as Mrs. Sumner's.[1] I cut out of the Galignani the other day, to send you, a paragraph on Miss Lowe's marriage, at Venice; and have stupidly lost it.[2] You have of course heard of the event, but this had some account of the happy man's pedigree and affiliations. He is apparently a reputable British gentleman—and so much for Bellay! I call him— the husband (I forget his name)—the happy man: but is he, *con rispetto,* so ideally happy? By which gross speech I mean is his wife, after all, the intensely interesting personage she seemed and generally passed for? Miss Lowe always reminded me somewhat of that Chief Justice of England, of whom some one said that "no man was ever as wise as Lord So-and-so looked!" Beautiful, mysterious, melancholy, inscrutable and all that—was it simply her way of seeming, or had she unfathomable depths within? Her

marrying a British consul seems a little of a prosy performance.—
But these are impertinent reflections, at this time of day, and she is
certainly handsome enough to have a right to be as much more or
less as she chooses.—*Àpropos* of the ancient Romans, do you continue
to hear from Lefèbvre? I suppose he is biding his time and clutching
at the skirts of fame. If the world is to hear from him, however, I
hope it will not be as the composer of another *Fille de Mme Angot*[3]—
the surest passport to glory, apparently, now possible in France. (I
speak with the echoes of last night's dreary performance of that
work in my ears.)—But I must pull up. I remain here a few days
longer and then go down the Rhine to Holland, to take a look at
Dutch pictures, which I adore, and thence cross to England for a
fortnight before sailing. I shall see no one, save the Tweedies who
have taken a house in the country for the summer. Think of me
after that as in a not-to-be-thought-of-state for ten days, and then as
doing battle with first impressions at Cambridge. It would be a
blessing if ten lines from you were to arrive there (at 20 Quincy St.)
to help the good cause. Farewell! My friendliest regards to Dr.
Wister and kind remembrances to your mother if, as I suppose,
she is still near you. Yours, dear Mrs. Wister, most faithfully

Henry James jr.

That mention, by the way, of my story for the *Atlantic* was premature. Would you kindly forbear to allude to it? I have lost your
Philadelphia address and must risk another.

1. Probably an allusion to Mrs. Sumner's divorce.
2. The paragraph about Elena Lowe appeared in *Galignani's Messenger*
9 July 1874. It read as follows:

MARRIED—At the British Consulate in Venice on the 20th June, by the
Rev. J. D. Mereweather, Gerald Raoul Perry, Esq., H.B.M.'s Consul in the
Island of Reunion, and Elena, daughter of the late Francis Lowe, Esq., of
Boston, Mass. U.S. Mr. Gerald Perry is the son of Sir William Perry (for
many years H.B.M.'s Consul-General at Venice) and of his wife the late
Geraldine de Courcy sister of the present Lord Kingsale.

3. An operetta popular at the time with music by Alexandre-Charles
Lecocq.

6
The Choice

1874-1875

6
The Choice

Henry James's return to 20 Quincy Street in 1874 had none of the gloom or melancholy that had attended his return four years earlier after his grand tour. His forays abroad had been, in reality, attempts to leave the parental roof, to find means of self-support. He had demonstrated that this was possible. He was thirty-one, a time when most young men were married and settled in life. Henry James now took a series of steps to settle into his career. He was still writing *Roderick Hudson*; and after visiting his parents and savoring American domestic life and domestic cooking, he moved to New York to test that city as a domicile for an active bachelor writer. He was also establishing a pattern of work: his running start on his serialized novel gave him margin for other writing; and in Manhattan, where he lived on the east side, off Madison Square (he placed his hero of *The Bostonians* in that environment), he wrote reviews and art notes and without joining the staff of the *Nation* became one of its regular contributors. He found, however, that agreeable as Manhattan life was in some ways—the easy bohemianism of the writing set, the dinners at chop houses, the hospitalities of cultivated houses—he had little time for fiction. Reviewing books was a burdensome undertaking; and the pattern of travel and writing, so easily possible in Europe, was not available to him once he was caught up in the urbanism of Manhattan.

In New York he put together his first three books. He had been publishing short stories for ten years; he now collected those dealing with Americans abroad in a volume called *A Passionate Pilgrim* and sold it to a Boston publisher. He also collected his travel sketches of the preceding months, when he had journeyed with his sister and aunt, in a volume he called *Transatlantic Sketches*. Finding no publisher for this sort of book, he had it printed at his own expense (borrowing as usual from his father). In a very short time he not only repaid the debt, but earned royalties on the work. Finally he revised *Roderick Hudson* for book publication. The year 1875 launched Henry James with his three books—an auspicious debut for a writer published largely anonymously in the magazines, and known only as a writer of skillful tales.

His winter in New York demonstrated to him that he would be committed there to constant drudgery and hack work. Moreover he found life in Manhattan expensive compared to life in the capitals of Europe. By early summer of 1875 he had formed his plan; he would return to the Continent in the fall, as soon as he had read final proofs of *Roderick*. He would try Paris—having already tested Rome. To this end he induced the New York *Tribune*, which had always featured its foreign correspondence, to appoint him Paris correspondent-at-large—a contributor on the arts and general topics in the French capital. In the autumn he sailed as he had planned. Howells rightly foretold that James would stay abroad a long time. The thirty-two-year-old American had undergone an arduous apprenticeship. He had now made his choice. He was launched at last in the world, and he embraced Europe—he "inhaled" it and "took possession"—with an ardor that would endure a lifetime.

To Robertson James

Ts Vaux

Cambridge
October 13*th* 1874

Dearest Bob:

I have not written to you for so long that I am afraid that you will think that I have abjured correspondence, on principle. This is not the case, and I may truly say that during the last half of my stay in Europe there was a certain intended letter to you which continued to get put off from day to day and from week to week. I find so much writing, epistolary and other, to attend to that it never came to the light. You know of course of my being at home and have, I hope, received good accounts of me. My arrival is now a month old, first impressions are losing their edge and Europe is fading away into a pleasant dream. But I confess I have become very much Europeanized in feeling, and I mean to keep a firm hold of the old world in some way or other. But home seems very pleasant after the lonely shiftless migratory life that I have been leading these two years. Cambridge has never looked so pretty as during the last month and I have seen nothing in Europe in the way of weather equal to the glory of an American autumn. I have extracted from mother and Alice all the gossip they could furnish about you and Mary and (conjecturally) about your infant son, and of course I feel nearer to you than I did on the other side of the Atlantic; but after the modest little railway journeys of Europe, you seem still to be divided from me by a formidable gulf of time and space. Gradually, however, I shall get reaccustomed to the American scale of things and then, I trust, I shall pick up energy (to say nothing of funds) to come out and take a look at you.—I should like to share your daily life for a while and have a glimpse of Western civilization I never think without silent applause of your hard laborious career: fortune and fame, I doubt not, will crown it in the end. Meanwhile you are happy as a husband and a father, and with these blessings, one can live with life. They have been coming lately to Wilky too . . . we are all extremely glad he has got a boy. I should like hugely to see you, dear Bob, and to make the acquaintance of Mary and the Babe. Some day I will. Love and blessings to them meanwhile and a line from you when you have time. Ever your brother

Henry James

To H. W. Longfellow

Ms Harvard

Cambridge
Wednesday A.M.

My dear Mr. Longfellow—

I had hoped last evening up to the last moment to enjoy your supper and your society; but I was kept within doors by a bad cold, which would have made me poor company and little better than a skeleton at your banquet. I shall give myself the pleasure of seeing you when I am in better condition—

Yours very truly
Henry James jr.

To H. W. Longfellow

Ms Harvard

Quincy St.
Thursday A.M.

My dear Mr. Longfellow—

I found the volumes of Tourgéneff of which we spoke the other evening, were in the hands of a friend, but here they are at last—to be kept during your uttermost convenience.—Three or four of the *Nouvelles*, I think, are the best short stories ever written—to my knowledge.

Yours very truly
H. James jr.

To William Dean Howells

Ms Harvard

[New York]
111 east 25*th* st.
Jan. 13*th* [1875]

Dear Howells—

I have just received your telegram about the proof, which went this A.M. I was in the country when they came, and they had been lying two days on my table, but I despatched them as soon as possible on my return. Don't lose courage about sending me more; I have made probably my only absence for the winter. I hope this has not seriously bothered you.—I found also your letter which gave me all the pleasure I had given you. My notices of the *Foregne Conclusion* were written most pleasurably to myself.[1] I am glad you are dining out and liking Boston. I'm afraid the tender grace of a day that is dead will not revisit *this* stagnant heart. But I come back to New York (from near Philadelphia, to be sure,) with a real relish. I feel vastly at home here and really like it. *Pourvu que ca dure!* I have been staying at Mrs. Owen Wister's and having Fanny Kemble read Calderon for me in *tête à tête* of a morning. How is that for high? She had on a cap and spectacles, but her voice is divine. I see a little of Sedgwick and dine with him at theatrical chop-houses. Naughty Bohemians! Would that I were either! Farewell.—I seem to have books enough on my hands for the *Nation* just now, but if you would like a notice of Emerson's *Parnassus,* I might try it.[2] In a week or two begins the annual exhibit of water-colors at the Academy. Would you like a couple of pages on it, if I can supply them?—It may interest you to know that the *Nation* has dropped noticing the magazines, a competent hand not appearing. I have looked up Lathrop,[3] but hardly seen him and I'm afraid he finds his experiment here not a bed of roses. With love *a casa*—

Yours H. J. jr.

1. HJ wrote two reviews of Howells's *A Foregone Conclusion* (1874), both unsigned. The first appeared in the *North American Review*, CXX (January 1875), 207–214; the second in the *Nation*, XX (7 Jan. 1875), 12–13.
2. So far as we know HJ did not write the review of this work.
3. George Parsons Lathrop (1851–1898) was at this time associate editor of the *Atlantic Monthly*. He was Hawthorne's son-in-law and editor of his collected works.

To Sarah Butler Wister

Ms Congress

111 east 25*th* St.
Jan. 23*rd* [1875]

Dear Mrs. Wister—

Butler Place and my visit there have had time to become a part of the "dreadful past" as Tennyson says—but I want to keep them a bit longer in the present if writing to you will help me to do so. It has been on my pen's end to write before this—any one of half a dozen recent evenings when I have come in from the outer world to my smouldering fireside, put myself into slippers and felt the need of spending a rational hour before going stupidly to bed. That my letter didn't get written was I think in a great measure owing to the fact that, sitting down by my fireside as before mentioned, I fell a-musing about you and prolonged my vigil in a sweet inaction which I really felt loath to interrupt by the (to me now-a-days) very vulgar act of scribbling. I came nearer doing so the other evening, however, on coming back from a dinner at Mrs. Lockwood's.[1] I have seen this lady twice, in her own tranquil home and have felt, after each occasion, burdened with emotions which it would have been a relief to tansfer to a sympathetic ear. They were emotions of high admiration and they were commingled with a very lively gratitude to you for having made me know her. Most truly, she is a remarkable woman and a very exquisite creature. I think I may say that she gives me an impression of a finer intelligence, a finer mental machinery than any woman I have known. She strikes me as rather too tense—too *tendue*—too *in*tense; but I find it does not at all keep my relations with her from being easy, and the stuff she is made of is so thoroughly superior and the *person* is so singularly lovely that a *tête à tête* with her is a great bliss. I hope to have many.—Except those I speak of I have had nothing since my return to town that is worth your hearing of. I have seen a certain number of ordinary people and read some dullish books, and walked in Broadway and eaten some good dinners and worried through the days in one way or another. Life, alas, isn't all resting on one's oars and staying at Butler Places and breathing the atmosphere of intelligent hospitality. Since I came back I have liked New York decidedly less—so little in fact that *hideous* is the most amiable word I can find to apply to it. If one could only get over the trick of judging things aesthetically!—With you, pray, how have things gone? Are you alone—that is *en famille?*—or have you had any more guests, punctual or otherwise? Especially, have you danced the tight-rope over the snow again to Germantown—alone, or with a companion of a dancing disposition? I have thought a good deal about that *premier mouvement* of mine and on the whole I don't repudiate it. Properly looked at it had its fine points. Your mother, I hope, is well and serene. I should like to send her my most cordial salutations.[2] I hope Dr. Wister has worked off his patriotic wrath. Since my return here I found people trampling on Grant very comfortably indeed.[3] Pray give my kind regards to your husband and lay my blessings on the head of that charming boy, if he is still at home. I have been out tonight among some people who were telling ghost stories, and heard for the first time a young woman maintain that she had seen a ghost with her own eyes. It was a very pretty story—only too pretty to be true.—But I see ghosts all the while over here; I live among 'em: the ghosts of the old world and the old things I left *là bas*. I hope nothing disagreeable has yet crossed the threshold of that little grey room,—or any of your thresholds.— I wish I could tell you all the good wishes I have for you. Find a few between the lines here and believe me always yours very faithfully

H. James jr.

1. Florence Bayard Lockwood (1842–1898), wife of Major Benoni Lockwood and friend of Mrs. Wister. She was a member of an old Delaware family and attracted wide attention by her statement of religous beliefs in *The Penn Monthly*, IX (March 1878), 177–200, "A Positive Creed." HJ remembered her as "one of the big figures of one's experience" and as "thoroughly in the grand high style."

2. Mrs. Kemble was living in Philadelphia. There are echoes of this visit in HJ's memorial of the actress in *Essays in London* (1893).

3. An allusion to the serious scandals in the administration of President Grant.

To Elizabeth Boott

Ms Harvard

111 east 25*th* [New York] Tuesday
[Jan. 27, 1875]

Dear Lizzie—

A hundred thanks for your letter, and for the charming news that you are coming to this place. I will give you an ardent welcome and spend the whole period of your visit at your feet, even tho' they be clad in Arctics. You have very strange notions of my gayeties here. Pray on what are they based?—I am leading the quietest and most humdrum of lives seeing few people and those very stupid. You will be indeed an enchanting apparition. I will take you any-where you want to go—even to J. La Farge's studio, though he is out of town and it is closed. But we will manage to get in. I am curious to know what you think of N.Y. It's a rattling big luxurious place, but I prefer F—Excuse me! I can't trust myself on that chapter. I am enchanted that things are so well with you in Cambridge and that you're having such comfortable dances. I wish I had been there that night to share your joy. Methinks that in a waltz with you I might have renewed for an hour my lost youth and fancied I was again in R—! It will out, you see. *La nostalgia non i ni melio ni peggio. Non puo ne crescere ne gudrier. Cè un solo rimedio! Ma il vedervi cara almeno per l'ora una consolazione.* I suppose you see my people often and I am glad you are coming to report of me to them. I hope your father is well and happy and I wish he were coming with you. My affectionate salutations to him. On you, dear Lizzie, my blessings and a speedy meeting.

Yours ever—
H. James jr.

To Welch and Bigelow

Ms Harvard

New York
111 east 25th st. [1875]

Messrs. Welch and Bigelow—
Dear Sirs:

Will you be so good as to insert in the copy of *Transatlantic Sketches,* which you are now printing, the enclosed fragment, originally omitted? I am unable to page it: but it belongs in the series entitled *Florentine Notes,* and had best be numbered IV or V. If these numbers have been set up, it may go last—as the VIII or IX.

Yours very truly
Henry James jr.

To Elizabeth Boott

Ms Harvard

New York, March 8*th*. [1875]
111 east 25*th* St.

Mille grazie, cara Lisa,[1] di vostra graziosa lettera, scritta nella vera lingua di Dante—Dio la benedica! Sapete che la vita di N.Y. é nemica di tutta occupazione seria e simpatica e potrete dunque perdonar al mio silenzio fin'ora. Penso spesso a quelle poche orette che abbiamo potuto passare insieme un mese fa,—mi rammento specialmente quella cara collazione da Delmonico. Dico *cara* senza *pun*—non ho mai avuto tanto piacere a cosi basso prezzo! E per provarvi che non mi ha rovinato vi diro che vi prendo ancora la collazione ogni domenica nello stesso posto! I giorni vengono e vanno, sempre aspri e selvaggi, mutando dalla pioggia alla nevica e *vice-versa* senza apportarmi nessun avvenimento di vero interesse. Ora che non posseggo piu un orecchio amichevole, per ricevere le mie confidenze *nostalgiche,* sono forzato di seppellirle in mio tristo cuore, e temo molto che mio carattere non ne prendi un brutto piego permanente. Scrivete mi dunque, vi congiuro, qualche parole consolatrici il più spesso che potrete; farete veramente opera di carità. Andai una sera cercar consolazione dai Botta;[2] trovai invece un *German,* ballato da giovani newyorkesi dei due sessima ma d'Italiani, mica! Cercar un Italiano e trovar un "Tedesco" é veramente crudele! Ho passato le mie sera recenti a sentir la Ristori, che ci da delle rappresentazioni da una settimana. Donna vecchia e faticata, ma grand' artista, gran *stile,* e atmosfera Italiana.—Cosi vi diro? La Wister ha passato un giorno a N.Y. poco tempo fa, ed io ne ho passato la maggior parte con lei, rinchiuso in vettura sotto pretesto di *errands.*—Questo é un racconto romantico! Il vero dell'affare fu molto prosaico.—E voi cosa fatte ed a che santo vi indirizzate per soccorso in questi giorni uggiosi? Lavorate senza dubbio splendidamente e vi fate una vita col aiuto dei vostri talenti artistici e sociali. Vedete spesso, io spero, la mia famiglia e loro dite del bene di me. Il padre—il vostro—beve il caffé, passegia e fa la musica, piaceri sufficienti per un filosofo. Io che non ho un caffé in America

—ho bisogno, delle volte, di tutta la mia filosofia. Addio, cara Lisa. Spero coi primi giorni di *vera* primavera di darvi un colpo d'occhio a C. Tanti complimenti al onorato padre. Vi auguro tutto il bene del mundo.

e rimango il vostro amico—H. James jr.

[Many thanks, dear Liz, for your gracious letter, written in the true language of Dante—God bless it! You know that N.Y. life is hostile to every serious and sympathetic occupation, so you can forgive my silence up to now. I often think of those few hours we were able to spend together a month ago,— I remember particularly that dear lunch at Delmonico's. I say *dear* without pun—I never had so much pleasure at such a low price! And to prove to you that it didn't ruin me, I'll tell you that I still lunch each Sunday at the same place! The days come and go, always harsh and wild, changing from rain to snow and vice-versa without bringing me any event of real interest. Now that I have no longer have a friendly ear to receive my nostalgic confidences I am forced to bury them in my sad heart, and I fear lest my nature take a bad turn permanently. Write to me then, I implore you, some consoling words as often as you àre able; you'll truly perform an act of charity. One evening I went to seek consolation at the Bottas; instead I found a *German*, danced by young New Yorkers of both sexes but of Italians, nothing! To look for an Italian and find a "Tedesco" is really cruel! I spent my recent evenings listening to Ristori, who has been giving performances for the last week. An old and worn-out woman, but a great artist, grand *style,* and Italian atmosphere.— What shall I tell you? Mrs. Wister spent a day in N.Y. a short time ago and I spent most of it with her, shut up in a carriage under pretext of *errands.*—What a romantic story! The truth of the matter was more prosaic.—And you, what are you doing and to what saint do you address yourself for help during these bleak days? Doubtless you work splendidly and are making a life with your artistic and social talents. You see my family often, I hope, and tell them good things about me. The father—yours—drinks coffee, takes walks and makes music, sufficient pleasures for a philosopher. I who take no coffee in America sometimes need all my philosophy. Goodbye, dear Lizzie. With the first days of *real* spring I hope to see you at Cambridge. My compliments to your honored father. I wish you all the good in the world, and remain your friend.]

1. Although there are a number of HJ letters in French, this is one of his rare letters in Italian—an Italian of a simple and tourist kind. His proficiency in that language improved with the years.

2. Anne Charlotte Lynch Botta (1815–1891). Her house on Waverly Place was a center of intellectual and artistic life and among her guests were Bryant, Greeley, Màrgàret Fuller, Willis, Poe, Bayard Taylor, R. H. Stoddard. She had married Professor Vincenzo Botta (1818–1894) who taught Italian at New York University. The Bottas later lived and entertained at 25 West 37th street where HJ visited them. Mrs. Botta published verses and painted. Her canvases are not extant.

To William Dean Howells

Ms Hayes

Friday evening [19 or 26 March 1875]
111 east 25*th* st.

Dear Howells,—

I read this morning your notice of *A Passionate Pilgrim*[1] and—well, I survive to tell the tale! If kindness could kill I should be safely out of the way of ever challenging your ingenuity again. Never was friendship so ingenious—never was ingenuity of so ample a flow! I am so new to criticism (as a subject,) that this rare sensation has suggested many thoughts, and I discern a virtue now in being overpraised. I lift up my hanging head little by little and try to earn the laurel for the future, even if it be so much too umbrageous now. Meanwhile I thank you most heartily. May your fancy never slumber when you again read anything of mine!

I hope to be in Cambridge for two or three days about April 10th, if by that time there is any symptom whatever of sprouting grass or swelling buds. We will take a walk together and you will help my town-wearied eyes to discover them. I will bring with me the "balance," as they say here, of my novel,[2] or at least the greater part of it. I hear rumors that you are coming this way (i.e. to New Jersey:) I hope it won't be at just that time; of course you won't be here, with whatever brevity, without looking me up. The wheel of life revolves here, but it doesn't turn up any great prizes. I lead a very quiet life and dwell rather in memories and hopes than in present emotions. With love to your house,

Yours ever—more than ever—

H. James jr.

1. *A Passionate Pilgrim*, HJ's first book, was published 31 January 1875 by Houghton Osgood & Company. It contained certain of his tales dealing with Americans in Europe which had appeared in magazines during the previous decade.
2. *Roderick Hudson* was being serialized in the *Atlantic Monthly*.

To John Hay

Ms Brown

20 Quincy St.
Cambridge, Mass.
July 21*st* [1875]

Dear Mr. Hay[1]—

Sometime before leaving town (which I did a few days since,) I called in 42d St., to find, to my regret, that you had already migrated for the summer. I had considerable discourse with the worthy woman who keeps your door (and for whose circumspection in opening it to able-bodied men in the dusky hours I can answer,) and she intimated that you had left town earlier than was natural, on account of some indisposition of your own. I hope the remedy has been effectual, and that you are now in the best of health; and that Mrs. Hay and your daughter share this blessing with you.

If I had seen you, perhaps I should not be writing to you now, and I am glad of a pretext for doing so. I have had it at heart for some little time to ask you a question or two; and perhaps it is prudent not longer to delay.

I have a tolerably definite plan of going in the autumn to Europe and fixing myself for a considerable period in Paris. I should like, if I do so, to secure a regular correspondence with a newspaper— non-political (I mean of course the correspondence,) and tolerably frequent: say three or four letters a month. When I say a "newspaper" I have an eye, of course, upon the *Tribune*. To my ambition, in fact, it would be the *Tribune* or nothing. There is apparently in the American public an essential appetite, and a standing demand, for information about all Parisian things. It is as a general thing rather flimsily and vulgarly supplied, and my notion would be to undertake to supply it in a more intelligent and cultivated fashion— to write in other words from the American (or if it doesn't seem presumptuous to say so, as far as might be from the *cosmopolitan*) point of view a sort of *chronique* of the events and interests of the day. I have thought the thing over in its various bearings, and have satisfied myself that I could put it through. Indeed I have a dazzling vision of doing very good things. I should have a fair number of strings to my bow, and be able to write on a variety of topics—"social" matters, so called, manners, habits, people etc, books, pictures, the theatre, and those things which come up in talk about rural excursions and dips into the provinces. I should come to the matter with a considerable familiarity with a good many points in French civilization, and should, I think, always feel pretty sure of my ground. Lastly, I should be likely to produce a tolerably finished piece of writing, and my letters would always have more or less the literary turn. I think I know how to observe, and may claim that I should observe to good purpose and chronicle my observations agreeably.

This very handsome account of myself is prefatory to an interrogation which you must answer at your convenience. Could the *Tribune* make any use of these brilliant gifts? Would it enter into its economy for the coming winter (to begin with) that I should address to it the weekly masterpieces of which I have given a hint? Two obvious reflections of course occur to me. One is that the *Tribune* has its regular political correspondent, whose province may not be invaded. I should have no fear of ever having to warn myself against trespassing on his field; our two lives would remain naturally so distinct. The other is that perhaps Arsène Houssaye is giving, and is to continue to give, the *Tribune* all it wants. In this last case of course I am anticipated; but if his relations with the paper are destined within the coming couple of months to terminate—and let me not seem obtrusively to assume that they are—, or you are weighing the question of resuming them,—my proposition may have a certain timeliness. *J'ai dit!*—I hope not too diffusely. I don't know that there is anything to add, save that my letters would of course be welcome to whatever credit my signature might bestow upon them—and that during three months or so of the year, I should be glad to date them from other places—out of the way ones, sometimes, where I might have gone in pursuit of the curious. If I had not seemed already to have blown my trumpet so lustily I would super add that I "calculated" to produce, every way, a very good style of thing.

Such answer, more or less conclusive, as you may be good enough to give to all this will find me *here* for some time to come. I have chiefly wished, for the present, to register myself in the *Tribune's* books. With kind regards to Mrs. Hay, and the best wishes for the prosperity of your business.

Yours very truly—
Henry James jr.

1. John Hay, assistant to the publisher of the *Tribune,* urged the appointment of HJ to write Paris letters for the newspaper. See *Parisian Sketches,* ed. Edel and Lind (1957) for a full account of HJ's relation with the *Tribune* and the texts of the twenty letters he wrote for the newspaper.

To John Hay

Ms Brown

20 Quincy St.
Cambridge
Aug. 5th [1875]

My dear Mr. Hay—

I find your note of July 30th on my return from a short visit to the country.—First of all let me thank you heartily for the trouble you have taken and for your sympathy and good will. May I ask you to render me a further service. Will you be so good as to let Mr. Reid[1] know that I accept his offer of $20—gold, and that I expect to be able to write my first letter by about October 25th. It is a smaller sum than I should myself have proposed, but being, as you say, good newspaper payment, I summon philosophy to my aid.

Your account of your own situation made me feel as if it had been very stupid in me to lay my case before you. But indeed it was only the day before that I had scurrily snubbed Howells for intimating that you had begun a flirtation with business, and I appealed to you with a perfect good conscience. May you have all the pleasures of the "avarice" you speak of, and some of its pains— its apprehensions and alarms about your money-bags; and may these speedily become full to bursting! I feel as if my sails had caught a very liberal capful of wind, in this epistolary enterprise, from your good wishes. Were I disposed to doubt that I should put it through, I should reflect with satisfaction that at any rate *your* perspicacity believed in it. You fill me with regret that I should not have caught a glimpse of the Giorgionesque daughter of your portress. Her golden hair would have done something to console me for not finding you.

Will you kindly add in communicating with Mr. Reid, that I shall endeavor to see him before I leave America. With many thanks, once more, and kind regards to Mrs. Hay—yours very truly

H. James jr.

1. Whitelaw Reid, editor of the *Tribune*.

To John Hay

Ms Brown

20 Quincy St.
Cambridge
Aug. 18*th* [1875]

Dear Mr. Hay—

I must acknowledge the receipt of your last note and thank you for it—the more so as I have it on my conscience to say that I shall find myself obliged to leave America a couple of weeks later than I expected, and to begin the immortal letters at a date correspondingly posterior. But I shall not be a day later than I can help.[1]

I appreciate the force of your reflections about the letters proving (potentially) a (relative) gold-mine in the long run; and if the run is long enough quite expect to be coupled anecdotically with Milton in all allusions to the £5, or whatever it was, he received for *Paradise Lost*.

I am very glad to hear you have hit *upon* your pretext for going to Paris. The honor of your ingenuity awaited it! I am also delighted that Mrs. Hay keeps abreast of the age as regards dados. If you can purchase a second-hand one out of the *Earthly Paradise*,[2] of course you will do the right thing. The great point however is to have one, of some sort or other, and to have mastered the art of attending to it as if you had had it for twenty years! I can talk about them very

479

prettily, but to this hour I am not sure that I know what they are.
With cordial good wishes—

> Yours very truly
> H. James jr.

1. HJ's first Parisian letter was of 22 Nov. 1875.
2. William Morris' narrative poem on Norse themes. Two unsigned reviews of this work were by James, in the *North American Review*, CVII (July 1868), 358–361 and the *Nation*, VII (July 9, 1868), 33–34.

To J. R. Osgood & Co.

Ms Yale

> Cambridge, Aug. 18*th* [1875]
> 20 Quincy st.

Dear Sirs,

I have just received your account of date Aug. 16th. for the stereotyped plates of *Transatlantic Sketches*, etc: the whole amounting to $555.07.[1] I have received no account on the sale of the "*Sketches*" and of a "Passionate Pilgrim," and I beg you to send me one, balanced, as regards my own profits, against the amount of the present bill. I will then settle the latter, so modified.

> Yours very truly
> H. James jr.

1. HJ paid for the printing of *Transltantic Sketches* but recovered his investment. His volume of fiction, *A Passionate Pilgrim*, was published by Osgood on a royalty basis.

To H. O. Houghton & Co.

Ms Harvard

> Cambridge 20 Quincy St.
> Aug. 24*th* [1875]

Dear Sirs.

I desire to make a request of you which I hope you will find convenient. It would be a service if you would advance me the balance of payment due on my story of *Roderick Hudson*, now running in the *Atlantic*. It has been paid for up to this time month by month, and there are four numbers (one just published) yet unpaid for. I sail for Europe in a few weeks and if I might be put into possession without delay of the outstanding four hundred dollars I should consider it a favor.

Faithfully yours
H. James jr.

To H. O. Houghton & Co.
Ms Harvard

20 Quincy St.
Cambridge
Aug. 30th [1875]

Dear Sirs.

I beg to thank you extremely for your cheque for $400—the remainder payment of *Roderick Hudson*, which I find on my return from the country. I was aware that it was not usual with you to advance money on *MS*; and I am therefore proportionately grateful to you for making an exception in my behalf.——

Yours very truly
H. James jr.

To E. C. Stedman
Ms Private

Cambridge Sept. 1st [1875]

My dear Sir:[1]

I find on my return from an absence in the country your very gratifying and interesting letter. I am very glad that my notice of *Queen Mary*[2] gave you any pleasure and greatly indebted to you for taking the trouble to express it to me. I find it, I confess, rather confusing, even, to be complimented on the article in question; especially by one who speaks on poetic matters with authority. My pretentions, in attempting to talk about Tennyson, were very modest, and I made no claim to express myself as anything but, as it were, an outsider. I know him only as we all know him—by desultory reading—and indeed from a comparative and categorical examination of any great poet I would always earnestly shrink.

I know poets and poetry only as an irredeemable proser! So if I have seemed to you to hit the nail at all on the head, in speaking of Tennyson, I am only the more thankful for my good fortune.—

I need hardly say that your own observations strike me as very much to the point—both those in your letter and those in the enclosed extracts from your book. The latter, on its appearance, I shall be very glad to see. I hesitate to agree with you in your forecast of what Tennyson will hereafter attempt and what English poetry is likely to come to. Not that I have an opposite opinion, but simply because these are questions on which I find myself much at sea—the whole poetic mystery and its conditions being emphatically a mystery to me. I can only say that were I myself capable of using the instrument of flexible verse I should go in with great good will for the dramatic form. Your prevision two years ago of Tennyson's putting forth a drama is very noticeable; and noticeable also your mention of the exceptional originality of the fable of the *Princess*.— I quite sympathise with you in your wonder that Browning should have never felt the intellectual comfort of "a few grave, rigid laws." But Browning's badness I have never professed to understand. I limit myself to vastly enjoying his goodness.

With many thanks and good wishes I remain, my dear Sir,

Yours very truly

Henry James jr.

1. Edmund Clarence Stedman (1833–1908) was a prominent figure in Wall Street and in the New York literary world. He was a writer of lyrics and edited the *Library of American Literature* in 11 volumes (1189–1890).

2. "Mr. Tennyson's Drama," *Galaxy*, XX (September 1875), 393–402.

To H. O. Houghton & Co.

Ms Harvard

20 Quincy St. Wednesday—[Sept. 1875]

Dear Sirs.—

I yesterday revised the proof of the *Atlantic*'s last part of "Roderick Hudson," which I suppose you will directly send to be composed.[1] I would like here to suggest a small change. This last Part is numbered XII. Please divide it in the plates into XII and XIII. Let the division come where I marked on the *Atlantic* proof a red cross—that is about a third of the way down the slip numbered 5, and at the words (which shall begin Chap. XIII) "Roderick on the homeward walk that evening . . ." Pray substitute the following in the volume: "*The Princess Casamassima.*"[2] And pray transfer in the volume the title Switzerland to Chapter XIII. This I think I have made plain.

Yours very truly

Henry James jr.

1. HJ first wrote "directly send to press for printing the plates" but crossed out "press for printing" and inserted the words "to be composed" and forgot to cross out "the plates." From these changes it is clear that HJ was then confused about the printing process—as between typesetting, composition, and stereotyping.

2. *Roderick Hudson* is the sole novel of HJ's which has chapter titles, and these imitate Hawthorne's way of naming chapters. HJ's decision to divide the final chapters makes clear for the readers Christina Light's becoming "The Princess Casamassima" and foreshadows the novel he would write about Christina as Princess ten years later.

To H. O. Houghton & Co.

Ms Harvard

20 Quincy St. Cambridge

Oct. 7*th* [1875]

Dear Sirs.—

It would be a great favor if you could let me have each day *considerably more* proof of "Roderick Hudson." I am afraid otherwise I shall not be able to finish revising before the 17th, on which day I leave Cambridge for Europe. About two-thirds (or a little less) of the volume remain to be seen thro' the press in these coming ten days. I shall need at this rate to see upwards of 30 pages a day, instead of the usual 12. I have not yet had proof of the XIIth part of R.H. from the *Atlantic*—so that if you will have that put thro' with as little delay as possible it will also be a service.—I delivered copy for the press only up to one half of part X. Having the sheets of the

Atlantic in your hands it will save time if you will please to use them simply as they stand for the remainder. I can easily make the few needful alterations in the proof of the reprint.—The matter of giving me more proof is, as you see, very urgent.

Yours very truly
H. James jr.

To The James Family

Ms Harvard

Story's Hotel, Dover St.
Piccadilly Sunday Nov. 1st [1875]

Dear People all—

I take possession of the old world[1]—I inhale it—I appropriate it! I have been in it now these twenty-four hours, having arrived at Liverpool yesterday at noon. It is now two o'clock, and I am sitting, in the livid light of a London November Sunday, before a copious fire, in my own particular sitting-room, at the establishment mentioned above. I took the afternoon train from Liverpool yesterday, and having telegraphed in advance, sat down at 10 P.M. to cold roast beef, bread and cheese and ale in this cosy corner of Britain. I have been walking up Piccadilly this morning, and into Hyde Park, to get my land-legs on; I am duly swathed and smoked and chilled, and feel as if I had been here for ten years.—Of course you got my letter from Sandy Hook, and learned that my voyage began comfortably. I am sorry to say it didn't continue so, and I spent my nights and my days declaring that the sea shouldn't catch me again for at least twenty years. But of course I have already forgotten all that and the watery gulf has closed over my miseries. Our voyage was decently rapid (just 10 days) owing to favoring winds; but the winds were boisterous gales, and after the second day we tumbled and tossed all the way across. I was as usual, but I kept pretty steadily on deck, and with my rugs and my chair, managed to worry thro'. The steamer is a superb one, but she was uncomfortably crowded, and she presumably bounced about more than was

Catherine Walsh (Aunt Kate)

needful. I was not conversational and communed but little with my multitudinous passengers. My chief interlocutor was Mrs. Lester Wallack,[2] whose principal merit is that she is the sister of Millais the painter. She offers to take me to his studio if he returns to town before I have—which he won't. We had also Anthony Trollope,[3] who wrote novels in his state room all the morning (he does it literally every morning of his life, no matter where he may be,) and played cards with Mrs. Bronson[4] all the evening. He has a gross and repulsive face and manner, but appears *bon enfant* when you talk with him. But he is the dullest Briton of them all. Nothing happened, but I loathed and despised the sea more than ever. I managed to eat a good deal in one way and another, and found it, when once I got it well under way, the best help to tranquillity. It isn't the eating that hurts one, but the stopping.—I shall remain in this place at most a week. It is the same old big black London, and seems, as always, half delicious, half dismal. I am profoundly comfortable, thanks to Mr. Story, the usual highly respectable retired butler, who gives me a sitting room, a bedroom, attendance, lights and fire, for three guineas a week. Everything is of the best, and it is a very honorable residence. Why didn't Aunt Kate and Alice bring me here in '72? I shall probably start for Paris a week from tomorrow, and hope to find there a line from home. If anything very interesting befalls me here I will write again, but in my unfriended condition this is not probable. I hope the Western journey has been safely and smoothly executed and count upon hearing full particulars. If Aunt Kate has gone to New York let her see this. Each of you hold Dido an hour against your heart for me.[5] The sight of all the pretty genteel dogs in Hyde Park a while since brought tears to my eyes. I think that if I could have had Dido in my berth I would have been quite well. But perhaps *she* would have been sea-sick. I have been haunted since I left home by the recollection of three small unpaid bills, which I pray mother to settle for me.

1. At Dollard's, the cobbler's. About 2 dollars.
2. Schönhof and Moellers. About $3.00
3d. At Smith's, the tailor's, 7$ for that summer coat: not 7.50,

as his bill said, which I left on my bedroom table. Excuse these sordid details. This sitting still to write makes me swim and roll about most damnably. Your all-affectionate

H. James jr.

1. The statement was prophetic: this was indeed the beginning of his expatriation.

2. Wife of the English actor Lester Wallack (1820–1888). The actor wrote popular plays as well as acted in them.

3. HJ would later recall this voyage in his essay on Trollope in *Partial Portraits* (1888).

4. Katherine de Kay Bronson, wife of Arthur Bronson and future hostess of James and Browning in Venice.

5. The James family pet.

INDEX

James, Henry (Continued)
RETURN TO CAMBRIDGE AND NEW
YORK (1874–1875), 465–466;
family letters, 466, 484; letters to
friends, 467, 468, 469, 471, 473,
481; letters to publishers, 468, 472,
475, 476, 478, 479, 480, 481, 482,
483
TALES: At Isella, 128, 133n, 259;
Eugene Pickering, 424, 426n, 437,
440n, 445; Gabrielle de Bergerac,
114n, 126 and n; The Last of the
Valerii, 336n, 426n; A Light Man,
357, 358n; Madame de Mauves,
282, 408n; The Madonna of the
Future, 334, 336; My Friend
Bingham, 70n; Owen Wingrave,
41–42; A Passionate Pilgrim, 111,
114n, 237, 255, 257, 262, 357;
Poor Richard, 70n; The Story of
a Masterpiece, 73–74; The Story of
a Year, xxxvii, 50, 51n, 56, 57;
The Sweetheart of M. Briseux,
336n, 394, 395; A Tragedy of
Error, xxxvii, 50, 51n
NOVELS: The Ambassadors, 288n;
The Bostonians, 48n3, 465;
Confidence, 282; Ivory Tower,
xviii; The Portrait of a Lady, 3;
The Princess Casamassima, 483;
Roderick Hudson, xxxviii, 142n,
171n, 249, 282–283, 440n, 465,
466, 475 and n, 480–481, 482–484;
Washington Square, 3; Watch and
Ward, xxxvii, 238, 248–249, 262,
263n, 267n
ESSAYS AND REVIEWS: Azarian, 55 and
n; A Chain of Italian Cities, 271n,
397 and n, 402, 403n; Dumas and
Goethe, 411, 412n; Emily Chester,
55 and n; Essays in Criticism,
58n; From Chambéry to Milan,
133n, 302n; Florentine Notes, 419,
433 and n, 454 and n, 472;
Howells' Poems, 411, 425; Journal
of Guérin, 54 and n; Lichfield and
Warwick, 114n, 289n; Lindisfarn
Chase, 57, 58n; London, 97n;
Merimée, 411, 435; The Parisian
Stage, 332–333; From a Roman
Notebook, 399, 400n; Roman
Rides, 399, 400n

OTHER WORKS MENTIONED: Italian
Hours, 271n, 419n, 433n; The
Middle Years, xviii, xxi, 97n,
119n; Notes of a Son and Brother,
xxi, 41, 48n2; A Passionate Pilgrim
and Other Tales, xxxviii, 465, 475,
480; A Small Boy and Others, 5;
Transatlantic Sketches, xxxviii,
465–466, 480
James, Henry (Harry; nephew and
executor; 1879–1948), xvi, xix–xxxi;
passim, xxxiv
James, Howard (uncle; 1828–1887), 56,
57n
James, John S.R. (1915–1969), xxxi
James, Mary Walsh (mother;
1810–1882), 4; letters to, 33, 102,
122, 149, 172, 193, 218, 283, 285,
290, 295, 302, 304, 316, 330, 341,
354, 375, 387, 410, 429, 431, 434,
448, 452, 458
James, Margaret Mary (Peggy; niece;
1887–1952), xiv, xvii, xviii, xix–xx,
xxi, xxxiii
James, Robertson (brother; 1846–1910),
3, 9, 43, 311–312, 314n; letter to, 466
James, William (brother; 1842–1910),
xiv, xxvi–xxvii, 3–4, 9, 41, 48, 85,
282, 412–414; letters to, 79, 98, 108,
136, 158, 159, 179, 200, 206, 223,
298, 311, 320, 363, 383, 390, 392,
440, 455
James, Mrs. William (Alice H.
Gibbens; sister-in-law; 1849–1922),
xiv, xvi–xix, xxi, xxxii
James, William (Billy; nephew;
1882–1961), xxi, xxxi–xxxii, xxxiv

Keeler, Ralph, 396–397
Kemble, Frances Anne, 318, 322, 328
Kingsley, Charles, 287
Kronenberger, Louis, xxxi

La Farge, John, 4, 14, 50, 52–53;
letters to, 119, 133
Lathrop, George Parsons, 469
Lecky, W. E. H., 206
Lefèbvre, Jules J., 400
Leverett, Rev. W. C., 13, 14n
Lewes, George Henry, 91, 117
Lincoln, Abraham, 48n1
Lockwood, Florence Bayard, 470